MW01222812

CONTROLLING CONFLICT

Alternative Dispute Resolution for Business

by
Edward J. Costello, Jr.

CCH INCORPORATED
4025 W. Peterson Ave.
Chicago, IL 60646-6085
1 800 TELL CCH

Editorial Staff

Editor: Fran Jacobs

Indexer: Nancy Hagler

This publication is designed to provide accurate and authoritative information in regard to the subject matter covered. It is sold with the understanding that the publisher is not engaged in rendering legal, accounting, or other professional service and that the author is not offering such advice in this publication. If legal advice or other expert assistance is required, the services of a competent professional person should be sought.

ISBN 0-8080-0088-8

Printed in the United States of America

TO

KARIN B. COSTELLO

CATHARINE A. COSTELLO

KRISTIN M. MACK

KATHERINE E. MACK

ROCCO M. SCANZA

SCOTT E. WOOD

WITH LOVE AND THANKS

EJC

About the Author

EDWARD J. COSTELLO, JR., is a full-time arbitrator/mediator/private judge with over 30 years experience in the practice of law and alternative dispute resolution. In addition to his practice and service as Judge Pro Tempore for the Los Angeles Superior and Municipal Courts, Mr. Costello is an adjunct Professor of Law at Loyola University School of Law.

Preface

The idea for this book was given to me in 1984 by an experienced business trial lawyer when we were flying across North America after having attended the same deposition. We each represented different parties, whose positions were, more or less, allied, and had suggested to our clients (the general counsels of two large corporations) that only one of us really needed to attend this deposition. Both clients had insisted on having separate and independent representation. Those decisions, of course, meant that one of us was going to make more money than had our advice been taken. Nonetheless, our return trip was not a happy one. My colleague said, "Correct me if I'm wrong, but we've wasted three days in a conference room, listening to four other lawyers ask some poor accountant questions that had no bearing on the case." I offered the slight correction that our questions and those of one other lawyer had had something to do with the case. "Okay," he said, "two and a half days!" We ruminated about the state of dispute resolution in American business. Each of us had some familiarity with dispute-handling methods in foreign business, but saw flaws in those systems as well. Finally, in exasperation, my colleague said, *"There must be a better way!"*

In the intervening eleven years, I have returned to his exclamation many times in my mind. On one of those occasions, six years later, a professor at a prestigious business school who approached the civil justice system as a method of resolving business disputes from a different angle than had my lawyer colleague, said, "Businesses are abandoning the courts as a place to get important disputes resolved." I asked why. He continued, "You know all about crowded courts, long waits, judges who know nothing about business, juries who know less, interminable appeals, and discovery costs the size of the national debt. What you may not know is what these all add up to. That's the real reason for wholesale abandonment of the courts by businesses: *We are using too many resources to resolve these disputes through the court system.*"

Two weeks later I began research on what turned out to be this book. The more research I did, the more convinced I became that both my "advisors" had been correct: We *are* using far too many resources to resolve civil disputes and that there *must* be a better way. I believe I have found the better way, and I know this way uses significantly less resources than the court system does to resolve the same dispute. But why should this be of interest?

Why business people should read this book

The purpose of this volume is to provide a tool to help organizations be better and more profitably managed in the years to come. Although this book may seem to be directed to a "business" audience, isn't everyone in business today? Ask the administrator of a hospital, the president of a small college, or the executive director of a charitable organization or trade association. Each one of them (and many more people who would not have thought of themselves as being "in business") now has to try to flourish in a world of diminishing resources. As a real estate developer I know said recently, "The gravy train has stopped. No, it's worse than that. The gravy train has been sold to a foreign company and they have turned it into a freight train." When I asked for an explanation of these railroad metaphors, he responded, "Look around. You can't raise the price of anything anymore. Even that famous maker of paper millionaires, California real estate, has gone in the tank." I thought he might be exaggerating, but I took his advice and looked around. The most compelling pieces of evidence I found were the advertisements for luxury cars. Historically, Americans who shopped for luxury cars were interested in just that: luxury. Price, maintenance costs, resale value, and gasoline mileage were all minor considerations, but now BMW, Mercedes-Benz, and Lexus are falling all over one another claiming how much "value" there is in cars that they make and sell. BMW's most recent ad campaign compares the resale values of its vehicles to those of Mercedes and Lexus—a full-page ad in most major newspapers that talks about nothing but resale value. The real estate developer was right; the gravy train has been turned into a freight train.

Elementary economics states that any organization can improve its profits (surplus, or whatever) in only two ways: increase revenues or decrease costs. In the '70s and before, American business boosted profits by raising the price of goods (sold mainly to one another). Since that avenue is decreasingly available, everyone is looking to cut costs and has had to become more competitive, cost-conscious, whether they wanted to or not.

Yet the cry "Costs are out of control!" is heard every day. It behooves American business, then, to control costs *in advance* to the extent humanly possible. At the same time, the advent of the "global village" and the breaking down of international trade barriers (NAFTA, GATT/WTO) have also forced more close competition in ways other than cost-cutting. As our Asian and European counterparts have been doing for years, American business people must now focus more on maintaining excellent, long-term relationships with both customers and suppliers. This book will help to:

- control most dispute resolution costs in advance;

- maintain those relationships of value;

- become more competitive, domestically and internationally; and

- save time and money in the bargain.

How the book is organized

After the introductory chapter, the book is divided in two parts. The first part, comprised of Chapters 2 through 4, takes a look at the history of business dispute resolution in America and how it affects the way business disputes are resolved today. These chapters also examine the state of our public court system, analyze its current and future ability to handle civil disputes, and give a comparative analysis of how two other major trading countries resolve their business disputes. Lastly, Chapter 4 gives an overview of alternative dispute resolution, what that phrase encompasses, and how ADR is used in America.

The second part (Chapters 5 through 16) devotes a separate chapter to each of the major alternative dispute resolution formats: negotiation, mediation, arbitration, private judging, mini-trial, and early neutral evaluation. Another chapter reviews various "hybrid" forms of ADR which have gained popularity. In each of these chapters, the process is explained, and its advantages and disadvantages are explored. At Chapter 12, suggestions are offered as to how ADR can be used to improve relations with an organization's three main constituencies: suppliers, customers, and employees. Chapter 13 gives a framework for choosing the appropriate ADR program for an organization, including numerous "forms" with commentary. Chapter 14 gives a guided tour through the major institutional providers of ADR services and some help in selecting among them. Chapter 15 discusses the role of ADR in international business. Chapter 16, entitled "The Future of ADR," examines the growing involvement of all levels of government in the ADR "movement," suggests how the "cause" of ADR can be advanced, and makes some predictions about the directions in which ADR will grow.

Appendices A through D include copies or summaries of useful legislation, rules, and international agreements. Right before the index, a glossary of ADR and other pertinent terms and a bibliography has been compiled for a more thorough examination of any of the topics in this book.

February 1996   E.J. Costello

Acknowledgments

This book could not have been written without the love and active support of my family and two close friends, to all of whom it is dedicated.

I was greatly assisted by the research help of Merrilee Goodwin and Larry Doan, both students at Southwestern University School of Law. They are thanked for both their hard work and their patience. Ideas which found their way into the book were germinated by dozens of people. At the risk offending some of them, I single out for thanks Joe Hartnett, Burt Nanus (himself a prolific author of business books), and Scott Wood.

Special thanks go to Larry Norris, acquisitions manager at CCH. Larry's belief in and unflagging commitment to the project, coupled with his patience and diplomacy, have made the process most enjoyable for me (if not for him).

Finally, but not least, three groups deserve special thanks. First, my teachers, whose inspiration remains with me more than thirty years after my last degree was awarded. Secondly, my students, past and present, who listened to my half-baked ideas and gave me great feedback, permitting me to fully bake some of the ideas. Thirdly, my colleagues, particularly those who share the pleasure of being full-time arbitrators, mediators, and private judges. You have been enormously generous with your time and ideas. I thank you, one and all.

Contents

A detailed Table of Contents for each chapter appears on page xi.

Table of Contents

"Achieving a consensus is not my style.
When I'm right, I'm right."

INTRODUCTION

The obscure we see eventually. The completely apparent takes longer.
   —Edward R. Murrow

A. Learning to Control the Dispute Resolution Process

When agreements are being negotiated, no one (except possibly the lawyers) ever expects that one of the parties will later break the agreement. Yet, unforeseen events often do occur. Contracts are breached, and problems of other kinds develop. Court litigation is one method of resolving these disputes, if one has the time, the money, and the burning desire to ruin the relationship with the opposing party permanently. Another method, advocated here, is the implementation of an alternative dispute resolution (ADR) agreement. In this type of agreement, the parties consent at the outset of their relationship to resolve disputes in a particular way. Such an agreement alone gives the parties to it more control than businesses which do not have one, because the parties *know in advance* exactly how disputes will be resolved. ADR procedures also offer the parties more control of business disputes than does traditional litigation in that parties can choose *which* process will be used in dispute resolution, an option not normally available with traditional litigation *after* the dispute arises.

1. Saving Money and Time

Including ADR in an agreement will save money and time as well. Taking a premeditated approach to dispute resolution permits parties to examine what ADR mechanisms will best suit their needs and wallets rather than the spontaneity of litigation. Parties are able to assess, before any dispute has broken out, the cost of different ADR methods and can select those which are most cost efficient for their businesses. Even if parties choose arbitration (the most expensive and time-consuming of ADR techniques), they will nonetheless save money compared to what would have been spent taking the same dispute through the litigation grinder.

By implementing an ADR system in their agreements and employment policies, organizations can avoid the temporal uncertainties of litigation. Not only does every ADR process save time versus litigating the same dispute, but in ADR an organization will not be faced with the repeated postponements for which law courts are justly infamous.

2. Becoming More Competitive

Litigation depletes the assets of businesses by consuming the time of the parties involved (and their employees), the financial resources used to pay costs and attorney fees, and the goodwill of a customer or supplier by permanently destroying the relationship. Alternative dispute resolution allows businesses to avoid these pitfalls by a more productive allocation of resources. The saved resources, of course, can be used in the normal work of making a profit (or providing a better public service or education, or obtaining more resources for a charitable program).

ADR engenders goodwill among business associates, who will come to recognize that those agreements which incorporate ADR among its terms provide for quick and fair resolution of disputes, something that is in everyone's interests. The inclusion of ADR programs in business agreements also demonstrates a high level of confidence in each party's goodwill.

For many defendants, litigation operates as a financing device. When a debtor is sued, he may do as little as possible to defend the lawsuit and still not pay what is owed. He may know that he owes money but will attempt to delay payment by using all the foot-dragging permitted by the court system. Although there is no good defense to the claim, it may take years for a court to recognize that fact. Parties who drag suits out normally hope that doing so will encourage settlement for an amount less than the actual debt. Where no attractive settlement is offered, such a party nonetheless avoids paying his debt until the civil suit is finally adjudicated (or the last appeal has been decided). When the matter is finally resolved through the court system, the result is hardly a victory for the "winner." The winning party in nine cases out of ten is not awarded attorney fees. This results in a loss of net revenue for businesses, and further encourages recalcitrant debtors to use the public judicial system as a financing device. While prevailing parties are normally awarded prejudgment interest, this is no panacea either. Most states have statutes which set the rate of prejudgment interest, which often is below market. A debtor is thereby further encouraged to delay because it is less expensive to wait and pay prejudgment interest than it is to borrow the money and pay off the debt. Even if attorney fees and costs are recovered, the winner will not be awarded the interest on *those amounts.* The attorney fees spent, however, were paid "up front" on a monthly basis. At minimum, the time value of the expenditures, from when they were paid until the judgment is entered, are lost. Even if a winning party *is* awarded costs and attorney fees, financing the litigation will likely cost more than the amount recovered. Therefore, a cost-effective way of resolving such disputes makes a business more competitive.

In all cases, ADR involves some costs itself, but parties recover these costs more quickly than in litigation. Additionally, ADR methods are not as limited as the judicial system in allowing for parties to be made whole. Those who use ADR may lawfully contract that *all* expenditures will be recovered in arbitration, for instance, including attorney fees. They may also provide in a predispute agreement that market rates will be used in calculating amounts of interest owing. As a result, the award obtained through arbitration may, in fact, make the recovering party whole.

Finally, these qualities, which are inherent in alternative dispute resolution, may also serve to deter debtors from delaying the payment of just debts.

3. Maintaining Valued Relationships, even During a Dispute

Those who have been through a serious litigation with another organization find that they rarely do business with that organization again, regardless of how the litigation came out. As one senior vice-president of a major specialty chemical manufacturer put it: "Once the litigation gets going, the atmosphere becomes absolutely toxic. And it has nothing to do with our chemicals. The damn litigation takes on a life of its own, and everybody gets nasty with everybody else. By the time it's over, settled or not, you not only don't want to see the other side and its lawyer again, but you frequently don't want to see *your* lawyer either." One might imagine that the word "toxic" would flow easily from the tongue of a chemist, but others have used it, too. The president (whose discipline was literature) of a university located in New York recently had this to say: "We were embroiled (literally) in a lengthy lawsuit with one of the university's long-time suppliers. I had my deposition taken. When I entered the room, the atmosphere was positively toxic. Even the exchanges of greetings sounded like fighting words." Almost everyone probably has his own litigation horror stories. The question is, how does alternative dispute resolution differ?

The answer to that question can be derived from the fact that:

(a) ADR processes, for the most part, are dispute resolution methods *which the parties themselves have freely chosen.* That fact alone reduces hostility, since no one will be experiencing the litigation "machine." A mechanism of one's own choosing, moreover, will always be preferable.

(b) ADR permits maximum party control during the proceedings as well, thereby enhancing stability and confidence and reducing tension and anger all around. In conducting most alternative dispute resolution processes, the focus is on a common problem and the quest for a common, agreeable solution to that problem in a distinctly non-adversarial setting. Indeed, the consensual nature of most ADR mechanisms *enables* the parties to have an honest, vigorous debate and to take a longer view.

The relatively informal atmosphere in ADR proceedings certainly helps to soften the edges of whatever happens. Parties, feeling more comfortable themselves, are inclined to be more cooperative with their opponents.

4. Imitating Foreign Business Solutions

Some elements of alternative dispute resolution, such as arbitration, have a long history in America. However, many nations that have a long history of ADR use have well-functioning, less wasteful economies. It would behoove American business people to want to learn to improve to be able to better function in the "global village."

B. Limitations

This book deals with a complicated topic, aspects of which can have serious legal and business consequences. Of necessity, it can only give general guidance. Nothing here will apply to everyone, and some of it may not apply to any one organization at all. Each organization has separate, perhaps unique, dispute resolution needs. Therefore, do not decide upon any ADR mechanism or program without consulting a *professional in alternative dispute resolution.* ADR requires expertise and experience to make the right choices.

Some chapters are more in summary form than others. A wealth of information is available on international ADR. Chapter 14 only covers the high points of adjudicative international ADR. Chapter 15 provides information on the institutional providers, much of it *furnished by them.* It also provides, however, a list of queries which will help choose among them.

C. Executive Overview

Reading this book will give business people and organization managers the means of controlling dispute resolution before disputes arise. By doing so, more managerial control over both the process and the outcome will be possible than with litigation. In addition, using alternative dispute resolution will save money and time which can be allocated to more productive activities. ADR is a catch-all phrase both for a less adversarial *approach* to dispute resolution as well as the specific optional *methods* of resolving disputes. These methods can maintain valued relationships and also lead to outcomes that are more rational than some jury verdicts. ADR can be generally divided into two categories: conciliatory and adjudicative. The conciliatory methods explored are negotiation, mediation, mini-trial, early neutral evaluation, partnering, and ombudsman. Adjudicative (meaning a third-party decision) methods discussed are arbitration, Med/Arb, private judging, and Arb/Med. The characteristics of each method are laid out, with its advantages and disadvantages. Techniques are prescribed for helping to decide whether ADR is right for certain types of organization, and, if so, what kind(s) of ADR. Ways of turning an ADR program into a marketing tool and an employment benefit are also discussed. ADR with various levels of government is assessed, and some predictions of the future of ADR are given.

"She is not my witness! She's your witness!"

BUSINESS DISPUTES IN AMERICA

A Very Short History

Discourage litigation. Persuade your neighbors to compromise whenever you can. Point out to them how the nominal winner is often a real loser–in fees, expenses, and waste of time. As a peacemaker, the lawyer has a superior opportunity of being a good man. There will still be business enough.
  —A. Lincoln

In the less complex economy of the early eighteenth century, American courts could handle the relatively few lawsuits brought to them. During that period the American business community did not recognize any need for alternatives to litigation. As the complexity of business disputes evolved, the necessity for alternatives to traditional litigation became apparent. Among the first communities to recognize the need for alternatives to court litigation were New York (1768), New Haven, Connecticut (1794), and Philadelphia, Pennsylvania (1801). They all created arbitral tribunals to settle commercial disputes. These tribunals concentrated primarily on dispute resolution in the clothing and printing industries. However, the courts remained hostile to arbitration, which removed disputes from their jurisdiction, and generally refused to enforce predispute arbitration clauses in contracts.

In the 1900s, America's economy continued to expand, and business firms became increasingly uncomfortable with the growing cost and delays of litigation. The business community began to lobby for legislation that would empower parties with the right to enforce arbitration clauses. In 1920, inspired by Julian Cohen's tract, *Commercial Arbitration and the Law,* New York enacted the first arbitration statute[1] which enforced predispute arbitration clauses in signed contracts.

In 1922, business leaders created an organization called the Arbitration Society of America, whose purpose was to educate people about, and advance the use of, arbitration. As a result of the Society's extensive lobbying, the Federal Arbitration Act (FAA) was passed in 1925. The FAA required Federal judges to recognize and enforce predispute arbitration clauses, thus providing business with a judicially accepted alternative to litigation.

Historically, the vast majority of business disputes have been resolved by negotiation. Most still are. Like other elements of our society, however, businesses have succumbed to the siren song of litigation. No further back than thirty years ago, litigation *between* business enterprises was relatively rare. Similarly, not many lawsuits were brought against business entities by others. There can be no question that *some* of the dramatic growth in lawsuits in the intervening years has produced socially worthy results. Some litigation has been deliberately encouraged by legislation, either in creating new rights or in providing for the collection of attorney fees and costs to the prevailing party. Other litigation has arisen from newly evolved rights of a political (civil rights) or social (entitlement programs) nature. While contingent fee arrangements (the lawyer gets paid nothing unless the case is won or favorably settled) *may* discourage the bringing of some frivolous lawsuits, the hourly fees charged by those lawyers who regularly represent defendants do nothing to shorten litigation. The rampant individualism and competitiveness fostered in our culture certainly encourage the knight-errantry of litigation. So, for all these reasons, more business disputes (between businesses and against businesses) are "resolved" by litigation today than ever before. Most are not resolved by litigation at all, of course, but settled by negotiation, frequently in spite of pending litigation. That's a capsule history, but what is truly important are the consequences of that history.

Every case that is (or will be) in the court system has at least five negative characteristics which conspire to impede efficient resolution. These characteristics are:

1. The people with the most direct interest in resolving the dispute (the "owners" of it) are removed from front-line responsibility for resolving it because all activity is "delegated" to the lawyer for each party;

2. The normally combative approach of the litigator infects his client: Disputes become personalized, and the opposing side demonized;

3. The communication problems associated with having two or more "outsiders" (the lawyers) to the dispute who are in charge of processing it are exponentially exacerbated by the lawyers' code of ethics which forbids any lawyer from talking directly to any party but his own client;

4. The vexatious and time-consuming nature of litigation frequently leads to exasperation on the part of the parties, with the result that they distance themselves from the dispute and "leave it to the lawyers," which is particularly appealing to those who are not spending their own money.

5. Almost unbridled "discovery" is available to every party, and it can be used to slow down litigation even when the court calendar is not clogged.

With these forces at work, it's a wonder any litigated disputes get resolved short of trial.

ENDNOTE

[1] New York, *Civil Practice Act,* art. 84, secs. 1448-1469. See, generally, American Arbitration Association, *Pioneers in Dispute Resolution: A History of the American Arbitration Association on Its 65th Anniversary (1926-1991)* (1991).

BUSINESS DISPUTES AND THE LAW

For most of the twentieth century, business disputes which could not be readily solved by negotiation headed for the courthouse. However, some industries saw that there were more attractive alternatives to a litigated resolution of their disputes, by disputes meaning those occurring between and among companies within a particular industry and not the disputes that such companies had with "outsiders." A number of these industries chose to set up arbitration programs whose common features included:

— industrywide agreements to refer disputes to the program;

— selection of arbitrators from within the industry itself; and

— predominance of nonlawyer arbitrators.

Generally speaking, these intraindustry arbitration programs arose because of perceived needs for:

— special expertise among those who decided the disputes (*e.g.,* construction, insurance industries);

— uniformity of result within the industry (*e.g.,* insurance); and

— speed of resolution (*e.g.,* textile/clothing industry).

Some of these intraindustry alternative dispute resolution programs are more than forty years old and have become established fixtures in the minds of industry members. Unfortunately, the industries which came to rely on arbitration of their intraindustry disputes did not have the same success in getting the "outside world" to accept arbitration or other ADR mechanisms as ways of resolving disputes with their members.

A. Current Status: the Lawyer as Specialist

One of the reasons why these industries could not succeed in persuading "outsiders" to use ADR for disputes with their members is the historic availability of our court system. In the late nineteenth century, for instance, courts were generally available to civil litigants without undue delay. Excluding some giant antitrust cases brought by the federal government, trials tended to be shorter than they are today. Because tax dollars support the court system, people with disputes felt entitled to "get their money's worth" by using it.

1. Why Businesses Turn to Lawyers: the Myths

Since the beginning of our republic (and earlier in England), lawyers have had a monopoly (really an oligopoly) on the courthouse. In order to be represented in court, a lawyer was required. True, parties were always in theory permitted to represent themselves. However, business enterprises always thought it prudent to hire a lawyer, and laws were passed which prohibited corporations from appearing in court *without* a lawyer. So, what started out as a prudent, self-protective measure for management quickly turned into a legal necessity.

2. Courts: the Only Way to Resolve Disputes(?)

Given the historic availability of the courts, the "requirement" that a lawyer represent a party before them and the inevitability of disputes themselves, certain consequences followed. The first was that many business people abandoned efforts to "keep up with the law." One reason was that the law itself started to proliferate wildly as the nineteenth century ended. Another was that a "dedicated" class of lawyers grew up whose *only* business it was to know the law. Within those ranks, a subclass emerged: the litigator. This group knew something about the general laws which applied to civil conduct, but their real expertise was in the rules, lore, and nuances of the judicial system. Keep in mind that this is not an exclusively American phenomenon. Indeed, large parts of it were imported, fully assembled, from the United Kingdom. Nonetheless, as business activity in America surpassed that of our former colonial power, so, too, did the ascendancy of lawyers. They functioned both as guardians of the court system, and as agents for it.

3. Public Has Been Trained to Turn to Lawyers

Our lawyers have instilled in us the notion that the court system is not only the best place to go for dispute resolution, it is the *only* place. Historically, courts emerged as places where the sovereign provided for "peaceful" resolution of disputes. Otherwise, disputes had been resolved by lobbing one of the disputants into boiling water or oil, having (nonlawyer) representative combatants fight to an obvious conclusion, etc. The only way that these relatively new inventions, the courts, could work was if the sovereign gave them coercive power over the (disputing) citizenry. It also followed that the coercive power given to courts had to be the exclusive (legal) coercive power for dispute resolution. If it were not, then the medieval equivalent of "loan sharks" would have continued to "resolve disputes" in private.[1] So, once the courts had exclusive (legal) coercive power to resolve civil disputes, they became indispensable to the resolution process. Why? For example, assume that two disputing parties decided to resolve their dispute by, say, mediation. An agreement was reached, but, shortly afterward, one of the parties did not honor its end of the mediated bargain. What was the other party to do? Barring an assignment for the medieval loan sharks, the only place that had the power to punish the derelict party for "breaching" the mediated agreement was the court (in actuality, its representative, the sheriff). Things are really no different today. If a party contracts to arbitrate its disputes with another and then refuses to go to arbitration, the court is the only place with the power to "order" that party to go to arbitration or risk loss by default if it does not. Similarly, at the other end of the arbitration process, the award an arbitrator makes at the end of his hearing does not enforce itself. If the parties do not comply with it, one of them must go to court for relief. So, our lawyers said, if the court is responsible for enforcing the decision anyhow, why not go there in the first place?

4. Disputes Are "Legal" and Not "Business" Matters

It is an axiom of life that acts have consequences. In our culture, there is a corollary to that axiom: acts have *legal* consequences. Like most axioms and corollaries, it is true, but its real meaning derives from conclusions drawn from it. In our business culture, the conclusion drawn from this corollary is that all disputes are essentially legal matters. Looked at squarely, this is patent nonsense, but no one asserts the conclusion that baldly. A business person who is in a dispute certainly would not mind, in most instances, having the help provided by a lawyer. Lawyers, in business to make a living themselves, certainly do not mind giving whatever help they can to remedy unfortunate actions of managers, if that's what is wanted, resulting in a symbiotic relationship. Tragically (and it is really no one's fault), business disputes (personal ones, too) have increasingly come to be seen as "legal" matters, meaning not only that a lawyer should be used in connection with disputes, but that a lawyer should, effectively, be *in charge of* the process of resolving the dispute. In fact, until about fifteen years ago, lawyers (either corporate staff or outside counsel) were controlling most business disputes.

5. A Lawyer Is Needed to Communicate with the Opponent

A rather awkward problem is the matter of who communicates with the opponent. In these circumstances, many American business people feel that they need a lawyer, if for no other reason, to interact with the other party. Lawyers are not necessarily to blame for this phenomenon; they simply move in to fill the "vacuum" that business people's own unwillingness to communicate directly with the other party has created. Regardless of who started this "tradition," it has a certain effect.

When people have a dispute with one another, one of the difficulties that got them there (and may be a barrier to resolution) is frequently a communication failure. The presence of representatives (whether they are lawyers or not) on one or both sides of the dispute may help to ameliorate the communications problems which the principals had, or it may not. Even if the representatives (assuming each side has one) are active listeners, have total recall, and communicate clearly, they nonetheless have placed two filters between the "owners" of the dispute. Also, if these representatives are getting paid (say, by the hour) for doing this job, they have little economic incentive to get the dispute resolved. Even if the representatives can put aside their own economic interests (as many lawyers/negotiators do), they still, in the words of a university vice president, "aren't playing with their own money." However, was the university v.p. also not "playing" with her own money? She frankly conceded the point, but added, "I am responsible for the tax money that comes in here (a public university), and my job depends on how it's spent. That's never going to be true of an outside lawyer whom I hire."

Should we then foreswear all legal assistance and go ahead without help? Of course not, but it would be a good idea to keep in mind the layers of filtration that are involved when lawyers (or other representatives) are used to negotiate a dispute. With the best will in the world, what a representative says may not be what the dispute "owner" said or heard.

B. The Public Court System: Core Meltdown

1. Court Congestion (State and Federal)

One reason for the growing popularity of alternative dispute resolution in America is the failure of the judicial system to provide adequate service to civil litigants. The public court system has become overburdened, resulting in delays of court hearings and the adjudication of disputes.[2] Parties may enter the judicial system seeking justice, but the time delays and costs of pursuing their case frequently put that goal beyond reach. After litigating a matter in the public court system, parties to the litigation, even the "winners," often question what they really got. In many cases, the process of taking a case to trial is so expensive that it costs parties more money than they win. Even if a party prevails at trial with costs that are reasonable, the losing party can often keep the "winner" at bay for years by using the appellate court processes. As a result, individuals and organizations alike have turned to alternative methods of dispute resolution. Arbitration, mediation, etc., offer parties more rapid and less expensive means of resolving their conflicts. Sadly, the current congestion on both the state and federal level is likely to get worse. Dwindling public resources, the escalating demands of the criminal side of the justice system, and recent "tough-on-crime" legislation all point in that direction.

2. Dwindling Public Resources

At the same time that civil court dockets are growing,[3] the funding of public courts has been dwindling, not because of competition for resources among various branches, levels, and departments of government, but because of a net decrease in the total of resources available for government services. One result of this is that while the number of cases within the public court system has increased, the number of judges appointed to the bench has not kept pace. So, the case load per judge continues to expand. In addition, lack of funding has thinned the number of clerical personnel and prevented long-overdue technological upgrades. So, even the judges on the bench become less efficient than they otherwise might be.

3. Escalating Demands of the "Criminal Justice System"

Another reason for the backlog in our civil courts is the increasing caseload of criminal matters. These higher numbers of criminal cases are soaking up judicial resources formerly available for civil disputes. Many states and the federal system have "speedy trial" laws which give criminal cases priority over almost all civil suits.[4] A state trial court judge recently told of having to declare a mistrial in a civil case which he had been trying for three weeks. The presiding judge called him and said, "I have a murder case down here where the defendant is going to go free if we can't get him out to trial today. Every other judge who's working has a criminal case, so I have to send this to you." The trial court judge protested that he had five parties and their lawyers before him, had been trying the case for three weeks, and knew that there was one party which would not agree to a postponement. "Tell them I'm sorry," the presiding judge said, "but I can't let this accused murderer walk out the door." The result was that the civil suit had to restart some time in the future when a judge was available, and run the risk of the same thing happening all over again.

4. The Effect of Recent Legislation

In the political scramble to be seen as tough on crime, elected officials have latched on to a new "panacea." This one uses a baseball metaphor, and is called the Three Strikes Law. This legislation puts the offender in prison after the third conviction for the rest of his life. While each state's version differs slightly from the other's, the effect of the laws is that a person convicted of (or who pleads guilty to) a third crime will be incarcerated for life. The merits of this type of legislation are questionable, at best.[5] One law enforcement official put it this way: "What we are doing is turning our prisons into the largest, most expensive set of male geriatric wards in the world. Except for the lunatic fringe, who are probably already in jail for long terms, no man over (age) 45 or so is likely to commit a violent crime. So, this isn't going to do a damn thing to reduce street crime." Nonetheless, criminal defendants and their attorneys are predictably refusing to plea bargain, fearing that a guilty plea will be one "strike" of the three allowed before life imprisonment. Historically, the vast majority of criminal cases were disposed of by these plea bargains. So, logically, the end result is a growing backlog of *criminal* cases. In 1994, for example, the number of felony *trials* increased by nearly 150 percent, mainly because of the three strikes law.[6] As a result, civil cases have been pushed to the back of an even longer line. Some jurisdictions have even shut down their civil courts to free up court space, personnel, and other resources to handle the criminal docket.[7] Since the passage of three-strikes legislation in California, approximately 2,500 three-strike felony cases have been filed in Los Angeles county alone.[8] Prior to the legislation, 75 percent to 80 percent of these types of cases were disposed of through plea bargains. However, today less than one percent of the three-strike felony cases are resolved by a plea. Instead, these cases are being sent to trial. To date, only 35 percent of these cases have actually gone to trial, leaving nearly 1,675 cases still pending—all of which take priority over civil trials.[9] One metropolitan trial court judge in California said, "In six months there will be *no* civil cases being tried in this courthouse. What's worse, I can't tell you when we will be able to start trying them again." As a result, for many people with a civil dispute, alternative dispute resolution is no longer "alternative"; it is the only practical choice.

C. Comparison with Other Industrialized Countries

1. Great Britain

Great Britain has essentially the same legal system as the United States does, largely because the American version is derived from the British. Yet many fewer business disputes find their way to—or through—the British courts. Arbitration is a popular avenue for resolving disputes, particularly international ones. Mediation takes place quite frequently, but not always in the same form as it does in the United States. In Britain, trade and community associations regularly provide the mediation "forum," and mediators are often people who know the parties (and even the particular dispute) quite well. When business disputes do go to court, they are heard by juries much less often than in the United States.

2. Japan

Japan is well known for its emphasis on consensus, and its statistics bear this reputation out. The number of civil suits filed in Japan varies from four to ten percent of those filed in other rich countries, not because the Japanese do not have disputes, but because of their strong cultural bias against confrontational activities. As a result, the Japanese have a highly developed ADR system which resolves the vast majority of disputes without anyone going to court.

The Japanese ADR system has three major forms: reconcilement, conciliation, and *chotei*. Reconcilement involves negotiation between the disputing parties with a view toward working out their differences. This process distinctly does not adhere to any legal rules or principles. Rather, the key to resolution is heavy reliance on the status of the social groups to which the disputants belong. The member of the more powerful group (*oyabun*) is supposed to act in the best interests of the weaker party (*kobun*). The practical result of reconcilement is that the decision of the socially superior (more powerful) party is imposed on the party with lower status.

Conciliation is really only a modified form of reconcilement, which involves an intermediary. Conciliation itself has two branches, which approximate American mediation and arbitration. Both branches emphasize mutual concessions rather than logical or legal considerations. The crucial difference from American (and European) practice is that the conciliator (not the parties) decides what the outcome will be in *both* branches of conciliation. This is no surprise when the intermediary is expected to act as an arbitrator, but very unusual (to us) when he is acting as a mediator. In practice, a "mediating" conciliator will give the parties time to negotiate their own resolution, but will suggest outcomes if he thinks things are taking too long or the party with the higher social status seems to be getting impatient. The only practical difference between the two branches of conciliation seems to be that the decision which results from the "arbitration" version of conciliation is accorded the effect of a final court judgment.

Chotei (for which there is no English word) consists of a hearing by a panel composed of a judge and two or more lay conciliators. This format seems to be more like a court-annexed process in America, as it is usually invoked only by parties who have filed a lawsuit or are contemplating doing so. The process may be invoked by any of the parties, or the judge. Its purpose is to achieve a compromise between the positions of the parties, put that compromise in writing, and file it as a final judgment of the court. If no acceptable compromise can be reached, the *chotei* committee will give its own opinions to the court, which may render a decision based on them.

It has been shown, in great oversimplification, that two other economically strong countries can and do resolve their business disputes in ways that are less confrontational and less expensive than the normal American methods of settling such disputes. One of those countries is culturally similar to our own. It can be done.

ENDNOTES

¹ They probably did then, and they certainly do now. This is not a criticism of the court system so much as it is a criticism of social hypocrisy.

² See William Ide III, "Summoning Our Resolve: Alternative Dispute Resolution Aims for Settlement Without Litigation," *American Bar Association Journal* (October 1993): 8. The average state civil court action takes nearly 14 months to conclude and the average federal case takes between seven and 11 months to conclude. This statistic, however, is not meaningful for organizations which are located in urban centers. For example, the Second (federal) Circuit Court of Appeals (covering New York, Connecticut, and Vermont) has reported a backlog of 3,600 cases which are *more than three years old.* See Doreen Carvajal, "Civil Verdicts Delayed for Years in New York's Clogged U.S. Court," *New York Times,* 17 April 1995, p. A1.

³ See, *e.g.,* "Judicial Statistics for Fiscal Year 1991-92," Judicial Council of California Annual Report, vol. 2, 1993. The number of cases filed in the California superior courts increased five percent. The number of new California judgeships filled in that year did not keep pace.

⁴ "Congress has effectively 'orphaned' the federal civil justice system to a secondary status. The developments that have contributed most to the delay and expense in processing civil cases are (1) the enactment of the federal criminal Speedy Trial act; (2) the promulgation of rigid, mandatory, and formalistic federal criminal sentencing guidelines; and (3) the increasing federalization of crime." Eastern District of Wisconsin, *Introduction to Civil Justice Expense and Delay Reduction Plan Adopted Pursuant to the Civil Justice Reform Act of 1990* (1991), p. 4. Apparently, things had not improved much three years later. Hon. J. Clifford Wallace, "Tackling the Caseload Crisis," *American Bar Association Journal* (June 1994): 88.

⁵ In 1993, 13 states, including Washington, California, Colorado, Connecticut, Georgia, Indiana, Kansas, Louisiana, Maryland, New Mexico, North Carolina, Tennessee, Virginia, and Wisconsin, had passed "three strikes" or similar legislation. See Richard C. Reuben, "Get-tough Stance Draws Fiscal Criticism," *American Bar Association Journal* (January 1995): 16.

⁶ Legislation mandating stiffer penalties in drug cases has also contributed to the backlog of criminal cases.

⁷ Richard C. Reuben, *op. cit.,* p. 16.

⁸ Interview with Sandy Gibbons, Public Information Officer, Los Angeles County District Attorney's Office, 25 May 1995.

⁹ Forty new deputy district attorneys have been hired in order to manage the increased caseloads.

Counselor, in case you're intending to rap your opening
statement, let me assure you the court will not be amused.

ADR IN AMERICA

Share everything. Play fair. Don't hit people. Put things back where you found them. Clean up your own mess. Don't take things that aren't yours. Say you're sorry when you hurt somebody.
—Robert Fulghum

A. What It Is and How It Is Used

Alternative dispute resolution, for purposes of this discussion, means nothing more than that collection of options available to parties to a dispute *other than court litigation.* Informal ADR, such as negotiation, has been going on throughout the ages.

While evidence of formal alternative dispute resolution (such as arbitration) is found as early as Plato's time and appears throughout Anglo-Norman history,[1] the intellectual birthplace of the alternative dispute resolution movement in America has been routinely traced to the Pound Conference, sponsored by the American Bar Association in 1976. In that year, seventy years after Roscoe Pound himself delivered a lecture on public dissatisfaction with the legal system, Professor Frank Sander delivered a paper entitled "Varieties of Dispute Processing." In it, Prof. Sander reminded the legal community—and anyone else willing to pay attention—that court-centered litigation was only one way to resolve disputes. From that conference sprang increased interest, both academic and practical, in noncourthouse processes for resolving disputes. Surprisingly, those with the most to lose in alternatives to court-based litigation, business litigators, moved first. In 1977, the mini-trial was invented by lawyers involved in a seemingly interminable patent case involving Telecredit and TRW. In parallel with the development of the mini-trial, the dust was blown off mediation. Arbitration, which had long been used to solve labor and some commercial disputes, was tested in other areas, and given new forms. Finally, that oldest of dispute resolution techniques, negotiation, was subjected to unprecedented scholarly scrutiny and began to be seriously taught as a learnable skill.

Bear in mind that under English and American common law, courts were not thrilled about requiring parties to arbitrate their disputes. In general, the law was that an agreement to arbitrate could be revoked by any party, for no reason, right up until the award had been issued by the arbitrator. In the early part of this century, states began to enact legislation which provided for the enforcement of agreements to arbitrate *existing disputes only*. In the 1950s, a Uniform Arbitration Act was issued which provided that contracts to arbitrate *future* disputes were also legally enforceable. Many states adopted a version of the Uniform Act, while others chose to model their law after the earlier federal legislation. (See Appendix A for lists of these states.)

This earlier federal law took the form of the U.S. Arbitration Act (USAA or FAA), which was enacted by Congress in 1925. It provided that arbitration agreements (for existing or future disputes) were enforceable to the same extent as any other contract. Although the jurisdiction of the USAA was limited to transactions in interstate commerce, the reach of that jurisdiction broadened as this century reached its midpoint. In 1967, the U.S. Supreme Court came down squarely on the side of enforcing as many arbitration agreements as the federal courts could.[2]

Private sector developments were coinciding with legislation. In the late 1920s, the American Arbitration Association was founded in order to foster the use and study of arbitration (and other ADR forms) as well as provide an institutional venue and set of rules for those who wished to arbitrate. Still functioning, the American Arbitration Association's numerous offices provide panels of neutrals, administration of cases, education, and training in ADR.

As all the above events were happening, the various court systems in urban America were moving inexorably toward gridlock. As a result, even those disputants who originally had no interest in alternative dispute resolution were forced by circumstances to seek other means of settling their disputes. Many who did found the "new" ways superior. Others found certain ADR methods lacking, and modified them accordingly.

1. Strategies for Identifying Disputes Before They Become "Federal Cases"

Still others took ADR one logical step further and focused on dispute *prevention*. Two approaches which have benefited large organizations handsomely are legal audits and compliance programs. A legal audit involves taking a close look at all of an organization's practices (from contracting to product design to service guarantees) with a view toward identifying which of them may cause future liability (or just litigation). Once identified, these practices can usually be modified to make them less dangerous. Done well, a legal audit is a true implementation of the maxim, "An ounce of prevention is worth a pound of cure."

Compliance programs are similarly preventive in nature, but with a different emphasis. In a compliance program, employees whose daily responsibilities include living up to legal or regulatory requirements are instructed on the nature of these requirements and the reasons behind them (and, perhaps, the penalties for transgressing them). Thus empowered, these employees act in a way that ensures senior management of organizational rectitude in areas as diverse as antitrust, environmental, and securities laws.

Common qualities shared by all successful dispute prevention programs are:

— Unqualified commitment by ownership and/or senior management;

— Advance "amnesty" for employees who were "doing it wrong";

— Independent, unbiased legal and regulatory advice;

— Making dispute prevention an ongoing process, not just a one-time event; and

— Assistance from affected outsiders (government agencies, customers, suppliers, investors, etc.).

An important subset of compliance programs is the engineering audit. Conducted by business people, lawyers, *and* engineers, these programs try to anticipate and defuse problems in the areas of product design, product labelling, instructions and warnings, and warranties. While the goal of these audits is to eliminate future liability, it should not be surprising to learn that product improvement and increased customer satisfaction are important byproducts of this process.

2. Prevention and Resolution Begin at Home

The internal workings of organizations have been affected by the ADR movement as well. While this area still lags behind external relations in adopting user-friendly ADR systems, organizations are increasingly testing new methods of preventing or efficiently resolving disputes with their own employees. In this area, the internal "grievance" mechanism is probably still the most popular with employers who do not have collective bargaining agreements with their employees. (ADR in the collective bargaining setting is beyond the scope of this book.) Many long-standing grievance programs have been spruced up to make them more efficient, easier to use, and (a crucial consideration for their effectiveness) fair in both appearance and reality.

Some organizations, particularly in the education field, have installed ombudsmen (of both genders) in their organizations. These professionals, almost always employees themselves, are charged with receiving and investigating complaints by employees. After doing so, they report their findings—usually accompanied by recommendations—to senior management. Less frequently, the ombudsman tries to mediate the dispute himself. While the success of this institution depends greatly on the quality of the ombudsman, many organizations report tremendous satisfaction with it. To bolster the independence of the ombudsman, some organizations have turned to non-employee professionals or retired employees (whose pensions have fully vested).

3. ADR in Contracts: Preventive Medicine

Normally, the term "contract" is thought of as a written business agreement between two parties. In the ADR field, there is one contract that has many parties and should be mentioned first in discussions of business dispute prevention and resolution. The Corporate Policy Statement on ADR, which was issued by the Center for Public Resources (CPR) in 1984, commits the organizations who sign it to explore ADR options first in all future disputes with other signatories. Hundreds of major corporations have signed the Statement, but the effect on corporate behavior is not fully known.

One of the purposes of promulgating the Statement was to make it easier for executives of large organizations to avoid the "knee-jerk" selection of litigation whenever a dispute arises. One general counsel of a major computer company put it this way: "Don't forget, we have manhood at stake here, too. With the ADR statement now corporate policy, an executive or a company lawyer has a fig leaf to cover his making a phone call to see if a matter can be settled. Otherwise, making that same phone call might have made others in the company think he wasn't tough. I can't tell you how much money we used to spend on outside counsel just defending someone's reputation for being tough."

In the more mundane world of day-to-day contracts, preventive medicine can also be administered. ADR clauses can be placed in contractual documents as different as invoices, purchase orders, delivery contracts, product/service warranties, deposit receipts (in residential real estate), construction contracts, distributorship agreements, licensing agreements for technology or intellectual property, and so on. The important concept is that by placing these ADR clauses in such contracts, it is possible to *control* any dispute resolution in advance. Most people would jump at the chance to control any part of their future. To control a part of the future in a way which will save money, time, and headaches should be attractive. While the specifics of choosing ADR clauses will be dealt with later, a few guidelines can be given here:

    a.   A low-cost, low-hostility option should always be chosen as a first step. Most of the time, this will be negotiation. Only when that step fails should a contract clause require more expensive options. The reasoning behind this is not just to save time and money (although those might be reasons enough), but it is almost always true that the low-cost option will also be the less adversarial one. So, tensions as well as costs will be kept at the lowest possible level.

b. Ensure that the other parties to the contract understand the nature of the ADR clause and its mutual benefit. This does not mean simply complying with the legal minimum to make the ADR clause legally enforceable, although this should be done.[3]

4. When Being Sued

"It's too late for ADR," an oil company manager said, "we're being sued." Well, yes and no. It is certainly too late for a predispute ADR agreement, but it is not too late, however, to suggest ADR to the party bringing suit or to the court in which the lawsuit is pending. Currently, courts and their judges are rated on how many cases are disposed of. So, almost every trial judge will try to get a case disposed of by ADR. The judge will get a favorable statistic, and the parties will be saved the ordeal of litigation.

If a suing party seems immovable, the American Arbitration Association or other ADR agency can help in trying to persuade the opposition to use ADR. Although a first reaction to the lawsuit may be a desire to "smite" the opposition with litigation tactics, remember that lawsuits quickly take on a life of their own. Once they do, they tend to career expensively beyond the control of any one party or lawyer. The only way to be sure that this does not happen is to intervene early in the process and move to less toxic methods of resolving the controversy.

5. When Bringing Suit

To reiterate: ADR is not necessarily for every dispute. Certain types of disputes (criminal cases, for instance) and certain types of opponents who will not negotiate in good faith (bad-faith crooks, to take a random example) are just not amenable to low-hostility, noncoercive processes. As an example of a criminal dispute, a Taiwanese "businessman" came into the offices of a bank. He presented an International Letter of Credit for $500,000 for which this was the confirming bank, together with Oceangoing Bills of Lading that seemed to show that he had delivered to the United States a container of specialty chemicals of that value. Something made the bank officer suspicious, so he asked the businessman to come back later in the day. In the interim, customs officials "randomly inspected" the container, and found that it contained nothing but old newspapers. But the businessman's papers were regular on their face, and the rules of international credit would require the bank to pay the $500,000. Working with the general counsel, the bank officer prepared and filed an application for a temporary restraining order with the local trial court. When the businessman returned, the bank officer was able to say (truthfully, albeit misleadingly) that a suit had been filed to restrain payment of the letter of credit, and that the bank was compelled to await the court's decision. After some test ranting to see if the bank officer was firm in his position, the businessman left the bank, never to be seen again. The buyer of the specialty chemicals, of course, never had to fund the letter of credit. Would a different result have been obtained in arbitration? Hardly. The problem with arbitration in this setting is that it could not have moved nearly quickly enough to accommodate the needs of the wronged parties. Arbitrators are empowered to hear one dispute at a time. Unlike public judges, they have no continuing jurisdiction to hear claims generally. So, even if there were an arbitration clause in the letter of credit, an arbitrator selection process would have had to have been completed before anyone could act. In this case, it would have been too late.

So, in a dispute, a bit of preliminary analysis is required before any form of ADR is attempted. The first inquiry, of course, should be if there is an existing contract between the parties which *requires* ADR. If not, it should then be determined whether one of the parties is a signatory to the CPR Corporate Policy Statement on ADR (or something like it). Assuming the answer is no, then the next question is if there is some action which an opponent can take which will either determine the outcome of the dispute or give a party enormous leverage over another? If the answer is yes, then it must be determined whether this action is one which a court would likely prevent. For example, a business which makes computer chips owes $1,200,000, and its foreign owners have denuded it of cash. The only hope of collection of the debt lies in its inventory of chips. So, to the question of if there is some action which the opponent can take, the answer is a resounding affirmative. It could take all the valuable yet small chips and leave town with them! The next part of the question of a court being likely to prevent such an action must be left to lawyers. Unless there is an arbitrator in place presiding over a dispute, the only forum that will be able to act fast enough to help will be the courts. But ADR could still be used after a court has provided the needed preliminary relief.

B. Why Businesses Have Turned to ADR

There is always free cheese in a mousetrap.—Anonymous

Although the courts are a separate branch of government and lawyers belong to a profession, when viewed through the eyes of a client with a civil dispute, they are collectively in the dispute resolution business. This is a service business, although those who avail themselves of it sometimes feel as if *they are serving it.* In a very real sense, then, businesses with disputes are *consumers* of dispute resolution *services.* Unlike those with criminal complaints, organizations and individuals with civil disputes are not faced with a government monopoly. If an organization has a dispute which cannot be settled by unmanaged negotiation, dispute resolution services will be necessary. Most consumers of services have four basic concerns with every potential service provider:

1. how long it will take;
2. how much it will cost;
3. what the end result will be; and
4. why this service should be chosen over other providers.

In the normal world of commerce, these are four questions that any service-provider of quality is prepared to answer at the drop of a hat. Without the answers to these queries, any potential consumer of a service will be hard put to make a rational choice. With them, a comparison of the eligible providers can be made, with a resultant informed decision.

Sadly, answers to these questions are hard to come by from our public court systems. Even if they *wanted* to provide this information, the court system to which a dispute might be taken could only give information about one piece of the puzzle. The court, after all, is not the biggest factor in the cost of resolving the dispute. Nor does the court have full control over the time it will take. The court can list a wide array of possibilities, but it cannot predict with any certainty what the outcome will be.

For contrast, imagine being in need of some other service, such as a swimming pool service. Every community has its share (or more) of swimming pool maintenance companies. The barriers to entry are low. When solicited for an estimate, each will answer the basic four questions. Each candidate will state a monthly charge, how many service calls that charge will cover, how long each call will last, how clean the pool will be after treatment, and if the chemicals for the pool are included in the monthly charge. If they are not, an estimate of what the chemicals will cost and a guarantee that they won't exceed a certain cost under normal conditions would be made. Each candidate will give references as partial answer to the question of why this particular service provider should be hired. Comparatively, in choosing dispute resolution services, a business relationship with the service provider is *out of control* from the consumer's point of view, because the four basic concerns have no specific answers. Yet, this is essentially what parties to disputes do every day of the year.

As later chapters will show, there is "a better way."

> *Fraud and Falsehood only dread examination. Truth invites it.*—Thomas Cooper

Ten Rules of Dispute Resolution

1. All disputes are personal.
2. The best time to agree on how to resolve a dispute is before that dispute has arisen.
3. No dispute will end before the parties want it to.
4. Some disputes will not end even when the parties want them to.
5. Alternative dispute resolution should be considered for every dispute.
6. Alternative dispute resolution should not be used for every dispute.
7. The neutral is the most important component of every alternative dispute resolution mechanism.
8. The process of resolving every dispute has its own costs, independent of those of the underlying dispute.
9. The costs referred to in Rule 8 can be controlled.
10. Justice can be done outside the courthouse.

ENDNOTES

[1] See William M. Howard, "The Evolution of Contractually Mandated Arbitration," *Arbitration Journal* 48 (September 1993): 27; Edward A. Dauer, *Manual of Dispute Resolution* (McGraw-Hill, 1994), p. 2-1.

[2] See the Court's opinion in *Prima Paint Corp. v. Flood & Conklin Mfg. Co.,* 388 U.S. 395.

[3] Despite the oxymoronic quality of this outcome (mandatory mediation), courts have held that agreements to participate in *completely voluntary* alternative dispute resolution mechanisms (mediation, advisory arbitration) are legally enforceable. For an early example of this now-settled view, see *AMF, Inc. v. Brunswick Corp.,* 621 F.Supp. 456 (D.C.N.Y. 1985).

"Look, at least we're talking."

NEGOTIATION
The Mother of All Dispute Resolution Processes

You can't always get what you want;
You can't always get what you want;
But, if you try sometimes,
You just might find,
You get what you need.
　　—Mick Jagger & Keith Richard

A. Negotiation Defined and Explained

Everyone negotiates every day of their life. On issues ranging from "What movie shall we see?" to "Should we release the nuclear missiles?", two or more people are frequently negotiating. Indeed, negotiating is so familiar an activity that it doesn't receive much thought. This is true, even in an academic setting. One author on negotiation recently wrote the following:

> ... we should all be spending an awful lot of time studying negotiation. Yet it is amazing to me how few people have. In 1985, my daughter Julia graduated from USC [University of Southern California]. She graduated from the business school, one of the finest business schools in the country in fact, and certainly one of the most expensive. It cost more than $50,000 to put her through that school. But she didn't get one hour of negotiating training.[1]

All of us negotiate when necessary, do the best that we can, live with the results, and move on. One of the premises of this book is that the various mechanisms of alternative dispute resolution which are dealt with contain a core of learnable skills. Negotiation, as a dispute resolution process, is no exception.

This chapter will define and explain dispute resolution negotiation in a business setting, set some of the cultural parameters for negotiation, identify some important problem areas of the negotiation process, and set out some guidelines for successful dispute resolution negotiation.

The type and level of negotiation being dealt with here will be limited to *"conversation processes directed toward resolving initial differences."* Before getting into details, it is important to notice how the working definition of negotiation here differs from the common meaning of the term.[2] One limiting element is the word "conversation." This treatment will be limited to situations where people converse with one another, in person or by telephone. This does not mean to suggest that business negotiations are not conducted in writing or by electronic telecommunications (fax, telex, etc.). Of course they are. However, everyone's experience and the studies that have been done indicate that *there is no substitute for live human connection* in the resolution of disputes by negotiation.[3] One executive of a New York-based trading company told me: "I don't care if I don't know a word of the other person's language or one bit about his culture. If we have a dispute, I want to sit down across the table from him, say what I think, and listen hard to what he tells me."

Notice that the above quotation *presumes the existence of a dispute,* which is the second differentiating factor in this working definition of negotiation: "resolving initial differences." This phrase does not mean an "initial difference" regarding price, or delivery terms, or who pays for insurance during shipment. This refers to an actual dispute. The existence of an actual dispute presumes that both parties have identified at least one issue and, at least once, stated their own views about it, which are in conflict.

Here is an example which not only illustrates different negotiated resolutions of the same dispute but also demonstrates the value of keeping an open mind. It seems there were ten people and five oranges. Each person wanted an orange. They were paired off in twos. One member of each twosome had a coin. The other had a knife. Here is how each pair negotiated their dispute:

PAIR ONE: These people reached a compromise, with each agreeing to take half the orange. They then decided upon two coin tosses, one to resolve who would cut the orange with the knife and the second to determine who would get to pick the first half.

PAIR TWO: This pair, after a bit of bargaining, decided to cut the orange in half, too. Their resolutions were that one would cut the orange, and the other choose the first piece.

PAIR THREE: These two experienced negotiators discussed their interests in the orange before making any decisions. One mentioned interest in eating the fruit. The other wanted to use the orange peel as flavoring. As a result, they were quickly able to agree that one would take the fruit and the other, the peel.

PAIR FOUR: This pair, a bit more creative than their counterparts in the earlier pairs, used everything at their disposal to reach an agreement which satisfied both of them. One intended to squeeze the fruit for juice and keep the knife, while giving the remains of the orange to the other. His negotiating partner kept the coin and planned to sell the peel to a tavern nearby for flavoring drinks, then sell the orange seed to a nursery, and then sell the fruit to a pet shop (tropical birds love it), believing that the resultant cash would be enough to buy two apples.

PAIR FIVE: The entrepreneurial negotiators in this twosome reached an agreement that not only used all the assets at their disposal, but also created a situation of possible future benefit to both of them. They sold the knife to buy poster board and a marker. They used the coin (a 50-cent piece) to buy a glass. They squeezed the orange, lettered an advertising sign, and the glass of orange juice was sold for one dollar. This enabled them to buy two more oranges and a package of plastic cups. Soon, they had enough inventory (oranges) to use as collateral for an expansion loan. With it, they rented and furnished a small juice stand, and . . . .

In all five situations, there was the same dispute, two orange-wanters and one orange, but with five different resolutions. There probably could have been dozens more. The points to remember are these:

1. Disputes can be negotiated to a resolution that is beneficial to (as well as acceptable to) each party;

2. The more open the parties are to imaginative resolutions, the more likely a solution will result; and

3. Disputes tend to get resolved when the parties to them pay attention to getting them resolved.

Taking off from the point last above, the working definition of negotiation contains the phrase "directed toward" settling initial differences. What is meant here is that discussions between the parties must have, *as an acknowledged purpose,* resolution of the existing dispute. Usually, this takes the form of planned negotiations to try to obtain closure on a dispute, which gives everyone involved time to prepare themselves.

The dispute may, however, arise in the course of discussions about other things (which are not themselves in dispute). In this case, on-the-spot decisions must be made as to (1) whether sufficient preparation has been done in order to engage in negotiations about the dispute, as opposed to the original topic of these talks, (2) recognition of the fact that there may be some connection between the original topic of the talks and the dispute that has arisen in discussion, or (3) even wanting to negotiate at this point at all. It may be best to try to defer discussion of the dispute until the three items above are more or less decided or until the original topic is settled. On the other hand, it may enhance the chances of a favorable outcome on the original topic of conversation if the existing dispute is resolved *first.* These are just some of the on-the-spot judgment calls that a negotiator must make. Obviously, on the other side of this transaction, one might well be completely prepared for negotiations, hoping to catch an opponent off guard.

So, to review, this chapter will outline some concepts and techniques helpful to those who participate in conversations having the purpose of resolving an existing dispute.

B. Getting Started

Preparation and timing are the key elements of every alternative dispute resolution mechanism. However, some recent conversations with business people in the international arena may cause a redefining of what the threshold consideration in negotiation should be. For example, a recent conversation with an American agribusiness executive surfaced this report:

> Negotiators for an American company (called, for example, Nuts2U) were in China, discussing with their Chinese hosts the prospect of delivering and selling several million pounds of certain types of nuts to China each year. The Nuts2U negotiating team felt, after four days of tough bargaining, that a deal was near. There was one topic on their list of concerns that had not been broached, however. Since the nuts were to be delivered to China in bulk, and they were foodstuffs, Chinese regulations required that their cleanliness (absence of rot or bug infestation) be certified before the nuts could be sold in China. This certification process was expensive. It required either a series of labor-intensive samplings and analyses or a large bribe to the certifying official. Either way, the Nuts2U team thought that the process could add costs of as much as $20 per ton. Put together with the transportation costs, this could seriously erode the profitability of the venture. At the beginning of the fifth day of negotiations, one of the Nuts2U team, the only one who spoke Chinese, was conversing over tea with two of his Chinese counterparts while waiting for other members of the Chinese team to arrive. Since one of the Chinese team members was an engineer, the American asked her how difficult she thought the logistics of breaking down the huge bulk shipments into deliverable quantities might be. The engineer responded, "Well, we have to do it anyhow for inspection. When we go to have the nuts certified, they must be broken into quantities not exceeding 50 kilograms or the government inspectors won't even look at them."

What happened here? The American team benefited from the fact that one of their number studied the Chinese language. In the conversation, it became clear that the Chinese importers believed that the certification of the nuts was *their responsibility*. This, of course, was the desired outcome for Nuts2U. Stepping back for a longer look at these negotiations, however, it is apparent that the Nuts2U team *thought they had a dispute when they really didn't.*

The moral of this story is: Before you start negotiating to resolve a dispute, make sure you *have* one.

1. Control—Why Negotiation Is Always the Best Form of Dispute Resolution

A fundamental premise of this book is this: Both the outcomes and transaction costs of business disputes can be improved by better control (management). As shown in the introductory chapters, traditional methods of resolving business disputes (lawsuits) have several short-comings. Potentially, the most costly of those defects is *loss of control* by the parties to the dispute. Unwittingly or not, control of *lawsuits* passes, in large measure, to:

> → the lawyers representing the parties,

>> → the judges of the court in which the lawsuit is pending,

>>> → the clerks of the court in which the lawsuit is pending,

>>>> → the legislature, which passed the various measures known as the "Rules of Civil Procedure,"

>>>>> → the media, who might influence both judge and jury by what they present about a case, and *worst of all*

>>>>>> → the opposition, who can play the system just as advantageously.

Against that background, a method of resolving disputes where the parties *retain complete control* looks very attractive. Negotiation is not just one alternative dispute resolution mechanism where the parties retain control, it is the *only one* where they do. This is not a criticism of mediation, mini-trials, early neutral evaluation, or the many hybrid alternative dispute resolution mechanisms. The parties retain *ultimate* control in most of them. However, each of these processes involves the introduction of one or more third parties (lawyers, mediators, etc.) *who* inevitably (sometimes appropriately) *exert some control* over the process. So, if retaining the ability to manage both the costs and the outcome of a business dispute is desired, negotiation is the best process.

2. Why (Business) People Don't Want to Negotiate (Business) Disputes

By reason of the analysis given in the section immediately above, one would expect that negotiation would be the preferred form of business dispute resolution by a wide margin. In a sense, it is. Ulti-mately, most business disputes *are* resolved by negotiation, but that final, negotiated resolution may not take place until large amounts of money have been spent on lawyers, technical experts, courts, deposi-tions (see Glossary for explanations of legal and alternative dispute resolution terms), public relations experts, and so forth. Much of this could have been avoided had the business parties themselves negotiated at or near the outbreak of the dispute.

Yet, these early negotiations by principals seem to be going the way of the California condor—headed toward extinction. Why? Most thoughtful observers of dispute resolution come up with strikingly similar answers. A former professor at the Anderson Graduate School of Management at the University of California (UCLA) explained it this way: "We have developed a 'rights' culture. It started, I think, with the Civil Rights movement in the Sixties. That was great. Large wrongs started to be righted. But, in another example of the law of unintended consequences, we now find ourselves in a setting where everyone thinks, 'I've got my rights,' and that those 'rights' should not be trampled on by anyone. It is a short step to the courthouse, because that's where the Civil Rights movement accomplished most of its goals."

A law professor at New York University School of Law put it somewhat differently: "We have developed a 'sue the bastards' culture. It has three causes. One is the view, inappropriately derived from the Civil Rights movement, that everyone has a package of rights that no one else can fool with. The second cause is the increasing fragmentation of our society: everyone sees themselves as a member of a small and beleaguered group. In short, everybody's a 'victim.' Finally, there is the view that the executive and legislative branches of government—at every level—are ineffective at best, corrupt at worst. So, if something happens that you don't like, and you can afford it, you head right for the courthouse."

A third academic, this time an English professor, put it this way: "Personal responsibility has almost disappeared from our culture. Even if people don't perceive themselves as victims, they still do not want to step up to the consequences of their actions. Negotiation of a dispute [by principals] is the ultimate act of assuming responsibility for having done something that someone else didn't like. It doesn't surprise me that business people run to their lawyers when they have a dispute. If there were no lawyers, they would run to someone else to 'represent' them. It's just part of the demise of personal responsibility. Americans are getting rid of it like snakes shedding their skin."

Whichever bundle of reasons lies behind it, there is an observable decline in the willingness of (business) people to negotiate their own disputes. This is not to criticize the CEO of a Fortune 100 company for *delegating* the authority to resolve certain disputes to junior executives in the company and only retaining authority in "bet the company" situations. No, this criticizes *both* the CEO and the junior executive for an increasing unwillingness to get personally involved in the negotiation of disputes that *are at their level of responsibility.* Whatever the cultural, financial, or egotistical roots of this trend, it is costing them and their companies money and time. It may also be costing them valuable relationships.

3. Why (Business) People Should Negotiate Anyway

It certainly is easier—particularly if the corporate treasury is fat with cash—to let a lawyer or other surrogate negotiate disputes for a business. But is it good policy? Certainly not all the time.

First of all, in a business, assumption of personal responsibility is best reproduced in colleagues and subordinates by *being* the role model. One of the most thoughtful writers on leadership, Burt Nanus, calls it "personifying the vision." As Nanus sees it: "Leaders live the vision by making all their actions and behaviors consistent with it and by creating a sense of urgency and passion for its attainment."[4] So, if taking personal responsibility is a desirable business behavior, being a model of such behavior by taking personal responsibility for negotiating disputes might be a good choice.

In addition to leading by example, the negotiation of disputes by principals has other salubrious results. The retention of control, mentioned above, is one. The fact that the presence of a CEO will bring the other principals to the table is another. A third is that no commitments will be made that a company cannot live up to. No matter how carefully a surrogate's authority is circumscribed, it is impossible to predict what the hurly-burly of negotiations may "force" the surrogate to commit to. If a surrogate is in a responsible position in a company, it may be legally (or, dare it be said, morally) obligated to live up to what has been done. Plus, even if the desire for control is not motivational, there is the matter of knowing first hand what is happening in the negotiations. It has been said that knowledge is power, and power certainly leads to control. But is it better or worse for a business owner/principal to be personally involved in the negotiation of disputes to which the business is a party? Most of the time, better.

4. When the Other Party Won't Negotiate

Why should parties to a dispute even bother to negotiate? The bedrock motivator for many negotiations is the following: Normally, no party has the power to achieve all its objectives at the expense of the other parties *and be certain that the other parties will abide by that outcome.* For example, a young company is the proud possessor of a novel (but unpatentable) method for manufacturing widgets. The technology has been revealed to International Widget (IW), in a joint venture where IW is to fund some further research by the company. At the end of the first year of this joint venture, IW declines to renew the relationship. Shortly thereafter, the young company learns that IW is using the unpatentable process at all of their widget factories worldwide (with nary a dime of royalties to the company). The company informs the CEO of IW that it would like to set up a meeting to discuss the use of its manufacturing method. He agrees. Why? Because even though IW has (apparently) achieved its objective at the small company's expense, he cannot be certain that the company would not take some sort of action, such as a lawsuit, writing letters to IW customers, or perhaps selling the process to IW's competitor, or even giving the story to the media or, better yet, a television news program, and let them take it from there. The CEO of IW doesn't know that the company would do any of those things, he just can't be sure that it won't. And so, the meeting takes place.

Generally, the above principle works well enough to get most parties to the bargaining table. But not all parties. There are some who will assess the risks of another party not abiding their actions, find them small, and decide to, in effect, dare the other party. There are others who refuse to negotiate *as a negotiation tactic* (I call them chronic recalcitrants, or CRs). With such behavior, some or all of the standard get-them-to-the-table gambits may be necessary:

a.   Every party to this dispute will gain if this can be settled short of litigation (to which the CR may reply: *"I love court because I always win."*);

b.   A proposal has been put together that meets everyone's needs (to which the CR says: *"Needs? I don't have any. I like things the way they are."*);

c.   Before this dispute goes any further, there is a policy of seeing if the other party would like to resolve the problem now (to which the CR responds: *"Sounds like a nice policy, but I don't have a problem."*); and

d.   There is something each party wants that the other party has (to which the CR says: *"You're only half right. I have something you want."*).

In the event that these methods fail with the chronic recalcitrant, perhaps an illustration of what might have to happen next will be helpful. A farmer in Missouri had a young mule, born on her property, who was like a pet. She wanted to have it trained for work, and interviewed many mule-skinners to find the right one. She asked each one, "Will you be gentle with the mule?" Most of them that they would do their best, but experience taught them that some force was necessary in training a young mule. Finally, she interviewed a mule-skinner who seemed right for the job. "I have never used violence while training a mule, ma'am," he said, "and I don't intend to start now." Impressed, she hired the man on the spot and pointed him in the direction of a corral behind the barn. Heading back into the farmhouse, she couldn't resist the temptation to eavesdrop on this training session. So, she headed around the other side of the barn. When the mule-skinner and mule came into sight, she was appalled to see the mule-skinner smacking the mule on the head with a two-by-four. She rushed over, shouting at the mule-skinner to stop. He did, and she began to reprove him: "I thought you said you didn't use violence to train mules. What do you call this?" The mule-skinner responded: "Ma'am, I don't use violence when I train a mule. But, ma'am, you have got to get its *attention* before you can begin the training."

Getting the attention of the chronic recalcitrant, then, is the key to his appearance at the bargaining table. The first suggestion for accomplishing this is the silent treatment. If *all* communication with the chronic recalcitrant were suspended, lack of information could, perhaps, lead to curiosity as to what was happening. Then, an energized imagination may lead to suspicion that the other party may be taking retaliatory action of some sort. Ideally, this will have the desired result.

If the chronic recalcitrant still will not come to the table, then one or more retaliatory actions must be undertaken. Usually, the economic value of the dispute will dictate the action. It may be a lawsuit (to get his attention). But sooner or later, the CR's position regarding negotiation will likely change, and alternative dispute resolution can begin at any time.

If an opportunity arises to talk with the opponent (about something else), it may be helpful to ask some questions designed to see if there is an unknown reason why the other party will not negotiate. Perhaps if a reason can be determined, the obstacle to negotiation can then be removed.

5. The Shape of the Table

There are those parties that will only come to the table if it's octagonal. Those who remember (or have read about) the Korean War may recall that a major stumbling block to truce negotiations with the Communist forces was an argument over what shape the negotiating table would be! [5]

So, there are those parties that will routinely require negotiations about the negotiations. However, even when all parties are willing to negotiate, there are some details that may need to be finalized even before entering ADR negotiations, such as:

a.   if the talks will be on or off the record (that is, will what has been said in the negotiating room be on the evening news?);

b.   determination of the ground rules regarding information which may be exchanged in the negotiations (suppose, for instance, that sensitive financial data will be exchanged; will it be disseminated to anyone but the negotiators; if so, to whom, and with what safeguards?);

c.   if there will be a moratorium on litigation while negotiations are continuing (if so, when will that moratorium end?); and

d.   if there are any "back channel" negotiations going on between other representatives of the parties.

6. Alternatives when Negotiations Reach an Impasse: "Getting to Maybe"

Don't forget that everybody, including yourself, has only his experience to think with.—Rudolf Flesch

The word "impasse" is defined as a difficult situation with no apparent way out. For this specific purpose, a *negotiation impasse* is a point in the negotiation process where all parties perceive themselves as unable to reach agreement. Some of the literature and language of negotiation refer to an impasse as a deadlock, which is really the same thing.

After having invested huge amounts of time in trying to finish this deal, negotiations have stalled. Both parties have gone as far as they are willing to; no ultimatum has been thrown down by either party. This is not a confrontational impasse; it just seems that the negotiations have reached a state of inertia. Here are some techniques which might restart the process:

a. Discuss (or think about) how impasse was arrived at

There are, of course, myriad reasons why the impasse may have arisen. Here are some of the most frequent ones. Keep in mind that what follows are really assumptions or feelings, and that any one or more of them can be held by any member of the negotiating group. Please also remember that *unexpressed assumptions* are one of the biggest impediments to human communication. So, an impasse may have been reached because someone assumed or felt that:

— The other party is the one who must compromise if a deal is to be made;

— No one has ever solved an impasse this difficult;

— The opponents will not help break the impasse;

— The negotiations have failed unless a total resolution is reached;

— The interests or positions of the parties can only be described as they have been so far;

— The types of solutions presently "on the table" are the only ones which might be acceptable;

— Everyone in the room knows everything that everyone else knows (except where individual bottom lines are drawn, of course); and

— If the negotiations end now, there will never be a deal.

So, the first step in breaking an impasse is to determine whether any of the parties are harboring some or all of the above assumptions in their minds. If any of these impasse-causers seems to be present, try to test for the accuracy of this supposition by commenting (if, for example, the last listed item, above, seemed to be the prevailing atmosphere): "Well, it appears that we are not going to reach an agreement." If the universal response is to the effect of: "Yes, I guess we had better go home," then most parties share that view. However, if enough of the parties still want to reach an agreement and believe that everyone else does, some inquiry into how the impasse was reached might allow the negotiations to get back on track.

b. Return to prior agreements

An impasse implies recognition of non-agreement, and that recognition itself tends to lessen the chances of agreement. However, there are always the basic agreement to negotiate and the series of more substantive agreements that have already occurred during the process. These can be recited and pointed to with pride. Giving the apparently recalcitrant party credit for earlier agreement (whether deserved or not) can sometimes help to break a deadlock.

c. Recount the practical effects of nonagreement

William Ury uses Chrysler Corporation's seeking loan guarantees from Congress in the wake of its 1979 financial crisis as an example of this technique.[6] When Chairman Lee Iacocca appeared before Congress and asked the crucial question: "What will the costs be if we can't reach agreement?", he had some answers ready. One particularly telling "answer" was that it would cost the taxpayers $2.7 billion dollars if Chrysler went bankrupt (in welfare and unemployment insurance payments), while the loan guarantees being sought were only for $1.5 billion (and there was a fair chance that Chrysler would pay the loans back without invoking the guarantees). In every negotiation, the stakes may not be quite as high, but the principles are the same.

Ury also identifies two subsets of this technique: the questions "What will a party do?" (if there's no agreement) and "What does the other party think its opponent will do?" These questions need not—indeed, should not—be posed as challenges to an opponent. Rather, they should be honest, information-seeking inquiries whose purpose is to fully explore the (perhaps dire) consequences of non-agreement. After all, if there is no agreement, all sides will have to do *something* else to meet their needs. Examining what that something is often has a positive effect on the negotiation process.

d. Get some fresh air

This is a literal suggestion in order to give negotiation opponents time to wonder what, if any, ulterior motives there might be in taking this break. This action will have a positive influence, whether the negotiations continue or not. In addition to its healthful effects, taking a short walk outside the room will permit each party to think through its own positions and interests to see if there is some way to break the deadlock. Further, disappearing for a walk will permit the other parties to contemplate the possibility of a party's disappearance in a more permanent way.

e. Suggest a new topic to talk about

An impasse usually arises because agreement could not be reached on a specific point. Certainly, the unpleasantness of the deadlock was created by the discussions on that point. What is to be done now? When something unpleasant has been said in social conversation, the polite response is to change the subject. Remember, the working definition of dispute resolution negotiation marks it as "conversation." So, why not try a subject change when an impasse has been reached?

The first suggestions of new topics are other areas of the negotiation where agreement is almost certain to be easy. This keeps everyone working toward agreement, but on a "safe" topic. If agreement on the safe topic is reached, that fact alone may lead to a break in the deadlock. But if under-collar temperatures are warm, subjects which are not related to the negotiation and are not potentially explosive in themselves might be a better idea. For instance, a discussion of the perils of business travel (lost luggage, terrible food, etc.) is almost always a safe topic to which everyone present can contribute. On the other hand, shifting to a discussion of a highly controversial subject would probably not be a good idea. Sports is not always a safe topic because it engenders some fierce loyalties and emotions. There is always the possibility of an occurrence such as this: It seems a young man, let's call him Jed, was the junior member of a three-person negotiating team sent to visit one of an auto company's suppliers. The purpose of their visit was to obtain price and delivery schedule concessions from the supplier. Sam, the supplier's CEO, attended the negotiations, with his manufacturing supervisor. Before long, talks bogged down around the question of whether the supplier would shorten delivery time. This request seemed particularly to upset Sam. Jed, who had attended a negotiation seminar, saw that an impasse either had been reached or was looming. He remembered that shifting to a "safe" topic could help break a deadlock. Jed chose baseball. He asked the supplier's manufacturing supervisor what he thought the home town team's chances were for a playoff berth. The supervisor said, "I think they're pretty good. Particularly since they picked up that new pitcher, Graham." Jed, to keep the conversation going, opined that he thought the local team had overpaid for Graham, describing him as having a reputation for quitting in the middle innings and being something of a cry-baby. The supervisor fell silent, as did everyone else. Wanting to keep the conversation off delivery schedules, Jed then asked Sam what his view of this Graham fellow was. Sam replied, "I can't be too objective, Jed, he's my son-in-law."

Perhaps it's better to stick to the perils of business travel, but don't identify the terrible restaurant, as an opponent may own a piece of it!

f. Use history

This technique is actually a form of changing the subject, but with a specific new subject in mind. That subject is the history of an organization's relations with an opponent's. Needless to say, there is nothing to be gained from this procedure unless the history is a good one. But, if it is, the relationship history can be used successfully in at least two ways. First, some reminiscing might be in order, such as "Remember back in the '80s, when old Harry Forbis was on our negotiating team? He used to smoke those big cigars. I think we got some concessions from you guys just so you wouldn't have to stick around and get cancer," or, "Where is your CFO, Jeanie Light, now? She was such a pleasure to deal with. I hope you haven't lost her." Comments such as this usually lead to other reminiscences, all of which collectively create a warm feeling around the table. Second, there is the substantive history between the negotiating parties; the deals that *have been made* in the past, and how mutually beneficial those turned out to be. This topic, in both its incarnations (personal relations and prior deals) may serve to break the deadlock. At a minimum, however, it will have changed the atmosphere in the room for the better. That is sometimes more important than immediate progress in the substantive negotiations.

g. Suggest mediation

If the appropriate selections from items a. through f. on the menu above do not work, it is likely that the parties have gone about as far as they can go in normal negotiations. To press on under these circumstances is to risk developing a truly toxic atmosphere. Not only will the impasse not be broken, but the parties may end up hating one another.

Whether and when to suggest a mediator are two of the toughest judgment calls to make in a negotiation. It is not that the introduction of a mediator is going to make the atmosphere worse, but that his introduction *will* break the momentum of the negotiations and add a new personal dynamic to the (now mediated) negotiations which everyone will need to get used to. So, the suggestion should not be made lightly. But if a party proposes that a mediator be called in, it *will* send messages to its opponents that it:

— really believes that an impasse has been reached;

— nonetheless wants the negotiations to continue; and

— is willing to share some additional expense to see if a deal can be made.

These are all positive signals to send out to opponents. Perhaps those messages will serve as a catalyst in breaking the deadlock without actually having to bring a mediator into the discussions. If not, there may be valuable information from the opponent's reaction to the suggestion. Depending on how much they know about mediation, a response, such as "Oh, I don't think a mediator could do us any good," will call for different interpretations. Someone who is knowledgeable about mediation would probably only say that if they really didn't want the mediator. But why would they feel that way? Perhaps they *know* that the impasse is an artificial one because they deliberately created it. On the other hand, someone who is not familiar with mediation might make such a remark out of ignorance. So, an interpretation of their response depends on the opponent's level of knowledge about mediation.

7. Culture and Negotiation

Culture and negotiation does not belong exclusively in the context of international negotiation, because the United States has always been a nation of immigrants. But in fairly recent times four new things have happened:

1. The United States has become a nation of immigrants from exotic places (*i.e.*, not where our earlier immigrants came from);

2. National antidiscrimination laws have led to a greater cultural diversification of the work force (which can present problems in the negotiation arena);

3. Affirmative action programs have brought into the work force people who, while they are American born, may not be familiar with so-called mainstream culture; and

4. We now live in a truly global economy.

The consequences for negotiators (not to mention managers) are vast. No one can afford to remain ignorant of the basic elements of many "foreign" cultures. In laying out some guidelines for "intercultural" negotiations, keep in mind that such negotiations are as likely to take place on the other side of the *street* as they are on the other side of the world. Please also remember that this is not a book on cultural anthropology. Therefore, summaries of the various cultural approaches to negotiation will be just that—summaries.

a. Location, language, and lore

Before getting into specific cultural differences, here are some general precepts which will be useful in every intercultural negotiation: location, language, and lore.

i. Location

Remember the old adage: When in Rome do as the Romans do. It applies with equal importance today in international negotiations, as illustrated earlier by the delay in the start of the Korean War armistice talks because of arguments over the shape of the table on which negotiations were to be conducted. Do not get into discussions like this. Unless the suggested site for the negotiations presents the danger of physical harm, try to accede to a foreign host's suggestions or even visit the proposed location first with a translator/cultural advisor. In some cultures, business negotiations are properly conducted in the home. In others, a restaurant or sidewalk cafe will do. Yet, other cultures only negotiate business transactions in a conference room in a business building or hotel.

ii. Language

In almost every situation where all the negotiating parties do not share the same first language (the one they learned from their parents), there is a language barrier. It is the rarest of persons who can conduct a negotiation in a second language (for instance, Chinese) with people for whom Chinese is a first language. This is not due entirely to how difficult it is to become truly fluent in a second (or subsequent) language. As important as basic language skills are, the person's knowledge of the culture surrounding that language is even more crucial. To stay with the same example, there are currently at least five separate Chinese-based cultures, where Chinese is the first language of most of the business community:

1. The People's Republic of China (PRC);
2. The Republic of China (Taiwan);
3. Hong Kong (British Crown Colony, until 1997);
4. Macao (Macau, a Portuguese colony); and
5. Singapore.

All of the above mentioned places have Chinese as their first language, yet they have starkly different cultures. So, knowing how to speak Chinese (even assuming that it's the correct dialect) well will not necessarily equip one to negotiate with people from *any* of those places. The best advice, unless someone in a negotiating party has idiomatic fluency with the language and deep and current knowledge of the local culture, is to *get a translator!*

Even if many foreign business people speak English, there are several important reasons why it is still helpful to have a translator:

— It is a courtesy to foreign hosts that they not be expected to speak the guest's language (courtesy counts for more in every foreign culture than it does at home);

— Someone else may be on the other side of the table in addition to the person who speaks English and that someone else may be the one with the decision-making power;

— A good translator is also a good cultural consultant (who would render something said in English that would insult foreign counterparts harmless in translation);

— It helps to build trust between culturally and linguistically divergent parties (most people outside the United States wouldn't do business with anyone they didn't know and trust); and

— It gives a guest *significant negotiating advantage.*

Beyond trust-building, conducting the negotiations in the first language of the host:

— forecloses the possibility of later misunderstandings attributed to the fact that the negotiations were conducted in English;

— even more importantly, the oral translation process gives you more time to think during the negotiations; and

— if agreement appears to have been reached, an English translation will be prepared of any written agreement.

iii. Lore

If it is (or may be) economically advantageous to try to negotiate a deal in a foreign country, then it is important enough to *learn something about it.* Some of the implications of a global economy are that the United States is competing with countries where the labor costs are 10 percent of ours, where the citizens are taught two (or more) languages from early childhood, where serious study of other cultures is required in school, and, not least, where the native culture may well be more similar to that of the "target" country than American culture is.

All of this leads to the conclusion that studying the customs and culture of a host country is mandatory.

Not only is it mandatory, it's fun and easy. Every country with an embassy or consulate in the United States is pleased to distribute information on the business and general customs of their country. Many countries have printed information to help visiting business persons. In addition, there is a federal government Department of Commerce, one of whose mandates is to help U.S. businesses succeed in foreign countries. If products or services concern things that grow, the Department of Agriculture may also be able to help. Whatever kind of business, the Office of the Trade Representative is always up to date on the latest changes in our trade relations with many countries, especially in connection with problems with Japan and China (PRC). As if this cornucopia of assistance were not enough, the major international accounting firms all have booklets designed to acquaint one with various countries' customs (and with the accounting firm's expertise). If there is an area business school, its library may be open to the public. Public libraries and the major on-line services (at this writing, America On Line, Compuserve, and Prodigy) also have information about cultures and customs of various countries.

Here are some basic overviews of the negotiating styles some cultures have. Please keep in mind that all foreign people are *individuals,* even in countries known for group conformity, such as Japan. Each human being is going to be somewhat different from every other one, so these generalities, then, are useful only in an impersonal way.

b. Specific cultures

i. the Arab Nations

While there are some major differences from country to country (the best example may be the seriousness with which a given population takes its religion), some generalizations can be ventured about the Arab countries:

— the business week is Saturday through Thursday;

— negotiations may be interrupted as many as five times a day (for prayer);

— loyalty is prized;

— speaking even a little Arabic will be viewed as respectful;

— Arabs like to think they are helpful, so ask for help;

— delays usually have a tactical purpose;

— religion and business are inseparable for many (*e.g.,* a profit-participation may have to be offered in lieu of interest, as the latter is forbidden by the Koran);

— don't negotiate during the month of Ramadan (businesses usually are closed, and the hosts may be fasting until sunset);

— some countries still boycott those who deal with Israel;

— hire a local agent, but be prepared for some detailed negotiations with him (Arab countries usually do not have women in business); and

— be prepared for two basic bargaining styles: the haggler, who begins with an outrageously extreme proposal (fully expecting the same in return) and charms and negotiates to a deal, or the intermediary, where a go-between is used, who acts like a mediator and also assures that everyone retains his dignity regardless of outcome.

ii. China

As mentioned earlier in this chapter, there are a number of Chinese cultures around the world. This summary is limited to the People's Republic of China (sometimes still referred to as Mainland China). With nearly a quarter of the world's population, remember that generalizations about China are subject to even greater possibility for error:

— Chinese pride themselves on their worldliness;

— relationships and general postulates count for more than details and legalisms;

— opening negotiations usually are limited to the establishment of general principles which will govern what follows;

— the second phase of discussions usually involves testing (particularly of the patience of the non-Chinese participants);

— as agreement nears, junior people often insist on very favorable terms, but a senior person may intervene to "solve the problem";

— some socializing is expected;

— if agreement is reached, be sure there is understanding regarding things such as spare parts, insurance, freight, etc., because Chinese customs are different; and

— prepare to stay in China "as long as it takes."

iii. Japan

Japanese negotiators are usually governed by two conflicting types of training. From childhood, they have been taught to avoid social conflict. However, the males have also been taught to be fierce "warriors." To the modern Japanese, this means being an adroit negotiator. The trick for the guest negotiator is to figure out which of these "schools of thought" is in the ascendancy at a given moment. Some other generalities which may help:

— never do anything to cause embarrassment for foreign hosts;

— understanding and satisfying the concerns of others is a very positive character trait;

— the above trait manifests itself in never saying "No"; instead phrases such as "It is difficult" or "I will do my best" are used;

— fairness is almost as important as satisfying needs;

— consensus among themselves is very important; this may cause delays while the Japanese side caucuses to get everyone's agreement;

— it is highly likely that negotiations will begin with someone who does not have full authority; he will have to get consensus among his bosses before being able to make a deal;

— while much lip service is given (mostly sincerely) to relationships, it may not necessarily affect the economic outcome;

— Japanese take a more long-term view than Americans;

— instead of "horse-trading," the Japanese prefer to make rather vague proposals, revealing more details as the talks progress;

— be prepared to spend time and be patient;

— have business cards in Japanese and English, and hand them out with both hands; and

— more than occasional direct eye contact may be considered rude; this is normally a big problem for Americans.

iv. Koreans

Korean culture is derivative of Chinese culture, a fact that Koreans usually don't like to be reminded of. This results in their "natural" brashness being tempered by a Confucian desire to avoid direct confrontation. American hard bargaining would seem uncivilized to them. A few other comments:

— negotiations will include some socializing;

— Koreans are more impulsive than most Asians; if they are favorably impressed, things could move along at almost American speed;

— Koreans are generally more volatile than their Asian neighbors; strong emotions may be displayed (and quickly changed);

— Koreans are more individualistic than their Asian neighbors, though family loyalty is strong;

— Koreans have an American-like (short-term) time horizon; and

— Koreans are just as interested in not losing face as any other Asian.

v. Bribery

No overview of dispute resolution negotiation would be complete without some mention of bribery. Some incidents of bribery in connection with the making of international deals are already world famous. Indeed, one Japanese prime minister lost his job over a bribery scandal involving Lockheed. In the area of dispute resolution negotiation, the opportunities for bribery are also present.

No American *wants* to pay a bribe because, practically speaking, it only adds to the cost of the transaction. In a dispute resolution context, it detracts from resources that could otherwise be used to resolve the dispute. In domestic negotiations, the legal and ethical lines are pretty clearly drawn. Bribery is always illegal and almost always against the ethical norms as well. In an international setting, however, both the (foreign) legal and ethical lines become a lot fuzzier. First of all, it is common practice in many countries that a foreign businessperson hire a "local consultant."[7] Assorted things are expected of such a person, depending on the culture. Almost universally, however, the local consultant is expected to obtain for his principle access to the appropriate decision makers. There is nothing wrong with that, as long as that is all the consultant does. If the consultant gets you into the right room with the right people, he has earned his "commission." In many cultures, however, the consultant is also expected to carry a wheelbarrow full of cash to the decision makers. In the words of the old map makers: "Here, there be dragons."

First of all, an American businessperson is almost always going to be subject to American law with respect to these transactions, even though everything may take place thousands of miles from U.S. territory. The Foreign Corrupt Practices Act[8] was passed by Congress for the specific purpose of criminalizing transactions like these. It provides for *personal* as well as corporate responsibility. On the other hand, many foreign cultures not only permit these transactions, but expect them. What's an American businessperson to do?

The dilemma is a difficult one. So, unlike the counterparts who simply are trying to make a deal, visiting business people cannot walk away if the situation becomes dicey. Here are a few suggestions which may help.

(1) If it doesn't pass the "smell" test, don't do it. (A foreign agent asks for a fee of $8 million, an outrageous amount to pay for his services. He darkly hints that most of this money will be going, not to him, but to pay "commissions" to certain government officials who have the power to resolve the dispute. Either the American business-

person is going to pay the bribe or is going to get taken to the cleaners by the agent. The answer is to find another agent.)

(2) Don't sweat the "small stuff." (Moderately priced gifts, hotel rooms, meals, or entertainment are no more than what might be done at home.)

(3) Get some reliable local advice. (In some circumstances, an $8 million fee to an agent would be reasonable if he could get access to people who could resolve the dispute, but it's impossible to be sure where the money is going. Check in with the U.S. consulate, or, if there isn't one, with U.S. business people (not competitors, of course) working locally, and ask what the customs are.)

(4) Make foreign colleagues aware that a problem exists. (Many sophisticated foreigners know all about the U.S. Foreign Corrupt Practices Act. Some do not. Negotiations might be reopened with a "declaration of inability to pay the bribe" (phrased much more diplomatically, of course), or handing them a copy of company policy on bribes (carefully translated, of course). These tactics must be used with caution, however. Many countries have their own laws prohibiting bribery, but the practice flourishes nonetheless. So, a "declaration" may be misinterpreted as a willingness to pay someone off. Remember, an unsuccessful dispute resolution may end up in court somewhere. Under these conditions, it is even more important that nothing illegal occurs, especially under the laws of the foreign country, because even though their notions of due process *might* be different from ours, their notions on penology certainly *will* be different.)

(5) Make a donation. (Even in the United States, disputes are sometimes resolved by one party or the other making a contribution to charity. In foreign countries, it may be possible to avoid being caught between the law and violating local custom by offering to make a donation. Charities, as they exist in the United States, are not as highly articulated in many countries, so the donation of or to a civic project is frequently a good substitute. One company resolved a dispute in an Asian country by building a soccer field and supplying some equipment for the employees of the disputing entity.)

(6) Don't get caught on the receiving end, either. (Because of the historic strength of the American economy relative to most other countries, U.S. business people are most often regarded as bribe *givers*. But sometimes in a dispute resolution framework, an American businessperson may be on the receiving end. In the early '80s, an American was sent by his oil company employer to a Middle East country. His job was to try to resolve some damage claims arising from an explosion which had taken place in the host country. Shortly after he arrived, his foreign counterpart told him that the claimants were willing to share

(50/50) with him all amounts his company would agree to pay them over a certain minimum. It turned out that the "minimum" was well within his authority. The moral of this story is: Neither a giver nor a taker be.)

8. Gender and Negotiation

In a domestic business setting, consider the impact on negotiation of the growth of the number of women in America's work force. Start with the premise that women are just as accustomed to negotiating as men, but are usually taught a different *manner* of negotiation. Where men concentrate on the need to compete with others, women generally negotiate in a relationship context.

Many women bring several important talents to the table. Usually, they are more conscious of the relationship elements in the negotiation than men. They tend to be more inclusive of others, which creates a less hostile environment no matter how the substantive negotiations are going. And, women are usually considered less threatening than men. It is also thought that women are better at the brainstorming aspects of negotiation than men.

Because they have been discriminated against in the work force for so long, many women (however well-qualified otherwise) are really business negotiation novices. In fact, they sometimes have to be told that they are *in a negotiation*. Many women in this situation simply state their needs to another person quite clearly, and then are surprised when those needs are not met. Frequently, the reason for this is that the person whom the woman told was operating on a (male?) set of assumptions, one of which was that her request was simply an opening gambit in what would be a longer negotiation. The woman may well have felt she was being arbitrarily turned down.

In other portions of this chapter, disclaimers have been issued about the usefulness of the generalities which were presented. Take these maxims lightly, and treat every woman negotiator for what she truly is: an individual human being, worthy of respect, who is trying to obtain certain goals, just as her counterpart is. Some guidelines may help:

— Never patronize; do not use words like "sweetheart" and "darlin' " under any circumstances;

— Realize that "yes" may mean "I understand" (as it does when Japanese *men* say it);

— Women *may* overpersonalize (or even blame themselves for) conflict that arises at the bargaining table;

— Women usually do not see negotiation as a contest, let alone a blood sport;

— Don't be sexually obnoxious;

— Women's speech tends to be interactive; men tend to soliloquize;

— If a woman does exhibit an understanding of male negotiating tactics, don't become offensive; and

— Because of the prevalence of sexual predation in the work place, many women feel extremely uncomfortable in the social settings where business deals are often concluded by men, such as bars, restaurants, hotel rooms, etc.

9. Fifteen Guideposts to Successful Negotiation

As established early in this chapter, the focus here is with a narrowed definition of negotiation itself: *"conversation processes directed toward resolving initial differences."* So, the guideposts set forth in this subsection will be most useful in that setting. None of them, however, is inimical to "normal" negotiation. They are set forth, as much as possible, in the order in which they will come up in dispute resolution negotiation. Unlike earlier sections, these guideposts will assume that all parties to the negotiation are Americans and native English speakers. If these are not the facts of a particular situation, the materials on culture and negotiation given earlier should be used as an overlay.

Guidepost Number One: Be Yourself
Do not try to be loud, aggressive and domineering if one is normally soft-spoken, bashful, and submissive—and *vice versa*. Not only will an opponent likely see through this "act," but also the sheer pressure of putting the act on will diminish the ability to be a good negotiator.

Guidepost Number Two: Prepare
Preparation for negotiation, foreign or domestic, involves studying the opponent's positions and interests. If negotiating as part of a team, it also involves planning and deciding role assignments[9] and areas of responsibility.

Guidepost Number Three: Listen Actively
Instead of concocting counterarguments while the opponent is talking, try to really listen, and then demonstrate this by paraphrasing what they have said, asking clarifying questions, and endorsing elements of agreement. Keep in mind, however, that negotiation is supposed to be a dialogue and not a series of monologues.

Guidepost Number Four: Size Up Your Opponents
What kind of reputations do they have (in their field and as people)? What is the general outlook for their business? What experience has anyone had in dealing with these people before?

How important is this negotiation to them? Are any of them personally responsible (or perceived as being personally responsible) for the activities leading to the dispute? Do any of them stand to lose financially (personally) depending on how the dispute is resolved?

Guidepost Number Five: Depersonalize the Dispute

To a certain extent, all disputes are personal. It does not matter how large an organization is that is being dealt with or how long ago the dispute arose; there is always somebody whose ego is involved in the outcome. To the extent that this person (or his feelings) can be neutralized, resolution becomes closer. So, resist the temptation to assign blame for how the dispute arose or who caused the problem. Don't disparage anyone's character, and don't demand apologies, retractions, etc., except in libel or slander settings. In short, as Fisher and Ury have said: "Separate the people from the problem."[10]

Guidepost Number Six: Establish Parity of Authority

One of the oldest tricks in the negotiating "book" is to send someone to the table who does not have authority to resolve the dispute. This gives that side an automatic "two bites at the apple," because the negotiator can always say: "It sounds good to me but I'll have to check with the CEO," (or whomever). This is not always a trick. Some organizations (particularly in education and government) simply cannot give one person the ultimate decision-making authority. Legitimate or not, however, the only way to protect one's self from the "two bites" effect is to claim to have the exact level of authority a counterpart *alleges to have.*

Guidepost Number Seven: Bring Only the People Necessary

Human nature being what it is, the more people at the bargaining session, the more difficult it will be to reach resolution. Just as importantly, try to get an opponent to limit the number of people on its team. After all, the same principles apply to the opposition, but even more so!

Guidepost Number Eight: Keep Control of Emotions

Notice that refraining from expressing any emotions is not suggested, merely that they are kept under control. There are times when displays of emotion are perfectly appropriate during negotiations. However, there should be internal analysis of feeling the emotion, recognizing that fact, and then deciding to express it. This is especially true when the opponent deliberately provokes an emotional response. In the latter case, however, the normal counsel would be to ignore the emotional outburst, and perhaps comment (softly) on its unproductiveness.

Guidepost Number Nine: Paraphrase Events Aloud

Clear communication is always a *goal* of negotiation, but it isn't always achieved. So, it frequently helps to verbalize what seems to be happening. It is the rare negotiation that doesn't produce one moment where the thought, "This negotiation is going nowhere," occurs. Say it aloud, not as an accusation, but as an observation. Maybe the opponents think otherwise and can explain where progress has been made. Maybe they agree, and the discussion can fruitfully look at *why* things are going nowhere. At a minimum, feelings are expressed, which will make some parties feel better.

Guidepost Number Ten: Know Oneself, Act Accordingly

Socrates gave this advice long ago. It works as well for dispute resolution negotiations as it does for the rest of life. If, for instance, one has a fairly short emotional fuse, make sure that frequent breaks are taken. During those breaks, make sure that any emotions vented to a colleague (or to the wind alone) are well out of earshot of the opposition. If jet lag is a problem, try flying to the negotiation site a day or two in advance in order to be ready to negotiate when talks begin.

Guidepost Number Eleven: Burn No Bridges

Not every dispute resolution negotiation succeeds. It is possible that a deal just cannot be made at this time. But, circumstances change: attitudes, interest rates, raw material prices, and computer speeds. It is also possible that one or both parties are without some existing information which might change their view. Not least likely, it is possible that one or both sides need to experience the bracing effect of a large legal bill before they see the wisdom in resolving their dispute by negotiation. So, even if talks break off, leave the opponents with their dignity intact and a glimmer of hope that negotiations might be resumed in the future.

Guidepost Number Twelve: Color Outside the Lines

Most business disputes are about money. It is no shock, then, that negotiators seeking to resolve business disputes look to money as the means of doing so. Truly successful negotiators, however, are able to "color outside the lines." They look for nonmonetary elements of a solution, forcing themselves to think of things beyond the "normal." They search for ways of satisfying the opposition's needs without giving away the store. In presenting possible solutions to an opponent, let them know in advance that this is just brainstorming, or otherwise, the opponent's critical faculties may trash an idea before it has a chance. If possible, enlist an opponent in a session devoted exclusively to brainstorming new ways of reaching an accord. In such a session, everyone has permission to come up with the wildest ideas imaginable, and everyone commits to postponing all criticism to a later session.

Guidepost Number Thirteen: Trust, but Verify

These words crystallize a dilemma that every negotiator must face: on the one hand, an opponent must be trusted somewhat or there will never be agreement; on the other, a high level of awareness must be maintained to the possibility of exploitation. In a dispute resolution negotiation, this dilemma is sharper because reason for mistrust already exists—the dispute. So, good negotiators walk a tightrope, indulging a normal human tendency to like and trust people, but being realistic enough to verify the availability and value of promises emanating from the other side.

Guidepost Number Fourteen: Viewing the Dispute from the Opponent's Side

Successful negotiations usually depend on the ability and willingness of each side to fulfill the other's legitimate needs. This is almost impossible to do without some empathy. The dictionary defines empathy as: "the action of understanding, being aware of, being sensitive to, and vicariously experiencing the feelings, thoughts and experience of another of either the past or present without having the feelings, thoughts, and experience fully communicated in an objectively explicit manner."[11]

Guidepost Number Fifteen: Leave Something on the Table

Never leave an opponent with nothing. In *successful* negotiation, it is the decent thing to do. For the less altruistic, there is another, more practical reason. It is almost unheard of that parties never have to deal with one another again when the negotiation is done. At a minimum, there may be checks to write, agreements to draft and sign, or documents to exchange. At a maximum, performance of the agreed resolution may have to continue for years. In either event, having to rely on people who have just been totally humiliated to perform whatever has been agreed is not a good idea. For example, at the end of World War I, the Allies (lead by the United States) basically dictated the Armistice Agreement to the Germans. So thorough was the humiliation that the German representatives were forced to meet in a railroad car at the site of the negotiations which ended the Franco-Prussian War in 1871.[12] Not only was Germany forced to agree to reduce its military power, but it was robbed of all vestiges of national pride. In short, the Allies left nothing on the table. The result was World War II.

ENDNOTES

[1] Roger Dawson, *The Facts About Negotiation* (Nightingale-Conant Corp., 1989), p. 10.

[2] There are a stunning number of books about negotiation in general (see the Bibliography). Some of the principles and techniques explored in them translate well into a dispute resolution context. Some do not.

[3] One chief executive of a securities firm is praised, in a book about leadership, for his ability to communicate *by memorandum,* "stressing a vision of [Prudential-Bache Securities] as a swift light cruiser on the stormy seas outflanking the big battleships of Wall Street." Burt Nanus, *Visionary Leadership* (San Francisco: Jossey-Bass, 1992), pp. 138-39. Given the legal difficulties that company has had (*after* the book was published) things might have been better if the CEO had communicated his ideas *in person.*

[4] *Ibid.*

[5] The suggestion of an armistice was made by Gen. Matthew B. Ridgway to the Communist forces on June 29, 1951. The armistice agreement was not actually signed until July 27, 1953.

[6] William Ury, *Getting Past No: Negotiating with Difficult People* (Bantam Books, 1991), p. 114nn.

[7] This function has many names. "Agent," "representative," "partner," "counselor," "joint venturer," and "bag man" are just a few.

[8] The text of the Foreign Corrupt Practices Act of 1977 may be found at 15 U.S.C.A. § § 78dd-1 and 78dd-2 (1995).

[9] This advice is not inconsistent with **Be Yourself.** The roles being referred to are those of team leader and the subordinates.

[10] Roger Fisher and William Ury, *Getting to Yes: Negotiating Agreement Without Giving In* (Houghton Mifflin, 1981), p. 17.

[11] See *Webster's Ninth New Collegiate Dictionary* (Springfield, Mass.: Merriam-Webster, 1985) p. 407.

[12] The location was the Forest of Compiègne. The railroad car belonged to Marshal Foch, France's highest-ranking military officer.

"What's amazing to me is that this late in the game we still have to settle our differences with rocks."

MEDIATION

ADR Without the Risks

He who will not reason is a bigot; He who cannot is a fool; He who dares not is a slave.
—William Drummond

A. Mediation Defined

Mediation is a process of reaching a voluntary resolution of a dispute with the aid of a qualified neutral. It is sometimes called "managed, private negotiations." Unlike litigation and arbitration, each party remains in control of the process until final agreement is reached; the mediator has no power to impose a solution. Mediation proceedings are private, and many state statutes[1] provide that certain contents of mediation proceedings may not be used in later contested proceedings, *e.g.,* arbitration or litigation.

After the parties have agreed to mediate, it is usually advisable that they sign a written mediation agreement. This agreement will, of course, include their commitment to enter into the mediation process, and it will also include provisions for confidentiality, scheduling, and other "ground rules" which the parties may require. The mediation agreement may be entered into before or after the mediator has been selected, and the parties may be assisted in reaching such an agreement by the proposed mediator and/or the American Arbitration Association or other alternative dispute resolution provider.

Once a mediator has been selected, mediation usually begins with each party sending the mediator a confidential memorandum about the dispute and its settlement history. "Confidential" here means that the memorandum will *not* be shared with the other parties to the mediation. Such a memorandum is more likely to contain a candid assessment of the dispute than one which *is* going to be read by the other side. It is appropriate to include any information which may help the mediator assist the parties in reaching an agreement, such as an outline of the facts, and a statement of the party's legal position (particularly if the dispute is already pending in court or arbitration).

The next process, face-to-face mediation, now begins. Normally, mediation takes place at the office of the organization which is administering the mediation, *e.g.,* American Arbitration Association, or at a "neutral" site selected by the parties and the mediator, *e.g.,* the mediator's office. However, the mediation can take place at any location to which the parties and the mediator agree. Some very successful mediations have taken place at construction sites.

At least two offices or conference rooms are required (more if there are more parties or sides to a dispute), because the private caucus between the mediator and each side is at the heart of the process. While there is no law against it, experienced mediators discourage parties and counsel from conducting sessions at their own work places. Not only might the "visiting team" of parties and lawyers feel disadvantaged, but the "home team" frequently finds itself unable to conduct an uninterrupted mediation session. In short, the modest additional costs of mediating at a neutral location are more than worth it.

A meeting of the mediator and all parties (and counsel, where they are involved) is arranged at the selected location. There, the mediator explains the process and then invites each side to make a general presentation of its position. This session is frequently called the "general caucus," where the parties (or their lawyers) want to inform the opponent (and the mediator) as much as to persuade them. Each side also gets an opportunity, perhaps for the first time, to hear the other party's position in full. The mediator sets the tone of the proceeding with an opening statement of purpose (everyone working together toward resolution), congratulates the parties on their willingness to enter into mediation, describes the process in some detail and the opportunities it presents, and explains the private caucuses which will likely follow the general caucus.

Private caucuses are meetings between the mediator and *less than all of the parties (and lawyers).* The central feature of a private caucus is the *second layer* of confidentiality. That layer is created by the mediator's commitment that anything said in confidence during the caucus will not be revealed to the other party. For example, Ajax Widget sues CementHead, Inc. for breach of contract. They agree to try to resolve their dispute in mediation. All parties meet with the mediator, as described above; then the mediator confers with the people from CementHead *out of the presence of the other parties.* During that caucus, the spokesperson for CementHead says: "We know we're in the wrong here. It's just a question of how much we have to pay." The mediator will not reveal that statement to the other side (unless, for some reason, CementHead gives the mediator *permission* to reveal it). The significance of this second layer of confidentiality to the success of mediation cannot be overemphasized. One can hardly imagine any party making a statement like the CementHead representative did in a *general* caucus. So, by talking with and, more importantly, *listening to* the parties in this doubly confidential setting, the mediator undoubtedly learns more about the real positions, needs, and perceptions of the parties than would ever be revealed in the general caucus. Thus informed, the mediator is in a much better position to:

— Help the parties move in a direction that is likely to answer the needs of all of them,

— Probe the factual and legal basis for, and sincerity of, their positions, and

— Test their perceptions against reality.

While the private caucus is progressing, the side(s) not meeting with the mediator have an opportunity to analyze and discuss information from the general session (or from earlier private caucuses). Soon, the mediator moves on to the next side, and gradually promotes greater understanding, clarity, and realism on all sides. Depending on the circumstances, the private caucuses may continue, or there may be reason to have general meetings again. The process is quite flexible, sometimes involving meetings between the mediator and experts or counsel without parties, or *vice versa*.

If resolution is reached, all sides are recalled[2] to review the basic terms of the agreement and to make sure there is no misunderstanding. Keep in mind that the mediator has no power but the power of persuasion,[3] so the success of the mediation depends greatly on his ability to get to the crux of the dispute. However, a mediator can provide some other valuable services for disputing parties.

B. The Role of the Mediator

A good mediator may perform one or all of the following functions for the disputing parties and their lawyers:

— Clarify for all concerned what the parties really want;

— Listen carefully to each party and make sure that they understand each other's views;

— Be a locus of trust and confidence for parties and counsel;

— Remove artificial barriers to resolution, *e.g.,* the barriers created by posturing, pouting, and pontificating;

— Keep discussions going without requiring commitments from any of the parties;

— Remove or reduce personal hostilities by permitting parties to "vent" in private caucus sessions;

— Educate the parties about their costs (tangible and intangible) if the dispute goes forward to arbitration or litigation;

— Suggest new and imaginative ways to resolve the dispute;[4]

— Keep the focus on the parties' legitimate needs and interests, not their positions;

— Give parties (and their lawyers) an idea of how great a distance separates their articulated positions;

— Provide a "fig leaf" for a party who wishes to settle but has previously taken extreme positions from which it would be embarrassing to retreat;

— Provide a similar "fig leaf" for a lawyer who may have misevaluated a dispute or may not feel able to confront the client with their true judgments;

— If the mediator has the experience to do so, give the parties a candid assessment of the result that would be reached if their dispute were adjudicated;

— Act as a "bad news" messenger for parties or lawyers who cannot (or will not) deliver it themselves;

— Create a constructive atmosphere for later resolution of the dispute, if through additional mediation sessions or not; and

— Create an atmosphere in which valuable relationships may be maintained, even if the dispute is not resolved.

C. The Roles of the Parties and Their Lawyers in Mediation

As with most things of importance, preparation is essential to successful mediation, whether a party to a dispute is preparing itself or being prepared by its lawyer. To understand the nature of mediation is to realize that *it is an extension of the negotiation process.* This has several implications, the first of which is that mediation is sharply to be distinguished from litigation (and even arbitration) because it is essentially a non-adversarial process where no one but the parties is empowered to compel any particular outcome. Another implication is that mediation, being a *process,* has some identifiable components to it.

This is not to say that mediation follows a series of rules of procedure, but that it is, in fact, one of the most flexible of alternative dispute resolution mechanisms. The accepted description of mediation is that it falls into six recognizable phases. They are:

1. designing and convening the mediation,

2. opening statements,

3. information exchange,

4. reality testing,

5. option-generating, and

6. closure (if all goes well).

Since mediation is always a voluntary process,[5] the parties can agree to whatever process they want. These, however, are the normal phases of mediation and the necessary preparation for each.

1. Designing and Convening the Mediation

The indispensable first step to successful mediation is *getting the other party to agree to mediate.* Even if there is a mediation clause in the contract whose breach has caused the dispute, mediation remains a voluntary process. So, the opponent has to be persuaded that mediation is a tolerable thing to do. In the American culture, this can be a real problem. One predictable reaction from the lawyer for the opposite party in a dispute is, in essence, "if you want it, it must be bad for me." There are several ways to get over this hurdle. The most popular way is to use the good offices of an institutional provider of ADR services. By "institutional provider," nothing more is meant than those organizations who administer ADR mechanisms and provide help with the selection of the appropriate neutral. The oldest and largest of these is the American Arbitration Association, which has been in business for 70 years and has offices in most major cities. Others include the Center for Public Resources (CPR), established by general counsels of large corporations, and the Judicial Arbitration and Mediation Service (JAMS), founded by a group of retired judges. Of these organizations, the American Arbitration Association and CPR are nonprofit. JAMS is a profit-making enterprise. What these agencies (and some of their more short-lived competitors) can do is to persuade the opponent not only that mediation will not harm them, but that it has advantages for all who participate. Opposing parties usually find the same facts and arguments more persuasive if they come from a neutral party.

Another way of surmounting the "if you want it, it must be bad for me" reaction is to move the lawyers aside for a while and have the party whose dispute it is discuss the possibility of mediation with the other party directly. If this route is taken, it should be carefully planned. While it is normally good to have both parties to a dispute communicating directly with one another, that may not be the case if one of them is more sophisticated in negotiation (or more forceful in personality) than their opponent. In such a case, the weaker party may wish to have their lawyer speak for them. Assuming an approximate parity in these areas, the calling party should suggest mediation as a *mutually valuable option,* be prepared to say *why* the process may benefit both parties, and have something specific to propose if an opponent seems interested. Having a neutral "suggestion" usually will not elicit a negative response. For example, a party could suggest that the lawyers call the American Arbitration Association for a list of good mediators, and if they can agree on one, a meeting could be set up as soon as the mediator is available. If they can't agree, the parties could look at the list and perhaps reach an agreement. Even if immediate agreement on mediation is not reached, the parties *are* talking to one another. They might even settle it themselves!

Another method of getting the opponent to agree to mediation is to have someone who has participated in a mediation process (but is not involved in this dispute) contact them. Obviously, the more positive connection such person has had with the other party, the more highly his opinion will be valued. It is usually not hard to find someone for this job, because it is extremely hard to find someone who has had a bad experience with mediation. The key to success here is selecting an intermediary who will be respected—and listened to—by the other party. If a person who will certainly be accorded this respect and attention cannot be found, it is better to use another method. Even if such a person is found, it is most important the intermediary understands that help is needed *only to get the parties to mediation* and not to produce a particular outcome in the dispute itself.

Sadly, the method of persuading the other side to go to mediation that is most likely to succeed is the one that is least employed: *getting the proposed mediator to persuade an opponent.* While quite useful, this method has some potential pitfalls. First of all, the active party, in effect, must select a proposed mediator who will be perceived as a neutral by the opponent (or they won't even listen) and who will be acceptable to both (if the opponent does agree to mediate). In order to determine the mediator's acceptability, he must know *something* about the dispute. Yet, if he is told *too much,* the opponent may believe that the mediator has been "brain-washed" and reject mediation and/or him on that ground alone. This latter danger is particularly true of those parties (or lawyers) who are unacquainted with mediation and do not realize that a mediator does not ever have decision-making power[6] and would not even form an opinion until he had heard fully from *both* sides. In searching out a mediator, lists and associations of mediators (and, unfortunately, would-be mediators) abound. Many times, the institutional provider will invoke the help of one of its mediators should the staff be unable to persuade an opponent to go to mediation. In addition, some parts of the country have "neighborhood dispute resolution centers." While disputes brought to these centers tend to be family or neighbor-against-neighbor affairs, they are frequently a source of information on mediation generally and may be able to provide references to more experienced mediators in business disputes which arise.

Once the parties have agreed to go to mediation (or, perhaps, as a part of that agreement), a number of potentially critical decisions may need to be made. Singularly, the most important of these is the selection of the mediator. Second only to mediator selection is crafting the type of process suited to the dispute.

Earlier, a general description of the workings of a traditional mediation was given. The parties (and their counsel) are free, however, to fashion whatever process works best for them. Some considerations before making a choice of mediator *or* type of mediation are:

(1) *Who needs to attend the mediation?* Specifically, who *must* attend in order that a settlement may be reached, and who *else should* attend in order to increase the chances of success? As to who *must* attend, they are (a) the person having the authority to decide for a party and (b) the person who will do the talking for a party. With business organizations, usually a senior executive has the power of decision and a lawyer (whether working for the company or outside counsel) does the talking. This *may* be the same person. If not, then there should be clear agreement between them as to the role each will take. As to who *should* attend, the answer depends on the nature of the dispute. For example, in a multiparty dispute regarding who was responsible for the cleanup of a giant toxic waste dump, the successful outcome of the mediation rested upon answers to questions such as:

— How had the dumping of a particular chemical affected the surrounding area?

— How long would the effects of particular chemicals be?

— What would it cost to clean up the dump?

Neither the senior executive (who had a technical background but not in toxic waste clean-up) nor the company's lawyer (outside counsel who was expert in environmental law but not technically trained) knew the answers to any of these questions, nor could they assess the correctness of answers given by others. So, two company technical experts were added to the team, a chemist and a chemical engineer experienced in waste clean-up. The opponent had brought similar experts, and, after some preliminary discussions with all present, it was agreed that the "experts" would meet with the mediator separately from the principals and the lawyers for a few sessions. These sessions examined a number of unexpressed assumptions that both sides had had, and prepared the path for a comprehensive settlement reached in the following month, with all participants back at the table.

(2) *Where should the mediation take place?* A neutral location is usually suggested for the mediation sessions so that no party feels at a disadvantage by virtue of the physical surroundings. Selecting a neutral location not only excludes the premises of the parties, but their lawyers' offices as well. As with everything else in mediation, this is subject to the agreement of the parties. Sometimes, the parties have been willing to go to each other's location (or their lawyer's office) for convenience. In general, however, a neutral location is most likely to

create the appropriate (neutral) atmosphere for the sessions to take place.

2. Opening Statements

The opening statement is a frequently neglected aspect of mediation. Parties and counsel seem to feel that the opponents already know what the dispute is about. Hence, they speak in generalities and conclusory terms. In doing so, they miss an opportunity to:

— Explain in detail the basis for their views of the dispute;

— Demonstrate a detailed knowledge of the facts of the dispute;

— Show the opponents that they can *present* their side of the dispute cogently and persuasively;

— Display their level of concern by careful preparation; and

— Cause the opponents to consider information they had not heard before.

Therefore, the opening statement in mediation should be as carefully crafted as an opening statement to a court, arbitrator, or jury, but the mediation opening statement *should not be the same as* similar statements which begin adjudicative processes. Here, the audience (the opponents) is different, as is the process itself (a form of negotiation where the only ones who *decide anything* are the parties themselves).

3. Information Exchange

The exchanging of information, of course, has begun with the opening statements, but mediation ground rules (and common courtesy) require that each party listen to the other without interruption. After opening statements are completed, however, the mediator and parties may want to have an actual exchange of information. It is the rare dispute where at least part of the disagreement is not based on someone (perhaps everyone) being mistaken about something factual. It can be as simple as what the weather was on a certain day or as complex as how to remove calcium ions from a chemical solution, but the parties are going to have differences based on mistakes of fact. Frequently, these items can be cleared up early in a mediation session. In the easiest cases, it is simply a matter of one party providing the other with factual information that it did not have. More usually, the parties and mediator need to resort to sources of information which are widely accepted for their accuracy (the U.S. Weather Service, in the case of the simple item above).

Another kind of information exchange is the direct revelation of what documents and potential testimony a party has to support its position. Parties and their lawyers are much more wary about being forthcoming with these types of information—and for good reason.

While many states have statutes which make mediations confidential, and the parties will (at least if they have read this book) insist on a written confidentiality agreement anyway, these provisions *do not* protect *what is learned* in the mediation sessions from later exploration ("discovery") *if the mediation does not end in resolution.* This fact can present a real dilemma:

> if a particularly crucial document or fact or piece of potential testimony is revealed and the dispute is not resolved, the opponent can pursue what they were shown or learned about, but

> if this crucial bit of information is not revealed, the chances of resolving the matter at mediation are substantially impaired.

To extricate oneself from this dilemma requires a minute examination of the facts (and, perhaps, the law) surrounding the dispute, as well as the personalities and behavior patterns of the participants. Here are some possible considerations:

— If the information is revealed, how hard will it be for the opponent to combat it or explain it away?

— How much would it improve the bargaining position to reveal it?

— Is there a way of getting the mediator to convey the existence of this piece of information without actually revealing it?

— Is there a way of setting up bargaining so that a resolution can be agreed upon, depending on the disposition of an issue that the crucial piece of information will necessarily resolve?

— Is there information that one party may have (on the crucial topic or a related one) that another would bargain for?

4. Reality Testing

This part of the process can take many forms, and, like information exchange, goes on throughout the mediation. Reality testing means nothing more than "test driving" the parties' positions, issues, and ideas *under the conditions in which they would actually be applied.* The easiest example is a legal one. Suppose the two parties at Turbulent and Placid are at it again. They go to mediation, and Placid takes the position that Turbulent's claims would be time-barred in court because of the applicable statute of limitations. With the help of an experienced, qualified mediator, several questions can be explored:

— What is the *applicable* statute of limitations period, *i.e.,* how long *does* Turbulent have to bring a lawsuit?

— When should the clock have begun running on Turbulent, *e.g.,* when it first found out about Placid's allegedinfringement or when, if it had its eyes open, it *should have* found out?

— Are there any reasons why this period should be suspended?

— What are the consequences if the period *has* run out, *e.g.,* will *all of* Turbulent's claims get thrown out of court or just some?

Similar action can be taken with *proposals* that are made during the mediation. A party or the mediator can ask questions such as:

— How will that work?

— How is this coming about?

— Will the Board of Directors approve something such as that?

— What would the company role be if such an action were taken?

— Can it be done in that time frame?

The purpose of this exercise is to get the party who owns the position or proposal to focus on how realistic they are in light of their position or proposal working out *in the real world outside the mediation room.*

5. Option-generating

Here, it is important to reemphasize the fact that, in mediation, *the parties can craft whatever resolution they can agree to and are not bound by normal legal remedies.* This is one of the most frequently overlooked benefits of mediation. When parties take their dispute to arbitration or court, they are doing at least two unattractive things:

(a) they are putting the power to decide their dispute in the hands of a third party who is (almost always) a stranger to the dispute and the parties, and

(b) they are narrowing the possible outcomes of the decision to those commonly accepted "legal" remedies: money damages, restitution, injunction, etc.

In mediation, however, the parties not only continue to retain control over the outcome, but they are not constrained by traditional legal remedies. For that matter, they are not even constrained by the "four corners" of their dispute. If they wish, they can resolve the dispute by agreements about entirely unrelated matters.

So, it is crucial that *all* available options be considered, however briefly. This is sometimes difficult where the parties are represented by counsel or are familiar with arbitration or litigation themselves. Through training and experience both, they are likely to have a narrow view of what the outcome options actually are. This is one of the places where a good mediator can earn his money. As an example, in a sexual harassment dispute, the claimant was a young, hard-charging executive at a major industrial corporation, and the respondents were the company itself and the alleged harasser, an executive two levels above the claimant in the corporate hierarchy. After nine hours of mediation, the dispute was resolved by the alleged harasser agreeing to write a letter of apology to the claimant, specifically mentioning the offending conduct. The claimant and the company agreed that a copy of the letter would go in this individual's confidential personnel file—and nowhere else—so long as no more sexual harassment complaints were lodged against him. In this instance, *the solution which the parties chose was one which no judge or arbitrator would have the power to impose on them*. So, the resolution which the parties actually selected could *never* have been reached in court or arbitration.

As with the decision about revealing a crucial piece of information, the various options available will always depend on the particulars of the dispute. Here are some approaches that are effective, some of which have already been metioned in the chapter on negotiation:

— Thinking from the opponent's place—think about what options might be appealing to them and see which ones could be lived with;

— Seek the mediator's help—what solutions have worked in other mediations similar to this one;

— "Color outside the lines"—discuss (in private caucuses) new ways of dealing with the problem, then reality test them to see if they might work;

— Consider noneconomic factors—maybe there is something that can be given up (perhaps a letter of apology) which has no economic cost to the organization; and

— Break things down into small components, and try to treat each component separately.

6. Closure

For both psychological and legal reasons, closure, the process whereby the agreement is reviewed and assented to by all the parties and the mediation concluded, is very important. A certain sense of ceremony will help give the parties a stronger feeling that the dispute is indeed over. And, the ceremony of reciting, assenting to, writing down and signing the agreement gives the mediation resolution the legally binding character that all parties (presumably) desire. The mediator reviews what has been agreed to, point by point, and what the terms of that portion of the agreement are with all the parties. The mediator's purpose is twofold:

(a) to make sure that all parties *understand* every term of the proposed resolution, and

(b) to make sure that all parties *agree* to the proposed resolution now that all the "blanks" have been filled in.

Keep in mind that the parties have been *involved* in the process all the way along, so they are not likely to be surprised by something the mediator recites. However, this will be the first time that the *entire* resolution package has been placed on the table for examination. Cases of "buyer's remorse" tend to show up here. Parties who have agreed to each of the components of the proposed settlement may now exhibit a squeamishness about accepting the whole thing. Many reasons for this behavior are possible, not least a genuine concern that the whole package is less favorable than the individual components appeared to be. More often, however, a party has become "wedded" to the dispute itself, particularly if it has been wending its way through the court-house. With patience and careful explanation from both the mediator and the other parties (if they are present), the squeamishness usually passes, and everyone is back on board.

D. Costs

The question about any business expenditure is not so much what it will cost as it is if it will be cost-effective, *i.e.,* an economical return for money spent. An expensive overcoat, for instance, may be the cost-effective choice because it will last more than twice as long as the cheaper one at half its price. Mediation is similar. As of this writing, a good mediator charges between $250 and $400 an hour in urban centers,[7] and the average mediation takes about five hours. The cost is already into the thousands column. Then, an alternative dispute resolution provider may have to administer the process and provide the neutral ground on which the mediation can take place. These charges currently can range from $150 to $300 for an administration fee, to which may be added facilities charges for renting the neutral ground. There is also the cost of diverting people who would otherwise be working to make money for your business to the mediation process. And, last but not least expensive, if legal representation is required, the preparation time and mediation sessions attendance add up (not unrea-sonably) to about 15 to 20 hours of time, assuming the mediation session itself lasts the average five hours. Even for the simplest media-tion, out-of-pocket expense will be at least $1,000 and about ten hours of someone's time will have been lost. For the complex mediation, with counsel involved, total costs of $50,000 are not unheard of.

It can be expensive. But, remember that the longer a mediation takes to prepare for and to attend, the more likely it is that there are serious dollars and issues at stake in the underlying dispute. Even so, the true cost-effectiveness of meditation doesn't come into clear focus without using the punch line from a portion of Henny Youngman's signature (and sexist) joke: "How's your wife?", the straight man says. "Compared to what?", the comedian responds. A similar "analysis" must be made with mediation. "Is it costly?" "Compared to what?"

The other available choices for resolving disputes are few indeed. Negotiation must be excluded, because if the parties had been able to negotiate a resolution successfully without help, they would not even *be* in mediation. Arbitration (if it had been contracted for in advance or possibly persuading the other party to submit to it now) or a lawsuit are all that are left. These are the points of comparison, then, in assessing whether mediation is cost-effective or merely costly.

In researching this book, interviews with more than fifty business people and lawyers were conducted, each of whom had substantial experience *in all three forms of dispute resolution*. The questions were essentially a composite of the straight man's question and the comedian's response: "Is mediation costly, compared to the (available) alternatives?" Their answers took many forms, but had one simple, recurring motif: *"The cost of mediating a dispute will always be no more than a small fraction of the cost of resolving the same dispute through arbitration or litigation."* One senior executive went so far as to say: "Mediation is so cost-effective, I can't think of a type of business dispute where I would not *insist* on it *before* we headed down the litigation trail."

A *Wall Street Journal* article from 1993 sums up the experience of businesses with mediation:

> ... [E]very week, it seems, key players in another industry—from banking to food to insurance—announce that they will submit a major area of litigation to some form of mediation or arbitration.

> **Tremendous Savings**

> The savings for companies so far have been tremendous. Since 1990, 406 companies tracked by the Center for Public Resources, a non-profit group that provides mediators and arbitrators, saved more than $150 million in legal fees and expert-witness costs by using litigation alternatives. The cases involved disputes with more than $5 billion at stake.[8]

Notice that the quote contained the term mentioned at the top of this section, cost-effective. So, having itemized some costs, the "effective" part will be discussed next.

E. Effectiveness of the Process

Statistics on mediation (such as those of the American Arbitration Association) show that mediation has about an 80- to 90-percent success rate, measured by whether the mediation session(s) end in a *complete resolution*. This definition of a successful mediation leaves out the numerous disputes where mediation has enabled the parties to unravel significant *portions of the dispute*. This method of counting also presumably leaves out equal number of disputes in which the mediation process has so detoxified the atmosphere between the parties that they negotiate a settlement sometime after mediation.

Another informative statistic is that 80 percent of *all* civil disputes reach a negotiated conclusion before going to trial or arbitration hearing. The number of actual civil filings has decreased in recent years, and most civil cases are settled before the evidence is heard by the arbitrator or judge. So, how is this cost-effective? The answer lies, as with so many things in life, in the *timing*. The key to the cost-effectiveness analysis is the answer to the question: "When do all those civil disputes settle?" The answer is that the great majority of them settle *within weeks of the scheduled hearing/trial date.* So, in settling a litigated civil dispute, one can just *wait.* Sadly, this is really not a viable option. By the date of the hearing, most of the time and money have already been spent on discovery, preparation, and the like. So, the cost-effectiveness of mediation still compares favorably with arbitration and litigation, because, *even if mediation is one week earlier than when the case would have been heard, money and time will have been saved.* Moreover, many parties experience most of the costs of a dispute in the pretrial phase of litigation. So, a theorem emerges: *The earlier in the dispute one mediates, the more money and time are saved.* This theorem, of course, is only right about 80 percent of the time.

F. Mediation in Criminal Matters

Not only is mediation an advantageous method of resolving disputes in the civil arena, but mediation is also being tested as a method of resolving misdemeanor criminal disputes. Several states across the country have implemented voluntary victim-offender mediation programs in an effort to resolve criminal disputes which would not otherwise be adequately addressed in the court system. Many prosecutors and public defenders support misdemeanor mediation programs, believing them to create a win-win-win outcome for the following reasons:

— Unlike the normal operation of the criminal justice system where the victim often feels excluded and powerless, mediation may restore the individual's sense of control of their life;

— Because of the reduced workload, prosecutors and public defenders can concentrate their efforts on more significant matters;

— For offenders, mediation is an alternative to a criminal record and a chance to right a wrong;

— Victims may win restitution for the damage done or an agreement governing the offender's future behavior;

— The community benefits by greater compliance with the punishment formulated through criminal mediation than with a judicially imposed punishment;[9] and

— Taxpayers benefit from the cost savings, because the "transaction cost" of handling each case is reduced dramatically.

G. Six Reasons Lawyers Give for Not Using Mediation and Why They Are Wrong

Lawyers who represent businesses with disputes (as distinguished from those lawyers who help their clients *control* disputes by drafting alternative dispute resolution clauses for them) have a number of recurring themes as to why mediation would *not be* a good idea. Six favorites are set forth below:

REASON NUMBER ONE: Mediation will be a waste of time and money if the dispute does not settle there.

REALITY NUMBER ONE: Much is usually accomplished, even if the entire dispute does not settle at the mediation session. As mentioned earlier, parts of the dispute are sometimes resolved. Absent a partial resolution, the parties may still succeed in narrowing the issues between them or reducing the *number of parties* in the dispute. They inevitably emerge from the mediation with a heightened sense of where the strengths and infirmities of their side of the dispute lie. It is also possible that the parties will develop a discovery plan, in itself a significant saving to all sides. Interestingly, an unsuccessful mediation frequently tightens the bond between attorney and client, which is helpful in those rare instances where the dispute really must go to arbitration or trial. Lastly, but most importantly, even an unsuccessful mediation usually detoxifies the atmosphere between the parties and sometimes between counsel as well. While the economic benefit of this detoxification can rarely be quantified, it is certain to make for less truculent behavior on the part of all the parties as the dispute progresses toward resolution by a third party.

REASON NUMBER TWO: Mediation will be a waste of time and money because of some fault of the opponent's lawyer.

REALITY NUMBER TWO: Mediation directly involves the parties as well as their counsel. So, intransigence or incompetence is more likely to be overcome in a mediation, where a party can both have his say and hear what others have to say without the filter of the lawyer's interpretation. The reality testing and position evaluation that is routinely done in mediation may well change an unrealistic appraisal by one side. This is particularly so because a good mediator can "save face" for the party whose appraisal must change.

REASON NUMBER THREE: Suggesting mediation will be interpreted as a sign of weakness.

REALITY NUMBER THREE: When a party suggests mediation to an opponent, they are actually

— exposing their position to scrutiny by the other side and its counsel;

— exposing their views to scrutiny by a trained and experienced neutral; and

— committing themselves to a frank discussion of the strengths and weaknesses of their position.

These are not the actions of a weakling. (See the earlier section where it is explained how to get the institutional alternative dispute resolution provider and/or the mediator involved in the "creation" of the mediation.) Another problem with this reason is that it implicitly assumes that the best (only) way to resolve a dispute is in an evidentiary hearing presided over by a neutral third party. The truth is that parties to a dispute are much more concerned with results and costs necessary to achieve those results. It is the rare party who wants to finance a protracted litigation so that a lawyer can show off.

REASON NUMBER FOUR: Delivering information during the mediation will hurt the case in the future.

REALITY NUMBER FOUR: As pointed out above, many states have statutes which cloak what is said and done in mediation with confidentiality. Plus, parties can craft additional safeguards, by agreement, before the mediation begins. But, just as importantly, each party remains in *control* of *what information* is delivered and *when* it is delivered. So, tactical decisions can be made on the spot or after private consultation. Further, the parties in mediation have the ability to use the mediator as a means of controlling the dissemination of information and/or settlement proposals.

REASON NUMBER FIVE: The case is "open-and-shut," so mediation is unnecessary, which actually means that if mediation is used, the lawyer won't be able to charge as much in fees.

REALITY NUMBER FIVE: If the lawyer is in good faith (most are) and *really believes* the case is a winner and is correct, a favorable outcome in mediation should be rather easily obtained. If the analysis of the case is not correct, then it behooves the lawyer and benefits the client to learn that fact *at the earliest possible moment.* Besides, there is no such thing as a sure winner. Every case can be lost, and most experienced dispute lawyers will say that they have won many that they *should have lost*, and *vice versa.* In some cases, what the lawyer really means is that he will make more fees if the matter lurches on through the maze at the courthouse. Considering only the individual dispute, there is no refuting the factual accuracy of this observation. The lawyer most likely will make less in fees, maybe much less, if the case is mediated, but legal ethics would put client interests ahead of his own. Assuming, just for the sake of completeness, that this particular lawyer has never read the ethical standards and wouldn't abide by them if he had, the best response to such a person, of course, is to get another lawyer, pointing out the fact that the best way to increase long-term income would be to satisfy existing clients, causing them to come back for additional legal work in the future.

REASON NUMBER SIX: Mediation will coerce a party into "splitting the difference," or otherwise compromising their principles.

REALITY NUMBER SIX: As mentioned before, the mediator has no power except the power of persuasion. So, strictly speaking, nothing can be coerced in mediation. Even accounting for the extraordinary persuasive powers of some mediators, the parties and lawyers have nothing to fear. First, the resolution must come from the parties. So, a split-the-difference approach (or any other solution) will not occur unless *all parties* want it to. Second, the procedures of mediation—principled negotiation, careful review of options, and meticulous scrutiny of any resolution—all militate *against* the sort of capricious approaches which lawyers fear.

H. Guide to Assessing Mediation for a Dispute

1. Whether to Mediate

The decision to mediate depends very much on the individual facts of each dispute; therefore, only generalizations are possible here. But remember that mediation is a voluntary process. So, even if the decision to mediate was wrong, the minute events begin to go awry, the case can be withdrawn, unlike in a litigation setting.

Collected below are a set of considerations, each of which should be pondered carefully before the decision is made:

Economics—Mediation is almost always a cost-saver and time-saver. If mediation becomes lengthy (and, therefore, more costly), it is always because significant progress toward resolution (or partial resolution) is being made. Even the longest mediation is cheaper than litigating or arbitrating a significant dispute. As mentioned above, counsel's ethical obligation to help a client resolve disputes efficiently may conflict with counsel's economic self-interest (as it always might when disputes are litigated). Experience shows, however, that a every lawyer who guides clients to a relatively quick and low-cost resolution is a lawyer who not only has many repeat clients, but one to whom a client turns for advice on an ever-widening range of matters—and earlier in the course of those matters.

Timing—While there is hardly any "bad" time to mediate, it is usually best to begin mediation after all sides have some awareness of their opponents' claims. This does *not* mean that mediation should not take place before a formal litigation or arbitration is begun, but that there should be at least a moderate level of candid, prelitigation communication among the parties and their representatives. Many times, what is lost in depth of knowledge about the legal merits of the case is more than made up for by the parties' higher level of willingness and ability to settle early.

Confidentiality and privacy—While many negotiated resolutions of disputes can be made confidential by agreement, mediation can frequently conceal even the *existence* of a dispute from all but the disputants themselves. If mediation is begun early enough, there may be no trace of the dispute on the "public record." Also, the contents of the mediation process are often made inadmissible in later proceedings by statute.[10] Some states may give "common-law" (judicial law found in reported case decisions) confidentiality protection to mediation, but it is important to know what protections are available and which will apply automatically *before* beginning the mediation itself. Not every jurisdiction grants the same level of confidentiality, but since mediation is a voluntary process, the parties can fill in any gaps in the legislative or common-law protection by adding more confidentiality provisions to their agreement to mediate.

The mediated resolution can itself be made confidential by agreement. On the other hand, some disputes (particularly in the areas of politics and entertainment) may be precipitated *for the purpose of gaining publicity*. In the latter situation, mediation frequently takes place against a backdrop of public pronouncements by the parties. Even in this area, a mediated resolution is frequently achieved, although the result may have to be revealed to a waiting media and public. Even so, the way in which the results are revealed (timing, contents of press release, etc.) may also be the subject of the mediated resolution.

Unlimited options for resolution—When a resolution is negotiated, the parties may agree to many things which a judge or arbitrator would have no power to order. A good example (given in detail above) is a dispute which was resolved by a carefully drafted letter of apology. The nature of the case was such that a judge or arbitrator would only have been able to award money damages. Frequently, however, the more important aspect of this consideration is that the parties may reach outside the dispute itself for ways to resolve it. A favorite disputant, CementHead, Inc., sued a vendor for delivering a huge quantity of defective supplies. Tempers flared and egos preened on both sides. The vendor wouldn't admit the delivered items were defective, and CementHead wanted its money back. At the mediation, to which both parties were dragged kicking and screaming by their lawyers, it was arranged that the vendor would supply CementHead, on a particular future date, with a similar quantity of supplies whose specifications were carefully described. CementHead waived its claim to get its money back, but was allowed to retain title to the "defective" shipment (thereby being able to realize the "salvage value"). The vendor didn't have to accept a return of its goods; CementHead didn't have to admit they were not defective. No court or arbitrator could have *ordered* this result.

Party willingness—A common misconception is that all parties must be "in a settlement frame of mind" for mediation to work. Actually, the mediator's job includes being able to persuade everyone involved of the attractiveness (as an idea, at least) of a mediated resolution. Indeed, experienced litigators and mediators agree that the intransigence of a party (or counsel) on the subject of settlement is usually a good indicator that the matter is ripe for mediation. It is the rare party who really wants to maintain an acrimonious and costly dispute when a rational alternative is provided. If egos are involved, an experienced mediator can provide "cover" for those egos while the businesses they are part of reach a satisfactory resolution.

Party representative—In order to succeed in mediation, *each* party must be represented by a principal or other representative (*in addition to* counsel) who has the authority to conclude the dispute. Who will it be? How will they behave? While mediation is a much less formal and more flexible procedure than *any* form of litigation or arbitration, it is not without structure. Almost always, the parties (or their counsel) get to explain their side of the dispute to the mediator initially *in the presence of the other party or parties.* While a sincere and persuasive presentation is always desirable, a shouting match is usually not. Similarly, while candor is normally a positive attribute, there may be aspects of the dispute (both positive and negative) which should not be revealed or not *just then.* As with other alternative dispute resolution mechanisms, there is a substantial role for counsel to play in preparing itself *and the client* for participation in the mediation.

Relationships—Will some or all of the parties have (or want to have) a continuing business/professional/personal relationship *after* this dispute is resolved? If so, choosing the least incendiary way of resolving the dispute is most likely to permit that relationship to continue. Also, continued relationships are aided by the fact that mediation results in a party-crafted resolution. For example, long-term considerations (even though not now in dispute) are easily dealt with, which they could not be in normal litigation or arbitration. Just as important is the nontoxic atmosphere in which a mediation is held. Even the most lugubrious parties usually wind up finding a better way of dealing with their opponents than they had before the mediation began.

Opportunities lost—Frequently external factors (*e.g.,* changes in general interest rates, new manufacturing technologies, discounts on transportation, product obsolescence, changes in management or ownership, etc.) provide a "window of opportunity" for rational resolution. This window may well have closed by the time an adjudicated resolution is reached. In sharp contrast, the mere commencement of litigation/arbitration sometimes serves to harden the parties' positions and to personalize what are essentially economic disputes. While perhaps a subset of "Timing," above, these considerations are present frequently enough to merit special consideration on their own.

Freedom/Control—One can always walk away from a mediation proceeding with only a few hours of time and a fractional share of the fees "lost." The mediator has no power except the power of persuasion. So, if things get too unpleasant, or one of the participants appears to have permanently abandoned rational discourse and that there is no real chance of reaching a resolution, one can simply walk out. In addition, the mediator, although optimistic by nature, has no desire to waste the parties' money and everyone's time. Even though the mediator gets paid by the hour, the business is successful only with "return customers" (the parties and/or their lawyers coming back). As with the litigator, the mediator who drags out a mediation a few more hours for a short-term billing gain will be losing long term. If, after a reasonable period, the mediator concludes that no progress is being made, the mediator will say so, state the apparent reasons, and give the parties a last chance before terminating the session. These facts often cause parties and counsel to tone down their rhetoric and really listen to what their opponent has to say. Finally, a resolution can only be reached if all parties agree to it.

Setting—Sadly, the mediation session location sometimes becomes as critical as the discussion content. If this results, the importance of a neutral location may need to be reevaluated. If the opponent's office seems to be a possible site for negotiation without detriment, give in. At least, mediation will begin.

2. When Not to Mediate

There are times when mediation may not be an appropriate choice for resolving a dispute. If a legal precedent is needed (or really wanted), mediation may not be a solution. Unless the parties can agree as to a legal interpretation and have that interpretation included in the judgment of a court of record, mediation will not provide a reliable legal precedent for the resolution of similar future disputes. Even if these things can be accomplished, the reliability of the precedent obtained may be questionable, since it is subject to the accusation that it is the result of collusion between the parties.

Similarly, if publicizing the existence of a dispute and every aspect of it up to and including resolution is desired, mediation may be an inappropriate choice. For instance, a manufacturer of popular trademarked goods may find it necessary to sue infringers both vigorously and publicly. Otherwise, a substantial portion of the "value" of such litigation (the deterrent effect on other likely infringers) would be lost in the confidentiality of mediation. Along the same lines, some large corporations perceive the need to defend vigorously all lawsuits of a certain kind, lest the company be viewed as a pushover by potential plaintiffs and their lawyers.

In most instances, however, mediation is very much like chicken soup: it certainly won't do any harm, and it may do a world of good.

3. When to Mediate

Mediation may be an attractive dispute resolution option when:

— *Early* resolution is desirable for any reason;
— The disputing parties want to resolve their dispute and maintain their relationship;
— There is animosity between parties or counsel;
— *Adverse publicity* is likely if litigated or arbitrated;
— *Adverse precedent* could result from arbitration or litigation;
— Other dispute resolution forums may not provide an appropriate *remedy* for a dispute;
— Formal litigation/arbitration is undesirable for any reason;
— The cost of other resolution methods may be prohibitive;
— A party and its counsel cannot agree on an evaluation of the legal merits of the case;
— Opposing parties and/or their counsel disagree widely in their evaluations, for no apparent reason;
— The practical problems, potential solutions, or legal issues are complex;

— The lawyers tire of fighting and/or the parties tire of paying for their fighting;

— Negotiation is in process, but neutral evaluation might help;

— The case is too large or complex for settlement in the little time a public court judge can give to a conference; or

— There is a great disparity of power which might work to the disadvantage of a party in the public court system.[11]

4. How to Mediate

In the joint caucus which usually begins a mediation, everyone meets face-to-face, perhaps for the first time. Before such a meeting, careful preparation is required, such as by asking what the goals are for this event. The overall goal, certainly, is an acceptable solution, but within the context of the mediation meetings themselves, the following goals are suggested:

— Raise doubts in the opponent about the viability of their position;

— Convince all of sincerely desiring a reasonable resolution;[12]

— Present persuasive views;

— Avoid inflammatory language;

— Listen carefully;

— Be flexible;

— Ensure clear communication among party members;

— Don't take personally whatever is said (even if it is *meant* personally);

— Try to see things from an opponent's perspective; and

— Keep the overall goal in view: resolution.

How these goals are achieved depends on the various skills which a team brings to the table. Mediation preparation should carefully consider who should be principally responsible for what goals.

As a mediation progresses, assess the personality types that appear to be seated across the table and at its head, and act accordingly. Just as the opponents will have different personalities, so will mediators. Some, usually true to their pacific temperament, will "listen the parties to death" and seem rarely to interrupt, let alone intervene. At the other extreme, other mediators will try to use the force of their personality to move the parties toward settlement, whether the parties like it or not. Remember that it is the parties who are paying a portion (depending on the number of parties) of the mediator's fees. Although expected to lead the process, the mediator is still "in the parties' employ." If the mediator's behavior seems likely to damage resolution prospects, say so (politely, of course). Most good mediators are flexible (and secure) enough to take a critique and use it to *increase the chance of resolution.*

In the private caucus, the mediator will encourage a greater level of candor than normally (understandably) exhibited when the opponent was in the room. Be careful. Even though the mediator can certainly *be trusted* to keep confidences from the other party, one may nonetheless wish to *control the timing* of giving some data to the mediator.

Another element of the dispute mediation process, which generally takes place in the private caucuses, is the venting of personal feelings in some fashion. *All disputes are personal,* in that each party to a dispute has at least one person on it whose ego is involved. It may be the person who negotiated this (now gone sour) deal. No matter who or what, *someone's ego is on the line.* Therefore, it should not be surprising to learn that feelings sometimes run high in business disputes. It is often said that, at bottom, every business dispute is just about money. While this is generally true, *some people get very emotional about money.* What can be done about these emotions? Vent them.

"Venting" is the name mediators have given to the process whereby parties basically "let off steam" verbally. They let everyone know just how *wronged* they have been in the dispute, and just how *wrong* the opponent is. While some of this venting is permissible in the general caucuses (particularly the first one), parties should generally wait for the private caucus to really let go. Why do it this way? First of all, in conveying some of the depth of feeling to the other party, it is not desirable *to so anger them that they leave the mediation table.* Secondly, by venting in the private caucus, the mediator gets a good sense of the depth of emotions involved *and may communicate that depth to the opponent himself* (without the risk of running them off).

Another good deportment choice in mediation is to stress certain principles without insisting on a specific position, as mentioned earlier.

Finally, some advice: *Just be yourself,* or, in other words, do not try to change personalities for the mediation. Why not? First, the mediator (and probably everyone else) will sense something artificial. But, more importantly, it adds an extra burden when successful negotiating requires total concentration.

5. What to Get at the End

This subsection can be summarized in four words: *Get a written agreement.* It is quite true that the parties to most mediated resolutions would likely perform their part of the agreement without the necessity of a document, but a document adds some large benefits. The first of these is entirely consistent with the philosophy of mediation: participation in the preparation and signing of a written agreement gives the parties one more reason to have a sense of ownership of both the process and its result. Further, a written agreement tends to flush out any misunderstandings or unexpressed assumptions that the parties may have *while the mediation process is still able to work them out.* Thirdly, a written agreement is usually an enforceable contract. This permits court enforcement of a settlement[13] if the other party does not comply with its terms. (This rarely occurs.)

The same principles apply to a mediation where less than all of the issues are resolved. Record what has been resolved, and, if possible, agree on a protocol for continuing efforts to resolve the remaining issues.

6. Choosing the Right Mediator

In the next chapter, some generalizations in assessing prospective neutrals are listed. But not every good arbitrator is good mediator, and *vice versa.* Here are some necessary characteristics for a good mediator:

— Patient;

— Optimistic;

— Tenacious;

— Confidence-inspiring;

— Wise;

— Flexible (here's that word again);

— An excellent listener;

— Intelligent;

— Insightful;

— Honest; and

— Realistic.

Not all mediators possess these traits to the same degree. A choice of mediator, then, may depend on which of these traits are most important to a particular mediation.

Even before assessing whether a prospective mediator has all (or most of) the qualities mentioned above, there is the matter of "disclosure," *i.e.,* meaning the process by which the mediator informs the parties of any relationships he has (or had) with any of them or their lawyers which might affect someone's perception of his neutrality. At first glance, disclosure would not seem to be as important in mediation as it definitely is in arbitration. True, but disclosure remains important. First, and foremost, in order for the mediation to have the best chance of succeeding, *all parties and counsel* must have great confidence in the mediator's neutrality. An illustration of the potential problems using an extreme example would be a dishonest mediator revealing to the other party everything an opponent said to him in confidence in the private caucuses. Indeed, a mediator who is only slightly biased could affect the outcome of the mediation just by using his persuasive powers to get one side to take less or give more. Keep in mind that these mediators are likely to be very persuasive people indeed. Don't take any chances. Have the prospective mediator make the same level of disclosure that would be required of a prospective arbitrator.[14] Certain disclosed items which might be cause for disqualification of that same person as an arbitrator can be ignored, but that choice should not be the prospective mediator's.

Much heat and very little light have been generated by two parallel sets of arguments about the nature of mediation and the appropriate characteristics of a mediator. First, there is the controversy over whether mediation is a facilitative or a directive process. What this means, simplified, is that some see mediation as a facilitative process in which the only thing that should be happening is the mediator's assisting the parties to come to a resolution on their own. To those who subscribe to this view, a mediator sharing his judgments about aspects of the dispute would be anathema. To the adherents of the directive school of mediation, it is not only appropriate but desirable that the mediator share his judgments with the parties and try to move them in the direction of what he believes would be a fair and suitable resolution. In truth, both sides are partly right. Mediation *is* a facilitative process, but it is also a process (at least in the business context) where the parties have paid handsomely for the assistance of the mediator in getting to a resolution. Therefore, a mediator should be able to use both techniques and have the good judgment to know when to use one and put away the other.

The other great controversy in the science of mediation is whether the mediator should be someone imbued in the mediation process and committed to making that process work or should be someone having "substantive expertise" in the subject matter of the dispute. Ideally, if possible, a mediator should have deep learning in and commitment to the mediation process, but should also have some expertise in the subject of the dispute. It is the rare urban center in the United States where a mediator possessing both qualities cannot be found.

In selecting a mediator, it is helpful to know that anyone who wishes to call himself a mediator *is* one, *i.e.,* there is no licensing process as there is for lawyers, doctors, accountants, *et al.* So, how does one find an experienced mediator? It takes some effort, but it can be done successfully. First of all, what not to do is to assume that someone is a competent mediator because they have been certified or credentialed by some school or (nongovernmental) agency. Such certification may mean nothing more than that the "mediator" has taken that organization's course and paid their fees, which doesn't necessarily make a good (or, for that matter, even well-trained) mediator.

A thoughtful process of mediator selection can *begin* by soliciting the help of institutional ADR providers such as the American Arbitration Association. Each of them has a panel of mediators; some may have subpanels of people who purport to have special expertise, *e.g.,* in construction matters, securities disputes, etc.[15] Obtain as much biographical information about each candidate as possible to learn what his experience has been. Get references from the ADR provider and also from business associates and lawyers, and ask about their recommendations carefully. Find out how much they know about a mediator. Did they attend a mediation with him, or did they hear him speak at a convention? The depth of inquiry here should only be limited by the budgetary constraints of the dispute itself. After all, if this mediator isn't going to add something measurable to the chances of resolution, negotiation might just as well be used, and the money saved.

ENDNOTES

[1] See, *e.g.,* California Evidence Code, sec. 1152.5.

[2] This assumes that they have been together at the beginning and are willing to come together at the end. That is not always the case. While there is no substitute for the possible benefits of parties speaking directly to one another, in some disputes emotions are too highly charged for this to happen (at least initially). So, for example, in a sexual harassment dispute, the parties may meet separately with the mediator from beginning to (successful) conclusion of the mediation.

[3] Overburdened courts across the country are increasingly turning to what they characterize as "mandatory mediation," meaning that the parties to a lawsuit and their lawyers are ordered to meet with a mediator with a view to solving their dispute. The power of any court, however, is limited to "leading the horse to water" and no one can "make him drink," *i.e.,* the parties have to show up at the appointed day and hour, but no court in the land has the power to *make them* agree to a specific resolution. So, in the end, even this "mandatory" process turns out to be voluntary.

[4] It is worth repeating here that parties and the mediator can fashion remedies which go far beyond the four corners of the existing dispute—and far beyond anything that an arbitrator or judge could order.

[5] See n. 3, above.

[6] There is the possibility that the parties will, at some point in the process where impasse is reached, give the (former) mediator the power to decide the controversy (or those aspects of it that mediation has not solved). This series of events is generally called Med/Arb and will be dealt with in detail in a later chapter.

[7] The upper end of this rate range sounds expensive, and it is. As with most things in life, however, one gets what one pays for.

[8] Ellen Joan Pollock, *Wall Street Journal,* 22 March 1993, p. B1.

[9] The rationale is similar to that which explains the high compliance rate with mediated resolutions in civil matters: the offenders will be more apt to abide by the

terms of mediation rather than an imposed sentence, since they helped devise the mediated agreement themselves.

[10] See, *e.g.,* California Evidence Code, secs. 703.5 and 1152.5.

[11] It is not meant to imply that disparities in bargaining power disappear at the mediation room door. They do not. However, a less affluent company can afford a mediation better than it can afford a five-year trip through the courthouse.

[12] It is especially important to convince the mediator of the sincere desire for resolution. While mediators are trained to remain neutral as to the relative merits of the parties' positions, it is most difficult for a mediator to banish completely his annoyance with a party who speaks and acts as if they *do not want a resolution.*

[13] Depending on the applicable law, a settlement agreement may be able to be immediately turned into a court judgment. The resulting enforceable contract can be the basis of another lawsuit and a sure-fire winner of a case. If mediation takes place while an arbitration is pending, then the mediated agreement can be rendered as an award by the arbitrator. Good judgment should be exercised about asking that this be done, however, since it implies some remaining distrust of the other party.

[14] The American Arbitration Association, the American Bar Association (ABA), and the Society of Professionals in Dispute Resolution (SPIDR) have jointly issued a recent document called *Standards of Conduct for Mediators.* Section III of that document provides:

Conflicts of Interest: A Mediator Shall Disclose all Actual and Potential Conflicts of Interest Reasonably Known to the Mediator. After Disclosure, the Mediator Shall Decline to Mediate Unless all Parties Choose to Retain the Mediator. The Need to Protect Against Conflicts of Interest Also Governs Conduct that Occurs During and After the Mediation.

This document defines "conflict of interest" as a "dealing or relationship that might create the impression of possible bias."

[15] For the most part, securities disputes, *i.e.,* disputes where one party is a securities broker-dealer, are required by contract to be handled by arbitration under the Rules of the New York Stock Exchange or the National Association of Securities Dealers (NASD). Nonetheless, parties can mediate before arbitration if they choose.

"Whose idea was it to use an arbitrator, anyway?"

ARBITRATION

The "Traditional" Alternative to Litigation

I cannot emphasize too strongly to those in business and industry—and especially to lawyers—that every private contract of real consequence to the parties ought to be treated as a 'candidate' for binding private arbitration.
—former Chief Justice Warren E. Burger

Although the term "alternative dispute resolution" is probably no more than fifteen years old, arbitration has a much longer history.[1] Currently, our court systems embrace it, and there is legislation in all fifty states and federal law which permits turning an arbitration award into a court judgment (confirmation). Arbitration is the one element of alternative dispute resolution which everyone knows about—or thinks he does. Its long use in labor-management disputes[2]—especially in professional baseball—has guaranteed it a frequent place in the media. But, like mediation, arbitration takes many forms and is a more sophisticated process than it seems.

In most instances, however, it can truly be said that arbitration is a creature of contract, meaning that what disputes are subject to arbitration, which parties have to bring these disputes to arbitration, what rules govern the administration of the arbitration process itself, and what powers the arbitrator has *are all governed by the agreement of parties to a contract.* Most frequently, this contract has something other than arbitration as its main subject matter, but contains an arbitration clause. In other instances, the parties to a dispute do not have a pre-existing obligation to arbitrate, but agree to do so after the dispute arises. These latter agreements to submit existing disputes to arbitration are unsurprisingly called submission agreements.[3] That said, it follows that the parties can agree to create whatever arbitration process suits their needs, as long as it is legal. Following is a definition of what arbitration is generally, with some examples of how parties *have varied* the general model.

A. Arbitration Defined

Reduced to its most basic elements, arbitration is the *use of a private third party to conduct a hearing on a dispute and make a final and binding decision on it.* Each component of this definition deserves a more detailed look. Unlike most other alternative dispute resolution mechanisms, arbitration involves the complete disposition of a dispute by someone other than the parties to the dispute themselves, as in the saying, "the mediator suggests, the arbitrator decides." So, the specifics of the process become much more important than those of a procedure where the neutral has only the power of persuasion. Each element of this definition requires individual scrutiny:

(1) *Private* has two meanings in arbitration: (a) The person who decides the dispute is not someone whose government (public) job is to decide disputes, such as judges, administrative hearing officers, magistrates, etc. It is not that such persons are not qualified by experience to *be* arbitrators, but that having a dispute decided by one of them is usually not considered arbitration. The real distinction here is that the arbitrator is *chosen* to hear and decide a particular dispute (or a particular class of dispute), while the public dispute-deciders (judges, etc.) *must* hear and decide those disputes which are assigned to them (in other words, within their jurisdiction). So, for example, a lawsuit in a state trial court will be decided by a judge appointed to that court. That same (now former) judge, after having left the bench, may be chosen to serve as a private arbitrator. (b) The process itself is *private,* in that the public (including the media) is not permitted to attend, the records of the arbitration proceedings are not public records,[4] as all court records are, and the awards of the arbitrators are generally not published.

(2) *Third party* means, at least, someone who is not one of the parties to the dispute. While it is not always required, arbitration has evolved to a point where the third party is almost always expected to be *neutral, i.e.,* unbiased and with no predisposition as to how the dispute should be decided.

(3) *Conduct a hearing* means that the arbitrator must go through some information-gathering process before deciding the dispute, *i.e.,* making the award. The nature and length of this information-gathering are governed by the parties agreement to arbitrate, but almost always include the following elements: (a) notice to all parties concerning when and where the hearing will be held, (b) an opportunity for each party to the dispute to present evidence to the arbitrator, and (c) an opportunity for each party to be present while other parties are presenting evidence and to test that evidence with cross-examination of witnesses.

(4) *Make a final and binding decision* contains three important elements: final, binding, and decision.

Final, in reference to an arbitration award, means that the award normally cannot be appealed to some higher authority. This is an attribute which sharply distinguishes arbitration awards from trial court judgments, since the latter are almost always appealable to a higher court. It has been said that the best thing about arbitration is its finality, and the worst thing about arbitration is its finality. Whether that quality is viewed as the best or worst thing is likely to depend on whether a party won or lost the arbitration. This is not to say that there are no circumstances in which an arbitrator's award may not be overturned. Most state laws and the Federal Arbitration Act[5] provide a short list of narrow grounds on which a court may overturn ("vacate" is the legal term) an award. Usually, an arbitrator's award is going to be left alone by the courts unless someone can prove that the arbitrator's actions were "crooked or crazy."[6]

Binding, in reference to a decision, means one which can be enforced against a party, whether that party wants to comply with the award or not. Since the arbitrator has no power to enforce his decision (unlike a judge), the binding quality of arbitration awards depends on the public court systems. Every state court and the federal courts are empowered by legislation to take an arbitration award and turn it into a judgment of that court. The legal term for this process is "confirmation." Once an award has been confirmed, it can be enforced like any other court judgment, *i.e.,* property and bank accounts may be seized, etc.

For the dispute to be successfully concluded, the arbitrator must make a *decision, i.e.,* award. This seems basic, but much litigation and trouble have arisen around them. An award, to be legally appropriate, must *decide the dispute which the parties have submitted* to arbitration, and *not decide anything else.* If the award fails to decide the entire dispute submitted to the arbitrator or goes on to decide something that the parties did not submit, *the entire award* may later be overturned by a court.

To review: Arbitration involves a process where a stranger to the dispute, after notifying all concerned parties, holds an information-gathering hearing after which the submitted dispute is decided, and nothing else, and cannot be appealed, but may be overturned by a court on very narrow grounds only.

B. Variations on Binding Arbitration

As the thoughtful reader might suspect, the power of an arbitrator can be immense. Without appellate review,[7] the arbitrator's award is essentially unchangeable[8] once it is rendered. To some people, this fact is frightening. While appreciating the speed, informality, and privacy of arbitration, a few parties shudder at the prospect of one person having such unrestrained power over their disputes. As a result, variations on traditional arbitration have grown up over the years. Some are limited to specific industries, and others are in general use.

The best known of these mutations to the arbitration process is undoubtedly "baseball" arbitration. Quotes are used because "baseball" arbitration, while once the exclusive province of players and owners disputing over players' salaries, is now moving into more general use.[9] "Baseball" arbitration has only one feature which distinguishes it from traditional arbitration: each party submits a proposed amount for the arbitrator to award (in effect, its best settlement offer), and the arbitrator *must* award one amount or the other. The arbitrator has no power to award any other amount, including one that is between the amounts submitted by the parties. From the parties' standpoint, this type of arbitration prevents a "clearly unreasonable" award (from the owner's point of view, an amount *higher* than its number, and from the player's standpoint, an amount *lower* than the one selected), and forces the arbitrator to select the more reasonable of the two numbers. This type of arbitration, as Dr. Johnson said of being hanged in two weeks, "concentrates the mind wonderfully."[10] The minds of the parties are "concentrated" on the fact that the arbitrator *must choose* one number or the other. This has two effects: first, the parties are highly motivated to make their numbers reasonable ones, based on the evidence submitted to the arbitrator, because if they do not, the arbitrator will pick the *other* number; second, because of the pressure to reach a reasonable number before the hearing begins, many of these disputes are settled by negotiation *before* they go to arbitration hearing.

A variation on "baseball" arbitration which has recently gained some popularity is "*night* baseball arbitration." Under this form of arbitration, the parties exchange their proposed resolutions (best offers) but do *not* tell the arbitrator what they are. The hearing goes forward, the parties present their evidence, and let the arbitrator make an award. They agree in advance, however, that the prevailing party will get whichever of their proposed amounts is *closest* to the actual award of the arbitrator. In this way, the parties put a floor under and ceiling over the outcome, but still get the benefit of the arbitrator's unadulterated view of the evidence.[11] As one may have guessed by now, the word "night" is added because the arbitrator is "kept in the dark" about the parties' positions.

Similar motivations had given birth to what is called "high-low" (or, sometimes "mini-max") arbitration. Here, the parties submit their dispute to binding arbitration, but agree that the claimant (plaintiff) will recover no less than, *e.g.,* $52,000 but not more than, *e.g.,* $112,000. The $52,000 is usually the amount of the defendant's last offer, and the $112,000 is usually the amount of the plaintiff's last demand. Like "night baseball arbitration," the parties do *not* tell the arbitrator what these numbers are. A normal hearing is then conducted and an award made. If the amount of the award is between $52,000 and $112,000 (or whatever numbers the parties have selected), then that is the amount the claimant (plaintiff) will recover. If, however, it is more than the high value ($112,000 here), then the award is reduced to that amount. On the other hand, if the arbitrator's award is below the low value ($52,000 here), it is then increased to that amount.

The advantages of this process are similar to those of night baseball arbitration:

— The parties have a narrowed range of recovery/exposure;

— The arbitrator has no power to go "off the reservation" with an award that is distant from the parties' own evaluation of the dispute; and

— The hearing is likely to take less time and cost much less than a court trial of a similar dispute.

It should be noted that all three of the above-noted mutations of traditional arbitration are only useful where the positions of the parties can be reduced to specific dollar amounts. While many disputes are "just about money," not all are. Those that are not just about money would seem not to be good candidates for these varieties of arbitration. Such processes could still be used, however, to solve the "money" portion of the dispute, if the parties agreed to do so.

C. Other Forms of Arbitration

The above definitions and examples concern traditional, binding (or, as some say, "real") arbitration. As if these weren't complicated enough, there are several other subcategories of arbitration in general use today. The two major subcategories are "advisory" arbitration and "court-annexed" arbitration. "Major" should be taken as a relative term, because the number of arbitrations in these two categories *together* amounts only to a small fraction of the number of "real" arbitrations taking place every day. Advisory arbitration, as the name implies, reaches a result (sometimes called an award, sometimes an advisory opinion) which *has no binding force on the parties.* Until that "award" is reached, the process is similar to binding arbitration. The only reasonable explanation for the existence of this kind of arbitration is that the parties may want the "expert neutral views" of the arbitrator, yet still *not* want to delegate to some third person the actual power to decide important disputes. These same benefits are usually available to parties through the mediation process or sometimes through early neutral evaluation, so it shouldn't come as a surprise that the use of advisory arbitration is on the wane.

Court-annexed arbitration, unlike advisory arbitration, is increasing in frequency and usually involves a *mandatory* diversion of selected cases from the court system, well in advance of a date when they might go to trial. This diversion is done in the hope that the less formal and less costly arbitration process will resolve the dispute. In these situations, then, a lawsuit has already been filed, and the judge sends the parties to arbitration. The motivating force here is not the convenience of the parties (although this may be a byproduct of the process). Rather, the goal is to reduce the number of cases the court has to handle. However, because the parties in most lawsuits have a constitutional right to a jury trial, court-annexed arbitration *awards cannot be made binding*. To do so would rob one (or both) of the parties of their right to present their case to a jury. So, court-annexed arbitration is, in practical outcome, a form of advisory arbitration. Most state laws which create court-annexed arbitration provide that the court-annexed arbitration award *does become binding* after the passage of a certain amount of time, unless one of the parties formally indicates its displeasure with the award (usually by filing a simple form with the court in which the original case is pending). If this happens, the parties are then put back into the court system to await the further expense and delays of the "normal" trial process. One reason for adopting a process so apparently wasteful as this is that the process of court-annexed arbitration makes sense only because the court process is so enormously *more* wasteful of resources itself.

For instance, in one recent year, the Los Angeles County (California) Superior Court evaluated the results of its court-annexed arbitration program. All cases selected were ones in which it appeared that less than $50,000 was at stake. For that year, only *one out of three* cases selected for the program were finally disposed of by this arbitration process. That statistic accounted not only for those cases where the parties were satisfied with the arbitrator's award, but also those cases where one party was not satisfied, sought a return to the normal court processes, and the case was settled by negotiation before returning to court. Nonetheless, the court felt that these results were quite worthwhile because the expense of taking perhaps one thousand cases through the court-annexed arbitration process was believed to be significantly less than the expense of taking three hundred thirty-three (one of three, remember) cases through the normal court trial process. So, with an average of .333, court-annexed arbitration has become an economically supportable way to reduce the caseload in our courts. Nonetheless, in most jurisdictions, its use is currently limited to small cases which take up only a small fraction of the court's time in the first place. Some of the problems for the parties and their lawyers, at least, should be obvious:

— Each side must prepare and present a case before all facts are known;

— Each side must decide whether or not to use its "ace in the hole" evidence, because the opponent will not have to abide by the award and may thereafter neutralize this evidence in the court trial;

— Each party risks giving the other "free" discovery of its witnesses and evidences; and

— Each party experiences the costs (attorney fees, lost time of the party, costs of experts, etc.) of this process, with no assurance that the dispute will be ended by it.

D. Arbitration: A Creature of Contract

In the phrase at the beginning of this chapter, "arbitration is a creature of contract," traditional, binding arbitration, and not the court-annexed type, was being referred to. Specifically, the phrase means that, subject only to the broadest legal limits, the parties can agree to craft whatever kind of arbitration process suits them. Most frequently, this agreement is found in an arbitration clause, lurking at the back of a contract that has something other than arbitration as its main subject matter. It is understandable that parties who have just agreed to a contract are not disposed to think about the possibility of the other party breaching it. And, of course, they *know* that they themselves will never breach it. Nonetheless, far too little attention is paid to the arbitration (or other dispute resolution) clauses in most contracts. Indeed, when a dispute arises later, many parties are surprised to learn that their agreement *has* an arbitration clause. Yet, the provisions of such a clause can have a major effect on how—and how expensively and within what time frame—disputes will be taken care of.

Standard arbitration clauses in most contracts consider a number of issues,[12] such as:

1. Selection of the Arbitrator

Selection of the neutral[13] is the most important decision in any alternative dispute resolution mechanism. No other provision (or combination of provisions) can have as much effect on the working of the process as the selection of the presiding neutral(s). It is treated separately later on in this chapter.

2. Choice of Dispute Resolution Mechanism(s)

For the purposes of this chapter, the assumption is that arbitration will be the choice. However, decisions still need to be made about whether it will be used in combination with other ADR mechanisms[14]

and, if so, in what order and on what time schedule. There are also determinations to be made about whether there should be specific qualifications for the arbitrator(s) (*e.g.,* whether they should all be lawyers, engineers, or retired nurses), how they will be selected, and how many of them should be chosen (the traditional numbers are, of course, one and three, but parties may agree on any number and sometimes have even agreed on an *even* number).

3. Which Disputes Will Be Subject to Arbitration

Here, the initial bias is—and should be—in favor of *all* disputes.[15] If arbitration is such a good idea, then why not include all possible disputes within the scope of the arbitration clause? Usually, there is no good reason not to use an omnibus arbitration clause, but there may be reason to leave some classes of disputes out of the arbitration process, or perhaps even to create different types of arbitration for some types of disputes. As with all of the considerations listed here, it is important that the tail not wag the dog. If the agreement to which the arbitration clause is being appended is an important one, the last thing anyone needs is for the underlying agreement to be "busted" by one party's insistence on an elaborate (or one-sided) arbitration clause. This presents a dilemma for lawyers and their clients; they frequently have to draft or agree to a less-than-perfect alternative dispute resolution clause so that the agreement whose disputes are to be arbitrated will, in fact, be signed. Whatever the relative importance of the arbitration clause itself, however, there is no question that deciding which disputes are covered by it is second in importance only to the arbitrator selection process itself.

4. Which Parties Have the Right to Bring Disputes to Arbitration

The overwhelming majority of arbitration clauses give each signatory equal access to the arbitration process. There are some industries (*e.g.,* automobile distribution), where one party is given the choice of going to court or to arbitration while another party *must* submit all its disputes to arbitration. Similarly, some states use a comparable process to resolve fee disputes between clients and attorneys. The client may arbitrate the dispute or head straight to court. The attorney is bound to submit the dispute to arbitration. Such clauses are generally enforceable, as long as the party with greater power is not using that power to foist an *unfair* procedure on other parties to the contract. If that party gets to choose whether to go to court or arbitration, however, the opponent will not be able to control costs or time if (or when) a dispute does arise.

5. Rules Governing the Arbitration Process Administration

The technical phrases used in this area are "administered" and *"ad hoc"* (meaning unadministered). The former means that the administrative aspects of the arbitration process, *i.e.*, setting hearings and deadlines, giving notice, collecting fees, etc., will be handled by an organization with published rules. The "grandfather" of all such organizations is the American Arbitration Association. Its rules are the most comprehensive, well known, and widely copied. Not surprisingly, most arbitration clauses which select an administering agency select the American Arbitration Association. There are three signal advantages of choosing an administered arbitration:

a.   The arbitration clause becomes "self-executing": If the arbitration clause provides for the arbitration to proceed "under the Rules of the American Arbitration Association," for instance, then a party whose opponent simply ignores the process can have an arbitration award entered against it without the necessity of seeking and obtaining a court order requiring the recalcitrant party to arbitrate.

b.   The parties know in advance what the procedures will be should they have a dispute; and

c.   If the parties cannot or will not cooperate in the arbitration process, the administering agency can make decisions for them which will assure a timely hearing (*e.g.*, selecting the arbitrator, setting hearing dates, and sending formal notices).

6. Powers and Duties of the Arbitrator

Most arbitrators, when empowered to decide the dispute(s) submitted, will render a "bare bones" award, which simply notifies the parties who won and what they won. This may be sufficient for many disputes, but parties often would like to know how the arbitrator reached this particular conclusion. If that is desirable, then the clause should require the arbitrator to give a "reasoned opinion" or otherwise let the parties know the basis for the award. Parties contemplating such a clause should remember that a reasoned opinion will likely take an arbitrator longer to prepare than a bare bones award. So, the process will take a little longer and cost a little more.

7. Remedies the Arbitrator Can Award

Arbitrators are not limited by the traditional constraints of the judicial process when making an award. An arbitrator's authority to fashion a remedy derives from the arbitration agreement created by the parties, while a judge's power to make an award is based on the statutory authority of the court. Courts tend to deal with issues and specific pigeonholed claims. Parties can, on the other hand, determine from the outset of their contractual relationship the exact remedies that the arbitrator will have the authority to award in the event of a dispute. They can also prescribe which remedies he will not be at liberty to award.

Notwithstanding the fact that arbitration (including the remedies an arbitrator can award) is a "creature of contract," the vast majority of arbitration clauses do not deal with remedies beyond provision for the prevailing party to recover costs and fees. In those rare instances when remedies are treated at all, those remedies most often dealt with are specific performance, provisional remedies, punitive damages, attorney fees, and costs. Of course, any other remedy that the parties agree is appropriate may be covered in the arbitration clause.

a. Specific performance

No less a legal beacon than Oliver Wendell Holmes said that when a party enters a contract, he acquires two rights: the right to perform, and the right to breach and take the consequences. So, most claims for breach of contract end up with awards of money damages in lieu of performance. In court litigation, there are hardly any situations where the breaching party is made to fulfill his part of the bargain.

If the arbitration agreement provides for specific performance, however, the arbitrator can mandate that the party breaching the contract perform his obligations under the agreement. Even if there is no specific performance reference in the arbitration clause, the arbitrator will still be likely to have the power to grant it.[16] Also note that, merely by incorporating the AAA rules into an agreement, the arbitrator is given the authority to order specific performance as a remedy.[17] For example, suppose B, a buyer, contracts with S, a seller, to purchase property for $100,000. Between the date of the agreement and when S was to deliver title, O makes an offer to S to buy the same property for $120,000. S fails to produce title for B on the date required by the agreement, thus breaching the contract. B, wanting the property, would like to seek enforcement of the contract. The parties had included an arbitration clause within their agreement and now seek arbitration to settle their dispute. Specific performance was included as one remedy in their arbitration clause. Since land is a unique item which the loss of generally cannot be replaced by any other kind of damages, an arbitrator will likely award specific performance. Under the parties' agreement, the arbitrator can provide that S specifically perform by delivering title for the land to B. In addition, compensatory damages may well be awarded to B for the delay in delivery.

b. Provisional remedies

In most cases when a dispute begins, the arbitrator has not yet been selected. Some kind of immediate relief may be needed to preserve the status quo until the dispute can be resolved through arbitration. Generally speaking, these provisional remedies fall into two categories:

(1) Orders that one of the parties to the arbitration refrain from some act (such as removing securities from an account) until the arbitration can be heard, or

(2) Orders that some third party (*e.g.,* bank, escrow company, etc., which is *not a party* to the arbitration) hold on to something (money, property, or goods in a warehouse, etc.) until the arbitration can be heard on its merits.

While courts traditionally have been the place to go for provisional remedies, arbitrators can also grant them if that power is given to him in the arbitration clause. Some states have statutes which govern judicial and arbitrator authority to provide some kind of provisional relief until the arbitration proceeding.[18] While state courts may grant provisional remedies to parties who have agreed to arbitrate their disputes, it is not absolutely clear that all courts will. If the availability of a provisional remedy is important to the parties (the necessity of provisional remedies is best evaluated based on the type of business agreement being entered into), assurance of such remedy is guaranteed by inclusion in the arbitration agreement.

Typically, what occurs is this: The parties have an agreement to arbitrate their disputes, but, prior to beginning the arbitration process, a party seeks judicial assistance for a provisional remedy, such as an order of attachment or a temporary restraining order. The responding party will argue either that seeking a provisional remedy is a waiver of the right to arbitrate or that the court cannot provide such a remedy since the parties agreed to arbitrate their disputes. In the absence of state law governing provisional remedies when parties have agreed to arbitrate their disputes, these arguments may be successful. However, such arguments will fail where the parties' arbitration agreement provides for provisional remedies.

c. Punitive damages

One thing that can be accomplished in an arbitration clause is to let the arbitrator know what specific remedies may be imposed when determining an award. One such remedy is punitive damages. As the name implies, punitive damages are designed to punish offensive conduct by a party. An arbitrator awards punitive damages also in order to deter similar behavior in the future (as does a judge or jury). Punitive damages may normally be awarded when the arbitrator determines that one party has engaged in outrageous and/or willful misconduct. In some instances, a punitive damage award may exceed the amount of the actual damages awarded. The actuality and (real or imagined) threat of punitive damage awards have attracted much attention from the business community. Indeed, a desire to limit exposure to punitive damages has been a motivation behind the adoption of some ADR programs.[19]

For instance, there has been a widespread adoption throughout the banking industry of mandatory binding arbitration, the theory being that mandatory arbitration will limit the risk of punitive damage awards by eliminating the unpredictability of juries. In a suit against Bank of America, consumers challenged the unilateral modification of deposit account agreements by the insertion of mandatory arbitration clauses. The court upheld the change to the agreements, reasoning that the ADR clause was not inherently unfair nor was the modification unconscionable.[20]

Generally, if there has been no mention of punitive damages in the arbitration clause, an award of such damages is proper. However, parties to a contract may lawfully agree to waive any claim for punitive damages. It is also (theoretically) possible for one party to a contract to waive his right to assert a potential claim of punitive damages while the other retains that right. As a practical matter, however, most parties would not divest themselves of this right without a reciprocal renouncement. As a result, in order for a party to avoid potential punitive damage claims, in most cases, it will have to give up the right to assert such claims itself.

New York law contains an exception to the general rule that an arbitrator can award punitive damages unless specifically prohibited. The law of New York State specifically prohibits an arbitrator from awarding punitive damages.[21] However, if parties wish to include a potential claim for punitive damages within the remedies available to the arbitrator, an express agreement to do so will be enforced in New York.[22]

d. Attorney fees

When drafting the arbitration clause, parties may also wish to consider whether to include a provision that the losing party will pay the opposing party's attorney fees. As a general rule, arbitrators do not have jurisdiction to award attorney fees in the absence of an express grant of that authority in the arbitration agreement. Without that grant of authority, parties also cannot assert a claim of right to attorney fees after the arbitration in court. If the parties' agreement does not address the issue of attorney fees, then the parties are deemed to have waived any claim to have theirs paid by the other party.

If parties explicitly express their intention to confer upon the arbitrator the authority to decide the entitlement to attorney fees, they should also consider what fees should be recoverable. For instance, the parties may choose to limit recovery of fees to only those expended for the arbitration itself and not for the duration of the dispute.

Similarly, parties may wish to provide for recovery of "reasonable attorney fees" for the prevailing party. Modifying attorney fees with the term "reasonable" has two consequences. First, it makes it clear that the winning party is not necessarily entitled to recover all its attorney fees. Second, it furnishes the arbitrator with discretion to determine what fees are reasonable.

Despite the general rule mentioned above, some state statutes preclude an arbitrator from awarding attorney fees as a matter of law.[23] In these cases, even if attorney fees were recoverable pursuant to the parties' agreement, an award granting them presumably would not be enforced by the court.

e. Costs

As with attorney fees, each party usually pays for most of its own costs of arbitrating a dispute, unless otherwise agreed. Parties may contract to give the arbitrator the authority to award costs of the arbitration to the prevailing party. If it is decided to do so, it is important to know what will be considered a "cost." In many jurisdictions, for example, the statutory definition of costs (in court litigation) is quite narrow, normally limiting recovery to a fraction of what was actually spent. Parties negotiating an arbitration clause, however, may provide that *all* costs associated with the arbitration shall be paid by the losing party. The parties can define costs, as in the everyday meaning of the word, to include travel expenses, meals, lodging, etc. These items of expense are not normally recoverable under "costs" statutes.

In another analogy to attorney fees, parties may wish only to limit costs to what is reasonable. Including the term "reasonable" has the same two consequences: it makes it clear that arbitrator need not award the prevailing party all costs associated with the dispute; and it lets the arbitrator decide which expenditures were reasonable.

Another consideration is the costs of the arbitration proceeding itself, *i.e.,* the administrative and arbitrator fees. It is common that an agreement provides that each party will share these costs. However, in some instances, parties have contracted that the losing party will pay the entire cost of arbitration. In other cases, the party with the greater bargaining power will choose to cover the costs of the arbitration, including the arbitrator's fee and administrative costs, except for a *de minimis* amount which the other party will be required to pay in order to deter frivolous claims. For example, an employer who includes an arbitration clause within the terms of employment agreement may cover all costs of the arbitration as a benefit to employees. However, in order to prevent employees from asserting empty claims, the employer might provide that employees are responsible for the initial $250 of the arbitration costs. This amount operates somewhat like a deductible in an insurance policy.

Although the issue of what authority an arbitrator will be clothed with may be an important one, it should not dominate the concerns of the negotiating parties. Keep in mind that *almost every predispute arbitration clause is only a small part of an agreement about something else* and the remedies available to the arbitrator are themselves only a small part of the arbitration clause. The most important aim of business negotiations is to produce a contract with terms that both parties will agree to. So, the "tail" of the arbitration clause should never wag the "dog" of a comprehensive business agreement.

f. Post-dispute clauses

The above considerations also apply to parties to a dispute who *do not have a pre-existing obligation to arbitrate,* but agree to do so after the dispute arises. The process of post-dispute agreement to arbitrate is called *submission.* (Usually, the dispute is being *submitted* to the American Arbitration Association or other alternative dispute resolution provider.) All the same considerations are relevant as when an arbitration clause in a larger agreement is being negotiated. Indeed, it seems that these considerations are *more important* in a submission setting, since a dispute already has arisen.

This situation brings up the question of why one should put an arbitration clause in a contract when the parties to it can always enter into a submission agreement should a dispute arise. The obvious reason is that one of the parties may not agree to arbitration if asked to do so only *after* a dispute has arisen. A debtor, for example, may not wish to choose a speedy proceeding if he really believes that he will ultimately be required to pay. The more complete response is that the principal benefit (to all parties) of an arbitration (or other alternative dispute resolution) clause is that the parties know *from the outset of their relationship* how disputes will be resolved. Sometimes, the mere *presence* of an alternative dispute resolution clause in a contract will deter a party from making frivolous claims or produce a negotiated resolution before the ADR clause needs to be invoked. So, where alternative dispute resolution is thought to be desirable, agreeing to it in advance of any dispute always seems to be preferable.

If an arbitration clause has not been included in a contract, the submission route remains available, but only if all other parties to the dispute can be persuaded that it is a good idea. Since the submission agreement is itself a contract, arbitration's position as "a creature of contract" remains undiminished.

E. Consumer's Guide to Selecting an Arbitrator

It bears repeating: There is nothing more important in the arbitration process than the selection of the arbitrator. It is also worth remembering that arbitration is like no other adjudicative alternative dispute resolution process (except private judging) to the extent that the parties have a hand in selecting the arbitrator.

In that case, it seems that choosing the best arbitrator available at the time the arbitration clause (or, more likely, contract containing such a clause) is negotiated and put his name in the clause as the arbitrator (to be) would make sense, except for the fact that people can have a tendency to die unexpectedly. Arbitrators are mostly middle-aged or older, which ups the odds of their predeceasing any dispute which may arise. So, it is unusual to find an arbitration clause which designates a particular person as arbitrator.[24] The most parties usually try to do in this respect is to limit the universe of persons who might arbitrate their dispute by laying down some mandatory qualifications for the arbitrator. Usually, the most stringent qualifications still leave a "pool" of hundreds of potential arbitrators. The parties should agree on one (or, occasionally, three). If they do not, the administering agency (or a court) will appoint an arbitrator for them.

There is some difference of opinion about one-person versus three-person arbitration panels among both users and providers of alternative dispute resolution services. The "school of one" holds that a careful selection process will produce the best available arbitrator, and that person will decide the matter properly. One arbitrator also makes for even more savings of money and time. Money is saved because the parties must fund only one neutral. Time is saved because the deliberations of one arbitrator will almost always be quicker than if there were three. In addition, much time may be saved because scheduling is so *much* easier with one arbitrator. Participants in arbitration usually say that the addition of each person to a group exponentially raises the difficulties of scheduling that group.

The "school of three" concedes all the points made above and goes on to propose that all the supposed drawbacks of a panel of three arbitrators are more than overcome by the "comfort" the parties feel when their fate is not in only one pair of hands. Particular emphasis is placed on the large, multiparty arbitration or the international arbitration, where each of the three arbitrators may be able to make a separate and unique contribution. Also, there is the fact that any tendency on the part of one arbitrator to go "off the rails" will be moderated by the presence of the other two. Most arbitrators are members of the "school of three" because it reduces the loneliness of their work.

Clearly, the choice of one or three arbitrators involves some trade-offs. In a big case, however, the added expense may not be meaningful.

When parties are involved in public court litigation, state or federal, much time and effort are spent in gathering and evaluating information about the judge who might decide the case. Not infrequently, additional time and effort are spent in attempting to steer a case toward a jurist who is capable, fair, energetic, and, perhaps, just slightly inclined toward that party's side of the case. Leaving out the extreme forms of judge-shopping, all of this activity is an ethical and appropriate part of a lawyer's work on behalf of the client. Selecting a neutral to act in an alternative dispute resolution setting is an even more important task for disputing parties and their lawyers. In arbitration, making a fully informed selection of the appropriate neutral(s) is *more important* than the comparable process in public court litigation. This is so because the typical arbitrator, once appointed, has broader power than a judge, being less constrained by both rules of evidence and legal precedents, and subject to a much narrower review after decision.[25] So, in the appropriate case, taking some time to investigate and select or reject an arbitrator can be crucial.[26]

Most other common forms of ADR—mediation, early neutral evaluation, mini-trial, summary jury trial, fact-finding[27]—lead to a resolution/recommendation that will be binding only if all parties agree to it.[28] So, the power of the neutral in those settings is, quite literally, limited to the power of persuasion. Nonetheless, once the parties have decided to use a particular form of ADR, they want—and deserve—the best neutral they can get. This section will review the available methods for information gathering and sorting, and present a suggested line of questions for a hitherto under-used method: interviewing the neutral.

As the popularity of ADR has grown, both litigators[29] and scholars[30] have recognized that background information on prospective neutrals is inadequate from both a quantitative and qualitative standpoint. Correcting this inadequacy is in the interest of the institutional providers of ADR services,[31] the disputing parties and their counsel, and, usually, the neutrals themselves.[32] This lack of information is made more critical by the fact that arbitrators are not licensed, need not be attorneys, and are not subject to any generally accepted standards for training. So, the market for arbitrators is an open one, where (as in the securities market) good information is critical.

1. Information-gathering

A typical situation finds the disputing parties with a clause in their contract agreeing to arbitrate according to the procedures of an institutional provider of alternative dispute resolution services, such as the American Arbitration Association. At that early stage, counsel should (cooperatively, if possible; separately, if not) contact the appropriate staff member at the American Arbitration Association and make sure that they understand the case details that are not typically revealed by the document ("demand") which initiates an arbitration.

Most institutional providers draw from a large list of neutrals, whose qualifications, experience, and personal skills vary widely. The tribunal administrator will be in a much better position to present a list of proposed neutrals who are most appropriate to a case if advised as to the nature of the dispute and its issues, and the parties involved,[33] and even more so, if desirable personal traits can be articulated (and agreed upon by all).

If the parties cannot agree on the arbitrator's requirements, the next step will usually be the presentation by the American Arbitration Association of a list of proposed neutrals, accompanied by brief biographical information on each. Usually, a rather short time period is allowed before choices must be made and communicated. By agreement among the parties, by which the American Arbitration Association must abide, that period can be lengthened. It is during that period when most of the investigative work on proposed neutrals takes place.[34] Those neutrals who subscribe to the American Arbitration Association's Code of Ethics will voluntarily disclose any remembered relationship with any of the parties or counsel; others may, or may not.[35]

At this point, the parties and their lawyers find themselves sending memoranda to their colleagues, calling other lawyers who are experienced in alternative dispute resolution, or other neutrals, and researching the background of the neutral through available published sources.[36] An often overlooked source is the published work of the neutral (if any). Such work is routinely examined in the case of expert witnesses, so why not for neutrals? Included in published work by the proposed neutral should be all available opinions and awards, as well as cases in which an appearance as an advocate is recorded. Bearing in mind that most arbitration awards are private, the body of work may still be slim.[37]

Even if the institutional provider or the proposed neutral has already provided a biographical sketch or resume, more detailed, written background information may be available from both of them.[38] Indeed, one question that should always be asked of both is when the submitted biographical information was last updated. Public records[39] may help to add to the store of knowledge already gathered.

2. The Inside Person

It is important to remember here that the parties may not always be seeking a true neutral. Many arbitration clauses and post-dispute agreements call for the selection of "party-appointed" arbitrators. In all cases, a third true neutral is selected by the parties, the party-appointed arbitrators, or the American Arbitration Association. In these circumstances, the parties are free to select someone who will be sympathetic to their side of the case, and even act as a kind of advocate for them.[40] Frequently, the party-appointed arbitrators themselves will be given the crucial task of selecting the third (true neutral) member of their panel.[41] While the parties have wide latitude about the procedure they can choose and the persons or institutions who may be party-appointed arbitrators, their discretion is not limitless.[42] While party-appointed arbitrators are almost a contradiction in terms, some organizations do not feel comfortable entering into an arbitration clause which does not provide for them. So, unlike the dinosaur, although the numbers of clauses using party-appointed arbitrators will continue to dwindle, they will not become extinct.

Whatever procedures the parties have agreed to for selecting arbitrators, institutional providers will normally implement them.[43] Some providers, however, require that the arbitrator be selected from among their panel exclusively.[44]

3. Court-appointed Arbitrator

If no contractual method for selecting the arbitrator(s) is found and no institutional provider with selection rules is agreed to "or if the agreed method fails," any party may petition the court to appoint an arbitrator.[45] Statutes permitting a court to appoint an arbitrator for the parties are essentially a fail-safe mechanism. Nine times out of ten, the arbitrator is selected either by agreement on a specific person or by the operation of the Rules of the American Arbitration Association (or another one of the institutional providers). Normally, the reason parties have to go to court is because one of them is simply trying to drag out the process. A genuine inability to find *any* acceptable neutral is rare.

Even when the court is asked to appoint an arbitrator, the parties can—and should—have some influence over who is chosen. A typical statute provides for the court to nominate "from a list of persons supplied jointly by the parties ... or obtained from a governmental agency concerned with arbitration or private disinterested association concerned with arbitration." But, typically, the parties only have five days from receipt of the nominees to select an arbitrator jointly.[46] If they do not, the court will appoint from among the nominees.[47] Of course, if the list of nominees is one that was *supplied jointly,* the parties are guaranteed that someone acceptable will be appointed.

However, if one party is really trying to stall progress, that party may not participate in the cooperative effort to send a list of nominees to the court. In that case, *both* parties may get the "pot luck" of having the arbitrator picked from a list supplied by someone else.[48]

4. Networking

However the neutral is selected, additional information beyond that presented by the biographies disseminated by institutional providers, published "works" of the proposed neutral,[49] and the lawyers' informal network of contacts is still available. One potential source is the party. Frequently, the business party to an arbitration has an informal network of contacts different from that of its lawyers. That network may know the proposed neutral's reputation within the party's industry/field. In addition, the party may sometimes be in a better position than its lawyers to assess the raw data obtained about a proposed neutral. In any event, every party should be actively involved in the arbitrator selection process.[50]

Another excellent source of information on neutrals is references. While prospective arbitrators will seldom be able to give references of who worked with them in an identical setting (same alternative dispute resolution mechanism, same type of dispute),[51] they should be able to provide several references who know their work *as an arbitrator.* A neutral who refuses to give any references is probably a neutral to be avoided. If a part-time neutral is being considered, it is important that the references that are given be for disputes resolved *while acting as a neutral.* Top trial lawyers, astute business executives, even wise former judges, do not always make good arbitrators.

5. Interviewing the Prospective Neutral

Assuming the matters in issue warrant it, an *interview* with the prospective neutral can be an excellent experience for all concerned. Many business people and lawyers alike blanch at the notion of conducting an informational interview with a prospective arbitrator. A computer industry executive took a practical approach: "What happens if you decide *not* to hire this guy? Won't he have it in for you the next time?" There are several answers to that, such as:

— Unless specifically informed, the prospective arbitrator will not know *which party* rejected him;

— Full-time neutrals are regularly "rejected"; and

— If afraid of "retaliation," one can almost always decline to use this arbitrator.

Please remember that when an arbitrator is hired, the parties are not only going to be spending a lot of time with this person but also going to be paying him a lot of money to make an important decision.

Assuming that an interview is generally regarded as a good idea, an interview arranged and conducted jointly by representatives of all parties choosing the neutral is strongly suggested.[52] Although an interview conducted by only one side *might* pass ethical muster,[53] it is too important that all parties have no doubts about the arbitrator's impartiality. It is customary to compensate the neutral for the interview time.[54]

The interview (or interviews) should be conducted only *after* other avenues of research have been reasonably exhausted. This permits the parties to save the money and time which would have been spent interviewing some *unacceptable* neutrals by simply reviewing written information about them. More importantly, it permits those interviews which are conducted to be thorough, well-informed, and efficient.

What to ask the neutral varies with each dispute. Here are some general categories of inquiry which might prove helpful.

— Is this biographical data complete?

— Are there any health or hearing/vision problems?

— What is the range of flexibility on procedural and evidentiary matters?

— Is the proposed neutral experienced as a neutral in the type of ADR under consideration?[55]

— Does the proposed neutral have an appropriate understanding of the "industry" involved in the dispute?

— Has this "understanding" led to some conclusions or assumptions about the industry which are incorrect or potentially harmful in this dispute? (In theory, it is good to have someone who "knows what's going on," but if that knowledge has led to some unshakable conclusions, a less knowledgeable but more open-minded arbitrator would be the better choice.)

— How attentive to detail is this person?

— How open-minded is this person?

— Is there substantial ego-sensitivity?

— Has this person served as a neutral in similar situations, although not in the subject "industry"?

— What is the neutral's "philosophy" on recovery of attorney fees and costs (if there is a clause providing for it)?

— What is the neutral's philosophy on punitive damages? (Unless they are dealt with by the arbitration agreement or applicable law; in the latter case, one might still confirm that the neutral agrees on what the applicable law is.)

— Is there some written work of his of which the neutral is particularly proud?[56]

— What is the neutral's approach to questioning witnesses himself or, in other words, will the parties be allowed to present their cases without interruption as they see fit?

— Does the neutral think the contemplated form of alternative dispute resolution (arbitration here) is the best one for this dispute? (Despite their economic interest in not doing so, many arbitrators will suggest that a lengthy or complicated case go to negotiation or mediation first; some offer to mediate it themselves. Before accepting that offer, everyone's agreement should be obtained that the neutral will *not* serve as arbitrator should the mediation fail. Also be sure that the prospective neutral has as good a reputation as a mediator as he does an arbitrator.)

— Is the neutral available during the time when the parties want their dispute to be heard and decided? The line of inquiry should address several areas which affect both parties and their counsel:

- Will the neutral commit a sufficient block of days so that hearings may be concluded, as far as possible, without lengthy intermissions?

- How many hours a day will be spent in hearings?

- When will the normal meal and break periods be?

- Is there flexibility to conduct hearings on either side of "normal business hours"? (More and more parties request hearings in extended half-day sessions; everyone gets the other half to tend other things or prepare for the next day's hearing.)

- What is the cost of cancellation or, in other words, how is a fee determined if the dispute is settled before the hearing is scheduled?

— What compensation is required, including hourly rate, travel, and certain expenses, and how much of a deposit will be required?

— What is his ability or willingness to travel, if that becomes necessary?[57]

— Is the neutral fair and reasonably unbiased? (After integrity, this is singularly the most critical judgment to be made.)

— Does the neutral have the appropriate personality and temperament to preside at the arbitration of this dispute? (Certainly, someone with a confidence-inspiring presence is desirable; depending on the personalities of parties, counsel, and important witnesses, there may be more special concerns.)

— Are there parties and counsel who have used the neutral as such (recently) and could be contacted as references? (Of course, there are earlier references from the time before the decision was made to commit the resources for an interview, but now the proposed arbitrator will know a lot more about the dispute and may be able to give more useful specific references.)

— What is the neutral's approach to alternative dispute resolution generally, or arbitration in particular? (This open-ended question frequently brings answers to earlier questions.)

— How does the neutral envision the proceeding's progress if chosen as arbitrator?[58]

F. Mandated Disclosure by the Arbitrator

1. Disputes Where American Arbitration Association Rules Are Applicable

A prospective arbitrator is required to reveal (or else feels compelled to reveal)[59] information about personal and business relationships and experiences which might create the impression of partiality. American Arbitration Association Rule 19,[60] for instance, requires "any person appointed as a neutral arbitrator" to disclose *"any circumstance likely to affect impartiality, including any financial or personal interest in the result of the arbitration or any past or present relationships with the parties or their representatives."* (Emphasis added.)

Once a disclosure has been made, the American Arbitration Association sends the information disclosed to all parties. If one or more of them object to the disclosing arbitrator's continuing to serve, the American Arbitration Association "shall determine whether the arbitrator should be disqualified and shall inform the parties of its decision, which shall be conclusive." (American Arbitration Association Commercial Rule 19.)

But what happens when the American Arbitration Association is not used for an arbitration?

2. Disputes Where American Arbitration Association Rules Do Not Apply

If a domestic dispute is not controlled by the Rules of the American Arbitration Association, several of the following possibilities exist:

a. Applicable law requires disclosure

As of this writing, the Federal Arbitration Act[61] contains no disclosure requirements. Many states have adopted a version of the Uniform Arbitration Act to govern domestic (non-international) arbitrations, but only one, Minnesota, has added a provision requiring disclosure.[62] California, whose domestic arbitration law is generally modelled on the Federal Arbitration Act, has recently enacted not one but several arbitrator disclosure statutes,[63] each of which creates a slightly different disclosure obligation. The legislatures of other states are considering enactment of arbitrator disclosure laws as well. As a practical matter, the only ways a party can control these obligations in advance is to:

— Provide for the kind of disclosure that prospective arbitrators must make in an arbitration clause (making for a very cumbersome and unattractive clause),

— Select an arbitration clause which makes the American Arbitration Association *Rules* applicable, or

— Draft an arbitration clause which makes the disclosure requirements of a particular state's laws applicable (bearing in mind, of course, that the state's legislature could well *change* the disclosure requirements between the time the contract is signed with the arbitration clause in it and the time a dispute occurs).

Right now, especially in light of the unpredictable (and, in the case of California, muddled) condition of state law, an arbitration clause making the American Arbitration Association Rules applicable seems the best bet.

b. Neither applicable law nor the arbitration clause requires disclosure

Here, the parties may be described as being in a free-fire zone. Because the prospective arbitrator has no statutory obligation to make disclosure, there is only the ethical obligation to do so. There could be a chance that this person may be biased and, later on, it could develop that a party might discover some information about the arbitrator which could suggest a bias *in another party's favor.* In this situation, a favorable award could be overturned by a court after the expense and time of the arbitration hearing. So, it behooves one to learn if this prospective arbitrator has *anything* in his background which might suggest bias, and to learn this information *before* the arbitrator is appointed and conducts any business.

Earlier in this chapter, an interview with prospective arbitrators was suggested (if the economics of the dispute warranted it). Disclosure matters would certainly be an appropriate topic for such an interview, but the prospective arbitrator's responses would be limited to his memory at the moment. To rectify this problem, a written questionnaire should be sent to the prospective arbitrator, asking a series of specific questions. If possible, the questionnaire should be presented to the prospective arbitrator *jointly* by all parties to the dispute. This eliminates the possibility that the prospective arbitrator (who may become the *actual* arbitrator) gets the impression that a party is targeting him or searching for a way to remove him from consideration. The questions in this questionnaire should be designed to elicit information which would normally rouse suspicions of bias. As with other alternative dispute resolution features, the questionnaire will have to be tailored to the particulars of a dispute. A general questionnaire is set forth below.

Questionnaire for Prospective Arbitrators

1. Do you have any past or present relationship with the parties, their counsel, or any member of this arbitration panel, direct or indirect, whether professional, social or any other kind?

2. Is the your biographical information accurate and complete?

3. Are you aware of any circumstance that is likely to affect your impartiality, including any bias or financial or personal interest in the results of the arbitration?

4. Has your current or previous employer(s) represented or been adverse to any of the parties, counsel, or witnesses involved in this case?

5. Do you represent or have you represented any person in a proceeding adverse to any party to the arbitration?

6. Have you served as an arbitrator or mediator in another proceeding involving one or more of the parties to the proceeding?

7. Have you had any social or professional relationship with any relative of any of the parties to this proceeding, or a relative of counsel in this proceeding, or of the witnesses identified to date in this proceeding?

8. Please give the names of any prior or pending cases in which you have served or are presently serving as a party appointed or neutral arbitrator for any party to the arbitration, or for a lawyer for a party, along with the results of each case arbitrated to conclusion.

9. Are you aware of any permanent or temporary physical impairment which would make you unable to properly perceive the evidence or unable to properly conduct the proceeding?

10. Have you ever served as an arbitrator in a proceeding in which any of the identified witnesses or named individual parties gave testimony?

11. Do you have any personal knowledge of disputed evidentiary facts concerning the proceeding?

12. Have you ever given advice to any party in the present proceeding on any matter involved in the action or proceeding?

13. Do you have a financial interest in the subject matter in the proceeding or in a party to the proceeding?

14. Are you aware of any reason that a person aware of the facts might reasonably entertain a doubt that you would be able to be impartial?

Keep in mind, at this stage of the proceedings, that no arbitrator has been formally selected. So, if any information is disclosed that is disturbing about the prospective arbitrator's background or experience, thank him (and pay him) for his time, and move along to someone else.

If the prospective arbitrator is a full-time neutral, it is *likely* that the answers to the questionnaire will present some information requiring further thought, because a busy full-time neutral will be likely to know some of the lawyers taking part in this process or have presided over alternative dispute resolution mechanisms where some of the parties to the current dispute were involved, or both. Please note that these two things are frequently true of a judge in the public court system, and, by themselves, are *not* causes for disqualification. So, the question is, what information is cause for disqualification of a prospective neutral?

As always, the answer may depend on the details of the neutral's relationships. There are, nonetheless, some pieces of data which should make one think twice about accepting a person as an arbitrator. These include such facts, as the candidate's having:

— been engaged as a *party-appointed* arbitrator by one of the parties;

— been associated with one of the law firms which represents a party in the arbitration (or represents that party regularly in other matters);

— been engaged as a neutral arbitrator by one of the parties more than three times in any recent year,[64]

— a serious financial interest in the outcome of the dispute or in the ownership of one of the parties; and

— expressed doubt about personal neutrality.

G. Preparing for the Hearing

Take care of the means, and the end will take care of itself.
—Mahatma Gandhi

Assume that the struggle through the arbitrator selection process is finished, and an arbitrator has been chosen. The next step is to go through the normal stages of an arbitration proceeding, cataloguing what can be expected to happen and what action will be required.

1. Deciding What the Case Is

The next job, however, is to persuade someone *who knows nothing about* the dispute to accept this version of events, conversations, documents, applicable principles, etc., which requires the creation of a cohesive series of events, choosing among the various pieces of evidence and theories of why the facts support this version of the dispute, and putting together the most coherent and persuasive narrative possible. There are two elements to this critical job:

(a) giving the arbitrator the evidence necessary to rule in favor of this party, and

(b) presenting the matter in a way that makes the arbitrator *want* to rule in favor of this party.

In normal court litigation, a process of information-gathering (and money-spending) called "discovery" would begin. This is where the lawyers get to shower one another with reams of paper containing comprehensive written questions (interrogatories), which are then followed by comprehensive evasive replies (interrogatory objections and answers), which are then followed by written demands for the production of documents, which are closely followed by responses which attach a few documents and state that the others requested do not exist (or if they do exist they are "privileged" and do not have to be produced), which are then followed by depositions of the parties and witnesses during which exhaustive questions are asked, followed by noncommittal answers and legal objections.

Almost everything mentioned in the above paragraph does not take place in ordinary arbitration. Indeed, in garden variety arbitrations, the only thing remotely like discovery that takes place is an exchange of documentary exhibits before the hearing. So, the parties to an arbitration can have as much, or as little, discovery as they can agree on. Such an agreement, of course, can take place either at the time the original arbitration clause is being negotiated or after a dispute has arisen. Just as the alternative dispute resolution clause should be negotiated before a dispute has broken out, the level of discovery should be agreed upon then, too. If a dispute arises before agreement on the level of discovery, it is almost inevitable that one party will be more in need of discovery than the other, with the result that the other party, in most cases, will agree to little or no discovery.

There are some ways to avoid controversy about this at the original negotiation. Parties could include in their arbitration clause that:

— The American Arbitration Association's Supplementary Rules for Large, Complex Cases will apply to their disputes (these Rules provide the arbitrator with discretion as to how much discovery to permit);

— Discovery will be permitted, but only as to documentary evidence (basically, this rules out depositions, frequently the most expensive element of discovery); and

— Without reference to any rules, the arbitrator will have discretion to order discovery on a showing of [need, good cause, or inability to obtain the evidence any other way].

So, as with other elements of the process of deciding disputes, the parties can do whatever they agree upon, but agreement may be hard to come by after a dispute has ensued.

2. Deciding How to Present the Case

First, one must know the various ways that evidence can be presented in arbitration. They are:

Stipulations—agreements between the parties that certain facts are true or certain documents are authentic;

Live testimony—real people, whether experts or "lay" witnesses, who will show up at the hearing, to be examined and cross-examined;

Exhibits—usually documentary, but can be any physical object; may need testimony to show authenticity and completeness;

Documentary testimony—can take the form of written statements from witnesses who can't (or won't) attend the hearing, or the deposition of a witness, or the record of a witness's testimony in some other hearing (not necessarily an arbitration);

Arbitral notice—process akin to judicial notice, here arbitrator relies on well-known facts, or ones that can be verified easily and quickly (*e.g.,* that Easter falls on April 18 in 1999, or that the boiling point of water is 212 degrees Fahrenheit); and

Admissions—statements (not necessarily under oath) made by opponents which are against their interests in this arbitration (perhaps the most dramatic way to prove something, but to use it risks finding that the "admitting" party now has some other explanation for what was said).

3. The Law

Although arbitrators are not bound to rule according to law as judges are, the party going before an arbitrator should remember these practical facts:

— Most arbitrators *are* lawyers, so legal analysis and argument is likely to be persuasive; and

— Many arbitrators, whether lawyers or not, believe that an arbitration should be decided (though not conducted) similarly to a bench (nonjury) trial in a local courthouse.

So, some attention to the applicable law as it is referred to in the arbitration agreement itself must be paid. Whether it is a predispute clause in larger agreement or a submission agreement crafted after the dispute arose, if the parties freely chose what law they wanted to apply to the resolution of their dispute, an arbitrator will apply that law. If the agreement does not mention applicable law, the parties may choose what law to apply before the hearing. If they cannot, it is likely that the local law (the law of the state in which the arbitration is taking place) will govern as a practical matter.

4. The Arbitration Book

In all but the simplest of disputes, an arbitration book(s) should be prepared by a party for presentation to the arbitrator *before* the hearing begins. What is this book, and why is it such a good idea to prepare and present it?

The arbitration book is a collection of memoranda, exhibits, witness lists, etc. Its purposes are to:

— inform the arbitrator about the party's view of the dispute;

— catalog materials for ease of reference and to prevent loss;[65]

— assist the arbitrator in following testimony on the exhibits; and

— assist the arbitrator in finding and reviewing a party's materials when deliberating a decision.

All of these objectives can really be summarized by this statement:

Make it as easy as possible for the arbitrator to rule in the party's favor.

5. Pre-hearing Memorandum

As with the arbitration book (which may hold it), a pre-hearing memorandum should probably be filed in all but the smallest cases. It should, when used, clearly and concisely set forth:

— the submitting party's "story"—what happened, who is responsible, what the results were, all in an interesting and factual way;

— identification of witnesses (except for surprises), and what they are going to testify about;

— those legal points which are important to the outcome of the hearing; and

— *what the arbitrator should do in his award* (and, if there is any doubt, why he has the power to do it).

The importance of letting the arbitrator know before the hearing begins what is expected as to the outcome of the dispute cannot be overemphasized. (It is perfectly acceptable to suggest alternative outcomes to the arbitrator.) In a substantial case where the arbitrator has not held a preliminary hearing, all that may be in the arbitrator's file is the claimant's demand for arbitration and respondent's denial and, perhaps, a counterclaim. None of these three documents needs to be more than a page long! Even the claimant doesn't have to say much more than to give a rounded figure of how many dollars are requested and some generalities about being entitled to those dollars. All the respondent has to do is deny what the claimant said. Unless the respondent has a counterclaim (which would be subject to the same loose format as the claim), there is seldom reason for the respondent to go beyond a simple denial. So, absent a preliminary hearing, the arbitrator will know very little about what this dispute is about.

The opening statement is a good way to supplement a pre-hearing memorandum and answer any questions, but at this point, it is too late to be telling the arbitrator about one side of the dispute for the first time, especially if the other party *has* already presented a pre-hearing memorandum.

A pre-hearing memorandum should not include character assassination of the other party or counsel. In some cases such as fraud, breach of fiduciary duty, or libel, it is necessary to attribute some nasty words or actions to the other party, but in most disputes, demeaning and insulting remarks about an opponent or their counsel do not aid a presentation. Keep in mind that arbitration is normally not concerned with who is the bad person and who is the good one.

6. The Hearing Itself

While arbitration hearings lack the formality of court trials, they do have some structure. Normally, the arbitrator will sit at the end of a conference table with the parties arrayed on opposite sides. A chair near the arbitrator may be "reserved" for whoever is giving testimony.

a. Conduct

Because of its unfamiliarity to them, many parties (and some lawyers) are not sure how to conduct themselves during the arbitration hearing. These rules of arbitration behavior should help.

— Behave respectfully toward everyone.

— Do not engage the arbitrator in any conversation beyond an exchange of pleasantries, unless representatives of all other parties are present. (The arbitrator must be like Caesar's wife: "above suspicion."[66])

— Ask the arbitrator how he would like to be addressed. (This minor item has created unwarranted stress for lawyers and parties. Most lawyers who appear in arbitrations are more familiar with the courtroom, where "your Honor" is *de rigueur*. However, most arbitrators are not judges (some were) and do not need or want to be treated like one. Unless the arbitrator is specific, either "Mr./Ms. Arbitrator" or "Mr./ Ms. (last name) is suggested.)

— Be punctual, or if delayed, phone the hearing to inform others of the fact.

— In administered arbitrations, take any questions about the arbitrator's fees to the case administrator.

— Arrange for electronic, audio-visual, or similar assistance before the hearing begins.

— Cooperate in the little things. (For instance, there is usually no reason to refuse to let an opponent take a witness out of order, and the arbitrator would probably permit it anyway, since it is a money-saver for the parties. Being ungracious would not advance a case, even if the argument was technically justified and/or won.)

— Don't act. (Exaggerated facial expressions do nothing for a case and may distract the arbitrator.)

— Remember, everyone is just doing their job.

b. The evidence

Arbitrators are expected to hear all evidence relevant to the dispute. In fact, one of the few grounds for overturning (vacating) an arbitrator's award is to show that he refused "to hear evidence pertinent and material to the controversy."[67] Subject to that one possibility of later scrutiny, then, arbitrators determine for themselves what is relevant. Precisely because arbitration awards are not appealable in the normal sense, arbitrators tend to accept evidence that might not be admitted by a judge. It is generally said of arbitration hearings that the rules of evidence do not apply. However, from interviews with arbitrators and experience, nothing could be further from the truth.

It is undeniably true that *some* rules of courtroom evidence do not apply in arbitration hearings. (Keep in mind, though, that the parties could make them apply if they agreed to.) In general, it is critical to remember that the courtroom evidentiary rules are mostly ways of keeping otherwise relevant (but unreliable or prejudicial) evidence away from a jury. Arbitrators, presumably more sophisticated about the *value of* evidence than the average juror, are biased in favor of letting evidence in. This does not mean that arbitrators ignore the *reasons* behind the courtroom evidence rules.

For example, the most familiar evidentiary rule that is not enforced in arbitration is the Hearsay Rule. Oversimplified, the Hearsay Rule prohibits the introduction into evidence of testimony *about* what the witness heard someone *else* say. The basis for the rule (which is already riddled with exceptions in court) is that such evidence is unreliable. It is certainly *less* reliable than having the person whom the witness heard come in and testify himself. In an arbitration hearing, the reasons behind the various evidence rules affect the arbitrator's view of the *weight* to be given to evidence which would normally be excluded.

This is not to say that all courtroom evidence rules are disregarded. An informal survey of thirty arbitrators (of whom only two were retired jurists, and two others were not lawyers) gave some interesting information. Asked what they would rule if a certain type of evidence (which would be excluded in court) were offered, *and objected to,* the answers were:

1. Thirty out of thirty said that they would not permit evidence of settlement negotiations or mediations to be introduced;

2. Twenty-two said that they would honor *all* evidentiary privileges which were contained in the law applicable to the arbitration ("privileges" are powers given to witnesses (or others) to prevent certain testimony from being given; the most famous is the Fifth Amendment privilege against self-incrimination);

3. Eight arbitrators said that they would always honor an assertion of the Fifth Amendment privilege or the attorney-client privilege, but would decide whether other privileges should give way to a need for more evidence on a given topic;

4. Twenty arbitrators said they would admit a copy of a crucial document where the original was not produced; six more agreed, but only if the absence of the original was "satisfactorily explained"; the remaining four had the view that the copy

should not be admitted, "unless there was testimony that it was identical to the original";

5.   All thirty agreed that hearsay evidence would be admitted, but added that they would view hearsay "with skepticism"; and

6.   There was unanimity on admitting oral testimony to prove the contents of a document, but there was equal unanimity that such evidence would not be given weight unless the disappearance of the document itself had been explained.

Not a scientific survey, certainly, but some proof of the fact that the relaxed admission standards in arbitration probably do not affect outcomes very much.

Nonetheless, the infirmities of certain kinds of evidence should be brought to the arbitrator's attention. Most of the time, this task should be saved for closing statement (or post-hearing memorandum). In other cases, an objection may be made at the time the evidence is sought to be introduced, not to keep it out, but to make sure the arbitrator is mindful of its shortcomings. This latter tactic will be most useful when the arbitrator has not had legal training. Even if contemporaneous objection has been made, it can be reinforced in the closing statement.

The only certain "rule of evidence" in arbitration is that the arbitrator is only interested in hearing evidence that will help him make a proper ruling. So, it is not helpful to the arbitrator (or to a cause) to spend large amounts of time trying to prove that the other party is a *bad person*. In some cases, such as fraud, libel, or unfair competition, that kind of proof is required to make the case. In most others, character assassination tends to backfire on the assassin.

c. The witnesses

Witnesses in arbitration (as in the courts) can be divided into two major classes: "expert" and "lay." An expert witness is a witness whose specialized knowledge, training, and experience may assist the arbitrator in reaching a proper decision. A "lay" witness is any other witness. Whichever category applies, witnesses should:

—   listen carefully to the question, and answer only when it is understood;

—   tell the truth;[68]

—   speak clearly and audibly;

—   use their own words and descriptions;

—   make some eye contact with the arbitrator;

—   dress appropriately;

—   stop talking when lawyers object or arbitrators starts talking;

— answer "I don't know" if that is the truth;

— expect to be nervous; and

— remember, the arbitrator needs their assistance.

When a witness is cross-examined (questioned by the opposing party/lawyer), however, a few additional precepts must be added:

— do not guess, speculate, or assume anything;

— do not feel obliged to estimate;

— explain answers to "yes or no" questions, if possible;

— if asked about a document, ask to see the document;

— do not volunteer information unless asked by the arbitrator; and

— answer as simply as is consistent with truthfulness.

When the arbitrator questions a witness, the witness should be (or at least *appear*) as cooperative as possible. While witnesses should do this at all times, it is particularly important that the witness directly answer the question that the arbitrator asked.

Since arbitration hearings are relatively informal, witnesses (particularly those who are not associated with either party) are frequently "taken out of order." This means nothing more than that a witness's testimony is temporarily interrupted so that another witness can be examined (and excused) without delay.

d. The parting shot

After all sides have had the opportunity to present all their evidence, the arbitrator may ask for closing statements (also called "summations" and "closing arguments" depending on where in the United States the hearing takes place). If he does not and a summation has been prepared, it is acceptable to ask if closing statements would be appropriate. It is the rare arbitrator who will refuse a chance to have each side summarize the evidence and highlight its significance. In large, complicated matters, however, both counsel and arbitrators increasingly prefer a final *written* submission. The latter has several advantages:

— It permits the authors time to think about and organize their presentations (although arbitrators will frequently give counsel/parties a recess in the hearing to prepare a final oral statements, it is still not the same);

— It permits the parties to address evidentiary (or legal) "surprises" which came up during the hearing;

— The written memorandum reaches the arbitrator much closer to the time of decision making; and

— Parties can ask the arbitrator (at the close of the hearing) what subjects should be treated, then address those topics thoughtfully.

Seeking permission (only needed when all parties do not agree) to file a post-hearing memorandum seems to have only two possible disadvantages: (1) unless it is coupled with an oral closing statement, the opportunity to go over the interpretation of the evidence with the arbitrator while the evidence is fresh is lost, and (2) the hearings remain open longer, taking more time and money and delaying the award.

e. The award: when and what

The first question a party often asks, after the hearing of evidence is concluded, is, "When do we get the award?" The answer may be found in the usual sources of guidance in arbitration:

The arbitration agreement of the parties can specify a period of time within which the arbitrator shall make the award;

Rules chosen by the parties—the American Arbitration Association Rules (under which most commercial arbitrations proceed) require the arbitrator to render his award within 30 days of the date the hearings "close";

Applicable law—if no guidance is given by the above two sources, applicable law *may* set a deadline.

Having established when the award will be received, thoughts lightly turn to "What is it that we are going to get?" This again is a matter which can be addressed in the arbitration agreement (whether predispute or submission) and may be treated in the rules governing the arbitration. At a minimum, an award which decides all the issues submitted to the arbitrator should be given. The *form* of that award may vary substantially, however.

While customs vary somewhat from industry to industry, arbitration awards may be said to fall into three discernible categories: the "bare bones" award, the "reasoned opinion" award, and the "semifreddo," or "lukewarm" or "half-baked" award.

The bare bones award, by far the most common form, simply contains a concise recital of who won, how much the winner gets, who pays for fees and costs, and other nonmonetary remedies. No reasons are given, although some may be inferred, particularly from the amount of damages awarded. When the arbitration award is made, both parties know that their controversy is finished. Of course, this fact is more appealing to the winning party, but it also saves the losing party time, money, and aggravation that would be associated with the almost-always-fruitless appeal process in the courts. Also remember that the only exception to arbitral finality is if a court vacates (over-turns) an award based on a set of narrow statutory grounds (the arbitrator was "crooked or crazy"). Against this backdrop, the clear advantage of a bare bones award is that it provides the least possible ammunition for a successful attack on that award in court. (Don't lose sight of the fact that the parties *could have* provided for whatever kind of award they wanted.)

The second major type of award is one which contains a reasoned opinion. This sort of award may well begin like a bare bones, clearly stating who won what. It will always go on, however, to present the arbitrator's reasons for coming to the conclusions he did. This type of award is gaining in popularity, despite the fact that it still accounts for only a small percentage of the awards made. One reason for this is that the number of international arbitrations conducted in the United States is growing, and the most widely used set of international arbitra-tion rules *require* that a reasoned opinion accompany the award. Another reason for the trend is that parties are becoming more desirous of knowing the arbitrator's reasons. Some pure inquisitiveness may underlie this change, but it is also based on the fact that parties can more easily change their business practices or conduct *if they know precisely why the arbitrator ruled against them.* Another reason why the number of reasoned opinion awards is growing may be that par-ties—and the lawyers advising them—have become more sanguine about repelling an attack on the award by the losing party. The judicial trend in this area seems to be in the direction of confirming the award *even if mistakes of law are made.*

Last, and statistically least, is the "semifreddo" award, so-called by a colleague, Richard Chernick. This type of award is really a compromise between bare bones and reasoned opinion type of awards, in that it contains a concise statement of who won and what, but also goes on to explain the ruling. For instance, claims may have been made in arbitration that the respondent infringed the claimant's copyright to computer software *and* engaged in unfair competition against the claimant (with the same actions). A semifreddo award in this case, assuming the evidence warranted it, might give the claimant "$482,700 damages for copyright infringement." Assuming for the sake of example that these words were all that was in the award, it must be concluded that the arbitrator found that the claimant *had* a valid copyright and the respondent *infringed* it. Because arbitration awards may be used against other disputants in the future,[69] this slight amplification of the award may be useful to the claimant. It is also useful to the respondent, in that it can be inferred that this arbitrator did not find its conduct to be unfair competition.

It has been noted with other elements of arbitration procedure that post-dispute agreement between the parties is much harder to come by than a predispute arrangement. That observation is not true to the same extent when the subject of discussion is types of awards.

Regardless of what type of award is issued, it should be in writing and signed by the arbitrator (or a majority of the arbitrators). Awards are still available to the parties if they settle their dispute while the arbitration is pending. These are called "consent awards" and are generally drafted by the parties and presented to the arbitrator for signature in the form of a stipulation (agreement). The principal benefit of having a consent award is that it may be converted into a court judgment by either party should the other not abide by the settlement terms.

f. Before the ink is dry: the winner

Once the award arrives by mail (or fax), the paths of the winning and losing parties tend to diverge. For the winners, the following course is suggested:

1. Celebrate;

2. Ask the opponent to comply with the award (This happens more frequently than one would think.);

3. If the opponent refuses to comply voluntarily (within the short deadline that has been politely set), petition a court to confirm the award. (The United States and all states have laws which permit an award to be turned into a court judgment and enforced like one.[70]);

4. Enforce the award as quickly as the law of where the petition has been filed (and, perhaps, the law of another jurisdiction where the opponent has assets) will allow; and

5. Add to the judgment whatever interest, fees, and costs the applicable law may allow (in addition to what may originally have been awarded).

g. Before the ink is dry: the loser

For the losers of an abritration award, this course of conduct is suggested:

1. Don't dwell on the loss;

2. Scrutinize the award for areas where the arbitrator may have made a mistake (Arbitrators usually have a short time after issuing the award when they can correct certain errors in it.);

3. If an error is found (the correction of which would make the award more bearable), petition the arbitrator to make the

correction[71] (The other party, of course, will be given an opportunity to respond to the petition.); and

4. Scrutinize the award and the conduct of the hearing for reasons why a court might vacate or correct the award. (Here, the applicable law must be checked as well. Some grounds for vacating an award that are found in many jurisdictions are:

   — There was no valid agreement to arbitrate in the first place,

   — There was an agreement to arbitrate, but it wasn't complied with,[72]

   — Fraud, misconduct, or corruption infested the proceedings,

   — The arbitrator exceeded the powers given him by the agreement (or law),

   — The parties did not get a fair, impartial hearing,[73]

   — The claim was barred by the applicable statute of limitations, and

   — The arbitrator refused to hear relevant evidence, which refusal substantially prejudiced the party offering it.);

5. Try to negotiate a more favorable outcome with the prevailing party (Sometimes parties will "discount" an award to avoid the time and expense associated with enforcing it. Be prepared to tender a cashier's check, however.);

6. If it is a cost-effective and an otherwise viable choice, do not comply with the award (It *is* an option, but it may cost more long term than the short-term delay in collection will save.); and

7. Rethink the decision not to comply voluntarily with the award.

H. Advantages and Disadvantages

Instead of using judicial proceedings for business disputes that take years to reach a final result and leave all parties financially and emotionally drained, negotiation or mediation of a dispute or using one of the other voluntary alternative dispute resolution mechanisms, avoids this scenario. Experience shows, however, that there are some disputes which are just not amenable to those kinds of solutions. In those cases, arbitration is the fastest, fairest, and most final of alternatives. However, arbitration has its detractors as well as supporters. Here are summaries of both views:

1. In Favor of Arbitration

— Faster results than court,

— Shorter and less expensive hearings,

— Savings of time and money,

— Ability to choose the arbitrator,

— Privacy,

— No "irrational" verdicts,

— Involves parties and community more,

— Lessens burden on courts (tax dollars), and

— Finality (no appeal).

2. Against Arbitration

— The perception that arbitrators always render a "compromise" award,[74]

— No discovery,

— No jury,

— No summary disposition (since arbitration awards can be overturned for refusal to hear evidence, pre-hearing dispositions, like summary judgment, are usually not available),

— Some arbitrations are more costly than court (filing fees may be higher, but the real difference is in paying for three arbitrators),

— Cannot be certain that the arbitrator will apply the law,

— Very limited judicial review, and

— Arbitrators may have relationships with parties or law firms that they do not have to disclose.

After listing the pros and cons, here are a few more observations:

— Some characteristics of arbitration, saving time and money, should be a benefit to all parties (although perhaps not to their lawyers).

— Support people for parties who are usually complainants protest the lack of extended discovery and the right to appeal an unfavorable award. Both these processes (discovery and appeal) are ones in which the party with the largest amount of resources (presumably the respondents) have an enormous advantage over their more impecunious opponent. While the absence of complete discovery may permit a respondent to "hide" documents which otherwise *might* have been unearthed by complainant, it can also be supposed that, if there were full discovery, respondent might have been able to "bury" the complainant before ever getting to a hearing on the merits.

— The practical unavailability of summary judgment-type remedies gives a complainant an enormous advantage over proceeding in the court system. Perhaps this advantage is overcome by the ability of respondents to avoid "irrational" jury verdicts, but this is just a guess.

— Opponents of arbitration seem to overlook the psychological (and social) value that accrues to everyone (not just the parties) when a dispute is *over.*

— Many proponents of arbitration are not doing enough to ensure that the arbitrators are competent and the processes are fair.[75]

— Nondisclosure of arbitrators' affiliations and relationships has been a problem, but not as widespread or serious as opponents of arbitration may believe. Keep in mind that most judges will know many of the lawyers who appear before them (both professionally and socially) and that fact (alone) is not considered grounds for judicial disqualification. In addition, subscribers to the American Arbitration Association's Code of Ethics for Arbitrators and Mediators, for instance, undertake to disclose any and all relationships with the parties or their lawyers which might give the impression of partiality. Some states have also enacted legislation specifying the disclosures a prospective arbitrator must make before his appointment may be confirmed.

— No one seems to have asked claimants if they would be willing to give up the chance at punitive damages (rarely awarded anyway, even in jury trials) and the right to appeal in return for getting a process that is fundamentally fair and which gets a case to a hearing on the merits more quickly, less expensively, and more certainly (no summary judgment, remember) than the court system does.

The debate over the appropriateness of arbitration (both at all and for particular kinds of disputes) will continue, as it should. All participants of that debate, however, should answer this question: In a world of shrinking governmental resources, fierce competition from foreign competitors, and growing division of our own country into various "special interest" groups (business, ethnic, racial, gender, sex preference, nativist, religious, etc.), just how much of society's resources should be allocated to resolving a particular dispute?

ENDNOTES

[1] For an entertaining and informative look at arbitration in England from the fifth to the fifteenth century, read Douglas H. Yarn, "Commercial Arbitration in Olde England," *Dispute Resolution Journal* 50, No. 1 (January 1995): 68.

[2] While most of the observations in this chapter apply to it, the subject of arbitration under a collective bargaining agreement is a separate specialty and will not be given detailed treatment in this book.

[3] The American Arbitration Association, which has been written into many contracts as the administering agency, estimates that only 18 percent of its 1994 arbitrations resulted from submission agreements. The rest arose from predispute arbitration clauses contained in contracts.

[4] A very small number of arbitrations are made public by statutes. For example, the results of arbitrations conducted by the American Arbitration Association for the U.S. Olympic Committee and its various single-sport committees are made public by federal law.

[5] 9 U.S.C. § § 1 *et seq.*

[6] Generally speaking, the grounds for vacating an award are what one would expect them to be, but one ground that surprises some is that the arbitrator refused to hear relevant evidence. For example, California's Code of Civil Procedure, sec. 1286.2 (e), empowers the court to vacate an award when "[t]he rights of the party were substantially prejudiced by the refusal of the arbitrators . . . to hear evidence material to the controversy . . . ."

[7] Since arbitration is "a creature of contract" in most instances, the parties could provide for appellate review if they chose to. To do so, however, would take away from two of the features which most attract people to arbitration in the first place: speed and economy.

[8] There are procedures for an arbitrator to correct an award, but the matters which may be "corrected" are few.

[9] The one area, outside of baseball itself, which is using "baseball" arbitration most frequently is personal injury claims. Most of these disputes start out in court, but are frequently diverted, by agreement, to a "baseball" arbitration process. Many insurance companies which insure automobile drivers have been a "driving" force in this movement.

[10] Boswell, *Life of Samuel Johnson* (19 September 1777), p. 167.

[11] If (and only if) the arbitrator's award in "night baseball arbitration" is *exactly* half way between the two proposals, then the amount of the award stands.

[12] The question of whether or not an arbitration clause should be insisted on (or agreed to) in the first place will be dealt with later in this chapter.

[13] The trend in alternative dispute resolution is very much in the direction of a single neutral arbitrator. Traditions exist in some areas, however, that "require" the use of three arbitrators. Examples of such areas are: international commercial arbitration; construction arbitration; and, legal/medical malpractice insurance coverage arbitration.

[14] As mentioned in other chapters, parties frequently employ more than one ADR mechanism in their dispute resolution clauses. The most popular "model" is currently the NEMA (NEgotiation-Mediation-Arbitration) clause, in which the parties exhaust one mechanism (usually with deadlines) before going on to the next. There is also the possibility of including nonbinding arbitration in the clause.

[15] The "industry standard" arbitration clause, created by the American Arbitration Association (and copied by many other ADR providers), is set forth in a later chapter.

[16] The question of arbitrator's powers usually arises when the losing party goes to court to vacate (overturn) the award. Two recent California cases illustrate (1) the reluctance some courts have in overturning anything the (honest and diligent) arbitrator does (see *Moncharsh v. Heily & Blase, et al.*, 10 Cal.Rptr.2d 183 (Cal. 1992); and (2) the broad powers to fashion an appropriate remedy that courts believe arbitrators should have (see *Advanced Micro Devices, Inc. v. Intel Corp.*, 36 Cal.Rptr.2d 581 (Cal. 1994).

[17] See *Island Creek Coal Sales Co. v. City of Gainesville, Florida*, 729 F.2d 1046 (1984).

[18] See, *e.g.*, West's Annotated California Code of Civil Procedure, sec. 1281.8 and New York Civil Practice Law and Rules, sec. 7502. These state statutes generally provide that provisional remedies are available to parties who have agreed to arbitrate their disputes and that seeking them in court will not operate as a waiver of the right to arbitrate.

See also AAA Commercial Arbitration Rule 34, "Interim Measures," which provides that the arbitrator may issue such orders for interim relief "as may be deemed necessary to safeguard the property that is the subject of arbitration". This language leaves open, however, the question of exactly what provisional relief can be awarded, particularly in disputes where there is no "property that is the subject of the arbitration."

[19] The threat of excessive punitive damage awards may be exaggerated. One study demonstrated that the total punitive damage awards at major securities firms is not as outrageous as one is led to believe. See *Business Week*, 20 March 1995.

[20] *Badie v. Bank of America* has not been published but can be found on Westlaw. It was decided in 1994 and has been appealed.

[21] See *Garrity v. Lyle Stuart, Inc.*, 353 N.E.2d 793 (N.Y. 1976).

[22] See *Mastrobuono v. Shearson Lehman Hutton, Inc.*, 115 S.Ct. 1212 (1995).

[23] See *J.M. Owen Bldg. Contractors, Inc. v. College Walk, Ltd.*, 400 S.E.2d 468 (N.C.App. 1991). North Carolina arbitration law does not allow the award of attorney fees in an arbitration award. See G.S. § 1-567.11.

[24] Unusual, but not unheard of. Some industries get together with their major unions and agree, as part of their collective bargaining agreement, to have a particular arbitrator handle all their disputes. One example involves the producers of legitimate theater productions in New York City and the major craft unions which work on the productions. For a number of years, they had Professor Daniel G. Collins of New York University School of Law as *the* arbitrator for their disputes.

[25] In the United States, state laws, *e.g.*, California Code of Civil Procedure, sec. 1286.2 and federal laws, Title 9 of the United States Code Annotated, sec. 10, provide for very limited review of an arbitrator's award. For a federal case implementing the law, see *Botany Industries, Inc. v. New York Jt. Bd., Amal. Cloth. Wkrs.*, 375 F.Supp. 485 (1974). See, generally, Bayer and Abrahams, "The Trouble With Arbitration," 11 *Litigation* 31 (Winter 1985).

[26] Some experts have singled arbitrator selection out as the *most* important step in the arbitration process. See, *e.g.*, James Acret, *Construction Arbitration Handbook* (Shepard's/McGraw-Hill, 1985), sec. 1.08; Michael F. Hoellering, *Alternative Dispute Resolution Report* (Bureau of National Affairs, 5 January 1989), p. 13.

[27] The list is by no means exhaustive. Not only are new ADR forms evolving, but the flexibility of ADR is such that "custom" procedures are frequently designed which combine features of several ADR mechanisms. To the extent that the customization process includes a provision that the end result will be binding, then the neutral selection process immediately becomes as crucial as it always is in traditional arbitration.

[28] The exceptions are use of an attorney/judge as judge *pro tem* (temporary) of the public court (see, *e.g.,* California Constitution, Article VI, Section 21; California Rules of Court, Rule 244), or use of a voluntary (California Code of Civil Procedure, sec. 638) or involuntary (C.C.P. sec. 639) order of reference. These latter two procedures, in effect, delegate to a private person a portion of the judicial power in a particular case. It is, of course, arguable that any of these three procedures constitute *alternative* dispute resolution mechanisms. Technical questions aside, however, it behooves the parties to be as well informed as possible in choosing judges *pro tem* and referees, too. See Chapter 8.

[29] See E.J. Costello, *Focus Group Report: Business and Construction Litigators View Alternative Dispute Resolution* (American Arbitration Association, 31 August 1991), p. 7.

[30] See Brunet, *Questioning the Quality of ADR,* 62 Tul. L. Rev. 1 (1987); Stipanowich, *Rethinking American Arbitration,* 63 Ind. L.J. 425, 435nn. (1987).

[31] The American Arbitration Association, Judicate, JAMS-Endispute, and U.S. Arbitration & Mediation Service, to name a few, all purport to provide a broad range of ADR opportunities in most populous states.

[32] One exception might be those prospective neutrals who have limited qualifications, references, or experience. Typically, no state statute governs who may be an arbitrator, and no separate licensure is provided for. It is a credit to the screening performed (to widely varying degrees) by the institutional providers, and to the astuteness of the litigation bar, that most persons who offer themselves to the public as ADR neutrals are at least minimally qualified to so act.

[33] If one of the parties insists, the institutional provider may have to present a panel composed of neutrals from countries other than the home country of any of the parties. For instance, American Arbitration Association, Commercial Arbitration Rules, Rule 16, provides:

"Where the parties are nationals or residents of different countries, any neutral arbitrator shall, upon the request of either party, be appointed from among the nationals of a country other than that of any of the parties. The request must be made prior to the time set for the appointment of the arbitrator as agreed by the parties or set by these rules."

[34] Perhaps it is utopian to suggest, but if the parties can agree on whom they would like to serve as their neutral, it is the rare institutional provider which will not accept the parties' choice. And, of course, starting off with someone whom all sides affirmatively want greatly increases the chances for a smooth proceeding.

[35] Disclosure of information possibly bearing on their neutrality is becoming less voluntary all the time. Generally, this is a good development, as parties should not have to wait to find out if the proposed arbitrator has relationships or experiences which cast a shadow on his impartiality. In 1994, the California legislature passed a number of bills which call upon prospective arbitrators to make certain disclosures. The subject of disclosure will be treated in more detail in this chapter, below.

[36] While Directories, *Who's Who* volumes, biographical advertising, and the like are useful, they all have the same problems as many institutional-provider biographies:

the information contained in them is provided by the subject himself, is largely unverified, and frequently out of date.

[37] One notable exception to the privacy of arbitration awards lies in the area of disputes regarding our various Olympic teams and athletes. Awards in these cases are made public by federal law and must contain the arbitrator's reasons for making his decision. This fact alone makes these awards more informative about the arbitrator's thought processes than the usual bare bones commercial awards. *Note:* the Olympic arbitrations are done under enormous time pressure and thus may not be the arbitrator's best work.

[38] Rocco M. Scanza, Esq., Regional Vice-President of the Los Angeles Office of the American Arbitration Association, in an interview on February 16, 1995, advised that his office maintains a list of types of cases handled for arbitrators and mediators on the American Arbitration Association panel. Case administrators use the list to help the parties select the most appropriate neutral.

[39] Criminal and civil court indices are obvious, but things as mundane as voter registration, motor vehicle registration/licensing data, and property tax records can sometimes produce useful information.

[40] In international arbitrations, *all* arbitrators are required to be neutral. So, in that setting, the only "partisan" act of a party-appointed arbitrator maybe to choose the third arbitrator. However, do not forget that the opponents have a party-appointed arbitrator doing the same thing, and that the third arbitrator must act as a neutral in any event.

[41] It is customary in some industries for the parties each to select a true neutral, and for this panel of two to attempt to arrive at a decision. Failing that, the two original neutrals appoint a third, and all three then hear and decide those issues which the original two could not resolve. It is difficult to see how the parties are greatly benefited by this procedure, unless one invokes the old legal maxim "two heads [then, three heads] are better than one." This process also creates the exponentially greater scheduling/delay problems associated with all ADR procedures where there is more than one neutral.

[42] In *Graham v. Scissor-Tail, Inc.,* 28 Cal.3d 807, 825, the court refused to enforce an arbitration agreement contained in a contract of adhesion where the dominant party's union was selected to be the arbitrator. The court viewed such a process as not meeting the "minimum levels of integrity" required of arbitration provisions before court's will enforce them.

[43] AAA Rules, Rule 14.

[44] JAMS-Endispute Arbitration Rules, Rule 2.

[45] See, *e.g.,* California Code of Civil Procedure, sec. 1281.6.

[46] California Code of Civil Procedure, sec. 1281.6.

[47] Oddly, since the whole process created by section 1281.6 presumes an inability by the parties to act jointly, the section nonetheless gives the parties a brief opportunity to appoint whomever they want, *after* the court has gone through the nomination process.

[48] Each party could still affect the list of a nominees sent to court by the American Arbitration Association (or some other third party) by communicating to that agency the nature of the dispute and what qualities it thinks an appropriate arbitrator should possess.

[49] These "works" may even include former testimony of an arbitrator concerning a previous arbitration. See, *e.g., Carolina-Virginia Fashion Exhibitors, Inc. v. Gunter,*

230 S.E.2d 380 (1976); *Griffith Co. v. San Diego College for Women,* 45 Cal.2d 501 (1955). This book would also qualify.

[50] Some lawyers find that invoking the help of nonlegal employees of their arbitration client gets excellent results. The client's general counsel and staff may share some of the limitations of the outside lawyers, but they can usually put counsel in touch with line managers who may provide (or obtain) useful information about the proposed arbitrator.

[51] This is frequently so because the parties to earlier mediations and arbitrations wish to keep even the existence of their dispute confidential.

[52] Here, the lawyers' excellent judgment and diplomatic skills may both be tested. Should clients be included? Should there be "ground rules" for the interview which would, for instance, prevent anyone from communicating with the proposed neutral in writing before or after the interview? The answers to these and similar questions will depend on the nature of the case, the adversaries and the level of trust, and the type of ADR being contemplated.

[53] For instance, American Arbitration Association Rule 40(a) prohibits any direct communication between the parties and the neutral arbitrator. Causists might argue that the contemplated interview will take place before an individual *becomes* a neutral arbitrator. See *Canadian Indemnity Co. v. Ohm,* 271 Cal.App.2d 703 (1969).

[54] Many busy neutrals require a commitment to a minimum number of hours before they will take a matter on. When that minimum materially exceeds the amount of time anticipated for the interview, counsel should ask the proposed neutral if it can be relaxed. After all, if selected, the neutral will be engaged for far more than the normal minimum (4-5 hours). An informal survey among eleven professional neutrals (those who devote their full time to service as neutrals in dispute resolution matters) produced only two respondents who did not welcome the idea of a preselection interview.

[55] It almost goes without saying that a great arbitrator may not always be a great mediator, and *vice versa.*

[56] That work will usually reflect the author's best thinking on a subject. If the subject bears on the current dispute, the work may be more revelatory than the interview.

[57] If the witness is in federal prison, for example, or abroad, the hearing may have to come to him/her.

[58] This open-ended question may reveal information that bears on the earlier questions.

[59] There are three levels of compulsion at work on the prospective arbitrator. The first is his conscience, whose efficacy is known only to the arbitrator. The second level consists of codes of conduct which, while widely known, do not have the force of law. An example would be the American Arbitration Association/American Bar Association Code of Ethics for Arbitrators in Commercial Disputes. The third level consists of statutory law to which the prospective arbitrator may be subject. Examples include a series of California statutes which mandate certain disclosures in international arbitrations (California Code of Civil Procedure, sec. 1281.6), home construction arbitrations (California Code of Civil Procedure, sec. 1281.95), and disclosures that must be made in any California arbitration (California Code of Civil Procedure, sec. 1282(e)). Tragically, the authors of these pieces of legislation did not coordinate their efforts, so parties, lawyers, and arbitrators in California are faced with a hodgepodge of overlapping and mutually inconsistent legal rules. Help may be on the way, however. The California Dispute Resolution Council, a group of providers of ADR services in California, has proposed clean-up legislation which will homogenize the various existing

statutes while keeping full disclosure *if it is passed by the legislature and signed by the governor.*

[60] Rule 19 was originally drafted as part of the American Arbitration Association's Commercial Arbitration Rules. Today, it is found in numerous industry-specific rules which the American Arbitration Association has promulgated, as well as a number of rules issued by other alternative dispute resolution providers.

[61] The Federal Arbitration Act, 9 U.S.C. § § 1 *et seq.*

[62] These requirements are found in Minnesota Statutes, secs. 572.10(1) and 572.10(2). Currently, thirty-four other states have adopted the Uniform Arbitration Act, but without a disclosure requirement.

[63] The California arbitrator disclosure laws may be found in the California Code of Civil Procedure, at secs. 1281.6, 1281.9, 1281.95, and 1282(e).

[64] There is nothing magic about the three-times-in-one-year prescription. There are arbitrators who have only been hired by a party once before in their lifetime, but may be partial to that party. Similarly, there are arbitrators who may have been hired by a party numerous times, but still would remain impartial.

[65] This is not meant to be facetious. In a court trial, the judge always has a clerk, whose responsibility is to manage all the exhibits and other paperwork that flows the judge's way. Unless the parties want to hire a "clerk," the arbitrator has no such assistant.

[66] Attributed to Julius Caesar, based on Plutarch, *Life of Julius Caesar,* xxxviii, (North translation.), p. 3.

[67] The quoted language is from the United States Arbitration Act, volume 9, United States Code, section 10. Most states have a similar ground for vacating an arbitrator's award in their law.

[68] Practice throughout the United States varies as to whether the arbitrator will place witnesses under oath. If the parties ask him to do so, the arbitrator will. While lying under oath carries with it the possibility of perjury indictment, such prosecutions are so rare that any witness who is disposed to lie will not likely be deterred by being placed under oath.

[69] The legal principles that make this the case are called *res judicata* and collateral estoppel. While originally introduced for the benefit of the courts (to not waste the court's time with matters that had already been tried and decided), these doctrines have become very useful to parties in dispute. While it is well beyond the scope of this book to explain the two principles, most jurisdictions find them fully applicable to arbitration awards.

[70] Most jurisdictions give the prevailing party a much longer time within which to confirm the award than the losing party has to try to vacate (overturn) it. This is part of a general public policy favoring arbitration.

[71] This petition for correction process is also available to the prevailing party. Understandably, prevailing parties use it a lot less frequently than losing parties.

[72] This is a tricky ground. Unless what was not done (or done wrong) went to the heart of the process, a court is likely to find that the losing party waived its right to object by continuing with the proceedings. Obviously, such a waiver should not apply where that party did not know of the offending conduct earlier.

[73] As more and more matters are covered by contractual arbitration, the courts (and some legislatures) are becoming more concerned about insuring that there was a "level playing field" in the arbitration. This trend is another reason why the drafting of arbitration clauses (and alternative dispute resolution agreements, generally) is so

important. Most of the benefits of arbitration disappear when it must be begun again after a full hearing and award.

[74] This canard has been disproven several times by empirical independent research. Yet, it persists. The only rational basis for it is that arbitrators do not want to offend either party for fear of not being selected in that party's next arbitration. In the experience of 30 arbitrators interviewed, rendering "neither fish nor fowl" awards puts an arbitrator at a lot greater risk of not being selected again by both sides.

[75] Two examples of the opposite are recent policy changes by the JAMS-Endispute and the American Arbitration Association. Both will now refuse to administer any employment arbitrations where the process is inherently unfair. See *The Recorder* (San Francisco), 18 April 1995, p. 1.

"God forbid some poor wretch should throw himself on the mercy of the court today."

Drawing by Whitney Darrow, Jr.; ©1975
The New Yorker Magazine, Inc.

PRIVATE JUDGING

A. Private Judging: Defined and Explained

This chapter will explore the availability and use of private judging in resolving business disputes. For these purposes, private judging is defined here as:

> The adjudication of disputes by private persons who are given the approximate powers of a trial court judge, and whose decision is appealable.

That said, what most parties and lawyers think about when they use the phrase "private judge" is their ability to get someone who is not a sitting trial court judge to hear and determine a dispute in the same way in which that dispute would be determined in the court where it is pending. In some quarters, this process is called "rent-a-judge"; in others, "private judge," "temporary judge," or "judge *pro tem.*" Because the normal rules of court procedure and evidentiary law will usually be used, the parties will likely select someone familiar with those rules to be their private judge. So, most people who serve as private judges are either present or former trial lawyers, retired jurists, or, very occasionally, law professors.

Normally, there is an existing dispute in the form of a pending state court case, and the parties in that case agree that it may be handled by a private judge.[1] The existence of formal pleadings permits precise identification of what the dispute is that is being handed over to the private judge.

B. Procedures: How to Get a Dispute Before a Private Judge

Since the case is being taken "out of" the normal court system, compliance with the applicable state procedures for giving the case to a private judge is also required. While these procedures vary from state to state, it can safely be said that all have the following components:

— The parties to the lawsuit must all agree to transfer the case to a private judge;

— This agreement is signified by signing and filing a form with the court;

— The court in which the case is pending must approve the transfer; and

— The proposed private judge must accept the appointment, and file with the court an oath to act as a judge in the particular case.

Generally speaking, once the case goes to a private judge, that judge is the functional equivalent of a sitting judge for all purposes in the case, until a judgment is rendered, or, in some jurisdictions, until the parties withdraw their agreement for the private judge to act.

C. Pros of Private Judging

What makes private judging attractive? First of all, lawyers who are fond of the process (and it is lawyers who make up the bulk of private judging's fans) respond to this question in a variety of ways. Most lawyers involved in the resolution of disputes are more familiar with court litigation than alternative dispute resolution. So, for the lawyers at least, taking a case to a private judge is very comfortable. As lawyers educate themselves more about alternative dispute resolution, this bias will diminish, but probably never disappear. There was once another perceived advantage: that having a court hear and decide a dispute would permit its lawyer (and, by extension, the opposing lawyer) to predict more accurately what the likely outcome would be. If true, this *should* lead to early and successful settlement negotiations. But, even the best business litigators despair of predicting what a court (not what a jury) will do these days. Most trial lawyers are less confident than they used to be about predicting the outcome of a judge ("bench") trial as well.

Then, there is the matter of lawyer fees. A case heard by a private judge will, unless the parties agree otherwise, involve all of the discovery and other pretrial procedures which frequently add much to the cost of resolving a dispute. The actual trial itself will take the same amount of time as it would in the public courthouse with a "regular" judge. Therefore, on grounds of familiarity, slightly greater predictability, and their own economic interests, lawyers like private judging. But because it is good for lawyers does not mean it is bad for a client. There are reasons why private judging is attractive to parties as well.

At bottom, there seem to be five characteristics of private judging which are recurrent themes in the comments of those who advocate it.

(1) *Speed*—Once disputes are assigned to a private judge, they move outside the workings of the normal court calendar. Parties and counsel only have to agree on when they are available and then fit themselves into the calendar of the chosen private judge. These two tasks may, at first, seem daunting, but parties and counsel who have agreed to the private judge process are already committed to the relatively prompt disposition of the dispute. So, the "normal" foot-dragging associated with court cases will likely

be absent, or at least reduced. In addition, *availability* at convenient times may be one of the criteria used in *selecting* the private judge. So, cases normally get to judgment sooner than if they had stayed in the courthouse.

(2) *Selection*—The parties may select their own their private judge in most cases. In many disputes, both the parties (or at least one side) would prefer to have a private judge who is knowledgeable in their type of dispute. Assuming cooperation between the parties, they may be able to select such a person from among those eligible to serve as private judges. The parties and counsel are much more likely to have someone adjudicate their case who is both capable and knowledgeable and who will give their dispute appropriate attention, a fair hearing, and correct rulings on matters of evidence. So, even though the other party has to agree to the choice, the ability to select a judge is potentially very important.

(3) *Flexibility*—Normally, the hearings conducted by a private judge (such as arbitration hearings) may be held at any place and any time, subject to everyone's agreement. So, for example, the hearings could be held between 7:30 a.m. and 1:30 p.m., Mondays through Thursdays. Such a schedule would permit all concerned to have at least a part of every business day "free" and Fridays to catch up. Similarly, the trial (or any pretrial hearings) could be held in the private judge's conference room, or that of one of the lawyers in the case, or, if all agree, at any convenient location (including a destination resort hotel). Within limits which may be imposed by the legislation of the state in which the case is being heard, the parties may also agree to some modification of the existing procedural and evidentiary rules. These latter modifications are infrequent, however, because private judging is most often chosen over its more flexible cousin, arbitration, simply *because* the parties want a replication of a court trial.

(4) *Appealability*—Despite the fact that they have a larger hand in choosing their private judge than they ever would in the court system, many parties emphasize appealability as the *main* reason for choosing private judging over arbitration. In arbitration, the award can usually be overturned (under state or federal law) only if one of a small handful of narrow requirements is met. Basically, the award will be final unless the arbitrator can be proven to have been "crooked or crazy." This aspect of arbitration scares some parties, and many lawyers, too. What if the arbitrator goes "off the rails"? In the business world, however, this is not as big a hurdle as with others who find themselves in disputes. Most companies are familiar with arbitration. Indeed, their industry

group or trade association may have chosen arbitration as the method of settling disputes *between* industry members.

(5) *Predictability*—The "default setting" for a private judge is to conduct a hearing or trial *exactly* as it would be conducted if the parties were in court. While private judges vary in temperament and predispositions, the hearings a private judge conducts can usually be relied on to follow the same procedural rules and impose the same standards for the admissibility of evidence as a trial court would. This gives lawyers and some litigants a sense of comfort about the procedural aspects of the hearing that they sometimes do not have with arbitration. It is also true that a private judge would be bound to decide the case on applicable legal principles. In the minds of some, this contrasts sharply with arbitration where the arbitrator is empowered to do what is right and just—even if certain legal principles would point the other way. Predictably, those lawyers and parties who tend regularly to rely on technical legal points to prevail in litigation are usually the strongest supporters of private judging.

D. Costs: Will It Be Less Costly than Court?

For using up time and money and taking a long time to conclude, nothing can beat our state court trial courts, particularly in populous areas.[2] It is, largely, not the fault of the hard-working judges and court staff. Most state trial courts have been overburdened with criminal matters since hard drugs became very popular and illegal in America. And, in most jurisdictions, these criminal matters take precedence over *every* civil case, regardless of how old or close to trial it may be. Moreover, dwindling tax revenues and general voter "revolts" against taxation are forcing many state court systems to handle a growing case load with *smaller* budgets than in previous years. Finally, the passage of "three-strikes-and-you're-out" laws in many states (where persons convicted of a third serious crime will be locked up for life) is threatening to swamp state trial courts completely.

The practical impact of these laws is potentially devastating to every state which has one. The defendants are not only refusing to plea bargain charges which would be the third strike, but are understandably almost as reluctant to plead to first and second "strikes" as well. So, the number of *criminal* cases requiring a full trial is increasing exponentially, resulting in a further absorption of judges who normally would be available for civil trials. So, the thinking goes, parties will inevitably experience numerous delays and last-minute postponements if they remain in the public court system. Each delay "costs" them not only the time and expense invested in futilely preparing for the to-be-delayed event, but also the time and money which must be expended to prepare for the postponed event when it does (one hopes) take place in the future.

In theory, at least, all of these costs can be eliminated by choosing private judging. The private judge (if a full-time neutral) is in sole control of his/her calendar, and can be "booked" for whatever time is needed. So, even though the actual trial may be identical in length to the one which would have taken place in the courthouse, parties may save time and money because the trial and other pretrial hearings take place when they are first scheduled to take place.

It should be borne in mind, of course, that the private judge will be compensated directly by the parties (at hourly rates ranging from $200-$500), while the public court judge is paid by all the taxpayers.

Similarly, even greater savings may be experienced in a state which has a "master calendar" assignment system in its trial court. Under such a system, the case is not assigned to one judge until it is ready to begin trial. So, unless there are only one or two judges on that bench, no judicial officer becomes familiar with the case until it is time for trial. This fact makes greater expense inevitable, because each pretrial ruling must "explain" the case in detail to a judge who has either never seen the case before or is so inundated with other matters that the previous hearings on the case are nothing more than a vague memory.

After the foregoing paragraphs, it may be concluded that private judging is to dispute resolution what the invention of the wheel was to transportation. But, among business people and the lawyers who serve them, private judging appears to have more detractors than supporters. Not surprisingly, their comments fall into five categories which are almost the antithesis of those put forward by private judging advocates. These categories are:

(1) *Too slow*—Critics of the private judging process point to the fact that, overall, it takes much longer to reach a *final* ruling than arbitration. While frequently conceding that the privately judged case may win the race to judgment/award, they point out that the (almost inevitable) appeals from the judgment can add from two to five years more to the process. Some experienced lawyers believe that even the race to judgment/award is more frequently won by arbitration. Those who make this comment cite the time saved, first, by having an arbitrator knowledgeable in business law and practices ("we don't have to reinvent the wheel"), and, second, by the more flexible procedures in arbitration. It is, of course, possible to find a private judge with business experience, but not easily.

(2) *Reduced pool of neutrals*—Those involved in business disputes value neutrals (judges, arbitrators, mediators, and private judges) who

have knowledge of and experience in their world very highly. To them, the usual statutory restriction, which limits those who may serve as private judges to active members of the bar or retired judges, substantially reduces the available pool of desirable neutrals. First, all nonlawyers are excluded. Second, while there are many active trial lawyers who have vast experience in business-related disputes (and the requisite familiarity with procedural and evidentiary rules), most of them are closely identified with the interests of businesses or with those who regularly sue businesses. This identification makes it extremely difficult for parties to agree on one of them to serve as a private judge. Many of these lawyers are able to put aside past associations and positions taken, and decide the particular case in its merits, but the problem here is one of perception. Most of those representing businesses believe that someone who has spent all of his/her professional life suing businesses could not be truly neutral toward, *e.g.,* an insurance company or auto manufacturer. Those representing parties normally suing businesses feel similarly about lawyers who have regularly represented businesses. So, *de facto,* the pool of available private judges frequently excludes many otherwise qualified practicing lawyers, as well as all nonlawyers.[3]

Generally speaking, the remaining pool of available private judges includes full-time professional neutrals and retired judges. In the case of each of these subgroups, there is an analog to the "problem" with trial lawyers discussed above. In the case of professional neutrals, it is likely (since full-time work outside the labor area did not exist until about five years ago) that these neutrals will all have a history of representing one side or the other in times past. Similarly, it is the rare judge who, while on the bench, does not acquire a reputation as being pro- or anti-business companies, or pro- or anti-plaintiffs. So, the irreducible group whom all would agree are "neutral" will most likely include only a few persons of deep knowledge and experience in the business world, probably full-time neutrals or retired judges who have developed a reputation for neutrality over time.

Some of the above analysis, at first sight, would seem not to apply to disputes *between* businesses. Knowledgeable persons from both the "pro" and "anti" camps appear to qualify as neutral when the dispute is between business enterprises. Yet, some similar biases are sometimes found here, too. And so it goes.

In addition, many interbusiness disputes are already committed to an arbitration regime set up by intercompany agreements or traditions.[4] This latter group of agreements contains many which were entered into *before* private judging became popular. Thus, in most cases, the existence of an intercompany agreement to arbitrate certain disputes does not imply a considered judgment, at the outset, that private judging is not the appropriate form of alternative dispute resolution for these types of disputes.[5]

(3) *Inflexibility*—Just as proponents of private judging laud its relative flexibility versus the public court system, critics point to its relative inflexibility when compared to arbitration. In arbitration, they say, the rules—both procedural and evidentiary—can be crafted by the parties themselves.[6] Further, they maintain, the parties' ability or willingness to enter into stipulations is reduced in a private judge setting because the private judge is less likely than an arbitrator to "understand the import of" a stipulation. So, the parties are often "put to their proof" even on issues where there is no disagreement.

One "flexibility" that private judging may not create is the ability to turn an otherwise public proceeding into a private one. Arbitrations are, by their nature, private. Court proceedings, for many very good reasons, are not. While the use of a private judge may *reduce* the likelihood that a given case will come to public or media attention, it cannot eliminate the possibility. For example, conducting hearings at a private location surely reduces the likelihood that reporters assigned to the "court beat" will happen upon the hearings, but the pleading, motions, filed depositions, and exhibits in a privately judged case are nonetheless *public* records. So, an interested citizen or reporter would have the right to have access to them.[7]

(4) *Lack of finality*—To many in government, education, business, and industry, a high premium is placed on having a dispute concluded. This need is sometimes particularly pressing in cases where the dispute is with a customer, but is by no means limited to those situations. Similarly, parties suing business companies almost always anxiously await the day when their case will be finally finished, and even when immediate business needs do not command quick finality, the *expense* of continued litigation often does. So, the fact that a judgment rendered by a private judge is appealable is frequently viewed as a substantial disadvantage.

(5) *Too expensive*—Critics of private judging often assert that the supposed savings in time and money (over regular public court litigation) are illusory or, at best, negligible. First, they point to the fact that, private judge or not, the parties are duplicating the normal process of getting to trial in a civil case. Not only, then, do the parties experience all the costs of pretrial motions and hearings, discovery and its attendant disputes, pretrial conferences and the necessary exhibit-culling and brief-writing associated with them, but the parties are also paying by the hour for judicial time which is otherwise "free" at the courthouse. There is also the fact that the case is usually not "administered" (as it would be in court by the clerk or in American Arbitration Association arbitration by a case administrator). This usually means

that the private judge must administer the case at his/her high hourly rate. As mentioned, the actual trial before a private judge is not likely to be significantly shorter than one conducted in a regular courtroom. Are these costs overcome by the savings experienced in efficient scheduling and reduced number of postponements? So far, the evidence is entirely anecdotal, so no one really knows.

The foregoing look at the "pros" and "cons" of private judging suggests two conclusions:

1. It is impossible to generalize about the appropriateness of private judging: each dispute and the parties' goals regarding it must be carefully examined to see how private judging fits them; and

2. Once the determination is made to use private judging, the single most critical decision is the selection of the private judge.

E. Choosing the Private Judge

As mentioned in Chapter 7, when parties and their counsel are involved in public court litigation, state or federal, much time and effort is spent in gathering and evaluating information about the judges who *might* decide the case. Selecting the person who will decide a particular case is at least equally important work for disputing parties and the lawyers.[8] So, expending time and effort to learn whom to select or reject as a private judge is not only appropriate but crucial.[9]

Most other common forms of ADR, *i.e.*, mediation, early neutral evaluation, mini-trial, summary jury trial, and fact-finding,[10] lead to a resolution/recommendation that will be binding only if all parties agree to it. So, the power of the neutral in those settings is, quite literally, limited to the power of persuasion. Nonetheless, once the parties have decided to use a particular form of ADR, they want—and deserve—the best neutral they can get. *A fortiori*, then, parties entering a private judging arrangement should make an informed decision based on reliable data.

As the popularity of ADR has grown, both litigators[11] and scholars have recognized that background information on prospective neutrals is inadequate from both a quantitative and qualitative standpoint. Correcting this inadequacy is not only in the interests of the disputing parties and their counsel, but also of the institutional providers of ADR services and, usually, the neutrals themselves.

A typical situation finds the disputing parties and their counsel having agreed to have their case heard by a private judge.[12] If an institutional provider is involved, counsel should (cooperatively, if possible; separately, if not) contact the appropriate staff member at the institutional provider, at an early stage, and make sure that he/she knows more about the case than is typically revealed by either the document which initiates an ADR mechanism or the usual type of state court complaint.[13] Most institutional providers draw from a large list of neutrals, whose qualifications, experience, and personal skills vary widely. The administrator will be in a much better position to present a list of proposed private judges who are most appropriate to a case if advised as to the nature of the dispute and its issues, and the parties involved. Equally importantly, if desirable personal traits can be articulated (and agreed upon by all), the parties stand a better chance of being presented with desirable private judges to choose from.[14]

Whether an institutional provider is involved or not, the parties should gather as much reliable information as possible on the available private judges in their region. The first items of business would seem to be the elimination of those candidates whose present or past associations disqualify them either for ethical or practical reasons. Those who subscribe to the American Arbitration Association's Code of Ethics will voluntarily disclose any remembered relationship with any of the parties or counsel. Others may or may not. Some states have statutory requirements for disclosure by prospective private judges.[15] For example, a private judge under the California Rules of Court will be disqualified pursuant to the same rules which govern trial court judges. These rules require that a private judge (a privately compensated temporary judge) disclose to the parties any potential ground for disqualification and any facts which might lead a party to question the ability of the judge to be impartial. Under the California Rules, disclosure must include any compensation the prospective judge has received in the last 18 months by a party, attorney, or law firm involved in the dispute at hand. In the states which do not require disclosure, litigating lawyers may find themselves sending memoranda to their colleagues, calling other lawyers who are experienced in litigated matters or other neutrals, and researching the background of the neutral through available published sources.[16] An often overlooked source is the published work,[17] if any, of the neutral. It is routinely examined in the case of expert witnesses, so why not for neutrals? Included in published work should be all available opinions and awards by the proposed neutral.

Even if the institutional provider or the candidate has provided a biographical sketch or resume, more detailed background information may be available from either of them.[18] Public records[19] also may add to the store of knowledge already gathered.

Another potential source of information is the client. Usually, the client has an informal network different from that of its lawyers, and that network may know the proposed private judge's reputation, if any, within the client's industry or field. In addition, the client may be in a better position than its lawyers to assess the raw data obtained about a proposed private judge. In any event, every lawyer's desire for good and continuing client relations suggests that the client at least be consulted.

References provide another excellent source of information on neutrals. While some neutrals may not be able to give references who have worked with them in an identical setting (private judging in the same type of dispute), a neutral who refuses to give any references in the business area is probably a neutral to be avoided. If a part-time neutral is being considered, it is important that some of the references apply to work done *as a private judge.* Top trial lawyers, learned law professors, even retired judges do not always make good *private* judges.

It is also not necessary to rely exclusively on references given by the neutral or their institutional provider. Indeed, lawyers and parties who have dealt with the neutral, but whose identities have not been volunteered, can provide some of the most valuable information.

Assuming the matters in issue warrant it, an interview with the prospective neutral can be an excellent experience for all concerned. An interview arranged and conducted jointly by representatives of all parties choosing the neutral is strongly suggested. Please refer to the end of Chapter 7. Principles discussed there regarding arbitrator selection are generally applicable to the selection of private judges.

ENDNOTES

[1] It is possible to arrange for a case to be "assigned" to a private judge shortly after the first pleading has been filed. A court case must be in existence, however, for the private judge to be assigned *to it.*

[2] Metropolitan civil trial courts have been trying to become more efficient. Many of them have cut delays, but the wait is usually still long.

[3] I would not make too much of this point because, after all, if parties want an exact replication of a court trial for their dispute, it is the rare nonlawyer who can accommodate them. The point is really another argument in favor of arbitration.

[4] The textile and construction industries, for instance, have long histories of using arbitration in this way.

[5] There are some recent agreements that imply a conscious choice of the arbitration forum over private judging.

[6] America's largest and oldest provider of alternative dispute resolution services, the American Arbitration Association, promulgates Rules for arbitrations conducted under its auspices. Except for the Rules relating to the Association's own fees, however, all such rules may be (and frequently are) modified by agreement of the parties.

[7] The Judicial Council of California, for example, has promulgated Court Rules which provide, among other things:

For all matters pending before privately compensated temporary judges, the clerk shall *post a notice* indicating the case name and number as well as the telephone number of a person to contact to arrange for attendance at any proceeding that would be open to the public if held in a courthouse. (Rule 244(d) [Superior Court], Rule 532(d) [Municipal Court], California Rules of Court.) (Emphasis added.)

The presiding judge . . . on request of *any person* or on the judge's own motion, may order that a case before a privately compensated temporary judge *must* be heard at a site easily accessible to the public and appropriate for seating those who have made known their plan to attend hearings. . . . The order may require that notice of trial or of other proceedings be given to the requesting party directly. (Rule 244(e), Rule 532(e)), California Rules of Court.) (Emphasis added.)

[8] In arbitration, for instance, making a fully informed selection of the appropriate neutral(s) is probably more important than the comparable process in public court litigation or private judging. The typical arbitrator, once appointed, has broader power than a judge, being less constrained by both rules of procedure and decision and subject to narrower review after decision. See, *e.g.,* 9 U.S.C. § 10 and California Code of Civil Procedure, sec. 1286.2; and a reported case named *Botany Industries, Inc. v. New York Jt. Bd.,. Amal. Cloth. Wkrs.,* 375 F.Supp. 485 (1974). See, generally, Bayer and Abrahams, "The Trouble With Arbitration," 11 *Litigation* 31 (Winter 1985).

[9] So crucial that some experts have singled it out as the most important step in the arbitration process as well. See, *e.g.,* James Acret, *Construction Arbitration Handbook* (Shepard's/McGraw-Hill, 1985), sec. 1.08; Michael F. Hoellering, *Alternative Dispute Resolution Report* (Bureau of National Affairs, 5 January 1989), p. 13.

[10] The list is by no means exhaustive. Not only are ADR forms evolving, but the flexibility of ADR is such that "custom" procedures are frequently designed which combine features of several ADR mechanisms. To the extent that the customization process includes a provision that the end result will be binding, then the neutral selection process immediately becomes as crucial as it always is in traditional arbitration.

[11] See endnotes 29 through 59 following Chapter 7 and accompanying text.

[12] In the best of all possible worlds, the parties will preselect their private judge and condition their agreement to submit the case to private judging on the availability and willingness of that person to serve. It's frequently not that easy, however.

[13] Most complaints, state or federal, give the opposing party only the most general idea of what the dispute is about. Demands for arbitration are similarly uninformative.

[14] Perhaps it is utopian to suggest here, too, but if the parties can agree on whom they would like to serve as their neutral, it is the rare institutional provider which will not accept the parties' choice. And, of course, starting off with someone whom all sides affirmatively want increases markedly the chances for a smooth proceeding.

[15] See, *e.g.,* the California Rules of Court, Rules 244(c), 244.1(b), and 244.2(c).

[16] See endnote 36 after Chapter 7.

[17] See endnote 49 after Chapter 7.

[18] Some institutional providers maintain a database showing the types of cases "their" neutrals have handled. Others rely on the neutral to supply that information. If the candidate is a current or former litigator, or retired judge, some insight into previous work may be gained from the computer legal research services.

[19] Criminal and civil court indices are obvious, as are legal databases, but things as mundane as voter registration, motor vehicle registration/licensing data, and property tax records can sometimes produce useful information. For retired judges, their history on the bench will be mostly a public record.

"*The courts have ruled, sir, that we must divest ourselves of the Watson Company and Copper Fittings, Inc., sell off thirty per cent of our mining interests, and get you a smaller desk.*"

MINI-TRIALS
A Corporate Creation

A. Mini-trials Defined and Explained

The first thing that needs to be said about a mini-trial is that it is not a trial, but a process which is really a highly articulated form of mediation, usually used in high-stakes disputes. Since it is a form of mediation, it is voluntary and there is no binding result. What happens is that each party in the dispute presents a summary of its case *to the other party,* with the neutral taking the role of a judge/arbitrator *but making no decisions.* So, even though a form of "evidence" will be presented and a "judge" (or "arbitrator") may preside, there is no trial.

This ADR mechanism is *not* designed for those with a thin wallet or low bank balance. As will be discussed later in detail, it is quite costly but, even so, was developed to save large business enterprises from having to spend even more money. Therefore, relatively speaking, mini-trials save money and time the way other ADR mechanisms do. As with garden-variety mediation, the presence and participation of the principals (those with power to resolve the dispute) are crucial to its success. Given its high cost, it would seem foolhardy to take part in a mini-trial unless an opponent's principal was also present. As with all ADR mechanisms, *flexibility* is a hallmark of mini-trials in that, with the agreement of a dispute opponent, a mini-trial can be custom-tailored to suit the needs of the particular dispute (or the parties involved in it).

B. Method: Differences from Summary Jury Trial

The "standard" mini-trial normally takes place fairly early in the life of a dispute. Since one of its purposes is to save the parties time and money, it has to. Very little would be saved if a mini-trial were held on the eve of a real trial, after all discovery had been completed.

If the underlying dispute is scheduled to be heard by a jury, one might ask: "Why not have the mini-trial presented to a jury?", since it is a jury who will ultimately decide the dispute (and whose decisions the parties and their counsel have to evaluate in assessing settlement possibilities). Actually, there is a process whereby the parties may do just that. However, that process is *not* a mini-trial, but a summary jury trial. Frequently confused with mini-trials, this mechanism differs from that of a mini-trial in several important ways:

— Summary jury trials are sponsored and overseen by the court in which the dispute is pending; mini-trials are done privately (although the dispute is usually already pending in some court);

— Summary jury trials involve the actual use of a group of strangers (the jury) to hear the evidence; the audience at mini-trials is the parties themselves;

— Summary jury trials result in an advisory "verdict" which may help the parties settle; mini-trials *involve the parties* in the "trial" process, which usually makes them more receptive to, and realistic about, a settlement; and

— To be most effective, summary jury trials should be conducted when the parties and counsel are almost totally ready for trial, *i.e., after* all the expensive discovery has been completed; mini-trials, on the other hand, can function quite successfully with incomplete discovery.

So, it can be seen that summary jury trials will ordinarily be useful only when the parties face an enormously lengthy jury trial and large amounts or issues are at stake, something that mini-trials can only partially address.

C. Role of the Parties (and Their Lawyers) and the Neutral

As mentioned above, mini-trials can be organized in any way that all the parties agree to. Nonetheless, some common features of the process have emerged over the years:

(1) *The role of the neutral:* Usually, the neutral presides over the proceedings, rules on evidentiary objections, and, only if asked by the parties, gives his own view of what the outcome of a full trial might be. One neglected area of a neutral's usefulness is *in the crafting of the ground rules for the mini-trial itself.* It is the rare lawyer (and even rarer party) who is truly experienced in mini-trials. An experienced neutral can help the parties to shape the process to the needs of the particular dispute and save even more time and money. If the neutral is expected to function as a true mediator *after* the mini-trial part of the process ends, it would be better not to publicize any opinions for a while. If, however, the parties seek the neutral's reaction immediately, there are several forms that reaction can take. First, and least useful, the neutral can simply tell the parties what the likely trial outcome will be. This may be of some use to the parties, but is really just the neutral's estimation of the dispute and may tend only to solidify the position of the party whom the neutral thinks will win. More

useful, and therefore more popular, is to have the neutral explain his view of the particular strengths and weaknesses of each side's case. This explanation can take place orally and immediately, or it can take the form of an advisory written opinion, which the neutral can prepare within a short time after the mini-trial ends. This feature of the mini-trial should be agreed upon in advance, so that the neutral understands what is expected of him.

(2) *The parties agree to "stay" (temporarily stop) any court litigation or arbitration* that may be pending between them, either until the end of the mini-trial or a specific period after the mini-trial ends (perhaps 30 days, to permit additional negotiation in light of the mini-trial). This agreement not only saves the costs of continuing the litigation/arbitration while the mini-trial is in prospect, but also removes the possibility that something which occurred in the pending suit might tend to harden the position of one (or more) of the parties.

(3) *The parties agree on a panel of principals from each side.* It is possible that one person so dominates the affairs of a business or organization, there is truly only one decision-maker. Even in those situations, however, it is useful to have a panel (at least two or three persons) representing each side at the mini-trial. Unless the lone decision-maker values no one else's judgment, the ability to involve all key people (or, in some cases, all knowledgeable people) is crucial to a successful outcome. It is also important to agree on who will be present *in advance,* because otherwise one party might send a "messenger" and treat the whole process as nothing more than a preview of the opponent's case. Given the expense of mini-trials, this latter result is unlikely, but not impossible.

(4) *Post mini-trial negotiations* are scheduled for the panels representing each side, frequently without the lawyers who represent the parties in the underlying dispute or the presence of the neutral, either. The reasoning behind such a plan is that the parties have just had a sample of what is to come in the litigation/arbitration and will strive to resolve the matter as a *business* (as opposed to legal) dispute.

(5) *Confidentiality* is frequently agreed on in mini-trials. Indeed, in some cases, confidentiality can turn out to be one of the major benefits of the mini-trial process for at least two reasons: (a) a confidential mini-trial permits the parties to explore their dispute in depth, *away from media scrutiny,* and (b) the parties themselves will frequently be more pliable in negotiations *if they know that the result will not be widely publicized.*

(6) *Case presentation is in summary form.* In order to hold out the hope of some savings for the parties, the mini-trial cannot approximate the length of the actual trial it is supposed to help avoid. So, the parties' counsel (it is almost unheard of that the parties would participate in a mini-trial without lawyers) usually present their evidence in summary fashion. In the "miniest" version, counsel are the only ones who speak, summarizing the evidence and arguing from it as they would at the end of a trial. That procedure can be modified to include the presentation of some actual documentary evidence (usually the most crucial) and even a witness or two.

(7) *Early intervention:* While the parties should know something about each other's views before beginning a mini-trial, the purpose of this mechanism would be defeated if it did not take place until almost all of the expenses of trial preparation had been exhausted. So, mini-trials should take place early on if possible. The lack of full discovery will, in most cases, be more than made up for by the ability to resolve the dispute relatively early and inexpensively.

1. Variations on the Mini-trial Theme

As mentioned above, the parties can craft whatever sort of mini-trial they can agree upon. From this infinite set of possibilities, a few favorites have surfaced. As might be expected, these variations on the mini-trial theme borrow some of their features from traditional mediation, adding elements of other ADR mechanisms and even judicial remedies. Here is a brief summary of each:

a. Mini-trial with teeth

In this version, the parties agree that the presiding neutral will give a full opinion containing the decision he would reach on what was presented and the reasons for that decision. The parties may then accept or reject the neutral's recommendation. If all parties accept, there remains only to document the settlement and order the champagne. If one party does not accept, then this form of mini-trial puts that party at some risk of future penalty. In all cases, the party which rejects the neutral's opinion bears the risk that the result at the *real* trial or arbitration will be less favorable than the mini-trial neutral's recommendation was. If that occurs, then a previously agreed-upon penalty is imposed. Again, penalty possibilities are nearly limitless, but some choices have come into general use. The favorites are that the rejecting party must then pay:

— a specific sum of money,

— all attorney fees and court costs of the other party or parties, or

— attorney and/or expert witness fees of the other party or parties incurred during the mini-trial process.

b. Mini-trial/Arb

This variation on the mini-trial theme is quite simple. The parties are given an agreed-upon length of time within which to negotiate a resolution of their dispute after the mini-trial is over. The presiding neutral's opinion is *not* sought at the end of the mini-trial, but if the parties have not resolved their differences by the expiration of the agreed-upon time period, then the presiding neutral is given the power to become an arbitrator *and make a binding award.* This method has the virtue of putting the additional pressure on the parties that, if they don't resolve their own dispute in a certain time, it will be decided *for them,* and they *must abide by the decision.* For business people whose job it is to *manage* disputes and *control* risks, this additional pressure is highly motivating.

c. Conditional settlement mini-trial

Here, the parties agree in advance as to what the key issues in their dispute are. Based on that identification of issues, they further agree as to what the economic consequences will be to each side on each issue, depending on whether they win or lose on that issue at the mini-trial. So, for example, Turbulent Software Company, which thought that its copyrighted software had been infringed upon by its competitor, Placid Software, Inc., might agree that a key issue is whether Placid actually infringed on the copyright. Both parties would then agree that, if infringement were found at the mini-trial, Placid would pay Turbulent $4,000,000. But they would also agree that if no infringement were found by the presiding neutral at the mini-trial, Turbulent would pay Placid $380,000, the latter sum usually approximating Placid's attorney fees and costs of litigation. Needless to say, agreements of this kind are easier to describe than they are to *reach.*

d. Key issue mini-trial

As the name implies, this mutation of the mini-trial involves focusing on what all parties agree is the central issue of the dispute. Unlike the mini-trial with teeth, however, no decisions are necessarily made by the neutral and no penalties are imposed on the party whose position may have been wrong. The usefulness of this version of mini-trial is that the parties can potentially save even *more* money and time by not having to prepare or present a summary of their entire "case." All attention is devoted to evidence and argument on the key issue. For instance, in the preceding paragraph's dispute between Turbulent and Placid, they could have chosen simply to have a mini-trial on the key issue of infringement. Once a presentation on this issue had been made and the parties had assessed it, the likelihood of resolution may be significantly advanced. That is so because, until the mini-trial, Placid had steadfastly maintained that its actions had not constituted infringement at all (while Turbulent was sure that they *did*).

2. Costs of the Mini-trial Process

As noted at the beginning of this chapter, mini-trials are not for those on a tight budget. The costs, from start to finish, will include:

a. Executive downtime

It has already been remarked that the mini-trial itself will require the presence of several of the parties' most senior people. In addition to the attendance time, they will have to spend some time with their lawyers before the actual mini-trial. This time will be spent in two possible ways: (1) they may have to assist counsel in *preparing* for the mini-trial presentation itself, and (2) they will have to *be prepared* for the mini-trial and the ensuing negotiations by counsel. It is impossible to estimate the number of hours of executive time any particular mini-trial will take, but a good rule of thumb is that for every hour the mini-trial and negotiations themselves are likely to take, involved executives should plan to spend about three hours in preparation. Because the mini-trial will likely take place at a "neutral" location, involved executives should also look forward to losing some time in transit.

b. Lawyers' time

Even though a mini-trial is not a real trial, the parties' lawyers will have to prepare for it much as if it were. Indeed, because the presentation will be done in summary form and perhaps within an agreed-upon time limit, the lawyers will not only have to review carefully all the available evidence, but will have to *condense* that evidence into a summary exposition *that is still very persuasive.* This takes time and possibly also the help of experts, at their hourly rates. In addition to the time spent by the presenting lawyer at the mini-trial, many hours may have to be spent by junior lawyers or paralegals, gathering and sorting documentary evidence, summarizing deposition testimony, and the like. As with executive downtime, it is impossible to give a general assessment of how many lawyer-hours will be involved, but the rule of thumb suggested above might have to be expanded to a five-to-one ratio, *i.e.*, five hours of preparation for each anticipated hour of presentation.

c. Experts

It is the rare mini-trial that does not involve the use of an expert whose field may range from appraisal to zoology, but mini-trials tend to be about complicated subjects, which frequently need to be explained by experts. So, no appraisal of the costs of a mini-trial would be complete without mentioning them. The amount of time an expert will need to spend in a mini-trial setting depends upon if the expert will be preparing the lawyers and the principals for their negotiation or will be called upon to issue a report for use as "evidence" in the mini-trial itself.

Depending on which type of service is required, experience suggests a guide of two-to-one preparation-to-presentation hours be used for personnel preparation work, while a five-to-one ratio is more realistic with respect to writing a report.

d. Allocation of other company resources

Even after accounting for executive downtime, there are still more direct costs of a mini-trial that a company will experience. Record-searching, generation of computer reports, financial projection and analysis, interviews with other knowledgeable employees—all of these tasks may become necessary in the time preceding a mini-trial and will probably *not* be performed by the senior executives who will be attending. So, an added call would be made on the company's resources, both human and technological. Here, a generalization is impossible, but since it is likely that much is at stake in the dispute, it is also likely that many hours of staff work will be needed.

3. Effectiveness of the Mini-trial Process

Large business organizations continue to employ the mini-trial as a way of ending disputes, but since most mini-trials are confidential, almost all data on how many have been used is anecdotal.[1] The perceived advantages of the process are:

a. Voluntariness

As with many ADR mechanisms, a mini-trial is entirely voluntary, in that all parties must not only agree to it, but also to continue the process. So, some parties feel that they can engage in a (somewhat expensive) "test drive" of mini-trials, with the ability to stop at any time. A possible downside of quitting a mini-trial in midprocess is that one party may see the other as being in bad faith with respect to actually wanting to settle the dispute, but this impression can normally be changed by explaining the reasons for abandoning the process, unless the reason is that the other party *was acting in bad faith*, and then perhaps no explanation will be availing. For those parties who find a mini-trial wanting and still wish to achieve an economical, nontoxic resolution, all other ADR mechanisms remain available.

b. Confidentiality

As remarked earlier, the confidentiality of the mini-trial procedure is often considered its major benefit, as the process is voluntary and takes place out of sight (and hearing) of the public and the media, produces no public records, and, depending on the agreement which

launches the process, may never be mentioned again, whether successful or not. All these factors are very attractive, particularly to a large
organization which may spend millions each year in nurturing its
public image.

c. Potential savings

Since the matters in which mini-trials conceivably make sense are
usually quite large, the prospect of settling the dispute at the mini-trial
stage should offer the likelihood of substantial savings to the parties.
However, since the process is voluntary, no settlement can be guaranteed. So, the *unsuccessful* use of a mini-trial will increase the parties'
overall costs materially. Some of the mini-trial preparation will remain
useful in the event of court trial or arbitration, but parties and lawyers
will still have to prepare all over again for the upcoming battle.

d. Nonbinding result

Since the parties are really presenting streamlined versions of their
cases *to each other,* a mini-trial (unlike litigation and arbitration) does
not result in a binding decision regarding the dispute. This fact has
appeal to both parties and their lawyers in major cases. At an absolute
minimum, a mini-trial gives them an opportunity to have a "test
drive" of their case. Reevaluation of a position, if needed, can take
place immediately or later if circumstances require, because nothing
has been done that is irrevocable. Most mistakes can be repaired or
most expectations can be changed.

e. Informality

Although a neutral is presiding, the parties are represented by
counsel, and counsel summarizes and argues the evidence, the mini-
trial is immensely less formal than a court trial. It is also less formal
than arbitration. There are no rules of procedures, save those ground
rules which the parties have agreed upon in advance. Informal exchanges can take place with no formal record kept. As a result, the
process tends to be short (usually no more than a day or two), relatively
(to court proceedings) nontoxic in atmosphere, and conducive to the
negotiations which take place at its end.

f. Practice for litigation

As mentioned in the costs section above, much of the work that the
parties and their lawyers do in preparation for a mini-trial is the same
as preparing for a court trial. Indeed, the summary of evidence and the
arguments given by lawyers *at* the mini-trial are very similar to
opening and closing argument at trial. So, in this sense, mini-trials are
a way of getting ready for trial, albeit an expensive one. However,
there is another, more important aspect to the practice function of a
mini-trial, in that *the parties* are exposed to what the ultimate trial (or
arbitration) will be like. This has several possible ramifications, the

most important of these, from the standpoint of bringing the case to resolution, being the economic and psychological effects that participation has on the parties. On the economic side, the more deeply the parties get involved in the mini-trial, the more self-evident these issues become:

— If we go to trial, how much will it cost?

— If we go to trial, how much individual time will be taken up?

— If we go to trial, what are the chances of winning?

— If we win, what will we get?

— If we lose, what is the worst thing that may happen?

— What happens to my job if we lose?

On the psychological side, the parties experience in miniature many of the forces at work in a trial (or, to a lesser extent, in an arbitration). They feel the intensity of preparation, the uncertainty of not being able to predict the outcome, and the cathartic effect of hearing their position prepared and ably presented. Sometimes, this miniature experience is enough to convince all sides that the matter should be resolved *now*. As one thoughtful author described this benefit: "While a few kernels of popcorn cannot provide the same satisfied feeling as a whole bowl, they may spare the parties the indigestion that overindulgence can cause."[2]

What does this all add up to? No one really knows. Anecdotally, lawyers and parties who have reported results indicate about a 50 percent success rate. If accurate, this statistic might still be somewhat misleading. Success in mini-trials is usually measured by whether or not the dispute was resolved in the negotiations *which immediately followed the mini-trial.* Of those cases which do not get concluded at this point, no one can be certain whether the process may have resulted in cost savings because of issue-narrowing or simply an overall, more cooperative attitude. And, of course, no one can reliably measure what contribution the mini-trial may have made to a settlement that is arrived at weeks or months later.

4. Using the Mini-trial Process

a. Whether to use

The threshold factor as to whether a mini-trial should be used has already been hinted at: if the time and money spent on the mini-trial will be justified by the amount of money and/or important issues involved in the dispute when the probability of settlement is factored in. In terms of assessing the amount of money involved in the dispute, a party must consider both the worst-case *outcome* of the dispute (after trial or arbitration) and the *transactional costs* of getting the dispute to final resolution (attorney fees, expert fees, court costs, etc.).

A second, but no less important, consideration in assessing mini-trial use is whether the parties have (or would like to have) an ongoing relationship which may survive this dispute. If they have (or want) such an affiliation, this fact should weigh in favor of a mini-trial (or other forms of mediation). The benefits of this relationship are twofold:

(1) It acts as a brake on both histrionic behavior and the taking of extreme positions *by either side,* and

(2) It provides a broader range of possible solutions to the dispute, since the parties can *shape the future* and not just rectify the past in their negotiations.

It is also important to consider the relative economic power of the disputing parties. If, going back to the disputing software companies, Turbulent is a multinational operation with $3 billion in annual sales and Placid is an emerging company with $50 million in annual sales, this apparent disparity in economic power may make the parties (particularly the weaker one) think twice before agreeing to a mini-trial. The reason is simple. Back at the beginning of this chapter, it was suggested that mini-trials are a highly articulated form of mediation, *i.e.,* a form of turbocharged, managed negotiation. The amount of resources available to either party in a controversy may have more to do with the outcome than the merits. This seems especially true when the disparity between the parties is such that it is obvious to all and makes the weaker party feel relatively powerless. So, getting parties in these relative positions together for a mini-trial may be an exercise in futility. In other words, the odds of mini-trial success become more favorable when the economic power of the parties is more equal.

Another consideration is the nature of the dispute, which probably should be large and/or very important for a mini-trial to be considered seriously. However, the subject of the dispute also plays an important role. What little data there is suggests, for example, that complex technical cases get settled more frequently after a mini-trial than nontechnical matters of approximately the same economic value. Some examples of these kinds of disputes are:

— insurance coverage cases, where the precise meaning of several key terms must be applied to the facts;

— patent and copyright disputes, where both the law and the facts are likely to be highly technical;

— where responsibility is acknowledged, and the only question is "how much";

— construction "defect" or "delay" cases, where the details of the work of a number of design professionals and a number of different trades may have to be scrutinized;

— partnership dissolutions, where a multitude of transactions must be measured against the agreement and the practice of the partners; and

— antitrust and unfair competition cases, where both the facts and their economic consequences must be evaluated.

Another factor which may point toward a mini-trial is the presence of a foreign party to a dispute that may be unfamiliar with either a judicial or arbitration system. A mini-trial might give this party the necessary exposure as to how a dispute might come out without the anxiety of a binding hearing on the merits before a judge or arbitrator.

A final, yet potentially critical, consideration is whether one or more of the parties has misevaluated the likely outcome of the dispute. If all the parties are represented by lawyers, it is nearly impossible to tell who might be guilty of this misevaluation, since it cannot be determined whether the articulated positions are those of the lawyer or the party. So, this consideration is directed specifically to the lawyers who represent (and the junior executives who work under) particularly strong-willed chief executives or owners. If the CEOs have (or *appear* to have) misevaluted the case, sometimes the only way to move them from their beliefs is a mini-trial.[3]

b. How to use

Assuming a dispute has been analyzed and the conclusion is that a mini-trial is worth doing, the first question is when the mini-trial should be held. In order to maximize the benefits of this process by controlling the transactional costs, it would seem that the earlier a dispute can be gotten into a mini-trial, the better. The only considerations which *might* militate against that conclusion are:

(1) if more information about the dispute is needed, and

(2) an opponent's impression on the suggestion of a mini-trial.

Regarding item (1), all parties (and their lawyers) should be sufficiently informed about the dispute that the mini-trial process will be worthwhile. If a court case or arbitration is pending, some information exchange (discovery) has probably already taken place. Is it enough? Here, the intellectual and economic interests of the parties and their lawyers may diverge. By training, temperament, and desire for more income, many lawyers are disposed to use the available discovery tools until the chances of an opponent having some "surprise" evidence has been reduced to zero. For normal business people, such levels of certainty are not only unusual but truly unnecessary. Most business *decisions* would be made too late if the person making them waited until 100 percent of the available data had been gathered and analyzed. Business people react similarly to disputes. So, as clients, business people must maintain control of (manage) their lawyers' desire to "leave no stone unturned."

Regarding item (2), if a mini-trial seems as if it would be useful, it should be suggested. As more business people and their lawyers become familiar with ADR in general (or mini-trials in particular), the person receiving the suggestion of a mini-trial will be less likely to infer that the one making the suggestion is exhibiting a sign of weakness. If the perception of weakness is *still a concern,* involve the prospective "judge" in the process or the pertinent ADR provider who can make it seem as if the mini-trial was *their idea.* Remember that the process is one in which the case must be presented, in summary form, to senior management and the lawyers for the other party. Surely offering to do *that* is not a sign of weakness!

Assuming that all obstacles have been overcome and the parties have agreed in principle to a mini-trial, some ground rules for regulating this individual process must now be established. Here, the decision tree develops three branches. The parties and lawyers can:

(1) select an "off-the-shelf" mini-trial procedure, obtainable from the American Arbitration Association or other ADR providers; or

(2) design and negotiate the entire procedure themselves; or

(3) use the neutral who will preside at the mini-trial to help them design the process.

The best suggestion is to combine all three. Get whatever "off-the-shelf" products are available. The American Arbitration Association, Center for Public Resources, and other ADR providers are only too happy to comply with requests for materials. Their shortcoming, of course, will be that they were not—indeed, could not have been—designed with *a particular dispute* in mind. So, they will be useful only as a way of getting started or to provide a nonspecific checklist of items. Next, bring in the neutral to work *with* counsel, with a view toward using as many of the off-the-shelf mini-trial ground rules as possible. With a brief introduction to the facts of the dispute from counsel, an experienced neutral can select from among the off-the-shelf products and suggest additional areas which the lawyers can draft. Using this method, the *most* time an experienced neutral should spend working out ground rules for a mini-trial is about six hours. So, at modest expense, the parties can have a complete set of ground rules that covers everything needing to be covered. Two benefits of having counsel work with the neutral in crafting the ground rules are that the lawyers will likely be on their best behavior and not disagree for the sake of disagreeing (to save the parties money), and that the mutual work of negotiating the ground rules will likely build mutual trust between counsel. An added benefit is that involving the neutral in the rule-making part of the process gives counsel the opportunity to determine if the neutral possesses the necessary impartiality and other qualities needed for this mini-trial. If both parties agree that he does not, they can dismiss him, or even if only one lawyer concludes that the neutral is somehow lacking, his party can simply refuse to go forward with the mini-trial (being voluntary) unless the neutral is replaced. But if the neutral is carefully selected, the neutral will be a neutral that no one wants to dismiss.

The person who will help craft and preside over the mini-trial process, even though no binding decision will be made, must be able to be trusted to act honorably at all times. Next to integrity, true neutrality, meaning that the person has no predisposition to one party or the other and will base a decision on the facts presented, is most important in a mini-trial setting. Then, in no particular order, the qualities of patience, intelligence, experience, persuasiveness, humor and flexibility are helpful. Keep in mind that it is always better to spend time and money evaluating prospective neutrals than to settle for an unsuitable one.

ENDNOTES

[1] The Center for Public Resources is the biggest institutional proponent of mini-trials and has the most information about them.

[2] Lawrence J. Fox, "Mini-trials," 19 *Litigation* 4 (Summer 1993): p. 36.

[3] Mediation is frequently invoked for this purpose, as is (less frequently) early neutral evaluation. However, each of these mechanisms lacks an element which *may* be needed to move CEOs from their positions: a "hearing." Many parties who adopt an apparently inflexible (and mistaken) view of their case do so in the belief that everything will end up the way they predict (or perhaps wish) once they have their "day in court." The mini-trial gives a party this "day in court" to the extent that almost no other nonbinding ADR mechanism does. An advisory arbitration would, of course, produce a similar result but at even greater expense to all concerned.

"In the future, son, everyone will be an attorney for fifteen minutes."

EARLY NEUTRAL EVALUATION

A. Early Neutral Evaluation Defined

The three components of the term "early neutral evaluation" are perhaps the best way to define the process. "Early" means at or shortly after the beginning of the formal conflict, *i.e.,* the filing of a demand for arbitration with the American Arbitration Association or of a complaint with a court. "Neutral," to no one's surprise, means that the process should be presided over by a neutral person, unconnected to the parties or their lawyers. "Evaluation" retains its common meaning, with some additions. An early neutral evaluator will evaluate and also help the parties to:

— focus on the truly important, dispositive aspects of their case;

— construct a discovery plan, or informal information-sharing agreement;

— locate areas where they do *not* disagree, perhaps leading to stipulations; and

— reassess the dispute in light of new observations.

Early neutral evaluation originated in the United States District Court for the Northern District of California (San Francisco and environs) as a court-annexed program (and continues as such in that district). Court-annexed correctly implies that early neutral evaluation began as part of the formal workings of the federal trial court in San Francisco, but as a *mandatory* process, whose original purpose—and still the dominant one—was to help civil litigants manage the often cumbersome and costly discovery process. Resolution of the entire dispute was to be only a gleam in the presiding neutral's eye.

Early neutral evaluation leads to complete resolution of some few disputes and to a more focused—and, therefore, less costly—discovery period in the case. Adding to its attractive qualities, it does not take much time and does not cost much in comparison to litigation. So, today, early neutral evaluation is not only used by different courts, but is being increasingly used *voluntarily* by parties and lawyers in complicated cases.

The principal specific purpose of early neutral evaluation is to rationalize pretrial procedures in a case headed for trial. Settlement of the whole dispute is a subsidiary, and sometimes unmentioned, aim. That said, early neutral evaluation is further testimony to the value of disputants (or their representatives) talking with an experienced third party: almost every early neutral evaluation ends with general agreement that ample money and time will be saved as a result of it.

B. How Early Neutral Evaluation Works

This is how a typical voluntary early neutral evaluation would be conducted. Counsel for the parties to an arbitration or, more likely, litigation[1] realize that they have a long and complicated (and expensive) road ahead of them before a dispute would be resolved by adjudication. One of the lawyers suggests early neutral evaluation, and, after some inevitable deliberation, the other lawyers in the case agree. (Occasionally, encouragement from their clients is required to arrive at this agreement.) After they select a neutral person to assist them, then all counsel submit a written "brief" to the neutral (and to each other), putting forward their clients' views of the conflict and a discovery plan which emphasizes critical fact-gathering which might lead to early resolution. After that, all the lawyers (usually *with* the parties) meet with the neutral. Each presents a concise, 30-minute (approximate) oral presentation to the neutral (and the other lawyers), which approximates an opening argument in a bench trial. There is then some discussion among all present, which generally involves testing the facts (or law) underlying certain contentions that one lawyer or another has made. This can take the form of questions and answers, or more formal rebuttal statements, or both. Usually, the parties themselves do not have to participate except by their presence (unlike mediation). At this point, the neutral evaluates the dispute, identifies key issues in the case (and perhaps even predicts an outcome with respect them, based on observation), and sorts through the various proposed discovery plans, with a view toward:

— Encouraging each party to evaluate its position in the lawsuit;

— Helping the parties develop an approach to discovery[2] that focuses immediately on key issues, and promptly disclosing key evidence on those issues;

— Offering a confidential, candid, and thoughtful assessment of the relative strengths and weaknesses of the parties' positions and the value of the case overall;

— Getting all present to focus on the really important elements of the dispute, while identifying those matters that need not be seriously contested;

— Providing each with an opportunity to hear the other party present its view of the case; and

— Providing an early opportunity for a negotiated settlement.[3]

1. When Is "Early"?

In the federal court where it all began, early neutral evaluation was required before the parties had their first status conference before the judge assigned to their case. Typically, this was only a few months after the pleadings which initiated the case had been filed. Discovery, if there had been any at all, was in its infancy. Now that early neutral evaluation has gained modest popularity as a voluntary alternative dispute resolution mechanism, the lawyers tend to agree to it later on in the case, but usually before six months after the pleadings were filed. The precipitating event for voluntary early neutral evaluation is often that the lawyers are quarreling about discovery, and one or more of them would like, at least, to regularize the discovery process.

2. How to Get Early Neutral Evaluation of a Dispute

The first step is to obtain consensus that early neutral evaluation is a worthwhile thing to do. Early neutral evaluation is so inexpensive (relative to the alternative of slogging through discovery with no agreed plan) that the only disagreement may come from a lawyer or party who might *benefit* from the delay that would result from friction and confusion during discovery.[4] In multiparty cases, which frequently employ early neutral evaluation, the peer pressure of the other lawyers may make a recalcitrant lawyer come around. If there are only two parties, the suggestion might be made when counsel are in front of the judge or arbitrator. If he opines that it is a good idea, agreement will follow shortly in most situations.

3. Role of Lawyers (and Parties)

As mentioned above, early neutral evaluation is usually attended by the lawyers *and parties* in order for each party to have an opportunity to hear the other's case presentation (somewhat like a mini-trial). There is, however, a respectable minority view that only the lawyers should be present, since the bulk of discussion will be about discovery, and clients are either not interested in such detail or are unequipped to deal with discovery questions. The fact is that some of the stipulations which may be entered into at an early neutral evaluation session will need party approval; therefore, an attendant party representative should be a person who has sufficient authority to give that approval. It would help if the representative also had authority to resolve the case, since settlement discussions may evolve.

The lawyers must prepare the written submission to the neutral (and the other lawyers) and prepare themselves for the actual early neutral evaluation session. Self-preparation usually takes three forms:

a. Developing as thorough a knowledge of the crucial issues in the case as possible;

    b.   Deciding what discovery is important; and

    c.   Analyzing the opponent's case for weak points.

As for their performance at the early neutral evaluation session itself, lawyers will each present oral summaries of their factual and legal points, but the rest of the process really is *negotiation.* Therefore, it is important that the lawyers blend advocacy with cooperation.

4. Results

Early neutral evaluation is such an open-ended process, no one can be certain what, if anything, the results will be, once a session has ended. At a minimum, the parties should have obtained a better understanding of each other's view of the case *now* (keep in mind how early in the course of the dispute early neutral evaluation normally happens) not only from listening to the oral summaries, but also from studying the discovery requests which each party makes. The parties will also have had an opportunity to "sell" their current view of the case to each other *and the neutral,* whose reactions will augment various portions of each view. That much will likely happen at *every* early neutral evaluation.

Added benefits of early neutral evaluation may include:

— stipulations as to agreed matters, so no one has the expense of proving them;

— commitments to make certain witnesses available for deposition;

— commitments to set aside a certain time period exclusively for discovery in this case; and

— a comprehensive discovery plan, subscribed to by all.

5. Costs of Early Neutral Evaluation

As with any other alternative dispute resolution mechanism, the neutral must be paid for services rendered, which normally include an hour or two spent reading the written submissions of the parties, plus the time of the early neutral evaluation session itself. On this latter point, there seems to be general, albeit anecdotal, agreement that an evaluation session should take no more than about two to four hours. Participants (neutrals and lawyers alike) have concluded that a law of diminishing return sets in at the four-hour mark. Even if progress is being made but has not been fully achieved, it is usually better to adjourn after several hours. The lawyers (and parties), with or without the presence of the neutral, can meet again and finalize details. In that case, the neutral is likely to charge a minimum of five hours of time to the process. As with mediators and arbitrators, current hourly fees for neutrals qualified in business disputes ranges from $250 to $400 per hour.

To this must be added attorney fees. The time that the session will probably take is only the tip of the iceberg. The dispute must be written up persuasively for the neutral and opposing counsel, and a discovery plan must be thought out and outlined. Remember that the case is still at an early stage when this can all normally be accomplished at the cost of approximately ten hours or less of the lawyer's time.

6. Consumer's Guide to Early Neutral Evaluation

a. Amount at stake vs. costs to resolution

The economic calculus of whether early neutral evaluation should be considered seriously involves weighing what is at stake in the controversy (in dollars or other important issues) together with the costs of getting the case to resolution. Suppose, for example, that the dispute is pending in court and is worth net $2 million to a company. Before going any further, the company will need to get their lawyer to give the best estimate of what discovery and trial preparation fees and costs will be. Bear in mind that this is early in the lawsuit, and the lawyer's estimate may be far less than accurate (and should include a caveat to that effect). Nonetheless, it is the best information available to work with.

Still supposing, the lawyer estimates the total cost at about $300,000 through the end of the trial and then assesses the percentage chances of completely prevailing at trial. The $2 million should then be multiplied by whatever that percentage is, arriving at a *most probable outcome* scenario. Would early neutral evaluation (or any other alternative dispute resolution mechanism) be a cost-effective way of spending time and money? While not very successful at resolving disputes, early neutral evaluation is an excellent vehicle by which to *save a large sum of money* in attorney fees and discovery costs. So, if it would cost approximately $300,000 to have a *chance* at some *percentage* of the $2 million maximum benefit where one may or may not do little better than breaking even, then early neutral evaluation may be the solution.

b. Do others need to be given "bad news"?

A frequent reason for getting *any* sort of dispute before a neutral is that the person who ultimately makes the party's decision is not heeding the careful analysis of the dispute from others. For example, Plantation, Inc. is sued by its former employee, Fred Douglas, for wrongful termination. The records are reviewed by Plantation's general counsel, who then conducts several key interviews. A memo from the general counsel to Plantation's CEO, Simone Legree, gives a very pessimistic evaluation of the company's chances of prevailing against Fred Douglas. Indeed, reinstatement is deemed a strong possibility. Ms. Legree reads the memo, calls in the general counsel, and berates him.

It seems that Ms. Legree was the one who ordered Douglas to be fired "properly," and she will brook no views which question the propriety of the decision to fire or its execution. The general counsel retreats, considering himself quite lucky that he did not get fired, too. His dilemma has two prongs:

(1) He can press the conclusions of his memo on Ms. Legree, risking his own livelihood, or

(2) He can do nothing and watch the company be wiped out in the Douglas lawsuit, also risking his own livelihood.

Fortunately, the general counsel knows how to escape this dilemma and suggests early neutral evaluation. The prospect of saving a lot of money on discovery will get CEO Legree to approve it, even though she *knows* what the outcome of the trial is going to be. At the early neutral evaluation, of course, the neutral takes a dim view of Plantation's case in no uncertain terms. Ms. Legree gets to hear this dim view with her own ears. Given the strength of her conviction about what the outcome will be, she will likely disregard even the neutral's evaluation if it is given to her by someone other than the neutral himself.

c. Party candor

The question of the degree of candor legitimately arises in every non-adjudicative alternative dispute resolution setting. Whether it be in mediation, early neutral evaluation, mini-trial, or summary jury trial, each party must decide (1) how badly it and the other party or parties want to resolve the dispute now, and (2) if some confidential information exists that is not intended to be revealed at this time (or ever), what the chances are that another party might discover it.

It would seem prudent to refrain from any confessions of weakness during an early neutral evaluation session. If it is transformed into serious settlement negotiations, views may change. But, given the primary purpose of early neutral evaluation, which is *case management,* party candor should probably be limited to what various witnesses can testify about, generally what documents exist, time estimates for depositions of various witnesses, and so forth. Part of the reason for suggesting limited candor is that it is all a party will probably receive from their opponent(s).

d. Why not negotiation or mediation?

As previously suggested, early neutral evaluation is usually not the best vehicle for achieving an overall settlement of a case because that is not its purpose. Negotiation of important issues and the handling of discovery might be a perfectly acceptable solution in some cases, with highly professional counsel who know and trust each other. Unfortunately, negotiation does not require *a neutral* and, hence, no evaluation is delivered. In most cases, the neutral also functions as a "referee" to keep the advocative instincts of the lawyers within reasonable bounds and to suggest compromises in the discovery process which are fair to all.

Even though mediation is, after all, *designed* to create a cooperative atmosphere, energize and manage negotiations, and help the parties resolve the *whole* dispute, lawyers (and sometimes even their parties) would hesitate to negotiate a full resolution when they know so little about the dispute. One of the reasons that they know so little has to do with the legal rules of pleading in state and (especially) federal courts. Greatly oversimplified, they are these:

— A pleading need only give the other party adequate notice of the general nature of the claim (federal and some states), or need only contain allegations sufficient to bring the case within one or more legally recognized "causes of action" (most states).

— A responsive pleading (to one which makes a claim) need only affirm or deny the allegations in the earlier pleading.

— No precision is required in the calculation of alleged damages or the description of other relief sought.

So, even a careful assessment of the pleadings in a case may still leave parties and counsel without very many details. In this setting, mediation is less likely to be successful than if the parties had a better understanding of precisely what was being claimed; however, many mediators are skilled at discovery management, too. So, it would seem possible to craft a mediation or a hybrid alternative dispute resolution mechanism whose *principal* purpose would be to *resolve the entire dispute* while still enabling the parties to rationalize discovery if complete resolution was not attainable. These possibilities should at least be considered and discussed with legal counsel before early neutral evaluation is undertaken.

e. Selecting the right neutral

Previously, in Chapter 7, a general guide to selecting a neutral was given and should be referred to in the selection of any alternative dispute resolution neutral. Some characteristics which ought to be added when the neutral is being selected for early neutral evaluation[5] are:

Specific experience—While it is not necessary for the proposed early neutral evaluation neutral to have ever conducted an early neutral evaluation session, having a background in the preparation and trial of complex cases is crucial, since the neutral's principal responsibilities will probably be:

— Assisting the parties in hammering out a detailed discovery plan;

— Giving a reasoned evaluation of the case based on the evidence presented (rather like an advisory arbitration without the hearing); and

— Sorting through the rhetoric to identify key issues and facts.

So, although a proposed early neutral evaluation neutral need not be a lawyer, the experience mentioned above is a requisite. It is also possible that a retired jurist may be selected as the early neutral evaluation neutral. If the latter is envisioned, be careful to subject the candidate's experience to the same scrutiny as if a lawyer were being chosen. There are many retired jurists who have served on the bench ably for many years, but have had very little contact with complex civil cases.

Subject matter expertise—Depending on the nature of the dispute, parties may wish to insist that the early neutral evaluation neutral have experience in handling (as advocate or judge) cases where either the same kinds of legal claims were being made, the same business or industry was involved, or both.

This will usually not be necessary, but certain cases may make it desirable. For instance, a case where the customs and practices of a particular industry are at issue might benefit from a neutral who was knowledgeable about that industry. Or, on the legal side, a case where the validity of patents is in issue might profit from having a neutral with expertise in that area.

Impressive credentials—Normally, the proposed neutral need only be impressive enough that competence in the proposed task is assured. In early neutral evaluation, however, which is similar to advisory arbitration, the parties and their counsel expect a comprehensive evaluation of the entire case.[6] The more "convincing" the neutral's credentials are, the more convincing such an evaluation will be. It is nothing more than common sense to suggest that the parties will pay more attention to someone whose background commands greater respect. Care should be taken to insure that the credentials proffered by the proposed neutral are accurate and unembellished.

ENDNOTES

[1] The arbitration process normally involves dramatically less discovery than court litigation. So, it is with court litigation that early neutral evaluation can have the biggest impact on costs.

[2] As mentioned elsewhere, the desire by lawyers to take "unlimited" discovery is not necessarily (or even *usually*) motivated by the prospect of more fees. Lawyers, by training and experience, want to get to the bottom of the other party's case and avoid surprise at the trial. There is sometimes the additional, but no less important, consideration of avoiding malpractice claims by the client. These factors may be important in discussions with the lawyer, as lawyer and client frequently see the value of discovery differently, but don't know why they do.

[3] Wayne Brazil, *et al.,* "Early Neutral Evaluation: An Experimental Effort to Expedite Dispute Resolution," 69 *Judicature* (American Judicature Society, 1986): p. 280.

[4] Another situation where a party might not readily agree to early neutral evaluation is where that party plans to use its greater resources to wear the opponent down with discovery.

[5] In mandatory court-annexed early neutral evaluation, it is most likely that the judge presiding over the case will make the selection or may entertain a suggestion of who the neutral should be, but only if all parties suggest the same person. In some courts, even the parties' ability to suggest is limited: *e.g.,* the court maintains a list of approved early neutral evaluation neutrals from which list the selection *must* be made. This section covers the procedures for *voluntary* early neutral evaluation, where all parties must agree on the neutral.

[6] The advisory arbitrator has the benefit of full presentation of evidence, while the early neutral evaluator does not.

My client is requesting a trial by talk show host.

HYBRIDS
Building Custom ADR Processes

Much has been said and written about the obvious advantages of alternative dispute resolution, such as saving money and time, maintaining relationships, getting more rational results, etc. An often neglected advantage of alternative dispute resolution, however, is its flexibility. Starting with the premise that all alternative dispute resolution processes are, at least initially, consensual (all parties consent), there exists at that time an opportunity to shape the process being chosen to the disputes it will likely be called upon to handle. So, parties can choose:

— whichever alternative dispute resolution mechanisms make sense to them,

— whatever *combination of* alternative dispute resolution mechanisms seems to fit the situation, or

— certain *features of* different alternative dispute resolution mechanisms, which can be combined to form a new, unique mechanism.

So, the ability of the parties to fashion new alternative dispute resolution processes is limited only by their imaginations and good sense. One of the more popular of these hybrids is a combination of mediation and arbitration commonly known as Med/Arb (pronounced "meed-arb"). Med/Arb is gaining popularity in employment disputes and other business settings. This hybrid is sometimes confused with Arb/Med, of which there is more later in this chapter.

A. Med/Arb Defined and Explained

There is not much to say about Med/Arb by way of definition. It is an alternative dispute resolution process in which the parties commit to a mediation, and if that mediation fails to reach complete resolution, to an arbitration of all remaining issues in dispute.

It seems as simple as nothing more than tying two alternative dispute resolution mechanisms end-to-end and guaranteeing that the dispute will be resolved. However, there are many who believe that Med/Arb detracts from the values of *both* mediation and arbitration. Mediation is really a form of negotiation which includes the active involvement of the parties in crafting an agreed resolution. The value of mediation consists, in part at least, in the fact that the parties realize that it is up to them if the matter will be resolved this way or not. It is their dispute; they take responsibility for it and (with help from their lawyers and other experts) arrive at an acceptable resolution. But how might this dynamic change if everyone knew that someone would *decide for them* all aspects of their dispute which they had not been able to negotiate? Human nature being what it is, the parties (and their advisers) are bound to feel less of a responsibility and commitment to a negotiated resolution than if they were entering *only a mediation.* After all, why go through the rigors of negotiating every issue knowing that someone else will decide it? One answer is that the parties do not want someone else deciding dispute issues. True enough, but if that were so strong a motivating factor for the parties, why didn't they negotiate a resolution *without* the intervention of a mediator?

A second difficulty with Med/Arb is that it makes the parties very selective in proffering negotiation issues and somewhat squeamish about committing to a resolution of *any issue* before a comprehensive agreement is reached because no one can know in advance what issues will remain unresolved at the end of the Med/ portion of the Med/Arb. Therefore, each party must consider the possibility that it will compromise on a number of issues, only to *lose* on others in the /Arb segment later on. Since this is so, all parties will be understandably reluctant to commit to anything more than conditional resolution of an issue (conditional on the other issues being resolved to its satisfaction). However, on the assumption that not all issues are deciphered in the Med/ segment, what happens to all those "conditional agreements" when the Med/ segment comes to an end? Will there be agreement on them, or will the parties choose to go back to the beginning and have the /Arb segment decide everything? If the latter choice is made, the time spent in the Med/ segment has been largely wasted.

One of the strong arguments put forward in favor of Med/Arb is that since the parties have taken time and money educating the mediator about the ins and outs of their dispute, why not use that considerable expertise in *deciding* those aspects of the dispute which cannot be negotiated? Again, this argument is superficially persuasive. Alternative dispute resolution is about saving money and time, after all, but when parties choose arbitration, it is because they want a neutral to hear their cases and decide the dispute based upon evidence presented at the hearing. However, if the notion that the same person will serve as both arbitrator and mediator is accepted (these savings would not be experienced otherwise), then a potentially serious problem for the /Arb part of this exercise is presented.

Remember how the typical mediation involves private caucuses between the mediator and one party only? In those caucuses, the parties routinely share confidential information with the mediator who is committed to keeping it from the other (absent) party. So, in the Med/ portion of Med/Arb, both parties may have confided items to the mediator *on the very issues that a decision now must be made!* Keep in mind also that the matters confided by a party on these issues may not necessarily have been favorable to it. Indeed, it is equally likely that some of the weaknesses of the party's position may have been divulged. So, it is entirely possible—no, likely—that the mediator/arbitrator will be deciding issues based upon information that each party is not even aware of. Not only does this sound unattractive, it is beginning not to sound like arbitration at all.

So, in actuality, Med/Arb reduces the odds that the Med/ portion will resolve the entire dispute, while creating a high likelihood that the /Arb portion will be decided on confidential evidence, which is not what Med/Arb first appears to be.

There are ways of controlling this hybrid process so that parties may obtain the benefits of both Med/ and /Arb, but first, a piece of advice in this area:

Never agree in advance to Med/Arb with the same neutral.

Making such an agreement is not only dangerous, but also unnecessary. For example, the parties agree to a mediation with a specific neutral. Outcomes may be that the entire dispute is resolved during the mediation or that, at a point in the mediation when all parties (and the mediator) agree that nothing more can be done, some matters remain undecided. Then, a party could still offer to have the remaining issues arbitrated with the current neutral (the mediator), already having experienced his expertise during the process. Perhaps there has developed sufficient confidence in the neutral's integrity and grasp of the issues that there would be no objection in having him arbitrate the unresolved issues. So far, so good, but the opposite experience could have occurred during the mediation, in that concern increased about the neutral's intelligence or even neutrality. On that hypothesis, under normal conditions, the neutral would be dismissed. However, that option would not be available if the parties had committed to Med/Arb with this person *in advance.*

Even if the experience with the mediator is entirely positive, there remains an additional impediment to his arbitrating the unresolved issues. As honest and capable as the mediator may be, he may nonetheless be in possession of some confidential information from the other party which bears on the issues to be decided.

Here, the choice of courses of action broadens. Suppose that the only confidential information a party gave to the mediator regarding the (now) unresolved issues was entirely favorable to it. If the party takes a chance, it could agree to the neutral's assuming the role of arbitrator *without knowing if the other party had shared any confidences with him on the unresolved issues.* But, not being a gambler, the party prudently asks the mediator if he recalls *either* party giving him confidential information which might bear on the decision of the remaining unresolved issues. If the mediator appeared trustworthy enough to *consider* putting the arbitration in his hands, he can be trusted to give a reliable answer.

Suppose the mediator says, "Yes, I have received confidences which bear on the unresolved issues."[1] Now, one or a series of questions can be asked:

— Did you get such confidential information from both parties? (This is not a good choice of question, as a "no" answer by the mediator can tip the opponent off to the fact that such information was given, if not by them. That will probably end any chance that the opponent will agree to let this person /Arb.)

— Will you be able to decide the *unresolved* issues without reference to any of these confidences? (A good query, because if the answer is "no," this party probably doesn't want him to /Arb. If the neutral's response is "yes," however, further inquiry is necessary.)

— Would you feel comfortable revealing all the confidences which bear on the unresolved issues if all parties agree that you can? (This permits the mediator to make a judgment as to whether one or more of the confidences he has received is so inflammatory that the entire process may be derailed if he reveals it to the other party. However, *before* asking this question, be sure that there is no problem with the possibility that all of the party's confidences (on the unresolved issues) may be revealed. If the neutral responds that he would be comfortable making such revelations, then the next question can be directed to the other party.)

— Can we agree to give the mediator permission to reveal those confidences each party has given him which may bear on the unresolved issues? (It is advisable to be the one asking the questions, because, depending on the neutral's responses, the opponent may have been put in a difficult position (why would one party refuse permission if the other is willing to give it?), and, at a minimum, the reasonableness of the asking party's approach has been demonstrated to all concerned.)

At all events, the parties will be in a position to know *if* the mediator has heard anything privately which might affect his decision, and, unless one of them (or the mediator) is unwilling, they can learn just what that confidential information was. It would seem that most parties would not be comfortable turning a matter over for the /Arb segment if the opponent—or the mediator—were unwilling to reveal the confidences. So, assuming that the confidences are revealed by the mediator, they must be assessed in order to determine what the mediator was told by the opponent (presumably, a party would *remember* what they said). In this assessment, a party should consider if it can effectively counter what the opponent has told the mediator. If it can be done, go ahead. If it cannot or it is uncertain that it can be done, the party should consider how crucial to the (soon-to-be) arbitrator's decision the opponent's confidences will be. If it is concluded that they are likely to be crucial and the party cannot be sure of countering them, then clearly this matter should not go on to arbitration. At least not before *this* arbitrator.

There is, of course, the possibility that the mediator announces that he has received confidences from both sides but is able and willing to ignore them in deciding the /Arb portion of this process. If the mediator is experienced in serving as an adjudicative neutral (one who decides), it is probably safe to take his word for it. If he is not so experienced in adjudicative matters, it is possible for an unpracticed neutral not to really know how confidential information may affect the final decision (without intending to demean the mediator's integrity at all). So, for many of these reasons, one may wish to decline the opportunity to have the same person serve as the arbitrator who earlier acted as the mediator.

If the parties go ahead, the /Arb hearing will be somewhat different from a normal one, in that, since they have already spent some hours telling the neutral their stories, the "hearing" may be limited to a short (30-minute) presentation by each side, where certain key documents are introduced. In this setting, it is frequently the case that no witnesses are called. The principals are present, of course, so their testimony (or informal statements) can be reviewed if needed.

Another way of lessening the uncertainty of the mediator-to-arbitrator transition is to combine one of the more party-controlled versions of arbitration with mediation. The chances of the neutral rendering an improper award can be substantially reduced by combining, for instance, "baseball" or "high-low" arbitration with the mediation.

B. Arb/Med Defined and Explained

This is another combination of existing mechanisms, this time with arbitration coming first. The selected neutral conducts what would otherwise be a normal arbitration hearing, retires, and prepares a binding award. This binding award is not shared with the parties, but held in reserve as mediation immediately commences. If the mediation leads to a resolution of all issues, the "award" is simply discarded.[2] If it does not, the award is delivered and becomes binding on the parties. There exists a third possible outcome: The parties resolve *some* of their issues in the (post-arbitration hearing) mediation, but not all of them. This is where careful draftsmanship of the alternative dispute resolution agreement pays off. In the abstract, all would agree that the resolutions reached by the parties themselves should supplant decisions on the same points by the neutral. But, if no specific provision for this outcome is contained in the agreement, the neutral may be compelled to issue the *entire award* if only one issue remains undecided after the mediation segment.

There is a bias against this hybrid format because it is preferred that the parties be permitted a chance to work things out themselves before anyone conducts an evidentiary hearing and before the parties experience the costs of preparation for and attendance at that evidentiary hearing. That said, if the Arb/ part of the operation does not take too long (and therefore not cost too much), this process may have some usefulness.

Indeed, it would seem that the "ideal" dispute for an Arb/Med procedure would be one which could be arbitrated in the morning and mediated in the afternoon of the same day. With that limitation, however, only the smallest of cases (or ones where the issues had been winnowed down drastically) would qualify.

If choosing the Arb/Med process for a dispute, great care should be exercised in drafting the agreement to conduct an Arb/Med. (See Form No. 40 (Chapter 13) for a generic agreement.) As always, great care should also be taken in the selection of the neutral to preside at this Arb/Med. Obviously, the candidates for neutral should be trained and experienced as both arbitrators and mediators. It would be helpful if they were also experienced in the use of hybrid alternative dispute resolution procedures. The presiding neutral will have to be certain that this Arb/ phase of the procedure does not amount to mediation, and that it is possible that the misapplication of the /Med phase may reveal some of the contents of the Arb/ award.

There is also the question of what happens to the "award" while the /Med phase is being conducted. There is a possibility that the neutral may wish to change the award because of something heard in the mediation phase. At a minimum, the neutral should be asked to place the award in a sealed envelope, pending outcome of the mediation phase. Remember, as in Med/Arb, the neutral may hear something in the private caucuses of mediation (that the opposing party will never know about) which causes him to take a very different view of the merits of the case. So, temptation should be removed. After all, the parties contracted to have their /Arb decided on the evidence presented.

C. "Partnering": Lessons from the Construction Industry

Coming together is a beginning, keeping together is progress, working together is success.—Henry Ford

Partnering has been defined as "a long-term commitment between two or more organizations for the purpose of achieving specific business objectives by maximizing the effectiveness of each participant's resources."[3] However, a more concise and useful definition of partnering is "a team-based approach to getting things done on a construction project."[4] It is, in fact, not a dispute resolution process at all, but a dispute *prevention* process. Partnering is also another example of the old adage: Necessity is the mother of invention.

For example, the Army Corps of Engineers designs and manages some of the largest construction projects in the world. Among their ongoing projects is the control of the flow of the Mississippi River.[5] Needless to say, these mighty projects had disputes between the Corps and the various contractors, disputes among the design professionals, disputes between the Corps and various state and local government entities, disputes between the Corps and various elected officials, and even disputes among Corps people themselves. The delays and acrimony which these disputes caused were extremely costly and had a deleterious effect on project quality as well. To circumvent these problems, the Corps of Engineers developed what has come to be known as partnering. For better understanding, the project system can be broken down to its components.

Who is involved—All the stakeholders in a project should be "at the table." This includes the owner, all design professionals (architects, engineers), contractors, government agencies whose approval will be required, environmental groups, neighborhood associations, etc.

What the goal is—The goal of partnering is to build a cooperative, team-based, goal-oriented attitude among all the participants in the project. Historically, the prevailing attitudes on a construction project were that all relationships began and ended within the pages of a contract, each participant in the project took what it could and gave as little as possible to the others, whatever went wrong was someone else's problem, whatever was done or suggested be put in writing, and all other project participants were adversaries. With these attitudes, it is no wonder that projects suffered massive delays due to disputes.

So, partnering seeks to get those involved to do the following:

— Understand each other's interests and personalities;

— Recognize the mutual benefits of non-adversarial relationships;

— Discuss the various roles of the stakeholders in the project;

— Discuss potential problem areas in the project;

— Acknowledge common goals and establish objectives to attain them;

— Develop criteria for evaluating progress;

— Arrange follow-up meetings on a regular basis;

— Consider alternative dispute resolution techniques as a fail-safe mechanism to prevent delays; and

— Create a written partnering charter which summarizes goals and objectives and time milestones.

Where partnering takes place—Experience has shown that partnering works best if the initial sessions are conducted at a neutral location (not on the project site or the offices of any participant). Everyone feels freer when they are not on someone else's "turf." (Keep in mind, they all start with the *old* attitudes.)

When partnering takes place—Ideally, partnering begins before ground is broken for a project. At that time, a fresh approach is more feasible and new attitudes can be learned *before* the maelstrom of actual construction begins. Partnering can take place at any time within the life of the project, but its effectiveness diminishes with the passage of time and the reinforcement of old attitudes.

How partnering is accomplished—Partnering is a "facilitated process," meaning that the participants are assisted in identifying their goals and changing their attitudes by trained persons (usually two) who are not themselves stakeholders in the project (similar to neutrals).[6] This usually occurs over a two-day period.

Reduced to its simplest terms, partnering occurs when the major stakeholders in a project meet at a neutral location, under the guidance of at least two trained facilitators, in order to get better acquainted with one another and to share their concerns about the upcoming project, to establish mutually agreeable goals and the means to achieve them, and to design ongoing mechanisms to preserve and enhance the attitudes created at the partnering session. Put this way, it is easy to see that partnering could be applied to *any project of finite length*.

One "partnering" project involved the transformation of part of an urban "wilderness" into an mixed-use development. The developer took the partnering approach not merely with the construction phase, but at the very beginning of the project. Before final plans were drawn, the neighbors (both human and governmental), environmental groups, interested state and federal agencies, the proposed general contractor, and the developer all met at a destination resort about one hundred miles from the proposed development location. For two days (at the developer's expense), all parties were informed of the general development plan and had their reactions and comments solicited and fully discussed. The developer stressed its desire to make the development as "low-impact" as possible and to be a "good neighbor" both while the project was being developed and afterward. Each constituency voiced its concerns and proposed solutions to them. Everyone left the session feeling that they had been included, although skepticism remained in some quarters. Monthly follow-up meetings were scheduled, with one (or the other) of the original facilitators invited. The development was not problem free, but it was litigation free. To the developer, this result alone was more than worth the effort. At the ribbon-cutting ceremony, he said that "Partnering saved me at least a million dollars in litigation expense, based on our experience with other projects of this size. And, it made *supporters* of the project out of many people who would otherwise have fought it tooth and nail. Oh, and by the way, the incremental cost of the partnering to us was $82,000."

The above story is related to illustrate that the principles at work in partnering can be successfully employed elsewhere. In today's business climate, both domestic and international,[7] organizations are coming together for project-related cooperative efforts more than ever before. If an organization is about to begin a project where the cooperation of disparate entities is required, a partnering session before things get under way might be suggested. Or, as two construction experts put it: "An ounce of partnering prevents a pound of claims."[8]

D. Dispute Review Boards: More Lessons from the Construction Industry

Dispute review boards are a form of advisory alternative dispute resolution usually associated with large construction projects.[9] It is constituted as an ongoing body, whose existence extends for as long as the parties desire. The "parties" who usually appoint the dispute review board are the owner of the project and the prime contractor on it. Typically, they each appoint one member of the board, and those two appoint the third (neutral) member.[10] The functions of a dispute review board are to:

— Review the plans and specifications of the project and confer among themselves about them;

— Visit the project site on a regular, scheduled basis;

— Make themselves available for discussion of any problems; and

— Recommend immediate solutions to any problems.

The costs of the dispute review board are shared by the parties who appoint them. The board members normally have no power of decision. Nonetheless, the fact that they have been cloaked with authority by the owner and prime contractor, together with the persuasive power that their collective experience and expertise gives them adds up to a large amount of persuasive power. As with partnering, dispute review boards are truly a dispute prevention mechanism. Because they have no decision power, however, the prudent owner and contractor may wish to put an actual dispute *resolution* mechanism in place as well.

As with other alternative dispute resolution processes, flexibility is a hallmark of dispute review boards. So, the makeup of the board itself, how it operates, and what its powers are can all be tailored to the needs of the particular project. For instance, some parties believe a completely neutral dispute review board is preferable to one with two "party-appointees." They can create a board selection process which starts by seeking agreement on the identity of all three board members, and ends, if there is no agreement, in reliance on an outside agency (such as the American Arbitration Association) to appoint three board members.

Another variant on the dispute review board process which is gaining in popularity is the on-site neutral. This person, selected by the major stakeholders in the project, will usually be a trained mediator, whose job is to be present on-site a sufficient amount of time in order to help solve problems before they become full-fledged disputes. The neutral will be generally familiar with the plans and specifications of the project and will likely attend any "project meetings." The way most on-site neutrals work is to walk the project, observing the work and chatting briefly with key people (*e.g.*, job superintendent, project architect, concrete subcontractor, etc.). When the on-site neutral sees possible conflict developing, he does not try to resolve it among the personnel involved. Rather, he contacts the principals of the involved parties, explains the nature of the problem to them, and assists in reaching a solution which can then be communicated to the field. By working with the principals or their *authorized* representatives, the on-site neutral avoids conflict with the people in the field. But in order to maintain the confidence of those people in the field, the on-site neutral should only bring the problems to the principals after field personnel have had a chance to work them out themselves, and after field personnel have been advised by the neutral that he is going to bring the problem to "a higher court."

On-site neutrals definitely do not make decisions for the stakeholders, nor do they impose outcomes of their own choosing. If they are good at what they do, however, they can save enormous amounts of time and money for all concerned. As with dispute review boards, on-site neutrals can be used as a stand-alone process or in conjunction with other alternative dispute resolution mechanisms. Whatever the choices are for the project, they will all likely work better if partnering is introduced at the inception of the project.

The advantages of these kinds of project-specific alternative dispute resolution are that:

— Working relationships are maintained or enhanced;

— Project down-time is minimized or eliminated;

— Costs of protracted[11] litigation are avoided;

— The principals themselves are involved in the solution; and

— Quality of performance on the project is likely strengthened.

E. Ombudsman: Roving Mediator or Permanent Arbitrator

The word "ombudsman" comes from Swedish, where it meant a commissioned representative of the king. Currently, the word has come to mean a government official (in Sweden or New Zealand) who watches out for the interests of ordinary citizens. The use of ombudsmen has spread to North America, particularly in local governments and educational institutions. While the charter of the ombudsman will vary, there are several common characteristics:

— The ombudsman has no power to *decide* anything;

— While the ombudsman is expected to hold an organization to its own high standards, the ombudsman is, nonetheless, an *employee* of that organization;

— The ombudsman's principal job seems to be to help individuals cut through red tape and get an audience for their grievances and a prompt (though not necessarily favorable) decision; and

— The effectiveness of any ombudsman varies directly with the commitment of top management to his mission.

One of the common characteristics mentioned above was that the ombudsman does not have decision-making power, meaning that he does not have the institutional authority to resolve a grievance, but many ombudsmen and ombudswomen investigate complaints made by employees, students, or colleagues. In business, ombudsmen are generally empowered to speak with anyone in the company as part of their investigation, report to senior management concerning the complaint, and what they would recommend as a solution. So, the ombudsman resembles a neutral fact-finder despite being employed by the company.

It has probably become apparent that:

— A part-time ombudsman cannot be effective (too much opportunity for compromising the ombudsman's neutrality),

— Only a large organization can afford to sponsor a full-time ombudsman, and

— The whole process only works if it is voluntary and confidence-inspiring.

So, the threshold question for assessing whether an ombudsman might work for a business is the number of disputes per year that are likely to fall within his "jurisdiction."[12] If the numbers seem to indicate an ombudsman might be worthwhile, then this process must be assessed against other alternative dispute resolution mechanisms which might work for a business.

F. Which Procedure Belongs in a Contract

This section will not address the general questions regarding what alternative dispute resolution mechanism, if any, is chosen. The inquiry here is if one or more of the mechanisms reviewed in this chapter should be incorporated into a company's contracts. In order to do this, determine if there are any routine recurring contractual relationships. If such contracts exist, then determine the likelihood of disputes arising under them and the nature of those projected disputes. One good indicator may be the number of disputes which arose under a particular set of contracts in the past. If there were very many and they all carried high risks of alienating contract partners, a mechanism from this chapter would be worthwhile. Even if these disputes were low-risk, however, they might still be the kinds of disputes where the *transaction costs of resolving them are very high*. If the latter is true, they may be good candidates for having a particular alternative dispute resolution mechanism imposed on them by contract. Keep in mind that invoices, purchase orders, claim tickets, repair orders, etc. can all be contracts containing an enforceable ADR clause.

ENDNOTES

[1] The mediator, being no slouch himself, is not likely to reveal, unbidden, either whether both parties gave him such confidences or which of the parties did.

[2] The parties, having paid for it, would be entitled to see the "award" if they insisted on it. I always suggest that they agree in advance *not to look* at the "award" if the controversy is resolved by mediation. This agreement avoids interparty recriminations, and "buyer's remorse."

[3] Construction Industry Institute definition.

[4] Alan D. Silberman, *Implementing the Partnering Process: Guidelines for Facilitators* (American Arbitration Association, 1993), p. 3.

[5] John McPhee, *The Control of Nature* (Farrar, Straus and Giroux: 1989), pp. 3-92.

[6] Depending on how elaborate a partnering process is contemplated, the facilitators may have to be skilled in (1) conflict management training, (2) communications skills development, (3) drafting of goals statements, (4) personality testing, and (5) dispute resolution program design.

[7] A particularly fruitful use of partnering has been in the area of international projects (construction and otherwise). The "normal" differences expected in such projects are exacerbated by the cultural and language differences among the parties. So, getting to know the other stakeholders and establishing common goals with them before the project starts can pay handsome dividends.

[8] Keith W. Hunter and Jim Hoenig, "Construction Claims Management Through Partnering," (Private monograph, 1994), p. 3.

[9] As with partnering, there is no reason why the dispute review board concept cannot be adapted to any kind of project.

[10] There may be other requirements for serving on a dispute review board. For instance, many board members are required to remain free of any affiliation with any of the parties for the duration of the project and sometimes required that dispute review board members be familiar with the specific type of project involved.

[11] Construction disputes usually have three qualities which make them take longer and cost more than other disputes:

(a) They are fact-intensive, *i.e.,* they involve perhaps thousands of individual actions taken by dozens of different parties,

(b) They involve multiple parties, each of whom may seek coverage from one of many insurance carriers, and

(c) The disputes usually revolve around technical issues, which not only take a long time to present to a decision-maker, but also require the hiring and preparation of expensive experts.

[12] Whatever that jurisdiction is will ultimately be decided by senior management. When the ombudsman's charter is fixed, it should be as widely disseminated within the organization as possible.

IMPROVING BUSINESS RELATIONS & ADR

There is nothing to restrain use of that privilege . . . to get away from judges who are considered to be unsympathetic, and to get before those who are considered more favorable; to get away from juries thought to be small-minded in the matter of verdicts and to get to those thought to be generous; to escape courts whose procedures are burdensome . . . to seek out courts whose procedures make the going easy.
—Mr. Justice Robert H. Jackson[1]

In most circumstances, alternative dispute resolution is a good idea, and if true, then it would seem to follow that alternative dispute resolution can play a positive role in business relations. Not only is ADR (properly done) not something needing apology, it is a positive benefit to all who are involved, such as a business's three most important constituencies: its suppliers, its customers, and, by no means least, its employees.

A. Suppliers

Many businesses depend heavily on their suppliers. With recent innovations in manufacturing processes, *e.g.,* just-in-time components inventory, and the trend toward "out sourcing," that dependency has deepened. Similarly, other organizations, such as universities, rely heavily on suppliers of food services, computer repairs, and the like, and many large nonprofit organizations are similarly situated. Although large manufacturing companies may be able to "put the squeeze on" suppliers for lower prices and quicker delivery times, when the "squeezing" is over, their symbiotic relationship continues. Perhaps the worst case of a "supplier-dependent" business occurs in the defense industry, where some items are "sole-sourced," meaning that there is only one supplier available. But whether an organization has one supplier or ten for a needed product or service, the relationship remains an important one.

1. Preserving the Relationship

Just as a business may be dependent on a supplier to put their product together (or keep their service going), a supplier is dependent on business. Large and small customers are all important to its business as well. From this state of affairs, it is easy to conclude that a rupture in the relationship is in no one's long-term interests. However, suppliers sometimes deliver items that do not meet specifications or fail to deliver when something is needed. What is one to do? Well, the first step would seem to be getting what is needed as soon as possible, and ADR can help. Many dispute resolutions clauses between organizations with ongoing relationships contain a provision that performance of the contract *will continue* despite the pendency of a dispute. This may seem to detract from any leverage a business might otherwise have with the supplier, but the clause may be drafted in such a way that both are deprived of "leverage" regarding the transaction in dispute. For example, a large manufacturer settled on the following policy: if any supplier delivered goods that did not meet specifications or delivered them more than 12 hours (this is a time-critical business) after they were promised, then the manufacturer could either accept or reject what was delivered. If it accepted the goods, then it was obligated to deposit the full amount of the contract price in an "escrow account" with a local bank, and fax a copy of the deposit slip to the supplier. The manufacturer also had a NEMA (NEgotiation/Mediation/Arbitration) clause in all its contracts. In the contracts with suppliers, however, the time period available for each step of the NEMA was drastically shortened so that the parties would have to negotiate about the dispute "immediately," and, if a resolution was not reached "in 48 hours," the parties could (at the election of either one) go to mediation or straight into arbitration. This "fork-in-the-road" provision allowed either party to jump to arbitration if it concluded that either the negotiations would not be aided by the participation of a trained, neutral third party or the size of the dispute was such that the expense and time of mediation were not warranted. (Arbitration, after all, guarantees a resolution; mediation does not.)

This program has been in place for about three years, and *both* the supplier and the manufacturer are happy with it. As the president of the supplying company said, "The ADR program permits us to isolate a dispute, and go on about our business. It's a little like a quarantine for the dispute. It's put away until it gets better, and we don't let it infect everything else."

2. "Selling" ADR

At first glance, "selling" ADR to a supplier may seem difficult. After all, business people can sometimes be as skeptical as lawyers. So, the concern may surface that if a business perceives ADR as a benefit, it must be a burden to the supplier. One way of eliminating problems of suspicion regarding motivation is to *include the supplier* in the process of designing the ADR program. These negotiations will be like any others: one doesn't know in advance how things will turn out, but one can always refuse to agree to a plan that isn't fair (to both parties). If negotiations on ADR take place at the outset of a relationship, they can reveal much about the general business "style" of the (prospective) supplier. The real "clincher," however, is likely to be the fact that ADR will preserve the business relationship while getting the dispute resolved fairly and quickly.

3. Suppliers Like to Save Money, Too

One of the perennial problems of suppliers is cash flow. Many of them count on prompt payment so that they can pay their employees (and, perhaps, their suppliers). In addition, money spent on dispute resolution frequently comes right off their bottom line. So, any process that will speed payment (if deserved), reduce dispute resolution costs, and preserve the relationship should be very attractive. As with all other ADR programs, the dispute resolution process (particularly the part where third parties do the deciding) should be scrupulously fair. If it is, there should be no reason why every supplier would not want to sign on.

4. Power Projection

Implicit in any suggestion of an ADR program is the recognition that there may be disputes. Most business people understand this as a likelihood in any event, but the fact that a business would propose an ADR program to a supplier says some other things about it as well, such as that it recognizes the fact that there may be disputes as a normal part of a business relationship. Secondly, willingness to enter into an ADR program (where issues will be resolved faster than in court) sends the message of confidence in a business's ability to live up to its agreements. Finally, in suggesting ADR before a dispute arises, a supplier may infer that they are probably dealing with a fair person.

B. Customers

The wisdom of setting up an ADR program with customers will depend, to a large extent, on what the business does. If individual transactions with customers are for small amounts of money and tend to be one-time transactions, an ADR program might not be necessary. If, on the other hand,

— transactions with customers tend to be for large amounts of money;

— the items sold to customers carry the risk of great liability;

— customers are (or are hoped to be) repeaters who have a long relationship with an organization;

— the transaction costs of resolving disputes with customers may be prohibitive; or

— a small number of disputes with customers could bring ruinous publicity, then ADR should be seriously considered.

1. Proceed with Caution

Depending on who the customers are, they may not expect to *have* any disputes with a corporation. This is the attitude of most purchasers of consumable goods, for example, who want to buy a product, take it home with them, and consume it without any difficulties. Such a group might be put off if forced to think about the possibility of having a dispute with the producer (or seller) of these goods. Buyers of durable goods, however, expect the manufacturer to stand behind the product (guarantee) for a considerable period of time. To them, the *possibility* of a dispute probably already exists. If that is so, then proposing a fair, cheap, and quick way to resolve such disputes might give one a competitive advantage. Purchasers of systems may be on the opposite extreme from buyers of consumable goods. The former anticipate a long relationship with the seller, which will include some disputes, and also might look favorably on an ADR program which dealt with such disputes equitably and quickly. Whatever the customer profile, proceed with caution. Too much emphasis on the possibility of future disputes may send them packing to a competitor.

2. ADR as an Extra Service

No one is better equipped to be the Complaint Department than the owner or CEO of a business. Sadly, many of them cannot take the time to function in this capacity, for it is usually only they who can both project and embody the "corporate culture." If left to the rest of the employees, the Complaint Department (or its equivalent) must be given clear and easy-to-understand orders. The Complaint Department, after all, is where most disputes *begin*. In a perfect world, it would also be where most disputes end. But how can a business be structured so that no disputes emerge unresolved from the Complaint Department? One excellent example of a company which rarely has disputes with its customers is the Nordstrom department store chain. The reason is simple: everything is returnable. A Nordstrom executive proudly related the following story: An elderly lady came up to a sales clerk on the main floor of a Nordstrom's store in a large urban shopping mall. She complained that two steel-belted radial tires which she had bought at Nordstrom's were giving her "a terrible ride." She said she didn't know whether it was because they didn't fit or not, but she wanted to return them. The sales clerk, a Nordstrom veteran, asked her if she had charged the tires on her Nordstrom account. She said she had. "Give me just a moment, ma'am," the clerk said, "while I find something to carry those tires back with, and I'll go with you to your car and get them." The clerk reappeared in a few minutes and off the two went. He removed the tires from her trunk, thanked her for letting Nordstrom's know that she was not satisfied, and asked her if she remembered what she had paid for the tires. The lady mentioned a figure, and the clerk said, "I'll see that the amount is credited to your account as soon as I get back to the store." The lady was so happy with the way she was treated that she wrote a letter commending the clerk.

If this sounds like fairly normal customer service and return policy, reconsider this narrative with the added piece of information that Nordstrom's doesn't sell tires, and they never have.

That's one way of keeping customers happy, but it can be an expensive one. What about designating a sort-of ombudsman, instead? If in retail, this person could roam the premises (or be assigned a place in full view of the customers) helping to resolve any disputes which might arise. With some training and some common sense, such a person could be providing an extra service to customers. More importantly, that person would be *perceived as providing an extra service by the customers themselves.* Depending on the line of business, similar use could be made of a mediation program, or even arbitration.

3. Drafting Clauses for Customers

Drafting ADR clauses which cover disputes with customers is like rock-climbing: a worthwhile activity about which one must be exceedingly careful. The next chapter gives general guidance about when to choose alternative dispute resolution and provides a number of forms with commentary. Suffice it to say here that there are several special implications to the fact that *this* ADR clause is going to be for a customer. The obvious ones have been discussed immediately above; an implication not so obvious is that a business may have to be very sure that the customer knows about this ADR program when a dispute arises and his participation becomes necessary. Courts always look disapprovingly on contracts where one party has all the bargaining power and dictates all the terms of the contract (or relationship), and justly so, since the essence of contract is voluntary agreement, and it's hard to agree voluntarily when there is no choice. However, there is another situation when courts are reluctant to find agreement, and that is where one party does not know of the contractual provision. Indeed, some legislatures have felt strongly enough about this issue to require that arbitration clauses in certain contracts be in no less than a certain size type and be introduced with statutorily mandated language.[2] On the other hand, Bank of America recently had a trial court uphold its unilateral modification of relationships with customers by putting an arbitration notice in with their monthly statements. This may be legal, but could also be viewed as sneaky, since most banks only include fliers for insurance. The point is that no one needs to be ashamed of arbitration. Make *sure* that customers know!

So, when putting together an ADR clause, particularly one where arbitration is involved, make sure that the clause is placed so that the customer cannot avoid seeing it. Otherwise, there may be a fight with the customer about whether the dispute is or is not going to be arbitrated, and then start through the court system. This is not the idea of ADR, but that customer is probably lost, anyway.

C. Employees

For I submit that it is only by trial and error, by insistent scrutiny and readiness to reexamine presently accredited conclusions, that we have risen . . . from our brutish ancestors . . . .—Learned Hand[3]

As mentioned in the introduction, the relations between labor and management in a collective bargaining (union) setting are beyond the scope of this book. Union membership being at a modern low point still leaves a great majority of the work force to talk about. Alternative dispute resolution in the employment setting, however, is a somewhat perilous topic. Professor Laura Nader, University of California (Berkeley) anthropologist, recently said:

> Alternative dispute resolution is basically an attempt to destroy the rights movements of the 1960s: the civil-rights movement, the women's movement, the consumer movement. I've analyzed the development of ADR, particularly during the tenure of former Chief Justice Warren Burger. It's a pacification plan that has managed to suck in some very nice people. . . . In my anthropology research, I have found that alternative dispute resolution techniques were used by colonial powers from the fifteenth century to pacify natives, to quiet rights movements, and currently, to manage trade disputes through treaties like NAFTA and GATT.[4]

It should be noted that Professor Nader's comments were directed at *mandatory* alternative dispute resolution. However, that is exactly the suggestion: that employers establish an alternative dispute resolution program of which all employees (as well as the employer itself) will be the beneficiaries (or, as Prof. Nader would have it, the victims).

1. ADR as an Employee Benefit

In dealing with ADR for customers above, those businesses whose customers were one-timers are distinguished from those who had longer, repeat relationships with their customers. The latter seemed more likely to benefit from an ADR program. On that point, who has (one hopes) a more long-term association with any organization than its employees? If ADR is good for customer and supplier relations, then why not employee relations? Many companies are considering adopting ADR programs for their employees, and some already have. Out of about fifteen of those programs, here are some generalizations about those that are successful.

A working definition of a "successful" employer/employee ADR program, distilled from conversations with workers and managers at places where the program *seems* to thrive, is this:

— The program must be fair to all parties in any dispute;

— The program must be *perceived* to be fair by a substantial majority of workers and managers;

— The program must supplement (not replace) normal communication as a method of settling workplace difficulties;

— Outcomes unfavorable to the employer must be strictly adhered to;

— The program must save *all* participants time and money; and

— *All* participants should bear some share of the cost of the program.

2. ADR as Part of the Human Resources Function

These qualities are easier to articulate than achieve. For example, one financial services company employee whose company recently implemented an ADR program remarked: "When you get through the negotiation and mediation and finally get someone who is going to decide something, guess who that someone is? A senior HR (human resources) person whose check the company signs. How long do you think she is going to last if she keeps finding in favor of the employee?" If all of his fellow employees shared this view, the program would be a dismal failure. Sadly, many of them did. The lesson is a simple one: Where adjudicative methods of ADR (arbitration, usually) are used, the neutral must be—and be *seen* to be—independent of both employer and employees.

This is not to say that HR personnel (or other trained company employees) cannot have an appropriate and productive role in an employee ADR program, only that such persons (or anyone else "beholden" to management or workers) should not be the neutral who *decides* disputes. Many HR people are already excellent amateur negotiators and mediators; more could be trained to be. It is also appropriate that employees begin their access to the ADR program through the HR department, because ADR is an employee benefit. It is also the case that HR people frequently know what bothers the employees with more precision than senior management may. That is a reason to have HR people involved in the *design* of any employee ADR program, as well as its implementation.

3. Problems with ADR and Union Employees

Despite the disclaimer regarding ADR in a collective bargaining setting, a bit of guidance is helpful in this area. First of all, it is the rare collective bargaining agreement which would permit the employer to impose an ADR program unilaterally, so the union must be consulted. Before abandoning the project as hopeless, however, there are some home truths about unions to keep in mind. Most unions are:

— familiar with negotiating as a way to resolve disputes;

— familiar with mediation as a way to settle disputes which can't be concluded by negotiation;

— familiar with arbitration as a means of deciding disputes which can't be determined by negotiation or mediation;

— familiar with grievance procedures which may resemble mediation and arbitration;

— interested in having their members treated fairly; and

— pleased to be able to present their members with a new employee benefit.

So, in the abstract at least, unions should be knowledgeable partners in the design and implementation of employee ADR programs. In the concrete, however, unions may be more skeptical of management's motivations. However, employers should not reject the possibility that a union might be a willing and helpful partner in the development of an ADR program for all employees (unionized or not).

4. Timing and Applicability of ADR Programs

Because the relationship between employers and workers has been such a tumultuous one, much law has grown up around it, some of it legislative (federal and state) and some of it case law (likewise). This fact makes the process of designing and implementing an employee ADR plan more complicated than doing so in other contexts. So, the advice about consulting an ADR expert if an ADR program is wanted is applicable with equal (or greater) vigor here. There are many problems which are peculiar to a particular locale or industry, but there are two specific problems, however, which seem to be everywhere.

a. Unilateral implementation

Some states look on the (non-union) employer/employee relationship as a matter of contract, and some do not. Whatever the view in your locale, there may still be a problem associated with the employer imposing an ADR system for employees without their consent. The obvious answer is to *get* the employees' consent, but in a large, non-union organization setting, that task is time-consuming, expensive, and perhaps impossible. Another option is to make the ADR program a voluntary one, which employees may opt into if they wish. This option tends to defeat the purpose of an ADR plan, however, since the cost/ time savings cannot be assured in disputes with all employees, and, from the employees' standpoint, different employees are being treated differently. The fact that some employees have *chosen* to be treated differently may not lessen employee discontent. So, as a practical matter, if an employer (or, at least, one with more than 25 employees) wants to have an employee ADR program, it will have to just do it. Before installing such a program, however, please consult an expert to make sure that it is being done in a legally acceptable way.

b. New hires only?

Even if local law (or other contracts) prevent an employer from unilaterally implementing an ADR plan for the entire body of employees, such a plan can still be executed. The process will be a gradual one, but, if properly planned, presented, and implemented, it will ultimately secure the entire work force. Step One is always to construct a fair plan with employee input if possible. Step Two, in these circumstances, is to activate the ADR plan exclusively with new hires. It can become, if necessary, a condition of their employment. Step Three is to make the ADR plan available to existing employees as a voluntary employee benefit. Over time, of course, the existing employees will leave, retire, or otherwise become casualties of attrition, and so, in a few hundred years, all employees will be part of the program. There is hope between now and then, however. If the program is well designed and executed, many people who were employed before its introduction *will join voluntarily.*

5. Educating Employees Before Implementation

As previously mentioned, the "ideal" employee ADR plan will be one which was designed with employee input. Even if that ideal cannot be achieved and unilateral implementation is perfectly legal, it is still good business to educate employees about alternative dispute resolution in general, and their plan in particular, well before implementation begins. The work force may be happy, well-paid, respected, valued, and employees may even trust management. Nonetheless, there will always be someone who believes that management is hatching some new plot to victimize the workers. Sometimes this person is simply acting on experience or else is a chronic malcontent. Whatever the motives, such activities must be neutralized before they begin. In order to keep the trust of the majority of employees, it is important to let them know what's going on.

Education about alternative dispute resolution can take many forms. In some settings, an ADR consultant explains the virtues of ADR generally to the employees, while senior management explains the details of the company's new ADR plan. At other times, employees from other companies which have a successful ADR program may be invited to meet with the employees and management of a company which is about to implement a new plan. In yet other situations, HR and other management personnel have done the entire "education" job, with some outside help and a videotape or two. The means can be tailored to any employment setting, but the main idea is that the education process be completed *before* implementation. That is the time of maximum benefit.

As mentioned above, *all* participants should bear some share of the cost of the program. On this point, the need for fair employee cost-sharing is crucial. First of all, it gives employees a stake in the working of the program that they would not have otherwise. Strictly from a management point of view, requiring employeesto bear some share of the program's costs is a simple way to prevent the ADR system from being abused. The chronic malcontents will probably not invoke the program if it will cost them something to do so. On the other hand, making the program prohibitively expensive for employees is the same as not having a program. The solution adopted by most companies is to charge an employee a slightly more-than-nominal amount as a share of the process, with the employer picking up the balance. Keep in mind, of course, that these cost factors would all have been fully explored *before the plan was announced or implemented.*

ENDNOTES

[1] Quoted in Glendon Schubert, *Dispassionate Justice: A Synthesis of the Judicial Opinions of Robert H. Jackson* (Bobs Merrill, 1969), p. 276, from Justice Jackson's concurring opinion in *Miles v. Illinois Central Railroad,* 315 U.S. 698, 705 (1942).

[2] California law requires that all residential real estate contracts which contain provisions for binding arbitration of any dispute between the principals in the transaction, shall have that provision clearly titled "ARBITRATION OF DISPUTES" and shall be printed in not less than "8 point bold type or in contrasting red in at least 8 point type." Immediately before or preceding the space where parties indicate their assent to the arbitration provision shall the following appear:

"NOTICE: BY INITIALING IN TH[IS] SPACE [] YOU ARE AGREEING TO HAVE ANY DISPUTE ARISING OUT OF THE MATTERS INCLUDED IN THE "ARBITRATION OF DISPUTES" PROVISION DECIDED BY NEUTRAL ARBITRATION AS PROVIDED BY CALIFORNIA LAW AND YOU ARE GIVING UP ANY RIGHTS YOU MIGHT POSSESS TO HAVE THE DISPUTE LITIGATED IN A COURT OR JURY TRIAL. BY INITIALING IN THE SPACE BELOW YOU ARE GIVING UP YOUR JUDICIAL RIGHTS TO DISCOVERY AND APPEAL, UNLESS THOSE RIGHTS ARE SPECIFICALLY INCLUDED IN THE ARBITRATION OF DISPUTES PROVISION . . . ."

If the above provision is included in a printed contract it must appear in capital letters and be printed in at least 10-point bold type or in contrasting red print in at least 8-point bold type.

[3] From *A Fanfare for Prometheus,* collected in: Dilliard, Irving (ed.), *The Spirit of Liberty: Papers and Addresses of Learned Hand* (Alfred A. Knopf, 1959), p. 222.

[4] Nina Schuyler (mod.), "Coercive Harmony," *California Lawyer,* May 1995, pp. 37-39. (Yes, Professor Nader is Ralph Nader's sister.)

Chapter 13

SELECTING AN ADR PROGRAM

Life is the art of drawing sufficient conclusions from insufficient premises.—Samuel Butler

Aristotle could have avoided the mistake of thinking that women have fewer teeth than men by the simple device of asking Mrs. Aristotle to open her mouth.—Bertrand Russell

Until now, this book has analyzed the reasons why traditional court litigation is normally an unattractive choice for dispute resolution and introduced ADR, explaining its general approach to resolving disputes, along with detailed examination of the major mechanisms of which it consists. However, considering whether to adopt an ADR plan is a lot like considering funeral arrangements in advance. The latter is an inevitable need best negotiated before the fact, so it makes good sense to buy such a plan. It is much the same with alternative dispute resolution. Disputes are a part of business and the time during a dispute is the worst time to try to choose a way of resolving it, not least because that choice will have to include the agreement of the party who is *already in dispute.* So, a dispute resolution program needs to be planned *before* disputes arise.

This chapter contains information basic to:

— Examining the question of whether alternative dispute resolution is an appropriate choice for a business, and

— Beginning to choose among a wide range of alternative dispute resolution clauses.

The alert reader may have noticed some murky language immediately above. The phrases "examining the question" and "beginning to choose among" are not models of crystalline clarity. Unfortunately, it is impossible to write a book which (a) contains a foolproof formula for deciding if alternative dispute resolution is applicable to a particular situation and (b) permits clear choices of alternative dispute resolution clauses for each situation. However, this chapter attempts to detail the basic considerations when determining if alternative dispute resolution is appropriate. Further, it provides samples of clauses which can be used to memorialize all the most common ADR choices. What it cannot do, however, is to give advice specific to dealing with a unique situation. An appropriate alternative dispute resolution choice cannot be made with the tools given in this book *alone.* When making a decision to implement ADR in a business and how to do so, *a professional should be consulted.*

However, the information contained in this chapter alone will save the purchaser of this book more than ten times its price. This is so, because an organization's knowledge about ADR is generally so slight that it can take several hours (at $400 to $500 per hour) to explain what ADR is. Similarly, the back end of the consultation frequently has to start from ground zero in assessing the choice of clauses in implementing an ADR plan. So, a sophisticated consumer, coming to the consultation process with the information in this book, can save from $750 to $5,000, guaranteed.

A. Planning for ADR Before Disputes Arise

Later on in this chapter, a number of clauses will be offered for possible use *after* a dispute which might benefit from alternative dispute resolution has arisen. However, the time when disputes are most easily controlled is before they begin.

B. Choosing an ADR Program for an Organization

One fact about ADR clauses that cannot be overemphasized is that they almost always are negotiated in connection with a larger agreement which has a different subject matter. It can be a sale, a distributorship agreement, a contract for professional services, a long-term supplier-manufacturer arrangement, a software design contract, a movie deal, or a contract with an airline to send relief supplies to a war-torn country. Whatever it is, the *main* reason why it is important to obtain this contract must be kept in sight.

There are circumstances, however, in which an ADR program can be introduced outside the context of contractual negotiation about something else, for instance, the banking industry. In the '80s, banks felt the impact of some enormous jury verdicts in cases brought on a "lender liability" theory. They counselled with their lawyers (inside and outside the companies), and several of them came up with similar ideas of instituting companywide ADR programs, the centerpiece of which would be quick, inexpensive arbitration. It was also thought that these arbitrations would lessen the chances of huge awards similar to the ones juries had been rendering. So, the banks did their homework. They realized that any adjudicative ADR program would only withstand court scrutiny (and the scrutiny of their customers) if it was fundamentally fair and not tilted in the banks' favor. The problem became apparent then. How would these institutions, who numbered their customers in the hundreds of thousands, initiate their programs? Surely, they couldn't afford to have the general counsel speak to every customer. On the other hand, if they applied the program only to new customers, most of its value would be lost. Indeed, their efforts over the past few years had been pointed toward maintaining customer loyalty. So, just applying ADR to new customers might literally take forever.

The magical (so far[1]) solution came from another element of the banks' business: credit cards. For years, banks and other credit card issuers have been able to modify the rules under which they contract with their customers quite simply. They merely mail out the modifications or new rules with the customer's monthly statement, and give the customer notice that using the credit card again after receiving this notice would constitute agreement to the new or modified terms.[2] So, banks that wanted to implement their new alternative dispute resolution programs inserted a notice with the mailed-out account statements (large borrowers' accounts were more complex). One of the architects of the Bank of America's program pronounced it a great success. (Because of the privacy of these arbitrations, the customers could not be contacted.) He said that while the Bank's "won-lost" record was no better than at the courthouse, both the Bank and its customers had experienced the cost and time savings of the Bank's arbitration program. He also mentioned an unanticipated benefit of fewer claims being made against the Bank, because customers and staff both know that claims will be resolved quickly and relatively cheaply. So, on the customer side, frivolous claims disappear. On the staff side, employees try harder to resolve problems that customers have by negotiation, which is just what was wanted, anyhow. So, even if a company has thousands of customers or thousands of *suppliers,* there is still a way to implement an ADR program with them.

Things become confused where ADR programs for *employees* are concerned. The law in many states views the conditions of employment as a contract between the employer and the employee. On this analysis, those conditions of employment should not be changed without the consent of both parties. So, many large employers, although they are committed to ADR and want to offer it as an employee benefit, have been advised by their lawyers that they may only introduce mandatory ADR with new hires. In conversation, an aerospace executive said that they started their arbitration program with their newly hired employees about eighteen months ago. Since then, more than 40 percent of their *existing* employees joined up on their own because they were confident that it would work for them, and obviously, it is.

When progressing through this chapter, remember these two things:

1. Whenever a transaction or event is controlled in advance, there also exists the opportunity to control what will happen if things do not go as expected.

2. The same principles which apply to the selection of predispute ADR mechanisms also apply to already-existing disputes. The main difference is that there is more concrete information to work with in the latter situation.

1. Assessing Dispute Resolution Goals

To reiterate:

— Choosing to use an ADR program is not simply choosing to avoid litigation, but agreeing to something else which has characteristics and problems of its own;

— Choosing to use an ADR program allows for many alternative mechanisms to select from and also the possibilities of combining some mechanisms, and/or selecting one for a certain type of dispute, another for another type;

— The selection of an ADR program or process also selects a dispute prevention technique; and

— Since flexibility is the hallmark of every ADR mechanism, flexibility should be built into a program as well.

As with any other inquiry, the inquiry into whether to use ADR and, if so, how to use it should begin with goal assessment. In an excellent article, *Fitting the Forum to the Fuss,*[3] the authors have identified eight separate, unranked goals, listed below, that parties to a dispute normally have. Indeed, it is crucial to realize that selected goals may very well change during the course of a dispute. The classic goals of dispute resolution are:

1. Achieving the best result;
2. Maintaining privacy;
3. Obtaining a speedy resolution;
4. Controlling costs;
5. Securing (or avoiding) a legal precedent;
6. Maintaining valued relationships;
7. Justifying (vindicating) a position; and
8. Obtaining the view of a neutral person.

As can easily be seen, many of these dispute resolution goals would not be bad goals in a workplace, generally. The trick, however, is in *applying* this goal-identification work to an organization.[4]

The first step toward integrating chosen goals with ADR is in identifying the types of probable disputes. These may turn out to be the same sorts of disputes as in the past, but do not just assume that result. A local government official recently said, "For years, the most frequent dispute we would have would be a slip-and-fall claim. Somebody would fall down somewhere, and, sure enough, we'd be sued. But, lately, worker disability claims top the list. You figure it out." So, as the mutual funds salespeople say, "Past performance does not necessarily indicate future results."

2. Organizational Dispute Resolution Costs

Suppose a business may have either few or no disputes. If that's the case, it may not feel the need even to consider an ADR program. But is that wise?

First of all, some questions: How much did litigation cost the company last year and for each of the last five years? If the answer to either question is anything other than too much, ADR probably can't save the business very much money, at least, not the out-of-pocket kind. But, how many hours were spent on court litigation by people other than counsel? Those employees all cost money every time they spend one hour on something other than their normal responsibilities, and it doesn't matter if the organization is a for-profit business or not. The executive director of a renowned charitable organization said (some years ago), "I have just been through my annual review with the staff, and I discovered that we are producing more billable hours than a law firm." It seems that the charity had been sued by a former employee for religious discrimination. In defending the lawsuit, which the charity's board had determined to be frivolous, the executive director and his staff had logged 582 hours the previous year. "I get mad as hell," he said, "every time I think of the impact that time would have had if we could have spent it on our programs."[5]

Litigation has many costs, some of which are out-of-pocket and others, less visible, which cost the organization by diverting its talent from its main enterprise. Even if these economic costs are manageable, the user-friendly qualities of ADR may persuade a business to adopt a program, anyway. Every other person or organization is likely to save substantial sums by instituting some form of alternative dispute resolution.

3. Assessing Organizational ADR Needs

The following list of questions, in the approximate order that they should be asked, is designed to elicit information which will make it possible to determine if an ADR program is likely to be beneficial to a business (or nonprofit or government organization). Many of these questions will also extract data which will help decide what form or forms of alternative dispute resolution may be right for a corporation. Please bear in mind, however, that it is impossible to speculate on all the questions which might pertain to a specific business and its use of alternative dispute resolution. So, an important component of this exercise will be the questions generated while answering the ones listed, and, of course, the answers to those questions.

— Is the inclusion of an ADR program likely to enhance or detract from the chances of making this deal (for specific clauses in particular agreements)?

— What kinds of disputes are likely to occur, and with what frequency?

— Is the ADR mechanism chosen likely to fit a specific budget?

— Will preliminary relief (injunction, attachment, etc.) be required?

— Is the company more likely to be a claimant (plaintiff) or a respondent (defendant) if a dispute arises?

— Does it matter *where* the ADR mechanism takes place?

— Should provision be made for "discovery" (prehearing production of documents and taking of depositions)? If so, what forms? Should discretion be given to the neutral as to whether and how much discovery may be had?

— Does it matter which law applies?

— Will confidentiality be affected by choice of law?

— Is there a reason *not* to have a "self-executing" clause for any adjudicative ADR mechanism?

— Does it matter how the costs are advanced/allocated?

— Does it matter whether the neutral(s) have a particular expertise or experience, *e.g.,* architecture in a construction dispute?

— Does it matter (other than in the cost and difficulty of scheduling) how many neutrals there are?

— Should the neutral(s) be chosen from a particular group (*e.g.,* members of the bar or the Supreme Court)?

— Should an institutional provider, *e.g.,* American Arbitration Association, etc., be chosen to make an adjudicative ADR clause "self-executing" (see Chapter 7) or because of its rules, or its panel of neutrals?

— Is there some reason why alternative dispute resolution (or a particular ADR mechanism) is *not* a good idea?

— Should the prevailing party be entitled to collect—or the arbitrator be empowered to award—attorney fees? Costs? Which costs?

— If an adjudicative mechanism is chosen, should a detailed opinion be required?

— If a particular neutral is agreed on in advance, what happens if he/she is unavailable when needed?

— If ADR is desirable, how can draftsmanship (and other actions) educate and persuade the other party to see that it is?

— Are any of the parties nationals of other countries?

— Is the other (foreign) party more familiar (or comfortable) with the UNCITRAL rules or other international institution or rules, *e.g.*, International Chamber of Commerce, Paris?

— If the company arbitrates and wins, where would the award most likely need to be enforced? If outside the United States, is the country a signatory to either the 1958 U.N. Convention on the Recognition and Enforcement of Foreign Arbitral Awards (the "New York Convention") or the Inter-American Convention on International Commercial Arbitration?

— Does it matter which *language* the ADR mechanism is conducted in?

— Does the *citizenship* of the neutral matter?

— Does counsel or the company understand what they are getting into, how long it will take, and how much it will cost?

— If arbitration is chosen, is everyone aware that there is normally no right of appeal?

— If confidentiality is desired, has it been provided for?

— Will the ADR mechanisms chosen help maintain those business relationships desirable to keep?

— Are the ADR terms suggested so onerous to an opponent and relative bargaining power so much greater that a court may later void the result?

a. Predispute situations

The clauses in this section are suggested for use as part of a larger agreement, *before* any disputes have arisen. The clauses are deliberately "bare bones," because (1) the simplest possible ADR clauses should be used and (2) many of the clauses may be combined with others if the situation warrants. Before using these clauses, satisfactory answers to all the questions listed above should have been given, and any additional questions that answers may give rise to. And, there should be some expert advice on a specific situation.

Wherever the name of an institutional provider of ADR services is appropriate in the following forms, the American Arbitration Association (AAA) has been used for several reasons:

— AAA is, at age 70, by far the most experienced provider of ADR services.

— AAA has a time-tested and court-tested set of rules, the invocation of which can make ADR clauses "self-executing."

— AAA maintains panels of neutrals whose knowledge is broadly based, including industry experts as well as lawyers and retired judges.

— AAA's "prices" (for the administration of the ADR mechanisms; neutrals will charge separately by the hour) are reasonable.

If another ADR provider is selected, be certain that it has a fully articulated set of procedural rules, particularly if arbitration is one of the ADR choices. Whatever ADR mechanism is adopted, be sure the provider knows how to administer it and has neutrals who are qualified to do so. If it cannot be ascertained that the provider has qualified neutrals on its own panels, make sure that neutrals other than the provider's can be utilized in conjunction with the provider's administration and rules. In fact, any provider that tries to force the use of its own neutrals should be avoided. Certainly, every ADR provider should be proud of its panel of neutrals and recommend them highly, but when it stipulates that one of its neutrals must be employed in order to utilize its administrative services, it is time to move on to the next provider.

FORM NO. 1

CORRESPONDENCE—NEGOTIATION—MEDIATION— ARBITRATION

- Any party may initiate negotiation proceedings by writing a certified or registered letter to the other party setting forth the particulars of the dispute, the term(s) of the contract that are involved and a suggested resolution of the problem.

- The recipient of the letter shall respond within ten (10) days to the proposed solution. The recipient shall either agree to the proposed solution or explain any disagreement.

- If correspondence does not resolve the dispute, the authors of the letters or their representatives shall meet on at least one occasion and attempt to resolve the matter. The meeting should be at a place selected by the parties, or if they cannot agree, then at the nearest office of the American Arbitration Association.

- If meeting(s) do not produce a resolution within ten (10) days, [current CEO of one party] and [current CEO of the other party] or their successors will meet and confer in person, in a good-faith attempt to resolve the matter.

- If this step does not produce resolution within ten (10) days of the first meeting, the parties agree to commence mediation immediately, pursuant to the applicable Rules of the American Arbitration Association.

- If mediation does not produce resolution within thirty (30) days of the first mediation session, the parties agree to submit their disagreement(s) forthwith to final, binding arbitration pursuant to the applicable Rules of the American Arbitration Association. Judgment upon the award rendered by the arbitrator may be entered in any court having jurisdiction to do so.

[**Comment:** Correspondence frequently tends to shed more heat than light on a dispute. This clause is usually useful only where the disputes are likely to be technical in nature and soluble by scientific/engineering inquiry. Otherwise, going straight into negotiation by principals or mediation will be more likely to lead to resolution.]

FORM NO. 2

NEGOTIATION—MEDIATION—ARBITRATION
(NeMA Clause)

- The parties will attempt in good faith to resolve any disagreement or claim relating to this Agreement by prompt negotiations between [principals, senior executives, . . .] of the parties who have authority to settle the disagreement.

- If this step does not produce resolution within ten (10) days of the first meeting, the parties agree to commence mediation immediately, pursuant to the applicable Rules of the American Arbitration Association.

- If mediation does not produce resolution within thirty (30) days of the first mediation session, the parties agree to submit their disagreement(s) forthwith to final, binding arbitration pursuant to the applicable Rules of the American Arbitration Association. Judgment upon the award rendered by the arbitrator may be entered in any court having jurisdiction to do so.

[**Comment:** This form eliminates the correspondence element and the posturing that frequently is contained therein. It can be tailored to involve the appropriate level of management, depending on the nature of the disputes covered. As with most recommended clauses that contain an arbitration provision, this one is self-executing.]

FORM NO. 3

NEGOTIATION—ARBITRATION

- In the event of any dispute, claim, question, or disagreement arising out of or relating to this Agreement or the breach thereof, the parties hereto shall use their best efforts to settle such disputes, claims, questions, or disagreement. To this effect, they shall consult and negotiate with each other, in good faith and, recognizing their mutual interests, attempt to reach a just and equitable solution satisfactory to both parties. If they do not reach such solution within a period of [sixty (60) days], then upon notice by either party to the other, disputes, claims, questions, or differences shall be finally settled by arbitration in accordance with the provisions of the [applicable] Rules of the American Arbitration Association. Judgment upon the award rendered by the arbitrator may be entered in any court having jurisdiction to do so.

[Comment: Conspicuous by its absence is any mention of mediation. This clause is used mostly by organizations that not only have an ongoing relationship with one another, but also have a successful history of negotiating disputes between them. Their judgment is that if they cannot negotiate a resolution themselves, then mediation will not help or may take too long. If their own negotiations fail, the parties may need a swift resolution that arbitration can provide.]

FORM NO. 4
MEDIATION—ARBITRATION

- If a dispute arises out of or relates to this contract or the breach thereof, and if said dispute cannot be settled through direct discussions, the parties agree first to try to settle the dispute in an amicable manner by mediation under the Commercial Mediation Rules of the American Arbitration Association, before resorting to arbitration. Thereafter, any unresolved controversy or claim arising out of or relating to this contract, or breach thereof, shall be settled by arbitration in accordance with the Commercial Arbitration Rules of the American Arbitration Association, and judgment upon the Award rendered by the arbitrator(s) may be entered in any court having jurisdiction thereof.

[Comment: This clause eliminates negotiation as a first step. This could be for several reasons, but the most likely is that the parties know they will try negotiation first and, thus, do not feel that it is necessary to include it in the written agreement. Since mediation itself involves (assisted) negotiation, not much will be lost if the parties skip the negotiation step. Some executives have said that they dislike including the negotiation step in a clause because to do so "formalizes" negotiation in a way that they find counterproductive to the goal of early resolution. Others report that the negotiation step is left out because, in the words of one hospital executive, "If the other side is negotiating in good faith, you can always go along. If they are not, then you can invoke the mediation clause right away, avoid their ability to string things along, and get some help from the mediator." This clause also covers a larger number of disputes than those which contain the traditional "arising out of" language.]

FORM NO. 5
MEDIATION—ARBITRATION (MED/ARB)

- We, the undersigned, do hereby agree to submit all manner of disputes, controversies, differences, claims, or demands of any kind relating to or growing out of this [contract, relationship] to a two-step dispute resolution process administered by the American Arbitration Association (AAA).

- This two-step process shall begin with mediation before a mediator chosen from the AAA panel followed, if necessary, by final and binding arbitration pursuant to applicable AAA Rules. Judgment upon the award rendered by the arbitrator may be entered in any court having jurisdiction to do so.

[**Comment:** First, the reach of this clause is wider than any other in the book. It contemplates an ongoing business relationship, probably dealing with more than one product or service and perhaps more than one division or subsidiary of each of the involved entities. The principals wanted to ensure that any dispute that came up would be resolved in this way. The negotiation step is probably left out because the parties know each other well enough to be assured that negotiation will always be tried. Finally, the clause does not address the crucial question of whether the same person will serve as both arbitrator and mediator. See Chapter 11.]

FORM NO. 6

ARBITRATION—*AD HOC* ARBITRATION

Upon the request of either party, a dispute arising in connection with this Agreement shall be submitted to arbitration. The place of arbitration shall be [city, state, country] or such other place as may be agreed upon by the parties. Both parties shall attempt to agree upon one arbitrator, but if they are unable to agree, each shall appoint an arbitrator and these two shall appoint a third arbitrator. Expenses of arbitration shall be divided equally between the parties. The prevailing party [shall] [shall not] be entitled to reasonable attorney fees and costs not related to the administration of the arbitration.

In the event of arbitration, the arbitrator(s) shall pass finally upon all questions, both of law and fact, and his [or her or their] findings shall be conclusive. In the event of arbitration, pre-arbitration discovery shall be available to both parties and shall be governed by the Federal Rules of Civil Procedure. Information obtained by either party during the course of discovery shall be kept confidential, shall not be disclosed to any third party, and shall not be used except in connection with the arbitration proceeding. At the conclusion of the proceeding, all such information shall be returned to the other party. Both parties shall make their agents and employees available at reasonable times and places for pretrial depositions without the necessity of formal notices, subpoenas, or other court orders. Such discovery may be used as evidence in the arbitration proceeding to the same extent as if it were a court proceeding.

[**Comment:** This clause does not choose an administration body, but tries to set the necessary ground rules for the arbitration itself. This way of going about arbitration is generally called *ad hoc,* which Latin phrase means "for the specific incident." In ADR parlance, however, *ad hoc* has come to mean without specific rules or without having appointed an administering agency, *e.g.,* American Arbitration Association.]

FORM NO. 6A
ARBITRATION REMEDIES—OMNIBUS, INCLUDING PROVISIONAL REMEDIES

- The arbitrator shall have the authority to award any remedy or relief that a court of this state could order or grant, including, without limitation, specific performance of any obligation created under the agreement, the awarding of punitive damages, the issuance of a preliminary or permanent injunction, or the imposition of sanctions for abuse or frustration of the arbitration process.

[Comment: This clause grants the arbitrator broad, but not unlimited, powers. For instance, a normal arbitrator might be able to grant remedies that a state court judge could *not*. Nonetheless, the arbitrator is given some powers that he would normally not have, particularly the power to sanction parties for misconduct that abuses or frustrates the arbitration process. It is also unusual for the arbitrator to be given the power to specifically enforce compliance with a contract. Customarily, money damages would be awarded to the party who did not receive the promised performance.]

FORM NO. 7
ARBITRATION REMEDIES—PUNITIVE DAMAGES

- The arbitrators will have no authority to award punitive damages or any other damages not measured by the prevailing party's actual damages and may not, in any event, make any ruling, finding, or award that does not conform to the terms and conditions of the Agreement.

[Comment: This clause, of course, precludes punitive damage awards against either party in any dispute covered by the ADR agreement of which it will be part. To introduce this clause by itself, however, may be negotiation suicide. It sends the message, among others, that there may be worries about punitive damages because: (a) they have been awarded against that party before, and/or (b) that party may be planning something which might merit them receiving punitive damage. The *mutuality* of the clause should be emphasized.]

FORM NO. 8
ARBITRATION REMEDIES—SANCTIONS

- Arbitrators shall be empowered to impose sanctions and to take such other actions with regard to the parties as the arbitrators deem necessary to the same extent that a judge could, pursuant to the Federal Rules of Civil Procedure, the [state] Rules of Civil Procedure and applicable law.

[**Comment:** This clause has some of the same "me thinks thou dost protest too much" quality as the punitive damage clause immediately above. It is also largely unnecessary, *if* the right arbitrator is chosen.]

FORM NO. 9

ARBITRATION REMEDIES—COSTS AND FEES (EXCLUDING ATTORNEY FEES)

● All fees and expenses of the arbitration shall be borne by the parties equally. However, each party shall bear the expense of its own counsel, experts, witnesses, and preparation and presentation of proofs.

[Comment: The clause does not provide for any cost shifting based on who wins the most in the arbitration award. It is perfectly appropriate when it is reasonably certain that the other party will not try to abuse the process either by making numerous frivolous claims or by handling the preparation stages of the arbitration in a way designed to cause a party to spend more money. Keep in mind, however, that most arbitrations involve little or no "discovery," and it is discovery which accounts for most prehearing expenses in both arbitration and litigation.]

FORM NO. 10

ARBITRATION REMEDIES—ATTORNEY FEES

- The prevailing party shall be entitled to an award of reasonable attorney fees.

[OR]

The arbitrator(s) is authorized to award any parties such sums as shall be deemed proper for the time, expense, and trouble of arbitration, including arbitration fees and attorney fees.

[**Comment:** The principal practical difference between the two clauses above is the use of the word "reasonable" in the first of them. By incorporating that word, the parties give to the arbitrator the discretion to assess what fees of the prevailing party are reasonable before awarding them. Otherwise, an arbitrator could be bound to award the prevailing party *all* fees paid or incurred, no matter how unreasonable they might seem. These clauses are both unusual in that they treat attorney fees only and do not mention costs. See Form No. 11, below.]

FORM NO. 11

ARBITRATION REMEDIES—COSTS AND FEES (INCLUDING ATTORNEY FEES)

- The arbitrator(s) shall award to the prevailing party, if any, as determined by the arbitrators, all of its costs and fees. "Costs and fees" means all reasonable pre-award expenses of the arbitration, including the arbitrator's fees, administrative fees, travel expenses, and out-of-pocket expenses, such as copying and telephone, court costs, witness fees, and attorney fees.

[OR]

The parties shall each bear its own costs and expenses and an equal share of the arbitrator's and administrative fees of arbitration.

[OR]

The arbitrators shall award costs and expenses of the arbitration proceeding in accordance with the provisions of the [for example, loan agreement], which is the subject of the arbitrated claim or dispute.

[Comment: The first of the above clauses spells out what is meant by "costs." This is sometimes necessary because the state law definition of recoverable "costs" in *litigation* is very restrictive. For instance, many states have laws defining recoverable (litigation) costs to *exclude* travel expenses of parties, counsel, and witnesses, and the fees of expert witnesses. Depending on the dispute, these types of costs could be the major components of the costs experienced in arbitration.]

FORM NO. 12

ARBITRATION—PROVISIONAL REMEDIES (OMNIBUS)

- Any provisional remedy which would be available from a court of law shall be available to the parties to this Agreement, pending final award, from the arbitrator.

[**Comment:** This clause is the most sweeping of the provisional remedies clauses in these materials. Financial institutions (frequently claimants in situations where provisional relief is needed) prefer this clause. Any of these clauses, of course, should be used in conjunction with a clause choosing a particular method of resolving disputes. *Caveat:* This clause could reasonably be interpreted to make provisional remedies available in arbitration *under the same standards applicable in court.* Arbitrators might not otherwise be bound by those standards and could grant preliminary relief (particularly injunctions) on less stringent standards than a court might. If a party believes a clause should include arrangements for provisional relief, they should consult an expert.]

FORM NO. 13

ARBITRATION—PROVISIONAL REMEDIES (INJUNCTION ONLY—FROM ARBITRATOR)

- Either party may apply for, and the arbitrator may grant, injunctive relief to maintain the status quo until the award is rendered or the dispute is otherwise resolved.

[**Comment:** This clause limits the parties to a "status quo" injunction. This means that the arbitrator's power is limited to issuing preliminary injunctions *which preserve the situation between the parties as it existed before the dispute began.* If an opponent is truly slippery, it may be beneficial to consider what happens if the injunction is ordered "until the award is entered." At that point, the injunction would dissolve according to its terms and the losing party would be *unrestrained* for the time it took to get the award confirmed into a court judgment.]

FORM NO. 14

ARBITRATION—PROVISIONAL REMEDIES (OMNIBUS— BUT ONLY FROM COURT)

- Either party may, consistent with this Arbitration Agreement, seek from a court any provisional relief, pending

[either]

(a) the establishment of the arbitral tribunal,

[or]

(b) the arbitrator's determination of the merits of the dispute.

[**Comment:** Subclause (b) seems preferable, since parties choosing (a) might find themselves having to *reapply* to the newly constituted tribunal for the same relief which they had already obtained from a court. In addition to the extra expense involved in such a procedure, there is no guarantee that the outcome before the arbitral tribunal will be the same as it was before the court. In addition, there exists the possibility that parties subject to the court-granted provisional relief could use the "window of opportunity" between establishment of the tribunal and *its granting* provisional relief to do the otherwise prohibited acts. The phrase "consistently with this Arbitration Agreement" is added to prevent either party from claiming that the other had *waived* its right to arbitrate the dispute by going to court for preliminary relief. Please keep in mind that these clauses are used in conjunction with other provisions which govern *how the dispute will ultimately be resolved.*]

FORM NO. 15

MINI-TRIAL

- In the event of any dispute related to or arising out of any provision of the agreement, either party can initiate a mini-trial as a condition precedent to litigation or the continuance of litigation by serving written notice upon the other. Upon receipt of notice, the parties shall promptly attempt, in good faith, to resolve the dispute by a nonbinding mini-trial. A mini-trial shall be conducted by a neutral advisor and shall be attended by a senior executive officer from each party with sufficient authority to resolve the dispute. The neutral shall be selected in the following manner: the parties will agree upon a neutral themselves, or if they cannot do so within fifteen (15) days of the notice described above, the American Arbitration Association will appoint a neutral from its panel or a list of neutrals agreed upon by the parties. The parties shall agree upon the use of pre-existing rules governing the mini-trial process, or modifications to such rules, including the need for and extent of any expedited discovery, a schedule for an exchange of documents, the format and site of the mini-trial and the duties and responsibilities of the neutral. If they cannot agree within [30] days of the selection/appointment of the neutral, the American Arbitration Association Mini-trial Rules will apply. The senior executives of each party will engage in settlement discussions immediately after the mini-trial presentation. Either party can terminate the proceedings if it believes that negotiations are not productive.

[Comment: As previously discussed, this is a structured dispute resolution method in which senior executives and, if appropriate, technical advisors of the parties meet in the presence of a neutral and hear summary evidentiary presentations by all sides of the dispute. After this, the senior executives try to reach a voluntary settlement, with or without the neutral's assistance. If the latter part of this process sounds like mediation, that is because it *is* mediation. *Caveat:* Mini-trials are expensive. It is the rare contract or relationship where every dispute would warrant one. Use this mechanism sparingly, if at all, in ADR clauses that may not cover major disputes. The mere presence of a required mini-trial could add substantially to the cost of the deal being entered into. The parties can always agree to a mini-trial before (or during) other ADR processes.]

FORM NO. 16
MINI-TRIAL

● Any controversy or claim arising out of this [contract, relationship, etc.] shall be submitted to the American Arbitration Association under its mini-trial procedures. The result will not be binding on the parties.

[If the desired result is to *be binding*, then add: "Any court having jurisdiction to do so may enter a judgment upon the award made in this proceeding." However, it won't really be a mini-trial, but an arbitration based on truncated presentation of evidence.]

[**Comment:** This clause simply selects the American Arbitration Association rules. But if the parties agree, these rules can be modified to suit the specific dispute. It might be more advisable to use a short clause like this one, understanding that later modification is possible. The shorter the clause, the shorter the discussion concerning it.]

b. Submission clauses (post-dispute)

The term "submission" in alternative dispute resolution means that parties permit (submit) their dispute to be decided in a certain way, *without any pre-existing obligation to do so.* Obviously, at this stage of the proceedings, a dispute already exists. So, any power to steer the resolution of this dispute into alternative dispute resolution is severely limited by the fact that agreement on this issue is required from the disputing parties. But, more and more disputes are nonetheless being "submitted" to arbitration (and other forms of ADR) every day.

For example, International Widget and American Widget Distributors, Inc. (AWD) have signed a distributorship agreement which does not contain an ADR clause. Two years into their agreement, International Widget discovers that AWD has opened offices in Hong Kong and Frankfurt and is offering International Widgets to customers in those areas. International immediately notifies AWD that it has violated the distributorship agreement by distributing International Widgets outside the United States. AWD rejoins that nothing in the contract prevents this, and the only language bearing on the issue states: "Distributor will be limited to geographic areas within 2,500 miles of one of its offices." International has already entered into foreign distributorship agreements with several companies in Europe and the Far East and is receiving a great deal of pressure from those companies to protect their "exclusive" territories. So, a battle seems about to begin.

Executives at International consult with counsel as to how to bring the matter to a head. The first thing they learn is that the law in most American states would support AWD's position, not theirs. Secondly, they learn that there is a better chance of prevailing in Germany and Hong Kong, but that two very expensive lawsuits would have to be brought, simultaneously, to obtain rulings which would govern AWD's activities in both those jurisdictions. International's executives also learn that, while the court system moves rather smartly in Germany, civil cases in Hong Kong may take up to three or four years to conclude at the *trial* level. Both Germany and Hong Kong have elaborate (and slow) appellate processes.

Across the country, at AWD's headquarters, their executives have consulted with counsel as well. They learn that while U.S. law tends to favor their view as far as an ultimate ruling is concerned, many courts in the United States would grant a preliminary injunction preventing AWD from selling abroad until the final disposition of the case. They also are told that, in the United States, International could probably delay the beginning of a trial on the merits for three years or more by running up a huge discovery bill and using other delaying tactics that would cause AWD additional expense as well. AWD's CEO questions whether the prospective profits to be derived from foreign operations will exceed the cost of battling with International. No one can assure him that they will.

Unbeknownst to each other, the general counsel of each company has been instructed by the senior executives to call the other to see if something rational can be done, meaning to find some way of deciding the dispute in a inexpensive and not-so-time-consuming way. Neither party is in a position to negotiate/mediate a resolution because AWD won't give up its foreign outlets, and International must heed the call of its existing foreign distributors that it "squash AWD like a bug." As the two company lawyers talk together on the telephone, they quickly learn that their companies share some common interests in having the dispute decided quickly, relatively inexpensively by a third party (each company must be able to point to a binding decision should it lose) who knows something about the distribution of industrial products.

It will not be surprising to learn that they choose arbitration, and that this process can take place *even after a lawsuit has been filed* and some discovery taken. Since the parties are voluntarily submitting their dispute to arbitration, the question of "waiver" does not even arise. The only reasons for accomplishing this submission before a court case has begun are:

— to save some attorney fees and costs;

— to insure that the litigation does not "take on a life of its own," dragging the parties along with it; and

— to get the dispute finally resolved more quickly.

So, the clauses which follow are suggested for use *after* a dispute has arisen. Before using any of them, the questions posed at the beginning of this section should be answered and the additional questions that have emerged from answers to those questions. Then, negotiate accordingly.

FORM NO. 17

(FOR ILLUSTRATION ONLY—DO NOT USE)

MEDIATION—SUBMISSION TO MEDIATION

(a) **Agreement to Use Procedure.** The parties have entered into this Agreement in good faith and in the belief that it is mutually advantageous to them. Accordingly, they agree that the dispute which has arisen between them relating to [describe dispute generally here] (the "Dispute") will, prior to the commencement of any legal action concerning the Dispute, be submitted to the Procedure specified below.

(b) **Initiation of Procedure.** Each party shall initiate the Procedure by identifying one or more individuals with authority to settle the Dispute on such party's behalf, in writing, to the other party, within [five] days of the date of this Agreement. The persons so designated will be known collectively as the Authorized Individuals.

(c) **Direct Negotiations.** The Authorized Individuals shall be entitled to make such investigation of the Dispute as they deem appropriate, but agree, and in no event later than [thirty] days from the date of the writing which designated them, to promptly meet to discuss resolution of the Dispute. The Authorized Individuals shall meet at such times and places and with such frequency as they may agree. If the Dispute has not been resolved within [thirty] days from the date of their initial meeting, the parties shall cease direct negotiations and shall submit the Dispute to mediation as follows.

(d) **Selection of Mediator.** The Authorized Individuals shall have [five] business days from the date they cease direct negotiations to submit to each other a written list of acceptable qualified attorney-mediators not affiliated with any of the parties. Within [five] days from the date of receipt of such list, the Authorized Individuals shall rank the mediators in numerical order of preference and exchange such rankings. If one or more names are on both lists, the highest ranking person shall be designated as the mediator. If no mediator has been selected under this procedure, the parties agree jointly to request [the Presiding Judge of the District Court of Clark County, Nevada] to supply within [ten] business days a list of potential qualified attorney-mediators. Within [five] business days of receipt of the list, the parties shall again rank the proposed mediators in numerical order of preference and shall simultaneously exchange such ranking list and shall select as the mediator the individual receiving the highest combined ranking. If such mediator is not available to serve, they shall proceed to contact the mediator who was next highest in ranking until they are able to engage a mediator.

(e) **Time and Place for Mediation.** In consultation with the mediator selected, the parties shall promptly designate a mutually convenient time and place for the mediation, and unless circumstances require otherwise, such timeshall be not later than [45] days after selection of the mediator.

(f) **Exchange of Information.** In the event any party to this Agreement has substantial need for information in the possession of another party to this Agreement in order to prepare for the mediation, all parties shall attempt in good faith to agree on procedures for the expeditious exchange of such information, with the help of the mediator, if required.

(g) **Summary of Views.** At least [seven] days prior to the first scheduled session of the mediation, each party shall deliver to the mediator [only] [and to the other party] a concise written summary of its views on the Dispute and such other matters as may be required by the mediator.

(h) **Parties to be Represented.** In the mediation, each party shall be represented by an Authorized Individual and may also be represented by counsel. In addition, each party may, with permission of the mediator, bring such additional persons as needed to respond to questions, contribute information, and participate in the negotiations.

(i) **Conduct of Mediation.** The mediator shall determine the format for the meetings, designed to assure that both the mediator and the Authorized Individuals have an opportunity to hear an oral presentation of each party's views on the matter in dispute, and that the Authorized Individuals attempt to negotiate a resolution of the Dispute, with or without the assistance or counsel of others, but with the assistance of the mediator. To this end, the mediator is authorized to conduct both joint meetings and separate private caucuses with the parties. The mediation shall be private. The mediator will keep confidential all information learned in private caucus with any party unless specifically authorized by such party to make disclosure of the information to the other party. The parties agree to sign a document agreeing that the mediator shall be governed by the provisions of [*e.g.*, Chapter 154 of the Texas Remedies and Practice Code] and such other rules as the mediator shall prescribe. The parties commit to participate in the proceedings in good faith with the intention of resolving the Dispute if at all possible.

(j) **Termination of Procedure.** The parties agree to participate in the mediation procedure to its conclusion. The mediation shall be terminated by (1) the execution of a settlement agreement by the parties, (2) a declaration of the mediator that the mediation is terminated, or (3) a written declaration of a party to the effect that the mediation process is terminated at the conclusion of one full day's mediation session. Even if the mediation is terminated without a resolution of the Dispute, the parties agree not to terminate negotiations and not to commence any legal action or seek other remedies prior to the expiration of [five] days following the mediation. Notwithstanding the foregoing, any party may commence litigation within such [five]-day period if litigation could be barred by an applicable statute of limitations or in order to request an injunction to prevent irreparable harm.

(k) **Fees of Mediator; Disqualification.** The fees and expenses of the mediator shall be shared equally by the parties. The mediator shall be disqualified as a witness, consultant, expert, or counsel for any party with respect to the Dispute and any related matters.

(l) **Confidentiality.** Mediation is a compromise negotiation for purposes of the Federal and State Rules of Evidence and constitutes privileged communication under [*e.g.*, Texas] law. The entire mediation process is confidential, and no stenographic, visual, or audio record shall be made. All conduct, statements, promises, offers, views, and opinions, whether oral or written, made in the course of the mediation by any party, their agents, employees, representatives, or other invitees and by the mediator are confidential and shall, in addition and where appropriate, be deemed to be privileged. Such conduct, statements, promises, offers, views, and opinions shall not be discoverable or admissible for any purposes, including impeachment, in any litigation or other proceeding involving the parties, and shall not be disclosed to anyone not an agent, employee, expert, witness, or representative of any of the parties; provided however, that evidence otherwise discoverable or admissible is not excluded from discovery or admission as a result of its use in the mediation.

[**Comment:** This form is a disaster, an excellent example of how *not* to draft an ADR clause. Imagine two parties who *want to mediate* (keep in mind that this is a post-dispute submission agreement) being unable to agree on a mediator without these cumbersome procedures which, if really needed, would by that fact alone be conclusive evidence that one of the parties was stalling. Furthermore, if both parties want to mediate (and they do), why is it necessary for them to exchange a list of "Authorized Individuals"? Will the parties be likely to send the wrong persons to the mediation? Not really. The only circumstance where a mediation submission agreement *might* need to be this long and burdensome is where one of the parties is going to travel to the place of mediation from a great distance and doesn't want to undertake the time and expense of the trip without knowing exactly what to expect. Unless such a situation occurs, ***do not use this form.***]

FORM NO. 18
MEDIATION—SUBMISSION TO MEDIATION AND MEDIATION—CONFIDENTIALITY AGREEMENT

The undersigned parties have agreed to enter into mediation, pursuant to the American Arbitration Association's Mediation Rules, which are incorporated by this reference. They further agree as follows:

- That the mediator is a neutral intermediary who will assist them in reaching a resolution of their dispute and recording that resolution, but cannot impose a settlement, and will not render legal advice to any party.

- That the parties are free to consult with counsel during any phase of the mediation and are specifically advised to have any settlement agreement reviewed by their counsel before they sign it.

- That this mediation is conducted pursuant to [Section 1152.5 of the California Evidence Code or other state or federal confidentiality provisions], and each of the parties acknowledges that they have agreed to mediate for the purposes set forth in [that section].

- That any written settlement agreement resulting from this mediation shall be admissible in evidence in any proceeding to enforce its terms.

- That all the persons who will participate in the mediation have signed below, before the beginning of the mediation.

Dated: _____   _____
                            PARTY

_____   _____
PARTY   COUNSEL

_____   _____
COUNSEL   EXPERT

_____
MEDIATOR

[**Comment:** The reason this agreement can be as brief as it is can be traced to the selection of the American Arbitration Association Commercial Mediation Rules. These Rules, readily available to everyone and already known to most mediators and lawyers who practice alternative dispute resolution, are a comfortable "known quantity" by which the parties can assure impartial administration *and* an impartial neutral. Also note that there is no precise description of the dispute itself in the above form. Since the mediator has no power to determine a result, parties and counsel usually feel comfortable *not* defining the dispute in too much detail. This document, although only about one-fourth the length of the immediately prior form, is perfectly adequate for submitting a dispute to *mediation*. It does have some language which appears designed to advise the parties (and protect the mediator) concerning the fact that the mediator is not going to give anyone legal advice. If the parties take some or all of that language out, an experienced mediator may put it right back in.]

FORM NO. 19

MEDIATION—MEDIATION AGREEMENT

AGREEMENT, dated _____, 19____, between _____ and _____.

WHEREAS, the parties are presently [engaged in litigation] [involved in a dispute] relating to _____; and

WHEREAS, the parties desire to attempt to settle their dispute through nonbinding mediation with the assistance of _____ as mediator (the "Mediator");

NOW, THEREFORE, the parties hereby mutually agree as follows:

1. **Impartiality of the Mediator.** The parties and their counsel represent and warrant that they have made a diligent effort to determine all prior contacts between them and the Mediator, and all such contacts have been disclosed to counsel for the opposing party and the Mediator. The parties acknowledge that the Mediator is impartial and cannot act as advocate, representative, or counsel for either party and has no authority to make binding decisions, impose settlements, or require concessions by either party, it being understood and agreed that any agreements which may be reached between the parties as a result of the mediation process shall be embodied in a separate written agreement between the parties prepared with the assistance of their respective counsel.

2. **Caucuses and Conferences.** The parties understand and agree that, in connection with the mediation process, the Mediator may meet in confidential "caucus" sessions separately with each party. The Mediator will treat as confidential and refrain from disclosing to the other party or its counsel any information which any party or its counsel requests be so treated. The Mediator may, at the request of either party or on his own initiative, conduct any conference pursuant to this Agreement by telephone, facsimile transmission, or other means of communication.

3. **Confidentiality, Immunity, and Indemnification.** To enable the parties to discuss all aspects of their dispute freely and to enable the Mediator effectively to assist the parties in reaching a voluntary resolution of their dispute, the parties agree as follows:

   a. Conferences and discussions which occur in connection with mediation services provided pursuant to this Agreement shall be deemed settlement discussions, and nothing said or disclosed, nor any document produced, which is not otherwise independently discoverable, shall be offered or received as evidence or used for impeachment or for any other purpose in any current or future litigation, or arbitration, regardless of what law may apply to such proceeding.

b. The Mediator shall have the same common-law immunity as judges and arbitrators from suit for damages or equitable relief and from compulsory process to testify or produce evidence based on or concerning any action, statement, or communication in or concerning the mediation conducted pursuant to this Agreement.

c. The parties understand that there is no attorney-client relationship between the Mediator and any party to this Agreement, and each party acknowledges that it will seek and rely on legal advice solely from its own counsel and not from the Mediator.

d. The parties agree, on behalf of themselves and their attorneys, that none of them will call or subpoena the Mediator in any legal or administrative proceeding of any kind to produce any notes or documents related to his mediation services or to testify concerning any such notes or documents or his thoughts or impressions. If any party attempts to compel such testimony or production, such party shall be liable for and shall indemnify the Mediator for any liabilities, costs, and expenses, including attorney fees and lost professional time, which he may incur in resisting such compulsion.

4. **Participation of Parties.** At the request of the Mediator, each party shall have a corporate officer or representative, in addition to its counsel, in attendance at the mediation sessions who will have full power and authority to negotiate and conclude a binding settlement of the dispute on behalf of such party.

5. **Fees and Expenses.** The fee for the Mediator's services hereunder shall be computed at the rate of $__[400]__per hour for time spent in connection with the mediation, and one-half of the fees and expenses of the Mediator shall be paid by each party.

6. **Benefit of Agreement.** This Agreement shall inure to the benefit of and be binding upon the parties hereto, and the Mediator shall be deemed a third party beneficiary hereof.

IN WITNESS WHEREOF, the parties have executed this Agreement as of the date hereinabove first written.

PARTY

PARTY

[**Comment:** This form is somewhat elaborate, but it gets the job done. What "inure to the benefit of . . . the parties" adds is not certain. To whose benefit will an agreement inure, if not the parties? Note that the mediator's compensation and how it is to be allocated are covered here as well. It also might be useful as a "sales" tool for persuading a reluctant party to begin mediation.]

FORM NO. 20

MEDIATION SETTLEMENT AGREEMENT— CONFIDENTIALITY PROVISION

The parties and their lawyers agree that all terms of this Settlement shall remain secret and confidential and shall not be disclosed to any person or entity except by lawful process [subpoena] received by it or in the course of any action to enforce the terms of the Settlement.

[Comment: This clause may be inserted in the written settlement agreement which gets drafted at the *end of* a successful mediation, if the parties (or their lawyers) are uncertain whether the agreement they entered into to begin the mediation will provide confidentiality to the final settlement agreement. Care should be exercised that the language includes everyone who actually attended the mediation sessions. This form's most obvious deficiency is its lack of teeth. What happens if someone breaches the confidentiality? Should that (alone) unravel the entire agreement? Should the breaching party have to pay a penalty or forfeit some benefits obtained under the Mediation Settlement Agreement itself? These judgments can only be made at the time of negotiating the agreement. See also Form No. 21.]

FORM NO. 21

MEDIATION SETTLEMENT AGREEMENT—
CONFIDENTIALITY PROVISION

Each party agrees to keep this Agreement strictly confidential and not to transfer any copy of this Agreement or communicate the substance of this Agreement to any other person or entity, unless (a) the party is asserting a claim or defense arising out of this Agreement in any suit or proceeding; (b) the party is ordered to do so by a court [of competent jurisdiction]; or (c) the party is served with a subpoena or other request for discovery, provided that the party first gives prompt notice to the other parties so that the other parties may have an opportunity to quash or otherwise defend against the discovery request.

[**Comment:** As with Form No. 19, this provision will form a part of the final settlement agreement and should include in its ambit everyone who attended the mediation or who has come to know the terms of the settlement agreement, *e.g.,* a secretary at the office where the mediation is held who has typed up the final agreement. Note that the circumstances under which a party *can reveal* what he knows are set forth in more detail than in Form No. 19. Of particular potential benefit to the parties wanting secrecy is the provision requiring any party subjected to court process to notify the other parties and give them a chance to resist the court process (which the party who actually received it might not be motivated to do).]

FORM NO. 22

ARBITRATION—SUBMISSION TO ARBITRATION

We, the undersigned parties, agree to submit to arbitration, pursuant to the Rules of the American Arbitration Association, the following dispute [describe dispute *precisely* or refer to pending court case]. We further agree that any court having jurisdiction to do so may enter a judgment upon the award made in this arbitration.

[**Comment:** Unlike mediation, it may be *crucial* to describe precisely just what dispute is being submitted for decision by arbitration. If for no other reason, this agreement may be used to test whether the arbitrator has exceeded his/her powers. Note that this simple agreement is sufficient to bind a party to go to arbitration. If, for instance, one of the parties should resist arbitration later on, a court could—and would—compel that party to arbitrate. If the party continued not to participate in the arbitration, a hearing could be had and a valid award rendered *in his absence.*]

FORM NO. 23

ARBITRATION—HIGH/LOW CLAUSE (ARBITRATOR UNINFORMED REGARDING LIMITS)

In the event the arbitrator denies the claim entirely or awards an amount less than the minimum amount of $_____, then the minimum amount shall be paid to the claimant. Should the arbitrator's award exceed the maximum amount of $_____, then the maximum amount shall be paid to the claimant. If the arbitrator awards an amount between the minimum and maximum, then the exact amount awarded shall be paid to the claimant. The parties further agree that this Agreement will not be disclosed to the arbitrator. Any court having jurisdiction to do so may enter a judgment upon the award made in this arbitration.

[**Comment:** This mechanism is useful where liability is conceded, and where the parties wish to test their evaluation of the case against that of the arbitrator, *or vice versa*. It should also be considered where there is concern that the arbitrator's award will be influenced by the parties' agreement. This kind of arbitration is usually only useful where the matter can be decided by arriving at a specific dollar amount. Careful drafting could make it useful in other types of disputes as well. Its principal perceived benefit is that it permits the parties to control the extremes of possible outcomes, thereby reducing risk for both sides.]

FORM NO. 23A

ARBITRATION—NIGHT BASEBALL CLAUSE
(ARBITRATOR UNINFORMED REGARDING LIMITS)

Prior to the arbitration hearing, each party will give to the other its best offer, in writing. The arbitrator will not be informed of the contents of these best offers.

In the event that the arbitrator denies the claim entirely or awards an amount less than the claimant's best offer, the claimant's best offer shall be paid to the claimant. Should the arbitrator's award exceed the respondent's best offer, then the respondent's best offer amount shall be paid to the claimant. If the arbitrator awards an amount between the two best offers, then the amount of the best offer which is closest to the amount awarded shall be paid to the claimant. The parties further agree that this agreement will not be disclosed to the arbitrator prior to his rendering an award. Any court having jurisdiction to do so may enter a judgment upon the award made in this arbitration.

[**Comment:** This mechanism, like high/low arbitration, is useful where the parties wish to test their evaluation of the case against that of the arbitrator, *or vice versa.* It should also be considered where there is concern that the arbitrator's award may be influenced by the parties' agreement. This kind of arbitration is usually useful only where the matter can be decided by arriving at a specific dollar amount. Careful drafting could make it useful in other types of disputes as well. Its principal perceived benefit is that it permits the parties to control the extremes of possible outcomes, thereby reducing risk for both sides, while still getting the arbitrator's unsullied view of "the merits."]

FORM NO. 24

ARBITRATION—"BASEBALL" CLAUSE (PARTIES INFORMED REGARDING OFFERS)

Each party shall submit to the arbitrator, and exchange with each other in advance of the hearing, their last best offer. The arbitrator shall award only one or the other of the two offers submitted. Any court having jurisdiction to do so may enter a judgment upon the award made in this arbitration.

[**Comment:** This type of clause works best when the only (or only remaining) disputed item is an amount of money, as in an arbitration over back pay or termination benefits. Parties include this clause, under which they know each other's last offer before the submission to the arbitrator, because it frequently leads to eleventh-hour settlement. Obviously, both sides consider the amount of their offer most carefully when they know the arbitrator can only choose one or the other.]

FORM NO. 25

ARBITRATION—"BASEBALL" CLAUSE (PARTIES NOT INFORMED REGARDING OFFERS)

Each party shall submit to the arbitrator, but *not* exchange with each other in advance of the hearing, their last best offer. The arbitrator shall award only the amount of one or the other of the two offers submitted. Any court having jurisdiction to do so may enter a judgment upon the award made in this arbitration.

[**Comment:** This clause is frequently chosen by a party who firmly believes his evaluation of the dispute is closer to that of the arbitrator than the other party's evaluation will be. Otherwise, keeping the last offer from one another would seem to lessen the chances of a negotiated resolution.]

FORM NO. 26

ARBITRATION—SUBMISSION FOR INTERNATIONAL ARBITRATION

- We, the undersigned parties, agree to submit to arbitration, in accordance with the American Arbitration Association UNCITRAL Arbitration Rules in effect on the date of this Agreement, the following dispute(s): [describe dispute(s) with great specificity]. The appointing authority will be the American Arbitration Association (AAA), and the case will be administered by the AAA pursuant to its Procedures for Cases under the UNCITRAL Arbitration Rules.

- The arbitration shall be conducted in [city, state, country] and in the [English, or Italian, or Chinese] language.

- The matter shall be heard and decided by [one or three] arbitrator(s). All arbitrators appointed to hear and decide disputes submitted by this Agreement shall be [citizens of _____ countries] *or* [may be citizens of any country except the following: _____].

- We further agree that any court having jurisdiction to do so may enter a judgment upon the award made in this arbitration.[6]

   Dated: _____

[**Comment:** Parties, and/or their counsel, may be suspicious of prospective arbitrators who are nationals of the opponent's home country. So, many of these clauses contain a provision that no arbitrator may be a national (or permanent resident) of the home country of any of the parties. Some ADR providers, *e.g.,* the American Arbitration Association, have the same stipulation in their rules.]

FORM NO. 27

ARBITRATION—CLAUSES REGULATING PROCEDURE

- **Expeditious Resolution.** Prompt disposal of any dispute arising under this agreement to arbitrate is important to the parties. The parties agree that the arbitration process shall be conducted expeditiously to the end that the final award shall be issued in one year or less from the date of filing the demand for arbitration. The arbitrator(s) shall, upon acceptance of the appointment, certify that he/they have sufficient time available and shall give adequate priority to the process so that the goal of the parties as stated above can be achieved.

[Comment: Clauses like these are rare, but not unheard of. If the parties are choosing to submit their dispute to arbitration principally because of a desire for speed, such a clause could help. The question remains, however, what will the parties do if the arbitrator does not move fast enough for them? If they dismiss the arbitrator (which is perfectly proper if all parties agree), they may just have to start over with a new one. As mentioned in other chapters, most of these kinds of problems can be obviated by carefully screening the neutral *before his selection.*]

FORM NO. 28
ARBITRATION—DISCOVERY CLAUSES

- The arbitrator shall have the discretion to order a prehearing exchange of information by the parties, including, without limitation, production of requested documents, exchange of summaries of testimony of proposed witnesses, and examination by deposition of parties.

- The parties shall allow and participate in discovery in accordance with the Federal Rules of Civil Procedure for a period of ninety (90) days after the filing of the Response to demand for arbitration or other responsive pleading. Unresolved discovery disputes may be brought to the attention of the [arbitrator or chair of the arbitration panel] and may be disposed of by him.

- Limited civil discovery shall be permitted for the production of documents and taking of depositions. All discovery shall be governed by the [specify a particular State or the Federal] Rules of Civil Procedure. All issues regarding conformation with discovery requests shall be decided by the arbitrator.

FORM NO. 29

ARBITRATION—CPR[7] DISPUTE RESOLUTION INSTITUTE—NONADMINISTERED ARBITRATION CLAUSE

This dispute between [X Corporation] and [Y Corporation] concerning [here describe the dispute very specifically] shall be settled by arbitration in accordance with the CPR Nonadministered Arbitration Rules by [a sole arbitrator] or [three independent and impartial arbitrators, of whom each party shall appoint one] or [three independent and impartial arbitrators, none of whom shall be appointed by either party]. The arbitration shall be governed by the United States Arbitration Act, Title 9 of the U.S. Code, Sections 1-16, and judgment on the award rendered may be entered by any court having jurisdiction. The place of arbitration shall be [city, state, country]. The arbitrator(s) [are] [are not] empowered to award damages in addition to or in excess of compensatory damages [and each party hereby irrevocably waives any right to recover such damages].

The statute of limitations of the State of [_____] applicable to the commencement of a lawsuit shall apply to the commencement of an arbitration hereunder.

[**Comment:** This clause has the parties agreeing to arbitrate their disputes, but not agreeing on much more. When a dispute does arise, the parties will have to repair to the CPR Nonadministered Arbitration Rules (which, of course, are themselves a form of administration). Before considering a clause such as this, the parties should carefully read whatever "Rules" are referred to, or, if there are none, consider how smoothly proceedings will go with an intransigent opponent if there are no rules of procedure. One area where an administering agency can really help is when one party wishes to disqualify an arbitrator or lodge a complaint about the arbitrator's conduct of the hearing. In the first instance, the agency can (and the AAA does) investigate on its own and make an independent determination as to whether the arbitrator should be disqualified. The important benefit to the parties is that if there is no disqualification, the arbitrator will never know that someone was trying to have him removed or even who it was. Regarding the conduct of the hearing itself, the agency can discretely talk with the arbitrator without letting him know which party lodged the complaint (or, in some circumstances, that a complaint was even lodged). In a nonadministered setting, no entity is present which can perform this sometimes valuable function. This clause, with only slight modification, can be used in a *predispute* setting as well. From experience, nonadministered arbitration is usually *not* a good idea.]

FORM NO. 30

ARBITRATION—DISPUTE REVIEW BOARD (AMERICAN ARBITRATION ASSOCIATION)

The parties shall empanel a Dispute Review Board (DRB) whose objective is to assist in the resolution of disputes that would otherwise likely be submitted to litigation or other forums. If this objective is achieved, such disputes can be resolved promptly with minimum expense and minimum disruption to the administration and performance of the project.

It is intended that the mere presence of the Board will, in many instances, encourage the owner and contractor to resolve their disputes without resorting to formal application for rulings from the DRB.

Within [10] days after the contract is awarded, each party shall name its Board member and either the contractor or owner shall request in writing, accompanied by the appropriate fee, that the American Arbitration Association (AAA) nominate three individuals from which the party-appointed members will elect the Board chair. The Board chair shall be neutral and his/her appointment shall be subject to full disclosure of all relationships with the parties. The AAA will send its three nominees to both parties within [15] days of being requested to form the DRB.

The two party-appointed members will then have [15] days to select the neutral chairperson and advise the AAA. If they do not select the chairperson within that time, the AAA will administratively appoint the chairperson, and set the time and place of the first meeting.

The DRB will schedule and hold regular meetings consistent with project progress and any demands of the project or the parties. Each meeting will consist of a roundtable discussion and inspection of the project's progress. The meeting will be attended at a minimum by the project manager from the owner and the principal contractor.

The agenda will be as follows:

a. Meeting opened by the Chairperson of the Board.

b. Remarks by the owner representative.

c. A description by the contractor of work accomplished since the last DRB meeting, current status, and a forecast for the coming period.

d. An outline of any current problems and a description of the proposed solutions.

e. An outline of the project status as seen by the owner.

   f.   A brief description by either or both parties of potential claims
        or disputes that have arisen since the last meeting and the
        efforts to resolve them.

   g.   A summary of the current disputes and claims.

The DRB will give directions and recommendations to resolve open
claims and disputes which arise on the project. The DRB will encourage
the settlement at job level. Each DRB member will act in an independent manner and not act as a consultant to the individual parties. The
DRB members will refrain from voicing public opinions on merits of
matters in dispute.

When the parties are unable to resolve a dispute, either may file a
written request that the DRB issue a formal ruling. The moving party
will submit its position documented as it sees fit to the responding
party and to the AAA, which will forward a copy to each Board
member. The DRB will then schedule hearings at the next regular
meeting or will call a special meeting.

In addition to the submitted positions, the DRB may require
further information from either party which will be produced when
requested. In the hearings, which shall be attended by representatives
of both parties, the chairperson will preside. The claimant will discuss
its view with the DRB followed by the other party. Rebuttals will be
allowed until all aspects have been covered. Each time a person gives
information, the Board may ask questions, seek clarification, or request
other data. When all the evidence and argument is complete, the Board
will adjourn and prepare a written recommended finding within [30]
days. The Board's decision, if one of the parties requests, will be
reasoned [and in formats required by federal [or other] funding sources].

A refusal by a party to provide information or answer questions
from the Board may be considered by the Board in making its findings
or recommendations.

A majority of two members of the Board shall support the Board's
findings, though the DRB will endeavor to reach unanimous decisions.
Minority opinions, where appropriate, will be permitted.

Although both parties should place weight on the DRB findings,
they are not binding. Either party may file an appeal to the DRB if
new evidence is available. If the DRB's findings and recommendations
do not resolve the dispute, all records and written recommendations
including any minority reports may be admissible as evidence in
subsequent actions.

Payment

Normally, each party will bear one-half the cost of the DRB. [In
construction matters, this is often accomplished through a contract

allowance or change order wherein the contractor advances its funds to the AAA to organize and regulate the DRB. The contractor is reimbursed for these funds in the monthly job payment process.]

[Payment language to suit the parties' needs should be included at this point in the contract.]

[**Comment:** This form is designed mainly for construction projects, but may be adaptable to other projects of finite duration. At first reading, this process may seem unduly cumbersome and drawn out. The experience of people in the construction industry belies this conclusion, however. Many experts feel that it dignifies what is essentially a voluntary advisory arbitration, thus getting the parties to "go along" with recommended solutions more times than not. As with any group which does not have binding decisional power, the effectiveness of a dispute review board depends primarily on the respect which its members command and the reasonableness of its suggestions.]

FORM NO. 31

ARBITRATION—DOMESTIC *AD HOC* ARBITRATION

The parties who sign below agree to submit the following dispute to arbitration: [describe dispute carefully and specifically.] [*or* in a *predispute* setting: Any and all disputes arising out of or in connection with the negotiation, execution, interpretation, performance, or nonperformance of this agreement, including, without limitation, the validity, scope, and enforceability of this arbitration agreement, shall be solely and finally settled by arbitration.].

Within thirty [30] days of the date of this agreement [*or* for *predispute* clauses: [30] days from the date of the demand for arbitration] each party shall nominate one arbitrator, who shall be a [certified public accountant] and whose principal place of business is located within [Cuyahoga] County, [Ohio]. Such nominee shall be independent of the party appointing him, as that term is used in the accounting profession. The two arbitrators so appointed shall select a third arbitrator, who shall also be a [certified public accountant] whose principal place of business is located within [Cuyahoga] County, [Ohio] and who is independent of each of the parties. Should either party fail to appoint its arbitrator within thirty [30] days of notice of appointment by the other party of its arbitrator, then the requesting party shall name both arbitrators and they shall proceed to name the third arbitrator as provided above.

The arbitration shall be conducted in [county and state] in accordance with the [*e.g.,* American Arbitration Association, etc.] Rules. The arbitrators shall apply the internal law of the State of [_____] and shall have the power to grant all legal and equitable remedies and award compensatory damages provided by that law, including, without limitation, the right to order and provide for the [*e.g.,* dissolution of the partnership], but shall not have the power to award punitive damages.

The award of the majority of the arbitrators shall be final and binding upon the parties, and judgment upon any award rendered by the arbitrators may be entered by any state or federal court having jurisdiction thereof.

In their award, the arbitrators shall allocate against the losing parties all costs of arbitration, including the fees of the arbitrators, and reasonable attorney fees, costs, and expert witness expenses of the parties.

The parties intend that this agreement to arbitrate shall be valid, enforceable, and irrevocable.

[**Comment:** This clause contains some "new wrinkles." First, the parties have chosen to narrow the field of prospective neutrals by limiting their choices to CPAs who work in Cuyahoga County, Ohio. Secondly, if one party doesn't promptly name their arbitrator, the other party gets to pick two of the three members of the panel. Indeed, one could say that the lucky party gets to pick all three, since the two he chose get to pick the third arbitrator. This provision ought to get both parties to focus on their obligation to select an arbitrator in a timely fashion. Thirdly, the parties have chosen to have their arbitration governed by the laws of a particular state. Lastly, despite the fact that they have already chosen what law is to apply, the parties have furnished very specific direction regarding what remedies the arbitrator may award. As illustrated in the text of the form, this format is easily adapted to use in a *predispute* context.]

FORM NO. 32

ARBITRATION—*AD HOC* ARBITRATION—THREE ARBITRATORS

The parties to this agreement hereby submit [describe dispute carefully and specifically] to arbitration. The place of arbitration shall be [city, county, state] or such other place as may be agreed upon by the parties. Both parties shall attempt to agree upon one arbitrator, but if they are unable to agree, each shall appoint an arbitrator and these two shall appoint a third arbitrator. Expenses of arbitration shall be divided equally between the parties. The prevailing party shall [shall not] be entitled to reasonable attorney fees.

The arbitrator(s) shall pass finally upon all questions, both of law and fact, and his [or her or their] findings shall be conclusive. Pre-arbitration discovery shall be available to both parties and shall be governed by the Federal Rules of Civil Procedure. Information obtained by either party during the course of discovery shall be kept confidential, shall not be disclosed to any third party, shall not be used except in connection with the arbitration proceeding, and, at the conclusion of the proceeding, shall be returned to the other party. Both parties shall make their agents and employees available at reasonable times and places for pretrial depositions without the necessity of formal notices, subpoenas, or other court orders. Such discovery may be used as evidence in the arbitration proceeding to the same extent as if it were a court proceeding.

[**Comment:** This clause is the *post-dispute* kin of Form No. 6A, above. Please see the comments there. The biggest difference from Form No. 6A (and standard arbitration practice) is the inclusion of a provision permitting full discovery under the Federal Rules of Civil Procedure. However, don't expect to save much money/time unless the arbitrator is given power to *limit* discovery.]

FORM NO. 33

ARBITRATION—APPLICABLE LAW CLAUSES (AMERICAN ARBITRATION ASSOCIATION)

- All disputes . . . shall be resolved by arbitration in accordance with Title 9 of the U.S. Code (United States Arbitration Act) and the Commercial Arbitration Rules of the American Arbitration Association.

- This contract shall be governed by the laws of the State of [*e.g.*, New York].

- Any dispute . . . shall be settled by arbitration in accordance with [*e.g.*, Pennsylvania] Arbitration Law and administered by the American Arbitration Association under its [applicable] rules.

- In rendering the award, the arbitrator shall determine the rights and obligations of the parties according to the substantive and procedural laws of [*e.g.*, Illinois].

- The parties acknowledge that this Agreement evidences a transaction involving interstate commerce. The United States Arbitration Act shall govern the interpretation, enforcement, and proceedings pursuant to the arbitration clause in this Agreement.

[**Comment:** Each of these five clauses represents a decision to choose a particular body of law to govern the arbitration proceedings. A decision to include (or accept) such a clause should never be made without consulting an ADR expert.]

FORM NO. 34

ARBITRATOR SELECTION—NUMBER AND QUALIFICATIONS OF ARBITRATORS

- The arbitrator shall be selected from the panel of the Large Complex Case Program arbitrators of the American Arbitration Association.

- The sole arbitrator shall be a retired judge of the Supreme Court, Appellate Division, of the State of New York.

- The arbitrator shall be a neutral and impartial lawyer with excellent academic and professional credentials who has training and experience as an arbitrator [and who is a member of the _____ panel] [and who has been a practicing attorney specializing in general commercial litigation or general corporate and commercial matters for at least 15 years] [and who specializes in intellectual property and copyright matters].

- The arbitrator shall be selected in accordance with the AAA's Commercial Arbitration Rules [or the Arbitration Rules of JAMS/Endispute] except that each party shall be entitled to strike any or all of the names of potential arbitrators on the list submitted to the parties. In the event the parties are unable to agree on a mutually acceptable arbitrator from the first or second list submitted by [the American Arbitration Association] [or JAMS/Endispute], then [the regional director of the American Arbitration Association office] [or the Chief Judicial Officer of JAMS/Endispute] shall designate three persons who meet the criteria for appointment established by the parties. Each party shall be entitled to strike one name and shall state the order of preference for the persons not stricken, and the selection of the arbitrator shall be made from among those not stricken in their indicated order of mutual preference.

- (International)—Each party shall appoint one arbitrator in accordance with the Rules of Conciliation and Arbitration of the International Chamber of Commerce (Paris). The two party-appointed arbitrators shall select a presiding arbitrator. If they are unable to agree, the presiding arbitrator shall be appointed by the International Chamber of Commerce in accordance with its Rules.

- The arbitrator shall be a certified public accountant.

- The arbitrator shall be a retired insurance industry executive.

- The arbitration proceedings shall be conducted before a panel of three neutral arbitrators, each of whom shall be members of the Bar of the State of [specify], actively engaged in the practice of law for at least ten years.

- The panel of three arbitrators shall consist of one contractor, one architect, and one attorney who specializes in construction matters.

- Arbitrators must be members of the [specify] State Bar actively engaged in the practice of law with expertise in the process of deciding disputes and interpreting contracts in [the particular industry involved in the subject controversy].

- The arbitrators will be selected from a panel of persons having experience with and knowledge of computers and the computer business, and at least one of the arbitrators selected will be an attorney.

- One of the arbitrators shall be a member of the Bar of the State of [specify], actively engaged in the practice of law, or a retired member of the state or federal judiciary.

- The arbitration shall be before one neutral arbitrator to be selected in accordance with the Commercial Rules of the American Arbitration Association and shall proceed under the Expedited Procedures of said Rules, irrespective of the amount in dispute.

- In the event any party's claim exceeds $1 million, exclusive of interest and attorney fees, the dispute shall be heard and determined by three arbitrators.

[**Comment:** These clauses are examples of the myriad possibilities available, the most attractive prospect being that the parties will agree on the particular arbitrator(s) themselves. Failing that, a clause may control the choice (somewhat) by: (a) requiring a neutral from a distinguished panel; (b) listing qualifications for prospective arbitrators; (c) giving power to a trusted institution (or person) to narrow the choice; (d) mandating that the selection process be done according to a particular set of Rules; and (e) having the parties select two of the panel, and having those two select the third. Note that the "qualifications" clause (the third, above) begins with a rather vague and therefore fairly unenforceable set of criteria. Quantifiable standards finally appear at the bracketed phrases. When a dispute exists in a "submission" setting (*i.e.,* no predispute ADR clause exists), the selection of a neutral *should* be easy. The real art is in crafting an arbitrator-selection clause in a predispute setting when no one knows what issues *will* arise.]

FORM NO. 35

HYBRIDS: PARTNERING—CONTRACT PROVISIONS

1. The parties agree to hold a Partnering workshop within [60 days] of the Notice to Proceed. The workshop shall be attended by management-level representatives, who have the authority to enter into a Partnering Charter on behalf of their organizations. Attendance of similar representatives shall be required of any party who subsequently agrees to perform work on this project. The cost of the Partnering workshop, any follow-up workshops, and the implementation of any dispute resolution systems arising out of the workshop, will be shared equally among the parties to this contract with no change in contract price. Facilitators for the Partnering workshop shall be obtained from the [American Arbitration Association Partnering Facilitation Panel of the [city] Office]. Follow-up workshops will be held from time to time throughout the duration of the contract as agreed to by the parties.

2. **Partnering.** The parties agree to use Partnering for dispute avoidance. The Partnering process will be multilateral in makeup among [names of parties], and any costs associated with Partnering will be shared equally with no change in the contract price. Within [60] days of the Notice to Proceed [*or* other triggering event], the parties shall hold a Partnering workshop to be attended by each party's representatives as well as appropriate senior management from both parties. Management representatives of all subsequent parties to the contract will be required to attend the Partnering workshop. Follow-up workshops will be held from time to time throughout the duration of the contract as agreed by the parties. Partnering facilitators will be obtained through the Partnering program of the [U.S. Army Corps of Engineers] [*or* American Arbitration Association].

3. In order most effectively to complete this contract, the parties shall use Partnering techniques. The parties intend to draw on the strengths of each organization in an effort to achieve a successful project. Partnering on this project shall be multilateral in makeup, and any cost associated with effecting Partnering under this contract will be shared equally between the parties with no change in contract price. The parties agree to use the [Partnering Facilitation Panel of the American Arbitration Association] to effectuate this provision, and agree to hold periodic follow-up Partnering meetings. The Partnering workshops and meetings shall include key personnel from all parties. The costs for the Partnering workshops and meetings shall be borne by each party equally with no additional compensation for the individual participants.

4. Within ten [10] days of the acceptance of this contract, the parties shall meet and confer in order to commence planning the Partnering workshop.

5. In order to complete this contract most beneficially for all parties, the parties agree to form a Partnering relationship. This Partnering relationship will draw on the strengths of each party in achieving a quality project. Within [30] days of the date of execution of this contract, the parties will request from [the American Arbitration Association] the appointment of neutral facilitators for the Partnering retreat. The Partnering retreat will take place as soon as is practicable, but in any case within [60] days of the date of execution of this contract. The parties agree to participate in good faith in the Partnering retreat. Individual participation in the Partnering retreat shall be as agreed upon by the parties, but shall include at least the following project personnel:

[List names and organizations here.]

The cost of administering the Partnering retreat and the fees and expenses of the Partnering facilitator shall be borne equally by the contracting parties.

Provision for Project Specifications (Partnering)

[The following language may be used in the project specifications themselves.]

6. **Partnering.** [Party's name] intends to encourage the foundation of a cohesive partnership with [names of other parties in project]. This partnership will be structured to draw on the strengths of each organization to identify and achieve mutual and reciprocal goals. The objective is successful completion of the project within the provisions of the Partnering charter.

This partnership will be multilateral in makeup, and participation will be totally voluntary. Any cost associated with effectuating this partnership will be agreed to by both parties and will be shared equally with no change in contract price. To implement this partnership initiative, it is anticipated that within [60] days of Notice to Proceed [or other triggering event] the [representatives of each party] will attend a partnership development seminar, including a team-building workshop. Attendance is expected by [key personnel] as agreed to by the parties. Follow-up workshops will be held periodically throughout the duration of the contract as agreed to by the parties.

An integral aspect of Partnering is the resolution of disputes in a timely, professional and nonadversarial manner. Alternative dispute resolution (ADR) methodologies will be encouraged in place of more formal dispute resolution procedures. ADR will assist in promoting and maintaining an amicable working relationship to preserve the partnership. ADR in this context is intended to be a voluntary, nonbinding procedure available for use by the parties to this contract to resolve any dispute that may arise during performance.

[**Comment:** As with other ADR mechanisms, the clauses which create partnering vary widely in length and detail. In general, all they need to do is commit the signatories to a partnering program and indicate the origin or source of the partnering facilitators. Like other *voluntary* ADR processes, partnering is only going to work if all the parties want it to. As a result, no amount of draftsmanship can guarantee a successful partnering program.]

FORM NO. 36

HYBRIDS—LETTER TO AWARDEE REQUESTING A MEETING TO DISCUSS THE PARTNERING CONCEPT

[Name]
[Company]
[Address]

Dear [Name]:

Congratulations! I was delighted to find [addressee's company] the apparent low bidder on the [name] project. Your company has a reputation for excellence and we look forward to a mutually rewarding relationship with you.

I hope to have all the administrative formalities completed by [date], when I will make the formal contract award. In the meantime, I would like to propose a meeting with you within the next few weeks, at your headquarters, to discuss a "Partnering" approach to managing the project.

My concept of Partnering is recognizing shared risk and common objectives, promoting cooperation, minimizing confrontation, and eliminating litigation. Success is making all those having a stake in finishing the job a winner. It is a challenging endeavor that requires up-front agreement on expectations, helpful systems and, most importantly, the unqualified commitment of senior leadership.

I will call you to determine when a meeting may be convenient.

Sincerely,

[owner/contracting government agency]

FORM NO. 37
HYBRIDS—PARTNERING CHARTER WITH GOALS LISTED

We [the organizations], the partners in the [project name], are a trusting and cooperative team, committed to quality work, safety, timeliness, and within budget completion, so that all are proud to contribute. Our goals are to:

- Complete the project so that it meets the design intent.
- Complete the project without litigation.
- Achieve Value Engineering savings of $[_____].
- Control cost growth to less than [____]%.
- Finish the project [_____] days ahead of schedule.
- Suffer no lost-time injuries by promoting a safe job site.
- Ensure fair treatment for all parties.
- Solve problems at the first opportunity, at the lowest possible management level.
- Use alternative dispute resolution (ADR) if needed to aid problem solving.
- [Other objectives as defined by the parties at the Partnering workshop.]

[**Comment:** This charter is an example of a document which usually emerges at the end of the partnering session itself. Obviously, each one may be slightly different, depending on what the "partners" have decided. It does, however, show the typical kinds of goals set out in a Partnering Charter for a construction project. It is important that earlier Partnering documents (proposed clauses, letters of invitation, etc.) *do not contain* anything quite this specific. After all, the fundamental philosophy of partnering is that *all* stakeholders in the project *mutually* arrive at the statement of goals.]

FORM NO. 38
HYBRIDS—GENERAL PARTNERING CHARTER

Our Charter for success in [project name] is our commitment to work cooperatively and in harmony and to communicate openly in an atmosphere of confidence and trust. We will work as a team to build action plans, to break down communication barriers, resolve conflicts at the lowest possible level, to streamline the paperwork process, and build a team spirit to achieve maximum success for all: a quality project, a safe job site, and on-time completion within budget with a fair profit.

[Comment: While not as specific as Form No. 37, this charter, at least, sets general goals to which all have subscribed. A partnering session which ends with this general a charter has probably not been a very successful one.]

FORM NO. 39
HYBRIDS—PARTNERING STATEMENTS

- In order to accomplish this contract most effectively, [name of organizing party, usually owner] is encouraging the formation of a cohesive partnership with [other key organizations: in construction, usually with the general contractor, architect, engineers, and key subcontractors]. This partnership will strive to draw on the strengths of each organization in an effort to achieve a quality project, done right the first time, within budget, and on schedule. This partnership will be informal in makeup and participation will be totally voluntary. Any cost associated with effecting this partnership will be agreed to by all parties and will be shared equally with no change in contract price.

[**Comment:** This clause could be placed in every bid solicitation for a construction project. With slight modification, it could be used in Requests for Proposals or Requests for Tenders regarding almost any project.]

FORM NO. 40

HYBRIDS—AGREEMENT FOR ARBITRATION/ MEDIATION (ARB/MED)

The undersigned parties in the [identify lawsuit or other claims] controversy do request and appoint [name of neutral] both as our arbitrator and mediator with respect to the claims and counterclaims of the parties filed in the above-referenced matter. [Name of neutral] accepts the appointment. Hereinafter, [name of neutral] may be variously referred to as the "neutral," the "arbitrator," or the "mediator."

1. The parties agree to binding arbitration of any existing claim or controversy between the parties arising out of or relating to the above-referenced [litigation or claim] or the interpretation of this agreement. Subject to the provisions referencing mediation below, judgment upon the award rendered by the arbitrator may be entered in any court having jurisdiction thereof [add: including the court in which the above-referenced proceeding is pending, *if the controversy is a lawsuit*].

2. At the beginning of the arbitration, the parties will each pay the arbitrator an equal share of his estimated expenses as neutral plus $[_____] as a deposit for his fee, which will be $[_____ per hour].

3. The arbitrator, following the arbitration session, will prepare a written decision (award) granting any remedy or relief the arbitrator deems just and reasonable, including the assessment of the arbitrator's fees and expenses. The arbitrator shall not be required to assign any reasons, written or oral, for his decision.

4. Following the arbitration, the written decision will be sealed and placed in an envelope and held in confidence by the arbitrator pending the completion of mediation, which shall immediately follow the arbitration.

5. In the event the parties resolve the case voluntarily through mediation, the written decision in arbitration shall be of no force and effect and shall be discarded without disclosure to the parties. If, in the sole opinion and discretion of the mediator, the parties, after commencing mediation, are unable to resolve the matter through mediation, then the envelope will be opened and the written decision revealed and delivered to the parties.

6. The arbitrator will, in his sole discretion, determine what kind, manner, and length of presentation, argument, briefs, proofs, and other evidence he [she] will accept in the arbitration and what relevance or materiality any such evidence has. Conformity to strict legal rules of

evidence shall not be required. The arbitrator will also determine in his sole discretion all matters of procedure affecting the arbitration.

7. To the extent consistent with this agreement, both the arbitration and the mediation shall be subject to [state confidentiality statutes], the arbitration shall be conducted in accordance with the American Arbitration Association Commercial Arbitration Rules, and the mediation shall be conducted in accordance with the Commercial Mediation Rules of the American Arbitration Association.

8. All parties agree that the arbitration and mediation procedures shall be conducted on [date] and that the parties do not require any [additional] discovery concerning any matter in issue.

[Signatures of all parties and the neutral should be obtained.]

[**Comment:** This procedure, known as Arb/Med for short, is not widely used. It runs counter to the underlying outlook of alternative dispute resolution in several respects. The foremost of these is that the process seems to put the cart before the horse, *i.e.,* it requires the parties to go through an adversarial, evidentiary proceeding *before trying to work it out through mediation.*]

ENDNOTES

[1] A California Superior (trial) Court has upheld the Bank of America's method of introducing its program. The ruling is being appealed, however.

[2] If this process does not sound familiar, try reading all those little inserts that come with credit card bills. Who knows what has been agreed to?

[3] F. Sander and S. Goldberg, "Fitting the Forum to the Fuss: A User-Friendly Guide to Selecting an Alternative Dispute Resolution Procedure," *Negotiation Journal* 10 (1994): 295nn.

[4] *Id.* at pp. 299-301. The authors of the above article have tried to reduce the ADR selection process to mathematics by using the goals I have mentioned in conjunction with a number of factors which may get in the way of a dispute being resolved. While their work is thoughtful and, perhaps, useful, experience has taught me that every aspect of alternative dispute resolution is more of an art than a science.

[5] The executive director and his former employee eventually entered into mediation that resolved the matter, but that's not the point of the anecdote.

[6] Enforcement of awards in international arbitrations is covered by the 1958 United Nations Convention on the Recognition and Enforcement of Foreign Arbitral Awards which is commonly referred to as the "New York Convention." It has been somewhat supplemented [not all countries are signatories] in this hemisphere by the Inter-American Convention on International Commercial Arbitration. Before embarking on any international arbitration, the parties would be well advised to see whether the conventions apply to the dispute in question *and* whether the opponents are citizens of countries which are signatories to the New York Convention, and/or the Inter-American Convention.

[7] Center for Public Resources (CPR) is an organization, founded by general counsels of major corporations, whose stated purpose is to facilitate the cost-effective resolution of business disputes (usually between large corporations). This clause is one among a number of clauses which are provided without charge to interested parties.

*"I'm certain I speak for the entire legal profession when
I say that the fee is reasonable and just."*

CHOOSING THE RIGHT ADR HELP

There is one thing stronger than all the armies of the world: and that is an idea whose time has come.
—Victor Hugo

If anything has been repeated in this book, it is the advice that an alternative dispute resolution program should not be selected or implemented without getting advice on a specific situation. The forms contained in a previous chapter are "off-the-shelf" products which may or may not be appropriate to a situation, and the suggestions given throughout the book are necessarily general.

A. The Institutional Providers: ADR Supermarkets

There are a number of places to get ADR help and advice, where information (and some advice) is available without charge. The primary source of free information seems to be the American Arbitration Association. Not only is it the oldest and largest (by volume of cases, at least) provider of ADR services, it also provides the broadest *range* of services, which are:

— research in ADR;

— published materials on ADR and related topics;

— administration of ADR processes (arbitration, mediation, etc.);

— maintaining lists of qualified neutrals;

— training neutrals and ADR advocates; and

— informing the public about ADR.

The American Arbitration Association is a nonprofit organization, supported in part by fees for administrative and other services, and, in part, by membership dues, grants, and gifts. It has offices in all major (and some minor) cities in the United States, and affiliations with numerous counterpart organizations around the world. Initially, the AAA is useful as a storehouse of information about ADR. From pamphlets to books, the AAA has it all. Most regional offices are well stocked and have knowledgeable staff members who can answer most any question. Among its offerings, the AAA has sets of Rules of procedure for just about every ADR mechanism and just about every industry. In addition, the AAA produces pamphlets of suggested ADR clauses for all occasions. It is not surprising to learn that these clauses have the AAA identified as the administering entity (where administration is required). After having perused their materials and perhaps those of some of the "competition," some information specific to a situation may be necessary. A regional vice-president (as the head of an office is called) would be the initial telephone contact for inquiries about specific circumstances, as the line staff are not equipped to advise anyone on this level. Regional vice-presidents routinely call on the resources of the national office if they are needed. So, solid information and fairly unbiased advice can be obtained from AAA.[1]

There are two other organizations which provide ADR services and are national in scope. One is the Center for Public Resources (CPR), a nonprofit alliance of 550 global corporations and law firms that develops alternatives to litigation. Like the AAA, CPR is "engaged in an integrated agenda of research and development, education, advocacy, and conflict resolution."[2] Unlike the AAA, the focus of CPR is principally to aid large corporations and law firms in implementing alternative dispute mechanisms into the mainstream of their practices. This is not a criticism. CPR has excellent information available and is more than willing to share it. It is just that some of its procedures, *e.g.*, the mini-trial, are geared toward huge and costly litigation, and are quite costly themselves. That said, CPR has performed some real public service in educating the business community about the benefits of ADR, and creating industry-specific programs, such as the National Franchise Mediation Program to resolve disputes between franchisors and their franchisees.

CPR achieves corporate commitment to ADR through the CPR Corporate Policy Statement on Alternatives to Litigation. As of February 1995, more than 800 U.S. corporations with 2,800 corporate subsidiaries have signed the CPR statement pledging to explore alternatives to litigation when disputes arise with other signatories. In addition, 1,500 law firms have signed the CPR Law Firm Policy Statement on Alternatives to Litigation, whereby they have pledged both to be knowledgeable about alternative dispute resolution and to discuss ADR options with their clients when appropriate. Companies which have become signatories of the CPR Corporate Policy Statement may be influenced by the immense savings in legal costs reported by CPR. For instance, in 1994, CPR conducted a survey of disputes brought to them, and of the 109 companies which responded, an estimated savings in legal costs in excess of $75 million was reported.[3]

Perhaps the biggest distinction between AAA and CPR is the fact that CPR does not generally believe in or provide for administration of the ADR process. CPR advocates party-managed ADR (where the parties' counsel and the neutral, if requested, manage the process), regarding this method as the optimum way to achieve economy, control, and flexibility offered by ADR. However, a user of CPR highlighted a potential problem: "They say they want a party-managed process, but what they mean is a counsel-managed process." (There are other risks and extra cost in this approach, as previously discussed.)

Parties are assisted by the CPR Panel Management Group in choosing the neutral who will participate in the resolution of their dispute. When a dispute is brought to CPR, a member of the management panel reviews each dispute with counsel. Similar to the AAA, CPR maintains lists of neutrals, many of whom have specialized industry expertise. CPR policy states that the best way to realize full potential of ADR is to have a lawyer serve as the neutral. Like AAA, biographical information about the candidates, along with a fee schedule, are provided to the parties. Possible candidates are contacted to ascertain availability and potential conflicts of interest. The management panel member familiar with the dispute aids the parties in the final selection of a neutral, emphasizing the skills, experience, and substantive knowledge necessary for resolution of the dispute.

The third largest ADR provider is JAMS/Endispute. This is a for-profit business, which was started by a few retired California judges. For some years, its principal marketing tool was to emphasize that *all* its panelists were retired jurists. In 1994, JAMS (the Judicial Arbitration and Mediation Service) merged with two other ADR service entities, Bates & Edwards, a group of mediators named after its two founders, and Endispute, which provided a broader range of ADR services. Most of the neutrals in both of these organizations were *not retired judges.* Like its two big brothers (AAA and CPR), JAMS/Endispute will provide information about ADR to those who ask. Unlike the two others, however, the person responding to phone calls for information at JAMS is most likely to be a salesperson who tends not to know very much about ADR. So, the advice usually comes from a narrower knowledge base. Because JAMS is in business for profit, after all, it is the salesperson's job to sell JAMS. The AAA personnel are usually better informed, but they would also prefer their (nonprofit) organization be used.

Amongst the institutional ADR information providers, the American Arbitration Association has the top rating, followed rather closely by the Center for Public Resources, and, at a greater distance, by JAMS/Endispute. However, there are other names to consider:

— The National Institute for Dispute Resolution (NIDR), a nonprofit organization based in the District of Columbia, began in 1983 by five large foundations "to promote the development and use of dispute resolution locally, nationally and internationally." NIDR describes itself as focusing "special attention on lessening the conflict-based problems of the poor and other disadvantaged members of society."[4] The work of NIDR is largely educational, and it does not maintain a panel of neutrals.

— United States Arbitration & Mediation (USA&M), over ten years old, describes its role as providing "impartial administrative dispute resolution and consulting services," and is headquartered in Pittsburgh, Pennsylvania.

— Judicate is headquartered in Philadelphia, Pennsylvania, and describes itself as "The National Private Court System."

— Judicate West, apparently a split-off from Judicate, currently limits its activities to California.

— The Council of Better Business Bureaus, the umbrella group for local Better Business Bureau offices, offers dispute resolution services from its offices in Arlington, Virginia, and describes itself as "specialists in business-customer dispute resolution."

In addition to the above organizations, there are literally hundreds of local and regional companies, almost all of which are for profit. These companies range from one day to seven years old and encompass everything from sole proprietorships to an association of retired judges whose only joint activity is to advertise together. *Caveat emptor.*

B. The Neutrals

I am free of all prejudice. I hate everyone equally.—W.C. Fields

It should go without saying, but it needs to be said anyhow: Any alternative dispute resolution process is only as good as the neutral who is presiding over it. No amount of efficient administration, no set of well thought-out rules of procedure, no shiny new video-conference room, nothing can make up for an inept neutral. One, then, should choose a neutral for dispute resolution slowly and very, very carefully.

The first rule of selecting a neutral is to have nothing to do with an institutional provider of ADR which will *not* allow the parties to select the neutral, even if that neutral is not on their list. There is enough competition in this marketplace that consumers should be able to have the desired neutral. A clause which permits the institutional provider, *e.g.,* the AAA, to appoint an arbitrator if the parties can't agree on one is perfectly acceptable. Indeed, such a clause is desirable, since without it, one party to the dispute could delay things indefinitely and cause the other to experience the unnecessary expense of going to court and getting a judge to appoint an arbitrator. But if an institutional provider will not work with an arbitrator (or mediator or anything else) that the parties themselves have chosen, do business elsewhere.

Then, not being acquainted with hundreds of alternative dispute resolution neutrals, how does one find the neutral that is going to be right for *this dispute?* The first thing to know is that, as of now, anyone who wants to call himself an arbitrator or mediator or conciliator or ADR neutral can do so.[5] This fact gives the phrase *caveat emptor* rich, new meaning. Thousands (this is no exaggeration) of "wannabe" mediators are abroad in the land, many of whom have had no training or, at best, inadequate training. Even among those who have been exposed to good training, there is frequently a dearth of experience. Although their number is probably lower, the same thing is true of many "arbitrators"—no licensing, no standards, no training, and no experience. So, where does one turn?

The big three institutional providers are always good places to get some names and biographies. Describing the dispute and what type of neutral will be necessary will make the list of names they supply a lot more meaningful. Business associates who have been through the same type of ADR process may also be fertile grounds for developing referrals to competent neutrals. At this point, turn back to Chapter 7 of this book and reread the section on the selection of a neutral.

C. The Consultants

There are an astounding number of ADR consultants. For example, the 1995 Martindale-Hubbell Dispute Resolution Directory is indexed by "services provided." Under the heading "Case Evaluation," there are over 2,240 names.[6] Under "Program Design," there are about 520 listings, while under "Training," approximately 1,120 persons or firms are listed. All the listings in this directory are paid for by the providers.

Obviously, there are enough consultants to help design an alternative dispute resolution program that is right for an organization and the people it deals with. But how does one choose?

First of all, one hopes that reading this book has made the reader a more sophisticated consumer of ADR services. Secondly, the process for selecting a neutral can easily be adapted to the consultant-selection operation. Ask the institutional providers, who may (purport to) do it for free. Take what is free, keep what is needed, and discard the rest. But, before making a final decision, take the advice of someone who is truly neutral.

D. Neutrals as Consultants

A crank is a man with a new idea—until it catches on.
—Mark Twain

As with many fields, someone who is capable in one area of it may not be the best person to hire in another. In the selection of a capable neutral as consultant in designing an ADR program, not every capable neutral would make a good consultant. Many, knowing that they would not, decline to take such assignments. Other neutrals may have a wealth of experience in one or two ADR mechanisms, but do not know much about others. Still others may be so closely associated with one or the other of the institutional providers that they cannot give impartial advice. Others will truthfully say that they do not want to consult for fear of losing future "neutral" business if they do (not that they wouldn't be wanted, but that they would have to disclose the consulting relationship to the other party, who probably would not want them). The qualities which should be present in ADR consultants are that they should be:

— lawyers by training (Anyone suggesting an ADR program should be able to give advice on its legality and the appropriate way to implement it, as well as the enforceability of the outcome.);

— experienced in ADR, as advocates, parties, or neutrals (There is no substitute for experience here; the consultant will be relied on for the practical ramifications of various choices, and academic study alone will not give the necessary background.);

— interested in consulting (not just killing time until the next assignment as an arbitrator);

— reasonably priced (certainly no more per hour than the best neutrals charge);

— having a personal touch (This person will, in all probability, be laying the educational groundwork for an ADR plan with customers, suppliers, employees, outside counsel, or others; people skills will count.);

— willing to admit that there are times and situations when ADR is just not a good choice; and

— possessed of good references (certainly as a consultant, if possible; if not, then as an ADR neutral or advocate).

E. Managing an ADR Program

As previously mentioned, the importance of an educational effort to teach all concerned the values of ADR (and the specifics of a program and how it will be used) cannot be stressed enough. While this effort is important if ADR is being instituted with customers or suppliers, it is crucial if an ADR plan is being established for employees. This education campaign should precede any announcement of an ADR program, however informal. Indeed, the first battle of this campaign may be to convince others in management that ADR itself (or the particular program being focused on) is a good idea.

The next step in the managerial process should be some kind of policy statement. Depending on the size and type of organization, this statement will vary in both formality and detail. At a bare minimum, however, it should include a clear, unequivocal, and strong commitment by senior management. If there is a legal department and a human resources department in an organization, the heads of these departments should probably also be signatories to any policy statement. The human resources head will be a crucial signatory if an employee ADR program is being introduced. Policy statements frequently precipitate questions, so someone should be designated to answer them. A sufficient period should elapse between the policy statement and actual implementation so that no one gets the impression that the ADR program is being forced on anyone.

As with any organizational program, good management principles dictate that someone should be put in charge of it. Usually, that "someone" emerges from the group who was involved in designing the program in the first place. If an organization has a legal department, good candidates for the position will likely emerge from it. An ADR manager should ideally have several distinct responsibilities, the first of these being the administration of the program within the organization. This may sound like a bigger task than it is because many ADR programs turn to independent organizations (such as the American Arbitration Association) to administer the processing of the actual disputes themselves. So, an ADR manager will likely only be responsible for overseeing those aspects of the program that are internal to the organization. In addition to line management of the ADR program itself, an ADR manager will also be responsible for showing (by word and action) the organization's *continuing commitment* to ADR by developing *ongoing educational ADR programs* within the organization. This will take two forms:

(1) ADR basic education and the program for new hires and those existing employees who didn't understand the policy when it was first announced or implemented, and

(2) continuing education regarding changes in either ADR generally or the program itself.

This latter responsibility cannot be stressed too much. Unlike some companywide programs, ADR programs are dynamic, evolving organisms. The same is true of the field of alternative dispute resolution itself. So, the ADR manager must continue self-education and pass that new learning on to colleagues.[7] Last, but very important, is the responsibility for "financial management" of the ADR program. After all, some of the reasons this program was installed were the increased time and money savings, stress reduction, and reallocation of resources formerly dedicated to disputes to more meaningful activities. Someone has to monitor these results.

F. Financial Management of ADR Programs

"Financial management" of an ADR program will be difficult, because not all the results are easy to quantify. A good starting point will be the tangible costs of the program itself, which would include the costs of establishing the program (which should be amortized over a five- to ten-year period) and should include some allocation of cost for the time of employees and managers used in the design and set-up phases. However, the real key to whether the program is making sense financially lies in its long-term costs and benefits. Some of the ongoing costs which have to be captured include:

— Salary and overhead of the person(s) managing/administering the program internally;

— Time costs for those employees who participate in the program, *i.e.*, either as disputants in a employee program or as witnesses, negotiators, or the like in a program with "outsiders";

— The cost of whatever space may be dedicated to the program (not just the manager/administrator's office, but conference rooms, etc., which may be used part time);

— Printing costs for retooling contract documents or employee manuals to include ADR; and

— Fees for independent agency administration of some procedures, *e.g.*, arbitration or mediation, and the fees of independent neutrals.

This list may seem daunting, in the sense that all these expenses may add up to some large number. They probably will not, but that is not the end of the inquiry in any event. As an aerospace executive recently put it: "I almost don't care what ADR costs. What I care about is if we are saving money and time from the way we used to do things. We really are, and the bonus is that our employees like it, and our suppliers love it." The ultimate test, then, of the success of an ADR program is not how much it costs *per se* (although that should be carefully managed), but how much it costs compared to other available ways of resolving disputes. The most obvious elements of that analysis, time and money, were mentioned by the executive quoted above. However, there are more. Recall that he noted as bonuses the fact that the company's employees and suppliers both were satisfied with the program. (In the case of his industry, ADR with customers, mainly the government, is in its infancy.) While his approach characterizes employee (supplier, customer, or whomever) satisfaction as a bonus, that satisfaction is sometimes a principal motivator. Surely, there is no doubt that higher rates of satisfaction among an organization's various constituencies will sooner or later translate into a better "bottom line."

There is also the matter of privacy and how to quantify its benefits, and so on, until an ADR manager is able to make an "apples to apples" comparison of the costs of the ADR program and the costs of earlier methods of dispute resolution.

The ADR manager's work does not end there, however. Because one of the hallmarks of ADR is its flexibility, it follows that every ADR program may be easily modified. Even if a design phase was carefully done, there is no way to predict *exactly* how an ADR program will work in advance. Observant monitoring of all aspects of the program will show whether changes need to be made, or whether new developments in ADR generally should be incorporated into the program. In addition, with new legislation and court decisions regarding ADR arriving with increasing frequency, a regular "check-up" with the consultant who helped get the program started is almost a necessity.

G. Pitfalls to Be Avoided

As discussed earlier, arbitration agreements can limit the remedies available to parties, but such agreements should not be unfair. Parties who require mandatory arbitration as a condition of an agreement normally have a greater bargaining power, but they should not misuse this power to the detriment of the weaker party by forcing them to agree to terms which unfairly impair their rights. Although mandatory arbitration clauses are sanctioned by the courts, judges will not uphold arbitration agreements which purport to dispose of individual rights and protections mandated by statute.[8] If the courts were to enforce such agreements, parties with the superior bargaining power could compel their opponents to surrender their rights and Congress's efforts to protect certain classes of people would be of no consequence.

Attempts to limit individual rights contractually often arise in the employment contract setting. Since the Supreme Court upheld mandatory arbitration clauses for employment discrimination claims, many companies in different industries have required their employees to sign arbitration agreements for future claims, but some companies have gone too far. One company gave their employees five days to sign an arbitration agreement (which eliminated their right to bring claims against their employers in court and restricted their rights to collect damages) or lose their jobs.[9] Another company made employees sign a mandatory arbitration agreement which required that all *employee* claims be resolved through arbitration while retaining the right to sue employees in court. In addition, that same company gave employees less than one hour to sign the agreement or be fired. Employees were also told that they could not have their attorneys review the agreement, although the agreements stated that employees had been given that opportunity.[10]

Where employers have forced their employees to sign unfair arbitration agreements, they may be hard pressed to find someone to arbitrate claims. Some institutional providers of alternative dispute resolution have refused to accept arbitrations in which one party has attempted to restrict the remedies available to the other.[11] These institutional providers will only arbitrate cases where an employee retains most of the same rights as in court. When employee claims are arbitrated according to the terms of an unfair agreement, any award rendered under that agreement is seriously at risk of being overturned.

Don't risk forfeiting the right to arbitration or having an arbitration award overturned by entering into an unfair arbitration agreement with parties having disparate bargaining power. It is a waste of both time and money and will have gained nothing.

ENDNOTES

[1] Indeed, much of the information is available on-line in the WESTLAW research service.

[2] *Martindale-Hubbell Dispute Resolution Directory,* 1995, p. 2-5.

[3] The average saving per company was $695,000 when claims were $1.5 billion; for general commercial claims, the average savings was $366,000.

[4] *Martindale-Hubbell Dispute Resolution Directory,* 1995, p. 2-5.

[5] There is some limit to the pool of people who can call themselves "private judges," since, in most jurisdictions, service as a private judge is limited to members of the bar of that state. However, having a lawyer or retired jurist for a private judge does not necessarily ensure their competence *as* a private judge.

[6] *Martindale-Hubbell Dispute Resolution Directory,* 1995, pp. 5b-47—5b-56.

[7] Here, again, the institutional providers—especially AAA and CPR—can be excellent sources of printed materials explaining ADR.

[8] See, *Graham Oil Co. v. ARCO Products Co.,* 43 F.3d 1244 (9th Cir. 1994).

[9] Margaret A. Jacobs, "Workers Call Some Private Justice Unjust," *Wall Street Journal,* 26 January 1995, p. B1.

[10] Margaret A. Jacobs, "Mandatory Arbitration Agreement Faces Direct Challenge by EEOC," *Wall Street Journal,* 12 April 1995, p. B6.

[11] JAMS/Endispute issued minimum standards of fairness that prevent it from accepting arbitrations, for instance, where an employer has imposed restrictions on an employee's rights or ability to collect damages. The American Arbitration Association has also adopted a new set of rules governing wrongful termination, sexual harassment, and discrimination disputes. These rules provide that employees who have signed mandatory arbitration clauses as a condition of employment will get the same relief as they could in court. The rules were adopted to ensure fairness and are an effort to reduce the chance that an arbitration award will be overturned by the court.

"Officer, shouldn't this be a time for healing?"

INTERNATIONAL ADR

Improving Foreign Business Relations

A. A Climate of Acceptance: ADR in the International Business Community

The international business community has extensive experience with international arbitration and other ADR methods. This section introduces the international institutions and their rules which have established procedures to facilitate international ADR, such as the International Chamber of Commerce in Paris, the American Arbitration Association in New York (and other U.S. cities), and the London Court for International Arbitration (arbitration being predominant in international commercial dispute resolution). These major arbitral institutions offer organizational structures to provide assistance in initiating arbitral proceedings, appointing arbitrators, and taking care of concerns such as hearing rooms, translators, and secretarial services. Besides providing their own rules of arbitration procedures, some of these institutions accommodate the United Nations (UNCITRAL) Arbitration Rules, which were designed for widespread use in *ad hoc* arbitration, *i.e.,* arbitration which is unattached to any institutional framework.

1. The United Nations (UNCITRAL) Arbitration Rules

The United Nations Arbitration Rules[1] were adopted by the United Nations Commission on International Trade Law (UNCITRAL) on April 28, 1976. Unlike some other rules, such as the Rules of Arbitration of the International Chamber of Commerce (see below), the UNCITRAL Rules were not designed to be administered by any particular national or international arbitration organization, but were prepared for universal use. Most major arbitral institutions can provide administrative services to help parties and arbitrators conduct cases under the UNCITRAL Rules.

The parties can agree in a contract to use the UNCITRAL Rules for arbitrating disputes arising out of that contract. The Rules prescribe in detail the method of selecting the arbitral panel and the procedures for conducting the arbitral proceedings. However, in most instances, the parties may agree to modify the Rules and conduct proceedings accordingly (Art. 1(1) of Rules).

Under the UNCITRAL Rules, the parties agree to have one or three arbitrators serve on the arbitral panel. In most cases, they will also have agreed on an arbitral institution or person to act as the appointing authority, which has the power to appoint arbitrator(s) when the parties do not agree. If no appointing authority is agreed upon, the Rules provide that a party may request the Secretary-General of the Permanent Court of Arbitration at The Hague to designate the appointing authority. This, however, is more cumbersome than naming an "appointing authority" and usually delays the proceedings. When three arbitrators are to be appointed, each party appoints one arbitrator. These two arbitrators will choose the third arbitrator, who acts as the presiding arbitrator. If the two arbitrators do not make their selection within 30 days, the appointing authority will appoint the third arbitrator.

The arbitration proceedings will be held at the place agreed upon by the parties. If they have not agreed, the panel itself has the authority to determine the place under UNCITRAL rules. The proceedings are conducted in any way that the panel deems appropriate, as long as it gives equal treatment and opportunity to each party. Under the UNCITRAL Rules (unlike many U.S. states), the arbitral panel itself has the power to determine whether it has jurisdiction over the case. It can also rule on objections to the arbitration agreement's existence or validity (Art. 21). The panel will apply the law designated by the parties as applicable to the merits of the dispute. Without such designation, the panel will apply the law which it considers applicable (Art. 33(1)). In all cases, however, the panel must take into account the terms of the contract and the trade usages applicable.

The arbitral award is to be made in writing and (unlike American domestic arbitration) *must* state the reasons upon which it is based. It may be made public only with the parties' consent. Within 30 days after receiving the award, either party may request the panel to interpret the award or to correct any computational, clerical, or typographical errors in it.

More and more countries and arbitral institutions are adopting the UNCITRAL rules, such as Hong Kong in 1990.[2] Within the United States, Connecticut adopted the UNCITRAL rules in 1989, while California has international arbitration rules substantially similar to the UNCITRAL rules.

2. International Chamber of Commerce—Procedures and Cost

The International Chamber of Commerce (ICC) in Paris is a private nongovernmental association that promotes and facilitates international trade and commerce. Enterprises and organizations in over one hundred countries are members of the ICC.[3] The ICC operates what is probably the best-known international commercial arbitral institute, the ICC Court of Arbitration. The ICC Court of Arbitration is not really a court but an organization that provides administrative services to help parties conduct private international arbitration. It handles about 700 international arbitration cases per year.[4]

Parties who wish to specify ICC arbitration must put a clause in their contract to refer any dispute to the ICC. Arbitral proceedings conducted under the aegis of the ICC will follow the ICC Rules of Arbitration. Although the ICC's headquarters are located in Paris, the arbitral proceedings need not be held there. They can be held anywhere that the parties agree to and the ICC can accommodate. In fact, seven of ten cases do not take place in Paris.[5] If the parties do not agree, the Court (not the arbitrator) will decide a place, taking into account the convenience to the parties, the language and law of the contract, and attributes of national legal systems, among other things.

Arbitrators are formally appointed by the ICC Court of Arbitration, although the parties nominate them. An arbitrator must be "independent of the party nominating him." (Art. 2(4)). In case of a panel with a sole arbitrator, if the parties cannot agree on a candidate, the Court will appoint the sole arbitrator. If the panel is to be composed of three arbitrators, each party can nominate one candidate. The third arbitrator is appointed by the Court, unless the parties have agreed that their two appointees should agree on a third arbitrator within a fixed time limit. However selected, the third arbitrator will act as chairman of the panel. In practice, the Court does not appoint an arbitrator from a standing list, but determines that a particular nationality is desirable (generally a country other than that of any party) and requests the relevant National Committee (composed of ICC members from a given country) to make a recommendation. The Court rarely rejects a recommendation from a National Committee.[6]

The arbitrators, once impaneled, draw up Terms of Reference that describe both the parties and the claims. This practice also differs sharply from American domestic arbitration, but helps to clarify the issues involved. Unless the parties have agreed upon a law to be applied to the merits of the case, the arbitrators choose the law to be applied (Art. 13(3)). Procedural rules are those set by the ICC Rules of Arbitration, as modified by agreement of the parties.

Within six months after signing the terms of reference, the arbitrators must make their award, although this time limit can be extended by the ICC Court of Arbitration (Art. 18(2)). Awards are to be made by a majority of the panel, but the chairman is allowed to issue an award if a majority cannot be reached (Art. 19).[7] This power of the chairman seems likely to result in a compromise award in the view of at least one commentator. The ICC Rules do not require that the award state the reasons on which it is based. However, the ICC Court of Arbitration will inspect the award to make sure that it is enforceable at law (Art. 21). The Court does not review the award for errors in fact and law, but only reviews the formal sufficiency of the award. The parties, by submitting to ICC arbitration, agree to respect the award as binding and final.

Near the start of arbitration, after all the pleadings (claims and counterclaims) have been filed, the parties must pay at least half of the estimated arbitration fees before the claims are submitted to the arbitrators. These fees include the arbitrators' fees and personal expenses and ICC administrative fees. The ICC Court of Arbitration has the discretion to increase the arbitrators' fees to three times the amount paid to a sole arbitrator if the panel consists of three arbitrators. All the fees and costs are subject to allocation between the parties by the arbitrators in the final award, unless the parties agree otherwise.

The fees are based on a regressive percentage scale, set out in the ICC Rules' Schedule of Conciliation and Arbitration Costs,[8] and are as follows:

Sum in Dispute (in U.S. $)	Administrative Expenses
Up to 50,000	$ 2,000
100,000	$ 3,500
500,000	$ 9,500
1 million	$ 14,500
2 million	$ 19,500
5 million	$ 25,500
10 million	$ 30,500
50 million	$ 35,500
Over 50 million	$ 50,500 flat fee

Sum in Dispute (in U.S. $)	Min.	Arbitrators' Fees Max. with 1 Arbitrator	Max. with 3 Arbitrators
Up to 50,000	$ 1,000	$ 5,000	$ 15,000
100,000	$ 1,750	$ 8,000	$ 24,000
500,000	$ 4,950	$ 20,000	$ 60,000
1 million	$ 7,450	$ 30,000	$ 90,000
2 million	$ 10,450	$ 46,000	$138,000
5 million	$ 16,450	$ 63,000	$189,000
10 million	$ 21,450	$ 78,000	$234,000
50 million	$ 41,450	$138,000	$414,000
100 million	$ 51,450	$188,000	$564,000

From these tables, it is apparent that ICC arbitration is not cheap. A case with $100,000 in dispute will cost from $5,250 (all fees) to a maximum of $11,500 for a sole-arbitrator hearing or it may cost $27,500 for a three-arbitrator panel. A case with $1 million in dispute would cost from $21,950 to $104,500 for a three-arbitrator panel.

3. American Arbitration Association, International Arbitration Rules—Procedures and Cost

The American Arbitration Association (AAA), headquartered in New York City, was founded in 1926 and is the world's largest arbitral institution in terms of the overall number of cases. In the international arbitration field, the AAA handles about 200 cases per year, second to the ICC.[9] The AAA is a nongovernmental, nonprofit organization that supervises arbitration proceedings and provides administrative support under its own International Rules. The AAA also supervises arbitral proceedings using the UNCITRAL Rules at the parties' request. The AAA is also the North American administering body for arbitrations pursuant to the rules of the International Air Transport Association.

Parties who want their disputes to take place under the AAA International Rules can put a clause in their contract to that effect. The AAA recommends that the parties also add clauses regarding the number of arbitrators (one to three), the place of arbitration, and the language of arbitration.

The parties may modify the AAA International Arbitration Rules freely, subject to any conflicting provision of applicable law which they must follow (Art. 1). They have complete freedom in selecting the number of arbitrators and the method of appointing them. For example, they may agree that each party designate one arbitrator and those two will name a third, with the AAA making appointments if the panel is not promptly formed, or the parties may request the AAA to submit a list of arbitrators to them from which each can delete unacceptable names. In any event, one arbitrator will be appointed by the AAA if the parties have not agreed. If the case is large and complex, the AAA may appoint three arbitrators. Sixty days after the beginning of the arbitration request, if the panel has not been constituted because of disagreement, the AAA will appoint the arbitrator(s) and designate the presiding arbitrator (Art. 6(3)). In making the appointments, the AAA will consult with the parties.

The provisions of the AAA International Arbitration Rules regarding the arbitral procedures are very similar to that of UNCITRAL. The arbitration proceedings will be held at the place agreed upon by the parties. If they have not agreed, the panel has the authority to determine the place. The proceedings are conducted in the way that the panel deems appropriate, giving equal treatment and opportunity to each party. The arbitral panel has the power to determine whether it has jurisdiction over the case (Art. 15(1)). The panel will apply the law designated by the parties as applicable to the merits of the dispute. Without such designation, the panel will apply the law which it considers applicable.

The arbitral award is to be made in writing and must state the reasons upon which it is based. An award signed by a majority of the arbitrators is sufficient (Art. 28). It may be made public only with the parties' consent. Within 30 days after receiving the award, either party may request the panel to interpret the award or to correct any computational, clerical, or typographical errors in the award.

The AAA's administrative fees include filing and service fees. Arbitrator compensation is not included in the AAA schedule. These fees are subject to negotiation and allocation between the parties by the arbitrator in the award unless the parties agree otherwise. Proceeding under the AAA International Rules, the filing fees[10] are:

Amount of Claim	Filing Fee
Up to $10,000	$ 500
Above $10,000 to $50,000	$ 750
Above $50,000 to $250,000	$1,500
Above $250,000 to $500,000	$3,000
Above $500,000 to $1 million	$4,000
Above $1 million	$5,000

The minimum filing fee for any case having three or more arbitrators is $1,500.

The parties must also pay hearing and processing fees. These are $150 (per party) for each day of hearing before a single arbitrator, and $200 (per party) or each day of hearing before a multi-arbitrator panel. The processing fees are $150 (per party) 180 days after the case is initiated, and every 90 days thereafter for single-arbitrator cases, and $200 (per party) for multi-arbitrator cases. The parties must also pay rental fees for the hearing rooms. The AAA Rules seem unduly complicated, perhaps due to an effort to unbundle services. Whatever the AAA's motive, it is very hard to make an "apples to apples" comparison of its rates to other providers and even harder for parties to predict what their costs will be.

The AAA arbitrators' fees in international matters are set by the arbitrators themselves. Even so, a comparison shows that the AAA does not appear to have the same high-level fee structure as the ICC, resulting in relatively modest fees. For example, the filing fee for a $1 million case is only $4,000 as opposed to $14,500 with the ICC. One commentator believes that the low cost of its administered arbitration makes the AAA an "excellent choice for small and medium-sized businesses."[11] Since the AAA permits the parties to pick their own arbitrator(s), it would seem to be an equally good choice for large businesses.

4. Asia-Pacific Center for the Settlement of International Business Disputes

Based in San Francisco, the Asia-Pacific Center for the Settlement of International Business Disputes is an arm of the AAA which deals exclusively with international ADR in the Pacific Rim region. The Center has worked with Pacific Rim arbitral institutes to assist in the resolution of business disputes. For instance, the Center signed an agreement with the Center for International Commercial Dispute Resolution (CICDR) as part of an effort to make Hawaii the neutral center for resolving international commercial disputes in the Asia/Pacific region.[12] The Center's advisory council is composed of members from Asia, Australia, Korea, and the United States. More information about the Center can be obtained from the AAA's West Coast offices (Seattle, San Francisco, Los Angeles, and San Diego).

5. Investing in Foreign Countries: ICSID to the Rescue

When disputes arise between foreign governments and American investors in their countries, the parties can choose to take advantage of the institutional framework offered by the International Centre for the Settlement of Investment Disputes (ICSID). The Centre is an organization administered by the World Bank in Washington, D.C. and was set up in 1965 by the Convention on the Settlement of Investment Disputes Between States and Nationals of Other States. The Centre's purpose is to provide facilities for the arbitration and conciliation of investment disputes specifically between governments and private investors of other nationalities. While there are few cases before the Centre, each is significant beyond the immediate parties. The Centre does not arbitrate or conciliate but provides its own set of rules which the parties can follow if they choose to submit disputes to the Centre. The Centre maintains standing panels of arbitrators and conciliators, nominated by the Centre's member countries, to be available for conducting proceedings. Countries which are bound by the Convention pledge to accept arbitral awards rendered under ICSID as equivalent to final awards in their own courts. A more detailed discussion of the Centre and the ICSID Convention can be found below.

B. International Treaties and Other Laws

Before proceeding, some terms should be defined. Broadly speaking, a treaty is an agreement between two or more countries that legally binds those countries. A convention is a code of conduct presented by an international organization (such as the United Nations) or a group of countries, to which countries are invited to bind themselves. As a practical matter, once a country agrees to be bound by a convention, the effect is the same as being bound by a treaty.

In this chapter, when a country is bound by a treaty or convention, it will be called a "Contracting State" to that treaty or convention. In international law, the term "State" is used to mean country. A country that has merely signed the treaty, *i.e.*, a signatory, will not be referred to as a "Contracting State" since that country has not taken all the formal steps to consent to be bound by the treaty. The additional formal step is ratification or accession. Ratification involves a country that has played a part in the negotiation of a treaty, has also signed the text, and has adopted domestic legislation that manifests its consent to be bound.[13] Accession involves a country that did not originally negotiate, but later wishes to be bound by the treaty. That country would need both to sign the treaty and to adopt appropriate domestic legislation. Countries that have acceded to a treaty will have the same practical legal position as countries that ratified it.[14]

1. Convention on the Recognition and Enforcement of Foreign Arbitral Awards (The New York Convention)

a. Background

The Convention on the Recognition and Enforcement of Foreign Arbitral Awards[15] was completed at a 1958 conference in New York under the auspices of the United Nations Economic and Social Council. Since then, it has been known as the New York Convention. It was developed from a draft convention prepared by the International Chamber of Commerce in 1953. The United States ratified the Convention on December 29, 1970. As of January 1, 1994, 96 countries were parties to the Convention. Any member country of the United Nations may join the Convention.

b. Operative provisions

Main Provisions—The Convention applies to all arbitral awards made outside the country where the recognition and enforcement of such an award is sought. It also applies to awards not considered as domestic awards in the country where their recognition and enforcement is sought (Art. I(1)). In general, countries who are Contracting States of the Convention must "recognize" arbitration agreements in writing (Art. II(1)). The duty to "recognize" an arbitration agreement means that when a court of a Contracting State has jurisdiction over a case where there is an arbitration agreement, it must refer the case to arbitration at the request of one of the parties, unless the court finds that the agreement is invalid, *i.e.*, legally unenforceable, or incapable of being performed, *e.g.*, if a party to the agreement has gone out of business. "Agreement in writing" is defined to include an arbitral clause in a contract or an arbitration agreement, signed by the parties or contained in an exchange of letters or telegrams (Art. II(2)).[16]

As for arbitral awards, each Contracting State promises to recognize foreign arbitral awards as binding, *i.e.*, each party to the dispute may enforce it against the other. Essentially, "recognition" here means that the courts of a contracting state will accept the award as foreclosing relitigation of the issues decided by the award. So, even if enforcement of an award is not sought in a given country, "recognition" of the award will allow the winning party to prevent the losing party from relitigating the claims upon which the award is based. Each contracting state also promises to enforce the foreign arbitral awards according to the law of the country where the award is relied upon (Art. III). "Enforcement" means that the courts of the enforcing country will provide means for carrying the award into effect.

Two crucial qualifications of this general framework, or "reservations," which each country may adopt when signing the Convention are:

(a) *Reciprocity reservation:* A country may declare that it will apply the Convention only to awards made in the territory of another Contracting State. Thus, that country will not apply the Convention to its domestic arbitral awards nor to awards made in a country that is not a Contracting State of the Convention. "Reciprocity" basically means "I'll treat you in the same way that you treat me." For instance, the United States will apply the Convention to honor arbitral awards made in Country X (where X is a Contracting State of the Convention) only if X honors arbitral awards made in the United States.

(b) *Commercial reservation:* A country may declare that it will apply the Convention only to "commercial differences" as defined by that country's national law (Art. I(3)).

Many countries, including the United States, adopted both reservations.

Another limitation on the scope of the New York Convention is that a Contracting State cannot seek application of the Convention in other Contracting States except to the extent that it has bound itself to apply the Convention at home (Art. XIV), so-called reverse negative reciprocity. It works like this: Since the United States has bound itself to apply the Convention only to foreign *commercial* arbitral awards (the commercial reservation), only arbitral awards made in the United States that are commercial need be recognized and enforced by the other Contracting States of the Convention. Presumably, the country being asked to enforce the award will decide whether the U.S. award *is* commercial under its own national law. In plain language: "I can't force you to treat me one bit better than I treat you."

Refusal of Recognition and Enforcement of Award—As mentioned above, the Convention generally requires Contracting States to recognize and enforce awards made in other Contracting States. However, the Convention also provides for certain limited grounds that may be invoked by the losing party to prevent recognition and enforcement of an award in *any* Contracting State. These grounds deal with the formal validity of the award rather than the merits of the underlying dispute and are enumerated in Article V(1) of the Convention:

— legal incapacity of the parties (*incapacity*—one of the parties cannot legally be a party to an arbitration agreement because he is not (legally) old enough to contract);

— invalidity of the arbitration agreement (*invalidity*—a party who signed the arbitration clause was under threat or duress from the other party to do so);

— the losing party did not receive notice of the arbitrator's appointment or of the arbitration proceedings;

— the award falls beyond the scope of the agreement to arbitrate[17] (The arbitration agreement specifically prohibited the awarding of punitive damages, but included a punitive damages component.);

— the arbitral procedure or composition of the arbitration panel was improper (*improper procedure*—the arbitrators did not follow the procedures provided for in the arbitration agreement or the procedure followed was *not* in accordance with the law of the country where the arbitration took place; *improper composition*—an arbitrator on the panel is a citizen of Country Y, when the arbitration clause provided that no arbitrator from Country Y would be selected[18]); and

— the award has not yet become binding or has been set aside or suspended (*binding*—under the law of the country where the award is sought to be enforced, the winning party may have to wait a certain time before seeking judicial confirmation of the award, and that time may not have passed; *set aside*—the award has been declared unenforceable by another court which had jurisdiction to do so).

The New York Convention provides for two additional grounds for resisting enforcement that go more to the merits of the claim underlying the award (Art. V(2)). Recognition or enforcement of an award may be refused if a court of the country where either is sought finds that:

(1) the subject matter of the dispute cannot be settled by arbitration under the law of the country where recognition or enforcement is sought (Public law issues, such as whether a patent

is valid or whether antitrust violations that have occurred, are not arbitrable under the law of many countries.); or

(2) the recognition or enforcement of the award would be contrary to the public policy of that country (The public policy ground for not enforcing an award is rarely invoked successfully since courts have restricted it to the most basic questions of principle and justice.[19] As an example, an arbitral award that was procured by fraud or corruption will be vacated by United States courts.[20] In Germany, an arbitration agreement is void if it is the result of a commercially strong party applying undue influence upon an economically weaker opponent.[21] Therefore, an award arising from arbitration under such an agreement, even though the agreement was entered into in another country, would be contrary to the public policy of Germany and hence unenforceable there.).

c. Relationship of the New York Convention to other treaties and law

The New York Convention does not affect other multilateral or bilateral agreements on recognition and enforcement of arbitral awards entered into by the Contracting States to the Convention (Art. VII). For instance, the United States is also a Contracting State of the Inter-American Convention on International Commercial Arbitration, in company with 13 other countries in the Western Hemisphere.[22] Under U.S. law, if a majority of the parties to the arbitration agreement are citizens of countries that are Contracting States of the Inter-American Convention, that Convention will apply even if those countries are also Contracting States of the New York Convention.[23]

A party can obtain enforcement of an award in the manner provided by the law of the country where enforcement is sought, and the New York Convention does not affect that right (Art. VII). In plain language, this is saying that a party may have additional rights under the law of the country of enforcement which are wholly unaffected by the New York Convention. For example, although the New York Convention is silent about modification or correction of an award, United States legislation allows a party to petition a court for modification or correction under some circumstances.[24]

d. Survey of major trading countries

The United States—As mentioned earlier, the United States is a Contracting State, but has included both major reservations in its ratification of the New York Convention:

The United States of America will apply the Convention, on the basis of reciprocity, to the recognition and enforcement of only those awards made in the territory of another Contracting State.

The United States of America will apply the Convention only to differences arising out of legal relationships, whether contractual or not, which are considered as commercial under the national law of the United States.

United States courts enforce the New York Convention pursuant to federal law (Chapter 2 of the United States Arbitration Act[25]). Under this law, however, an agreement or award arising out of a commercial relationship *between U.S. citizens* does *not* fall within the Convention *unless* the relationship (a) involves property located abroad, (b) envisages performance or enforcement abroad, or (c) has some other reasonable relation to some foreign state.[26]

If the New York Convention applies, a U.S. court may direct arbitration to be held in accordance with the agreement and at the place provided in the agreement, whether in the United States or not.[27] The court may also appoint arbitrators as provided for in the agreement. Finally, federal legislation provides that any party who wishes a U.S. District Court to confirm an award under the Convention must apply to the court within three years[28] after the award was made. The court will confirm the award unless it finds one of the grounds for refusal of recognition or enforcement previously summarized above. (The normal U.S. Arbitration Act standards for refusing enforcement of "domestic" awards do not apply.)

Contracting States that Have Adopted Without Reservation

Chile	South Africa
Italy	Spain
Mexico	Sweden
Russian Federation	

*Contracting States that Have Adopted with **only** the Reciprocity Reservation*

France	Saudi Arabia
Germany	Singapore
Japan	Switzerland
the Netherlands	United Kingdom

*Contracting State that Has Adopted **only** the Commercial Reservation*

Canada

*Contracting States that Have Adopted with **both** Reservations*

Argentina[29]	Korea
China	Malaysia
India	United States
Indonesia	

Trading States that Are Not Parties to the Convention

Brazil
Taiwan

2. Inter-American Convention on International Commercial Arbitration

a. Background

The Inter-American Convention on International Commercial Arbitration[30] was adopted at Panama City in 1975. It was originally open for signature by member countries of the Organization of American States, but now also provides for any other country to join. The United States became a Contracting State of the Convention on October 27, 1990. As of January 1, 1995, 14 countries (all in the Western Hemisphere) were Contracting States of the Inter-American Convention.

b. Operative provisions

The Inter-American Convention specifically applies only to arbitration agreements concerning *commercial* transactions and recognizes such agreements as valid, *i.e.,* enforceable. An arbitral decision or award resulting from such an agreement will have the force of a final (court) judgment, and such judgment may be recognized or executed, *i.e.,* enforced, in the same way as decisions handed down by national courts (Art. 4). Where the parties do not expressly provide for the manner of arbitration, the Convention provides that the arbitration is to be conducted in accordance with the procedural rules of the Inter-American Commercial Arbitration Commission (IACAC) (Art. 3). The IACAC has its offices at the headquarters of the Organization of American States in Washington, D.C. Its Rules of Procedure are basically the Arbitration Rules of the United Nations Commission on International Trade Law (UNCITRAL), with only minor changes.

A major difference between the Inter-American Convention and the New York Convention is that the Inter-American Convention does not *require* that a court (with jurisdiction of a matter covered by an arbitration agreement) refer the matter to arbitration. The court has discretion to do so or not. Another difference is that the reciprocity reservation is not expressly provided for in the Inter-American Convention as it is in the New York Convention. Nonetheless, United States law implements the Inter-American Convention on the basis of reciprocity, as discussed below.

The losing party may invoke certain limited grounds under the Inter-American Convention to prevent recognition and execution (enforcement) of an arbitral decision. These grounds are almost identical to those provided for by New York Convention.

c. U.S. enforcement of the Inter-American Convention

United States courts enforce the Inter-American Convention as provided for in Chapter 3 of the United States Arbitration Act.[31] Under that Chapter, the United States applies the Convention on a reciprocity basis, *i.e.*, arbitral awards made in a foreign country will be recognized and enforced under the Inter-American Convention only if that country is itself a Contracting State of the Convention.[32] This is identical to U.S. enforcement policy under the New York Convention.

The U.S. enforcement of the Inter-American Convention is identical to the U.S. enforcement of the New York Convention in other ways.[33] For example, an agreement or award arising out of a commercial relationship between U.S. citizens does *not* fall within the Inter-American Convention unless the relationship meets one of the three conditions summarized above. The authority and procedure of a U.S. District Court to direct arbitration and appoint arbitrators is also the same as under the New York Convention.

Finally, if a majority of the parties to the arbitration agreement are citizens of countries that are Contracting States of the Inter-American Convention and the parties have not agreed otherwise, the Inter-American Convention will apply even if those countries are also Contracting States of the New York Convention. Otherwise, the New York Convention will apply.[34]

It is noteworthy that Argentina, Brazil, and Canada are not bound by the Inter-American Convention. Brazil has signed the Convention, but has not enacted necessary legislation to be bound by it. As of May 2, 1995, a request of consent for ratification of the Inter-American Convention is under scrutiny by the Brazilian Federal Senate.

3. Convention on the Settlement of Investment Disputes Between States and Nationals of Other States

a. Background

The Convention on the Settlement of Investment Disputes Between States and Nationals of Other States[35] (the ICSID Convention) was developed under the auspices of the World Bank and concluded in 1965 in Washington, D.C. Its goal is to provide an alternative to the always cumbersome litigation of investment disputes between private investors and foreign governments. The United States became a Contracting State of the ICSID Convention on October 14, 1966. As of August 1994, 114 countries were Contracting States of this Convention. It is open to any member country of the World Bank, although other countries may join by invitation.

b. Operative provisions

i. General provisions

The ICSID Convention applies only when a legal dispute arises directly out of an *investment* between a Contracting State (state, *i.e.*, country) and a national of another Contracting State and when the parties to the dispute *consent* in writing to submit for resolution under the Convention (Art. 25(1)). Thus, the operation of the Convention is not mandatory, but only comes into effect when the parties agree. However, after the parties have given their consent, no party may withdraw its consent unilaterally. (Art. 25(1)). "Investment" is not defined in the ICSID Convention but has been applied to both traditional investment such as capital contributions and newer types of investment, including service contracts and transfers of technology.[36] A "national of another Contracting State" is defined as a person or entity who has nationality of a Contracting State other than the State which is party to the dispute. However, an entity which has the nationality of the State party to the dispute but which is subject to foreign control may, at the agreement of the parties, also be treated as a national of another Contracting State (Art. 25(2)). For instance, a Zimbabwean subsidiary of an American corporation would be eligible for such treatment in a claim against the Zimbabwean government.

To provide facilities for conciliation and arbitration of disputes, the Convention established the International Centre for Settlement of Investment Disputes (ICSID), based at the World Bank's headquarters in Washington, D.C. However, the Centre itself does not conciliate or arbitrate. Instead, it maintains a Panel of Conciliators and a Panel of Arbitrators from which the parties can draw. Each Contracting State can designate four persons to each Panel. The designees do not have to be nationals of the country which picks them. In addition, the Chairman of the Administrative Council of the Centre (who is always the President of the World Bank) may designate ten additional persons, each having different nationality, to each of the two Panels.

It is important to note that a Contracting State may, at any time, notify the Centre of the classes of disputes which it would or would not consider submitting to the Centre for resolution (Art. 25(4)). Thus, not all investment disputes with that country might be submitted for resolution under the ICSID Convention, and what disputes the country will consider submitting may change from time to time. Of course, *all* submissions are ultimately voluntary.

To initiate conciliation or arbitration, a Contracting State or national of a Contracting State must send a written request to the Centre's Secretary-General (the principal officer of the Centre elected by the Administrative Council) who will send a copy of the request to the other party. The request must contain information concerning the issues in dispute, the identity of the parties, and their consent to conciliation or arbitration in accordance with the Centre's rules (Arts. 28, 36). If the dispute is accepted by the Centre, a Conciliation Commission or an Arbitral Tribunal is formed as the case may be.

The place of conciliation or arbitration proceedings will be at the Centre's headquarters in Washington, D.C., but may be held at another public or private arbitration institution if the parties agree.

ii. Arbitration tribunal

In the case of the ICSID Arbitration Tribunal, it may consist of a sole arbitrator or an odd number of arbitrators, appointed as the parties agree. If the parties do not agree on the number of arbitrators and the method of appointment, the Tribunal will consist of three arbitrators, one appointed by each party and the third appointed by the agreement of the parties who will act as the Tribunal's president (Art. 37). The parties may appoint arbitrators who are not members of the Panel of Arbitrators. In case the Tribunal is not constituted within 90 days after registration of the arbitration request by the Centre, the chairman will appoint the remaining arbitrator(s) upon request by either party and after consulting with both parties. Arbitrators appointed by the chairman must not have the same nationalities as the parties to the dispute (Art. 38).

The Arbitration Tribunal must decide the dispute in accordance with the law agreed upon by the parties, but if they have not, the Tribunal will apply the law of the Contracting State party to the dispute and international law (Art. 42). The arbitration proceedings are conducted in accordance with ICSID's Arbitration Rules, except as the parties otherwise agree (Art. 44). When the Tribunal renders an award, it must be in writing and contain the reasons for its decision. ICSID will not publish the award without the parties' consent.

When a party fails to appear, the other party may ask the Tribunal to decide the issues submitted to it and render an award. The Tribunal must give a grace period to the nonappearing party, unless the Tribunal is satisfied that party does not intend to appear (Art. 45).

The arbitral award is binding on the parties when rendered and is not subject to any appeal (Art. 53). Each Contracting State must recognize and enforce the award within its territory as if it were a final judgment of its own court (Art. 54). Unlike the New York Convention, the ICSID Convention does *not* allow a Contracting State the power to refuse the enforcement of an award on the grounds of public policy or nonarbitrability of the subject matter. As discussed more fully below, an award can only be annulled under very limited circumstances and only by another tribunal appointed by the chairman. A party seeking execution (enforcement) of the award must follow the law of the country where such execution is sought.

Interpretation of the Award—After the ICSID arbitration award is rendered, if there is a dispute as to the meaning of the award, either party may request interpretation of the award by a written application to the Secretary-General.[37] The request will be submitted to the original Tribunal that rendered the award, but if that is not possible, a new Tribunal will be selected under the same method as was the original Tribunal (Art. 50).

Revision of the Award—A party may request revision of an ICSID award on the ground that it discovered some fact that would decisively affect the award. That fact must have been unknown to the Tribunal and the party requesting the revision at the time the award was rendered. The requesting party's ignorance of that fact must also not have been due to its own negligence. The requesting application must be made within 90 days after the discovery of the fact and within three years after the date of the award. The application will be submitted to the original Tribunal that rendered the award, but if that is not possible, a new Tribunal will be selected under the same method as was the original Tribunal (Art. 51).

Annulment of the Award—A party may request annulment of an ICSID award by invoking one or more of the following grounds:

— The Tribunal was not properly constituted (The Tribunal was not selected in accordance with the proper procedure summarized above.);

— The Tribunal has manifestly exceeded its powers (The Tribunal upheld an illegal contract or rendered an award on issues not submitted to it for arbitration.);

— Corruption on the part of a Tribunal member;

— A serious departure from a fundamental rule of procedure, *e.g.,* failure to give notice of the hearing); and

— The award did not state the reasons on which it is based.

The request for annulment must be made within 120 days after the date the award was rendered. An exception is made when the annulment is requested on the ground of corruption, in which case the deadline is within 120 days after discovery of such corruption and within three years after the date of the award. Upon receipt of the request, the chairman will appoint from the Panel of Arbitrators a Committee of three persons to consider the request. None of the members of the Committee can be a member of the original Tribunal nor have the same nationality as any of the original Tribunal's members, or of the parties involved. The Committee, once appointed, has the authority to annul the award on the five grounds set forth above.

iii. Conciliation commission

The process for appointing conciliators to the Conciliation Commission is analogous to that of an Arbitration Tribunal. The Commission may consist of a sole conciliator or an odd number of conciliators appointed as the parties agree. If the parties do not agree on the conciliator number and the appointment method, the Commission will consist of three conciliators, one appointed by each party and the third appointed by the parties' agreement who will act as the Commission's president (Art. 29). The parties may also appoint conciliators who are not members of the Panel of Conciliators. In the case that the Commission is not constituted within 90 days after registration of the conciliation request by the Centre, the chairman will appoint the remaining conciliator(s) not yet appointed to the arbitration procedures.

The Conciliation Commission has the duty to clarify the issues in dispute and encourage agreement between the parties. The Commission may recommend terms of settlement to the parties at any stage of the proceedings. In practice, the Commission resembles a group of activist mediators. If the parties reach agreement, the Commission draws up a report noting the agreement. If at any time it appears to the Commission that no likelihood of agreement between the parties exists, the Commission will close the proceedings and draw up a report, noting the failure to reach agreement (Art. 34).

c. U.S. enforcement of the Convention

Under federal legislation, an arbitral award rendered under the ICSID Convention will be enforced as if it were a final judgment of a court in one of the 50 states.[38] The action to enforce the award must be brought in a U.S. District Court. The U.S. Arbitration Act will not apply to the enforcement of the award.

d. Trading countries not Contracting States of the ICSID Convention

Since there are 114 countries that are Contracting States of the ICSID Convention, it will be more worthwhile to point out the countries that are not.

Argentina, the Russian Federation, Thailand, and Venezuela have signed the ICSID Convention but have not become bound to it, *i.e.,* become Contracting States. Brazil, India, and Taiwan have not even signed the ICSID Convention.

4. The U.S. Arbitration Act

a. General provisions

The main portion of the U.S. Arbitration Act, Chapter 1, applies to *domestic* arbitration agreements and awards made in connection with interstate commerce.[39] The Act also has provisions which implement the New York Convention (Chapter 2) and the Inter-American Convention (Chapter 3).

When there is a written arbitration agreement, the Act mandates that a federal court must refer the case to arbitration at a party's request. However, the party resisting arbitration can dispute the validity of the arbitration agreement and is entitled to a separate trial on that issue.[40] A jury trial is available, except in admiralty cases. If the court (or jury) finds that there was a valid arbitration agreement, the court will order the parties to arbitration in accordance with its terms.

b. Confirmation, modification, and vacating of award

A party who wishes to confirm the arbitral award under the U.S. Arbitration Act must apply to the court within one year after the award was made. Note that this is two years less than the time a party has in asking a U.S. court to confirm an award under the New York Convention or the Inter-American Convention. If the arbitration agreement specified a particular district where the confirmation is to be made, the U.S. District Court for that district will confirm the award unless the award is vacated, modified, or corrected. If the agreement did not specify the district, then the District Court where the award was made may confirm the award.[41]

A party wishing the court to modify, correct, or vacate an award must apply to the court within three months after the award is rendered.[42]

The grounds for *modification or correction* of an arbitral award under the Act are:

— The award has an evident material miscalculation of figures or material mistake in the description of any person, thing, or property referred to in the award;

— The arbitrators gave an award upon a matter not submitted to them; and

— The award is imperfect in form, not affecting the merits of the dispute.[43]

The grounds for *vacating* an arbitral award under the Act are:

— The award was procured by corruption, fraud, or undue means (a witness for the winning party gave perjured testimony in the arbitral proceedings in regard to a highly important fact);

— Partiality or corruption in any arbitrator (an arbitrator did not disclose a significant business relationship with a party until after the award was made);

— Arbitrators' misconduct in refusing to postpone hearing upon sufficient cause shown, refusing to hear pertinent evidence, or any other misbehavior prejudicing the rights of a party (the arbitrators refused to adjourn the proceeding after one of the parties became seriously ill); and

— The arbitrators exceeded their powers or exercised their powers so "imperfectly" as to make the award not final and definite[44] (*exceeding powers*—the arbitrators rendered an award which includes the liability of a person not a party to the arbitration; *imperfect exercise of powers*—the award is ambiguous and contradictory on its face, and neither gave a clear interpretation of the award).

c. Residual application to other arbitral conventions

The U.S. Arbitration Act specifically provides that its domestic award-enforcement provisions will apply to any proceedings brought to recognize or enforce an award under the New York Convention.[45] The "domestic" provisions of the Act will also apply to any proceedings brought to recognize or enforce an award under the Inter-American Convention.[46] The Inter-American Convention is silent as to modification and correction of an award (as is the New York Convention). However, a United States appellate court recently ruled that a federal trial court had the authority to *modify* an award obtained by a Guatemalan party that was seeking to enforce an award against a U.S. party obtained under the Inter-American Convention.[47]

5. U.S. Foreign Sovereign Immunities Act

Under the doctrine of foreign sovereign immunity, foreign sovereigns, *i.e.,* foreign countries, are immune from the reach of another country's courts. Thus, for instance, a foreign country may not be sued by name in the courts of the United States. However, international law has developed certain exceptions to this doctrine, the most important being that a foreign government that engages in commercial rather than public activities is exposed to suit. The U.S. Foreign Sovereign Immunities Act[48] (FSIA) was passed in 1976. FSIA codifies the doctrine with its exception and specifies the circumstances under which a foreign sovereign is within the jurisdiction of U.S. courts.

a. Immunity from suit

Generally, under FSIA, a foreign state is immune from the jurisdiction of the courts of the United States and the 50 states.[49] "Foreign state" is defined to include: (1) a political subdivision of a foreign country, (2) an agency or instrumentality of such country, or (3) a state-owned company of such country. Under the following circumstances, however, the foreign state *will* be subject to the jurisdiction of courts in the United States where:

— The foreign state has waived its immunity, *i.e.,* agreed to be sued in the United States, either explicitly or by implication;

— A suit against the foreign state is based upon "commercial activity";

— The foreign state has taken property in violation of international law;

— The foreign state is sued for personal injury or property damage occurring in the United States; and

— An action is brought to enforce an arbitration agreement made by the foreign state or to confirm an award made pursuant to such agreement.

The FSIA's test of whether an act is commercial is to look at the *nature* of the act rather than its *purpose*. In general, an activity in which an individual might normally carry on for profit is a commercial activity. Such activity could include a joint venture with U.S. citizens to manufacture aircraft or a state-owned foreign company selling its products in the United States. If the activity is one which only a country can engage in, it is noncommercial. Noncommercial activities have included nationalizing the plaintiff's corporation and granting and revoking a license to export a natural resource.[50]

If subject to U.S. jurisdiction, the foreign state is liable in the same manner and extent as a private person. Punitive damages are available if the claim is against an agency or instrumentality of the foreign state, but not against the foreign state itself.

Where the foreign state itself brings an action in a U.S. court, the foreign state normally cannot assert sovereign immunity when the other party to the suit files a counterclaim.

b. Immunity from attachment and execution

The property of a foreign state that is located in the United States (and *not* used in commercial activity) is immune from seizure and enforcement.[51]

If the judgment is only against an agency or instrumentality of a foreign state which is engaged in commercial activity in the United States, *any* property *of that agency* or instrumentality can be attached. The property does not have to be involved with plaintiff's underlying claim. For instance, the plaintiff may attach a foreign state-owned airline's building in the United States to satisfy his or her judgment against the airline on a wrongful death claim.

Property of a foreign central bank or monetary authority held for its own account or military property, however, is always immune, unless the immunity is specifically waived.

C. ADR as a Marketing Tool in International Transactions

Business people from most parts of the world are familiar with international commercial arbitration and are generally willing to use it if the proceedings are perceived to be fair. An American business person can use his or her knowledge of ADR to win the confidence of foreign parties in business negotiations. For example, foreign parties will be understandably concerned about the fairness of ADR proceedings in the United States and would rather conduct them in their own countries. The American business person can point out that under the rules of the AAA, the neutral or arbitrator can be a person of nationality different from those of the parties to the dispute. Furthermore, the AAA's International Arbitration Rules easily accommodate arbitration proceedings in a neutral country, if desired. These neutral provisions may be important in reducing the foreign party's fear about the fairness of proceedings administered by a U.S.-based organization.

If the foreign party cannot be convinced of the AAA's neutrality, the ICC (Paris) or London Court of Arbitration can be suggested. Although the main objective in negotiating a business deal should be the deal itself, not the ADR clauses, those clauses should be carefully thought out since there will be disputes. The well-drafted ADR clause will be fair to both sides and will aid in securing international contracts. In that sense, ADR can definitely be a marketing tool.

D. Business Dispute Resolution in the Rest of Asia

Earlier in this book, it was shown how most *domestic* business disputes are resolved in Japan. However, in resolving disputes with foreign parties, the method used by most major Asian trading nations is arbitration, although the laws and practices under which these arbitrations take place do vary from country to country. As with other elements of this chapter, space permits only a summary overview of the applicable laws and customs. If entering into an agreement with companies (or governments) from this area, consult an expert for advice about a particular situation.

The countries included are the Republic of Korea, Taiwan (Republic of China), China (People's Republic of China), and Singapore.

1. Korea

While Korean businessmen (there are almost no Korean businesswomen) would prefer to resolve disputes through negotiation or mediation, commercial arbitration has a definite place in resolving disputes between Korean entities and foreign companies. Korea is now the eleventh largest trading nation in the world (judged by total trade in dollar value), and it is no exception to the norm that more trade brings more disputes. The fundamental law under which arbitration is conducted in Korea is the Arbitration Act of 1966 (KAA). While it has been amended as recently as 1989, the KAA was and is a comprehensive framework for the administration of arbitrations and promulgation of the Commercial Arbitration Rules. Like the private-sector International Rules of the American Arbitration Association and the Rules of the International Chamber of Commerce (Paris), the Korean Commercial Arbitration Rules are quite permissive about what procedures parties may agree upon and are similarly specific about what happens if parties do not agree on procedure, or if they have agreed but one party fails to comply with the agreement. The Korean Commercial Arbitration Rules (which have the force of law in Korea) have delegated the job of administering commercial arbitrations to the Korean Commercial Arbitration Board ("the Board"). The parties are free to agree upon the choice of arbitrators (both in a predispute agreement and by submission after a dispute has arisen) or upon a method by which the arbitrators will be selected. If there is no agreement (or implementation lags) the Board will send a list of prospective arbitrators to the parties, asking them to rank the proposed arbitrators in order of preference. Arbitrators with the highest rankings will be appointed. Where the parties cannot agree on, or the agreement doesn't provide for, the *number* of arbitrators, the Board will determine whether it is to be one or three. Of the list of almost 600 proposed arbitrators maintained by the Board, all but 20 (foreign businessmen and lawyers residing in Korea) are Korean nationals, who are mainly lawyers and academics. As a practical matter, almost every panel contains a lawyer who takes primary responsibility for administering the hearings, once the panel is constituted.

As with international arbitrations under the American Arbitration Association Rules, when one of the parties is not a Korean, either party may require that the sole arbitrator (or chair of a three-person panel) be a national of a third country, *i.e.,* neither Korea nor the country of the other party. It is not clear what happens if there is no third-country arbitrator on the Board's list that the parties can agree on.

The costs of arbitration, as always, vary greatly with the amount of time spent in preparation and hearing. The administrative costs include the arbitrators' fees (fixed by the Board and normally shared equally by the parties) and the administrative fee (US$2050 plus .25% of the amount by which the claim exceeds US$200,000, and normally apportioned by the arbitrators as part of their award). Large translation costs may also be incurred. The Board makes translators available, upon advance payment of their costs, and the Rules require that any document submitted in evidence which is not in Korean must be accompanied by a Korean translation (at the cost of the party offering the document). Proceedings are routinely tape-recorded, but a stenographic record is not normally kept.

As with most commercial jurisdictions, the parties will be directed to arbitrate only if they have agreed to do so. If they have such an agreement, access to the Korean court system will be foreclosed until arbitration is concluded. Attendance at the arbitration hearings is limited to directly interested parties and their counsel. Hearings may be conducted on the basis of written submission only, but most hearings involve the taking of oral testimony. Examination and cross-examination by counsel is permitted, but arbitrators themselves normally take a larger role in questioning witnesses than typical American arbitrators would (but about the same as European arbitrators). Comparable (or greater) speed may be expected as well. According to the Board's own figures, over 90 percent of all cases are disposed of within one year from the date the claim was filed.

Korean commercial arbitration, however, is vastly different from its Western counterpart. Even after the panel has been formally set up, an arbitrator may function as a mediator and actively involve himself in guiding settlement negotiations. It is quite common for the arbitrator to suggest possible outcomes to the parties—something that would be viewed as marginally unethical by many Western arbitrators.

In representing foreign organizations at arbitrations, normally non-Korean lawyers are not allowed to practice in Korea, but the Korean Arbitration Act permits representation in arbitrations by foreign counsel. As a practical matter, however, prudence would dictate having a Korean co-counsel work with the foreign lawyer.

2. Taiwan (Republic of China)

The currently applicable Taiwanese law is the Taiwan Commercial Arbitration Association Act ("Taiwan Act"), under which all commercial arbitrations must be conducted in the Chinese language, Chinese translations of all documents submitted may be required, and all arbitral awards must be rendered in Chinese. As in Korea, foreign lawyers may represent parties at arbitrations, but even if familiar with Chinese, foreign lawyers would be well advised to have associate local counsel. Parties to the arbitration are free to construct their own agreed-upon procedure, but if they do not, the arbitration panel will create one. In general, although the arbitrators are legally charged to "conduct inquiries," the hearings are about the same as a Western commercial arbitration, except in one respect: *cross-examination of witnesses is permitted only when the parties have agreed to it or the arbitrators insist on it.* As with European arbitrations, most of the questioning will be done by the arbitrators themselves. In a sharp break with accepted international practice, there is no restriction on the nationality of the sole arbitrator or the chair of a three-person panel. So, such a person could be a citizen of the same country as one of the parties. The timing of arbitration proceedings in Taiwan is quite tight. According to the Taiwan Act, the arbitrators must *render the award* within a maximum of six months (an initial three-month period which may be extended for another three months) from when they receive notice that they are designated as arbitrators. Given the complexity of many international commercial disputes, the busy schedules of both parties and their lawyers, and the lengthy travel which may be involved, this deadline, while laudable, seems unrealistic.

Early in 1995, some proposed amendments to the Taiwan Act were suggested by a committee of (Taiwanese) experts in an apparent attempt to make the Act more palatable to foreigners. The proposed amendments included a provision which permits the parties to agree to arbitral hearings conducted in any language (subject to the arbitrators' ability to order translations of evidence). While this proposal is a step forward, it is highly unlikely to turn Taiwan into an international center for commercial arbitration. As of this writing, the proposed amendments have not been passed by the Taiwanese legislature.

3. China (People's Republic of China)

Arbitration of international commercial disputes has a lengthy and mostly honorable history in China. The China International Economic and Trade Association Commission (inevitably shortened to CIETAC, and pronounced "see-tack" by Westerners) was established in the 1950s for the purpose of handling disputes between foreign and Chinese parties. While Chinese culture joins other Asian cultures in looking toward negotiation and mediation to resolve most disputes, arbitration through the CIETAC is encouraged when these other methods fail. A CIETAC arbitration clause once was mandatory in contracts between foreign parties and Chinese government trading agencies, but this requirement has been relaxed in the general effort to increase foreign investment in China. (Space does not permit treatment of the Chinese Maritime Arbitration Commission, whose jurisdiction can be guessed from its title.) While there is a substantial body of law and lore associated with arbitration under CIETAC, an arbitration law is scheduled to go into effect on September 1, 1995, under which the China International Chamber of Commerce (a quasi-governmental body) is permitted to set up (presumably new) procedures for CIETAC. The only restraint on the actions of the Chamber of Commerce is that any new procedures must be consistent with the arbitration law itself. Given the inherent conservatism of the Chinese business/legal community, radical changes in procedure are probably not forthcoming.

For now, a CIETAC arbitration is begun by applying for arbitration at one of the three CIETAC offices (Beijing, Shenzhen, and Shanghai). Written agreements to arbitrate, signed by all prospective parties, must be submitted to CIETAC, as well as a brief description of the dispute and claims. If the papers are in order, CIETAC undertakes the administration of the arbitration from then on, including the scheduling and hearing logistics. An arbitrator may be chosen from the CIETAC list, or the CIETAC staff will select one. As of early 1995, CIETAC boasted of having almost 100 non-Chinese nationals (from 15 countries) on its list of arbitrators, joining more than 200 Chinese nationals. Unlike Chinese domestic arbitration, the CIETAC arbitrators need not be legally trained and may include people with backgrounds in science, technology, and trade. The parties may agree on a language other than Chinese, but, if they do not, Chinese (Mandarin) will be the official language of the arbitration. Three-arbitrator panels are the rule, although a mutually agreed single arbitrator is permissible. The chairperson of CIETAC is empowered by the rules to appoint the chair of every three-person arbitration panel. Most of the time, that appointment goes to a Chinese national. Needless to say, a non-Chinese-speaking arbitrator will be of limited usefulness to the party appointing him if the arbitration is conducted in Chinese.

Arbitrator compensation is handled by CIETAC, which requires the parties to deposit their share. Foreign arbitrators are routinely compensated at a higher level than their Chinese counterparts, not including their greater expenses. As with most commercial arbitrations, the proceedings are private, but the hearings usually take the form of the arbitrators asking counsel for each side to state their party's position. The arbitrators will likely inquire extensively of counsel and may also question witnesses themselves, but cross-examination of witnesses by counsel is unusual. Either way, the presentation of evidence by testimony is much more limited than those familiar with Western commercial arbitration would expect. In a more radical departure from conventional international practice, the latest CIETAC Rules (1994) permit the arbitrators to conduct their own investigation into the dispute, in addition to requesting expert reports from the parties.

CIETAC rules require speedy action by both the arbitrators and the parties. For instance, a defending party has only 20 days from receiving notice of the arbitration to appoint its arbitrator, a mere 45 days to submit its position on the case to the CIETAC administrator, and only 60 days within which to assert any counterclaim. The arbitrators must render their award within nine months from the date the arbitration panel is set up. This latter period can be extended if the Arbitration Commission finds that such an extension is necessary.

4. Singapore

Singapore has had an arbitration law since 1953, but as of January 1995, the provisions of that law no longer apply to "international commercial arbitrations." The replacement Singapore International Arbitration Act of 1994 (the "Singapore Act") applies to all international commercial arbitrations which are held in Singapore. The Singapore Act gives the force of Singapore law to the UNCITRAL Law for International Commercial Arbitration (with some modifications), so international business people will be familiar with its provisions. The jurisdiction of Singapore courts to overturn an award is limited on the UNCITRAL model as well. If greater judicial intervention is (or might be) desirable, the parties may agree to be governed by the domestic Singapore Arbitration Law of 1953 (as amended in 1981), instead. Parties may agree on what law governs their dispute. If they cannot agree, Singapore commercial law will likely be applied.

As with other countries, there is a governmentally sanctioned body which administers international commercial arbitrations: the Singapore International Arbitration Centre (SIAC). SIAC was set up in 1991 (before the Singapore Act was passed) as part of a general upgrading of business service facilities in the country. SIAC has a panel of arbitrators which can be selected, but the parties are not limited to them. If parties cannot agree in advance on the identity of their arbitrator(s), SIAC sends them the now-familiar list of possible arbitrators from which they can strike objectionable names. If there is still no agreement, SIAC is empowered by law to appoint them. SIAC acts as the clearing house for arbitrator compensation, with the arbitrators being paid between Singapore$1000 and Singapore$3000 per day. Rules of procedure of familiarly UNCITRAL, and the rules of evidence are relaxed (the Singapore Evidence Act has a specific provision making it inapplicable to arbitrations). Written and oral testimony is normally permitted, as is cross-examination of witnesses. Unlike other Asian forums, all proceedings and correspondence are *in English* and the hearings are videotaped. No law imposes a deadline on the arbitrators, but the SIAC Rules require an award within 45 days of the close of the hearing. No reliable statistics exist regarding total time to complete an arbitration, but SIAC advises that a "typical" commercial dispute takes about six months from beginning to award.

ENDNOTES

[1] United Nations General Assembly Official Records, Session 31, Supp. No. 17 (A/31/17), p. 35.

[2] George W. Coombe, Jr., "State of the Art ADR: The Growing Influence of Asia," *American Bar Association International Commercial Arbitration Committee Newsletter* 4 (Fall 1994): 3.

[3] Jan Paulsson, *Arbitration Under the Rules of the International Chamber of Commerce,* as quoted in *Resolving Transnational Disputes Through International Arbitration,* Thomas Carboneau, ed. (1984), p. 240 [hereinafter cited as Paulsson].

[4] Graving, "The International Commercial Arbitration Institutions: How Good a Job Are They Doing?", *American University Journal of International Law and Policy* 4, (1989): 330.

[5] Paulsson, p. 235.

[6] Paulsson, p. 247.

[7] Ronald A. Brand, "Introduction to International Chamber of Commerce Rules of Conciliation and Arbitration," in *Basic Documents of International Law,* 1991 *BDIEL AD LEXIS* 36, available on LEXIS/NEXIS service.

[8] International Chamber of Commerce, *Rules of Conciliation and Arbitration,* Appendix III, Schedule of Conciliation and Arbitration Costs, table XV.A.1.a. 1 and 2.

[9] Meason and Smith, "Non-Lawyers in International Commercial Arbitration: Gathering Splinters on the Bench," *Journal of International Law & Business* 12 (1991): 31.

[10] American Arbitration Association, *International Arbitration Rules,* table XV.A.3.a., p. 17.

[11] John P. Karalis, *International Joint Ventures: A Practical Guide,* (West, 1992): Section 5.39.

[12] *Arbitration Times,* Fall 1991, p. 8.

[13] The United States manifests its consent to be bound by a treaty by first obtaining Senate approval by two-thirds vote, then passing federal legislation that implements the treaty within the United States.

[14] As an additional formality, most treaties and conventions provide that countries wishing to ratify or accede must deposit instruments of ratification.

[15] United States Treaties and Other International Agreements 21, *Treaties and Other International Acts Series* 6997, p. 2517.

[16] Although the Convention doesn't mention them, one hopes that faxes and E-mail would now be included in this definition.

[17] If the portions of the award beyond the scope of the agreement to arbitrate can be separated from the portions *within* the scope, the Convention allows the award to be recognized and enforced as to the latter. Thus, for example, above, a punitive damages portion may not be enforceable since it is outside the scope of the arbitration agreement, but the compensatory damages portion of the award would be enforceable.

[18] This fact would probably have been concealed by the arbitrator in question. Otherwise, a court would likely rule that the complaining party had waived the compositional defect in the arbitrator panel.

[19] Joseph W. Dellapenna, *Suing Foreign Governments and Their Corporations,* (1988), p. 400.

[20] 9 U.S.C. § 10(a)(1) (1990).

[21] German Code of Civil Procedure, Article 1025(2).

[22] These countries are Chile, Colombia, Costa Rica, Ecuador, El Salvador, Guatemala, Honduras, Mexico, Panama, Paraguay, Peru, Uruguay, and Venezuela.

[23] 9 U.S.C. § 305 (1990).

[24] 9 U.S.C. § 11 (1954).

[25] 9 U.S.C. § 201 *et seq.* (1970).

[26] 9 U.S.C. § 202 (1970).

[27] 9 U.S.C. § 206 (1970).

[28] This is not a statute of limitations which would bar a claim, however. In this context, there has already been an arbitral hearing on the merits. One purpose, of course, is to encourage arbitration generally. In the international context, the prevailing party may need more time to find the assets of the losing party.

[29] Argentina added the following language to its ratification: "The convention will be interpreted in accordance with the principles and clauses of the national Constitution in force or those resulting from modifications made by virtue of the Constitution." Argentine lawyers who were contacted advise that this language was inserted because of a political debate regarding whether the Convention impinged on national sovereignty. They are not sure if it has any substantive meaning.

[30] Organization of American States, Treaty Series No. 42, reprinted in 9 U.S.C.A. § 301 (West Supp., 1994).

[31] 9 U.S.C. § 301 *et seq.* (1990).

[32] 9 U.S.C. § 304. An award rendered *in* the United States that involves a U.S. company against a company with nationality of a Contracting State of the Inter-American Convention falls under the jurisdiction of the Inter-American Convention. See *Productos Mercantiles E Industriales, S.A. v. Faberge USA, Inc.,* 23 F.3d 41 (2nd Cir. 1994) (U.S. company against Guatemalan company).

[33] 9 U.S.C. § 302 (1990).

[34] 9 U.S.C. § 305 (1990).

[35] United States Treaties and Other International Agreements 17, *Treaties and Other International Acts Series* 6090, p. 1270.

[36] Stephen Zamora and Ronald A. Brand, gen. eds., *Basic Documents of International Economic Law 2,* (Commerce Clearing House, Inc., 1990), pp. 948-49.

[37] The Convention does not appear to specify the time limit in which the request for interpretation must be made.

[38] 22 U.S.C. § 1650a.

[39] 9 U.S.C. § 1 (1954). Maritime transactions also fall under the Act.

[40] 9 U.S.C. § 4 (1954).

[41] 9 U.S.C. § 9 (1954).

[42] 9 U.S.C. § 12 (1954).

[43] 9 U.S.C. § 11 (1954).

[44] 9 U.S.C. § 10 (1990).

[45] 9 U.S.C. § 208 (1970). To that extent, there is no conflict between Chapter 1 and Chapter 2 of the Convention. For example, Chapter 1's provisions for modification and correction of an arbitral award do not conflict with the New York Convention since the Convention does not mention modification and correction. Therefore, a party wishing to recognize or enforce an award under Chapter 2 has the right to ask a U.S. court for modification or correction of the award.

[46] 9 U.S.C. § 307 (1990).

[47] See *Productos Mercantiles E Industriales, S.A. v. Faberge USA, Inc.,* 23 F.3d 41 (2nd Cir. 1994).

[48] 28 U.S.C. § § 1330, 1332(a), 1391(f), 1441(d), and 1602-1611.

[49] 28 U.S.C. § 1604.

[50] Folsom, Gordon, and Spanogle, *International Business Transactions* (West, 1992), pp. 471-72.

[51] 28 U.S.C. § 1610.

"*Nowadays, Mr. Lambert, we practice preventive medicine. In laymen's terms, this means I don't do a damn thing until I talk to my lawyer.*"

THE FUTURE OF ADR

A. ADR and the Federal Government

The government of the United States is not unfriendly to ADR. Indeed, there is a federal agency called the Federal Mediation and Conciliation Service. Further, in 1988, the Judicial Improvements and Access to Justice Act was signed into law.[1] A part of this legislation provided for a committee to study various ADR options, recommended broadening of statutory authority for local (federal) court rules to establish ADR procedures, continued experimentation with and monitoring of ADR. While wholly voluntary forms of ADR receive some criticism on nonlegal grounds,[2] the legal atmosphere is favorable toward them at the federal level. The problems begin when government participation in *binding* arbitration is suggested.

To begin, several constitutional problems with binding arbitration arise when the federal government is a party. They are:

— Does the Constitution (Article I) prohibit Congress from delegating government functions to private parties (arbitrators)?

— Is binding arbitration (for the government) inconsistent with the President's executive power (Article II)?

— Is it inconsistent with the grant of *judicial* power to the federal courts (Article III)?

— Does it run afoul of the requirements of due process?[3]

1. Dispute Resolution Act: A First Step

In 1990, Congress enacted the Administrative Dispute Resolution Act (ADRA).[4] The Act was a product of congressional recognition that administrative proceedings had become increasingly formal, costly, and lengthy, resulting in both unnecessary expenditures of time and a decreased likelihood of achieving consensual resolution of disputes. During the hearings, Congress exalted the benefits of private sector alternative dispute resolution, noting that it has yielded processes that are faster, less expensive, and less contentious, which lead to more creative, efficient, and sensible outcomes.

ADRA is a five-year government experiment to use arbitration and mediation when resolving certain government disputes. The Act establishes a framework for government agencies both to train people in the use of ADR methods and to engage in arbitration and mediation when deciding disputes which the government is involved. Among its provisions, the ADRA requires each federal agency to promote alternative dispute resolution by appointing a senior official as an ADR specialist. That person's mandate is to oversee and encourage the use of alternative dispute resolution. The Act also requires that each agency review its contracts, grants, and other administrative programs to ensure that alternative dispute resolution is authorized and promoted.[5] It is important to note that ADRA is a voluntary program which allows private citizens the right to refuse participation in alternative dispute resolution. The Act prohibits the government from requiring consent to arbitration as a condition of being awarded a government contract.

Under ADRA, all arbitration agreements and arbitration awards are enforceable in federal court with one notable exception. Any government agency has the right (1) to terminate an arbitration while it is being conducted in order to protect essential government functions, or (2) to vacate an award within 30 days after it is entered. In the event an award is vacated, the government agency must pay attorney fees and costs of the other party unless there are special circumstances that would make such an award unjust.

It is also noteworthy that the Act does not encourage alternative dispute resolution in all situations. For instance, agencies are told *not to use* alternative dispute resolution when resolution is required to maintain either the "precedential value" of the agency ruling or "established policies," or where the matter poses "significant questions" or where "variations among individual decisions" should be avoided.[6] Given the breadth of this language, it is easy to see how an agency which was anti-ADR could avoid its use almost totally.

The net effect of ADRA on persons and organizations in arbitration with a federal agency is that the government has the power to turn the proceeding into a nonbinding advisory hearing. If the government likes the award, it can do nothing and the citizen will be bound, or if it doesn't, it can have the award vacated (for no reason) within 30 days. Advocates of real, binding arbitration can only hope that the government will move so slowly that the 30 days will pass unnoticed.

To make matters worse for parties facing off with a federal agency, the government does not even have to participate in an arbitration if it chooses not to. Here, at least, the statute requires a reason, *e.g.,* "protecting essential government functions," but that reason is so broad and vague that all of the employees of the Defense Department could pass through it.

2. ADR Atmosphere at Major Agencies

The Justice Department recently acknowledged the benefits of alternative dispute resolution by announcing that it will assign some of the 170,000 civil cases filed each year to outside arbitration. The arbitration plan will be implemented on a voluntary basis, where both the government and the private party concur on this alternative to litigation. On April 6, 1995, Attorney General Janet Reno signed the order implementing arbitration as a means of resolving cases more quickly and cost effectively, after noting that the Justice Department is the largest user of the federal courts. The Justice Department is not the first government agency to consider alternative dispute resolution measures. Successful ADR systems are already in place at a number of federal agencies, including the Environmental Protection Agency, the Federal Deposit Insurance Corp., the Army Corps of Engineers, the Department of Transportation, and the Department of the Navy. The ADR leaning of any given government agency can be assessed by contacting that agency's ADR specialist and by talking with people who regularly deal with that agency.

3. Negotiated Rulemaking: ADR or Another Venue for Lobbyists

Also in 1990, President Bush signed the Negotiated Rulemaking Act into law. The purpose of this law is to bring regulated industry members, trade associations, public interest groups, and unions together for (theoretically) cooperative drafting of proposed regulations. The salient provisions of the law are that:

— Where appropriate, any federal agency may establish a committee to propose a negotiated rulemaking procedure, whose establishment, agenda, and schedule shall be announced in the *Federal Register.*

— The agency may appoint an impartial facilitator to assist in deliberations, and the facilitator may be drawn from a list kept by the Administrative Conference of the United States (ACUS) in consultation with the Federal Mediation and Conciliation Service.

— A committee may propose a rule or other consensus reached and shall terminate when it presents a final rule or sooner.

— The ACUS will compile data on negotiated rulemaking and make biennial reports to Congress.

— Actions related to establishing, assisting, or terminating a negotiated rulemaking committee are not subject to judicial review, but rules resulting from negotiated rulemaking are subject to review if otherwise provided by law.[7]

Government agencies which have used negotiated rulemaking include the Environmental Protection Agency, the Department of Agriculture, the Department of Labor, the Department of Transportation, the Federal Aviation Administration, and the Federal Trade Commission. If an organization is regulated by a federal agency, the negotiated rulemaking process might be an appealing one. Even assuming that no more favorable regulation will result from using the process, the result can probably be reached with less time, money, and acrimony spent. If, however, access to regulators is already superb, an organization may not wish to share that access with others.

While many benefits can accrue from the adroit use of ADR by government agencies, there are some continuing overarching policy concerns, such as permitting any government agency to engage in essentially private proceedings while conducting public business. However, these agencies are already engaged in such proceedings by the process of lobbying, so why not formalize the process and require that all interested parties are allowed to attend it? The answer to this observation is one that comes up frequently in policy analysis, which is: who decides, *i.e.*, who decides when to use negotiated rulemaking, and who decides whom to invite to the negotiated rulemaking sessions when they are convened. As anyone who has engaged in the agency rulemaking process knows, the decision as to which "public interest groups" may be permitted to testify about a proposed rule can itself be crucial to the ultimate outcome. *Sed quis custodiet ipsos custodes?*[8]

4. Even Federal Government Litigation Has Not Escaped ADR

By Executive Order effective in early 1992, President Bush ordered government trial lawyers to place greater emphasis on seeking settlement of claims by or against the United States.[9] Federal government lawyers are required by the Order to:

a. notify defendants of claims and attempt to reach settlement before complaints are filed,

b. acquire training in ADR, and

c. suggest ADR mechanisms to private parties in litigation with the government.

Like its legislative counterpart, the ADRA of 1990, this Executive Order lists circumstances under which ADR is not recommended. Generally, these track the "exceptions" in the legislation and add "the impact of the dispute on nonparties" as an additional consideration.

B. ADR in State Government

State laws are gradually changing to encourage, provide, and regulate ADR through various avenues. For example, the Supreme Court of the State of Colorado adopted a Rule of Professional Ethics for lawyers in Colorado requiring them to advise clients in potential or actual litigation of the availability of ADR. California and Texas legislatures have long ago provided a role for ADR in their workers' compensation laws and, more recently, Alabama, New York, and Tennessee.[10] A number of state courts have changed their rules to accommodate programs where litigants are offered a menu of ADR options. Early neutral evaluation has caught on in state courts in both Colorado and Massachusetts. On the opposite end of the legislative spectrum, several states have begun to regulate out-of-court ADR activities. Both California and Minnesota, for instance, have passed laws requiring persons who are nominated to be arbitrators to disclose to the parties certain relationships with the other parties or their counsel.[11]

C. ADR in Society

Certain cultural tendencies in the United States were mentioned above which appear to work against ADR use. While ADR has made large inroads into the business world in spite of those tendencies, no similar progress has been made in society at large. Certainly, Community Dispute Resolution Centers have been set up in some locations, and many of them work well.[12] However, society generally appears drawn in the direction of using more combative measures to resolve disputes, and recent news reports seem to confirm this observation. Over the past several months, eleven separate news stories, from all over the country, have the following common facts:

— a subteen Caucasian from an affluent family is arrested for murder;

— the victim(s) are also Caucasian;

— the "reason" given for the murder was extremely trivial;

— the murder took place in an affluent, ethnically homogenous community; and

— all residents interviewed stated that they were shocked that such an event could take place in their community, and that "nothing like this has ever happened here before."

The phenomenon is fairly simple in its elements, if not its causes: violent death inflicted by someone who is young, economically well-off, not a member of a disadvantaged minority, and physically unprovoked. This, coupled with numerous similar stories that have crept into our media of the past few years, seems to be a trend *toward mindless violence as a remedy for almost any insignificant dispute.* This trend surely has many causes, whatever they all are, but some of this mindless violence may be reduced by giving citizens some other means of handling disputes.

1. The Role of Education

Reliable studies show that schools in other rich countries do a much better job at imparting basic knowledge to their students than our educational system. The same dwindling pool of public resources which affects the court system adversely also removes resources from schools, but the studies which highlight poor school performance additionally confirm that merely spending more money is not the answer. This is particularly the case in many middle and high schools, where the threat of violence is so real and imminent that no amount of money could create "a learning atmosphere." As with violence in society at large, the failure of our schools has many causes. However, all educators agree that a peaceful campus (or building or trailer) is an *indispensable* prerequisite to real learning. This presents a perfect opportunity and place for starting the ADR "movement."

Children need to be taught ways of dealing with conflict other than violence, ". . . that fighting isn't the solution to problems, and to get them to carry that idea into adulthood," said a spokesperson for a lawyers' association which implemented a mediation program in a public middle school.[13] The objective here is self-regulation, a developmental psychology concept that means nothing more than the ability of a person to behave in a socially acceptable way when not being watched by someone in charge.[14] From a parent's viewpoint, it would seem that any program teaching self-regulation which is completed before puberty would be a national asset of the first order.

2. The Role of the Legal Profession

Lawyers are the traditional gatekeepers of our justice system. By experience, if not training,[15] most lawyers know something about non-violent dispute resolution. They also, as a group, are prosperous members of their communities, with the ability to volunteer some time to "give something back." What a refreshing experience it would be for students or members of a civic organization or trade association to hear a lawyer speak to them about *alternatives* to lawsuits.

However, before beginning to convert society to ADR, lawyers might do well to clean house, starting with attorney-client fee disputes. While some jurisdictions already employ mediation and arbitration in this area, too many still have no institutional choice for the lawyer or the client other than suing each other. Introducing ADR in this area might also have the effect of polishing up the generally tarnished image of lawyers that the public now has.

3. The Role of Government

The use of ADR, particularly when its use is entirely voluntary, is a benefit to the body politic. If for no other reason, this is true because every dispute resolved by ADR is one more dispute that need not be resolved at the courthouse. However, there are other reasons.

a. Competitiveness in a global market

The existence of a "global marketplace," where every country's products and services compete with comparable products and services from other countries, has become a cliche. The implication of this global marketplace for American purveyors of goods and services, while not strongly ingrained in our national consciousness, is the added expense of high transaction costs of dispute resolution to many American products and services. The cost of the *outcomes* of these various disputes are deliberately not included because they would either have been experienced anyway through an ADR process or they involve societal costs willingly undertaken for goals more important than successful trade, *e.g.,* worker freedom from unnecessarily dangerous workplaces. However, the transaction costs of disputes are high enough in many industries to add significantly to the ultimate cost (price) of an American good or service. So, any method of lowering those costs, which is not anathema for other reasons, would be a worthy government goal.

b. The social value of strife reduction

Leaving aside the enormous economic costs associated with violence and stress in society (police, courts, hospitals, doctors, medicines, lost work time, etc.), there is a measurable benefit to be gleaned from any significant reduction in social strife. Whether a busy teacher feels free to walk in his neighborhood at night, or a busy business executive feels safe enough to walk to her car without an escort, society benefits when those feelings abound. And those feelings deal with the extreme end of strife-induced disturbances. What about the benefits of a populace which is *generally* less confrontational, more cooperative, and, at least, willing to give the other person a respectful hearing? If the government can spend hundreds of billions to make us "secure" from military attack by foreign countries, surely a few million on advancing the cause of cooperative dispute resolution would not be profligate.

c. "Court-annexed" ADR: the wave of the present

Courts basically approve of working with ADR, but they are not very familiar with their new tool. One recent meeting found that eight of thirteen federal judges present did not know the difference between arbitration and mediation. Yet, these same judges are being asked to design and implement ADR programs for their courts. This level of ignorance is being mended, however slowly. At another level, a lot is known about the ADR process, but there is very little scientifically reliable data on whether ADR *outcomes* are good, bad, or indifferent. Indeed, there may not even be consensus as to which outcomes are desirable. One of the keenest observers of our justice system, Judge William Schwarzer, put it in these terms:

> There is still a surprising dearth of information about the process of resolving disputes, either by traditional means or by the procedures we call alternatives. We know little . . . about the comparative costs and time effects of different forms of ADR and . . . traditional litigation . . . Much remains to be learned about assessing the effects of ADR. To begin with, we need to determine *what* we should be measuring. We have data, for example, on participant satisfaction, but we need to know what other indicia we should consider and what weight they should be given. By what standards should one measure the success of ADR? This, of course, brings us back to the question of the purpose of ADR; by defining the purpose, one also defines the criteria for measuring its effects.[16]

What Judge Schwarzer writes is true, but somewhat incomplete. While there is little data on some elements of ADR, there is an enormous body of what would technically be called "anecdotal evidence" which supports both the usefulness and attractiveness of ADR. In short, most people who use it, like it. It is most appropriate, however, that there be more research and dialogue on the question of what societal role ADR should play in the resolution of disputes. By that is meant, among other things, whether certain kinds of disputes are so affected with a public interest that they should *never* be resolved in a private process and whether the results of such private processes will ever be accepted by a skeptical populace.

For instance, a consultation with government officials from administrative agencies in Argentina, which is in the midst of massive privatization of many industries that it formerly owned and would now be regulating, resulted in many questions about whether ADR might work for them. Given the functions of the agencies, the consultants thought that the presentation should be divided about 50/50 between mediation and arbitration. After a preliminary overview of ADR as a whole, the consultants launched into a discussion of mediation, complete with examples of how it had worked in a regulatory context in both North America and Europe. At the next break, some of the Argentine officials took the consultants aside and explained, with exquisite politeness, that they believed mediation could not work for administrative agencies in their government because any time that a government official meets with a regulated party in private, the entire nation assumes that the government official had received a bribe. Needless to say, the rest of the time was spent exploring arbitration.

4. The Role of the Individual

Just as restaurants and auto mechanics do, ADR benefits from word-of-mouth communication. There are plenty of opportunities to advance general knowledge and understanding of ADR.

a. In an industry

If an industry has not already embraced ADR as the construction, real estate, and securities industries have, a union or trade organization or corporate human resources management can provide an introduction by inviting speakers to talk about ADR. The speakers should be given some advance information about what kinds of disputes are frequent and/or difficult and what the areas of specific interest are. As mentioned earlier, ADR is a broad name-band covering numerous techniques, not all of which are right for every dispute.

Getting people thinking and talking about ADR can be accomplished in many ways, from the suggestion box to the board room. Many law firms are pleased to give a free presentation to prospective clients about ADR. But remember that, before acting on what is heard, *independent* advice should always be sought.

b. In a community

With the help of a local or neighborhood telephone directory, see what (if anything) is listed under "community services" or other similar headings. There may already be a community dispute resolution center in the area. Religious communities frequently start ADR programs for their members. If there is a program, perhaps it needs volunteers. If no such program exists, do a "needs assessment" with other community leaders and members. Determine what the troublesome disputes are in the community. Are they political (neighbors vs. local government or industry)? Are they social (one neighbor's stereo is too loud for the other)? Are they ethnic (newly arrived immigrants act differently and aren't being accepted)? Are they educational (should the high school spend the money on a band or a football team)? Whatever the dispute, however simple or complex, ADR can help the community approach it peacefully and productively.

c. Communicating with government officials

Elected officials ultimately pay attention to what their constituents say. If that were not true, then why would all those religious and environmental organizations want their members to write to Congress all the time? The truth is, however, that most citizens and organizations do not have disputes with congressional members (at least not directly). Any disputes are more likely to be with various administrative agencies who depend on Congress (or state legislatures) for their budgets and are therefore most attentive when an elected official expresses an interest in their work. So, it is quite easy to bring some influence to bear on administrative agencies through elected representatives. Elected officials need to know that their constituents want action with respect to ADR and that the officials are being watched during the period before the next election.

A suggested list of action includes:

— Doing an independent study of the functionality of ADR and publishing the results (If ADR is as beneficial as believed, then there will be confirmation of that conclusion; if not, it can be remedied.);

— Inserting ADR provisions in new legislation (If everyone else is saving money using ADR, why not the taxpayers?);

— More vigorous oversight regarding implementation of the Administrative Dispute Resolution Act (ADRA), mentioned earlier in this chapter, or similar local legislation (Many agencies are themselves only paying lip service to the mandates of this legislation.); and

— Learning more about ADR themselves (or encouraging their staffs to learn more about ADR).

Most citizens live under four levels of government: federal, state, county, and city. Each level has a legislative body, which should be approached as vigorously as possible within ADR's ideals.

Other branches of government should not be neglected. Our court systems may be receptive to ADR out of necessity, but individual judges may not like it because they don't understand it. An explaination of the benefits of ADR needs to be available to them. Remember also that the executive branch (particularly at the state and federal levels) has enormous influence over the direction of administrative agencies. With a stroke of the pen (as in President Bush's Executive Order), governors and the President can set a course for ADR.

5. Conclusion

As with most things in life, influencing others takes persistence (unless one has a lot of money). Influencing organizations takes even more persistence. Indeed, as Calvin Coolidge said:

Nothing in this world can take the place of persistence. Talent will not; nothing is more common than unsuccessful people with talent. Genius will not; unrewarded genius is almost a proverb. Education will not; the world is full of educated derelicts. Persistence and determination alone are omnipotent. The slogan "press on" has solved and always will solve the problems of the human race.

So, press on.

ENDNOTES

[1] P.L. 100-702, 28 U.S.C. § § 651 *et seq.*

[2] These criticisms seem to fall into three categories: (1) fear of "second-guessing" of outcomes by agency higher-ups, inspectors general, or Congress itself; (2) doubt that ADR will really save time or money; and (3) concern that public interest may be injured through secret resolutions. See, *e.g., Paths to Justice: Major Public Policy Issues of Dispute Resolution,* Report of the Ad Hoc Panel on Dispute Resolution and Public Policy (National Institute for Dispute Resolution, 1983); statement of Marshall J. Breger, *Hearing on S. 2274 [ADRA of 1988] Before the Subcommittee on Courts and Administrative Practice of the Senate Committee on the Judiciary,* 100th Cong., 2d Sess., 1988.

[3] Harold H. Bruff, Administrative Conference of the United States, Sourcebook: Federal Agency Use of Alternative Means of Dispute Resolution (1987), p. 961ff.

[4] P.L. 101-552, 104 Stat. 2736 (1990).

[5] 5 U.S.C. § 581.

[6] 5 U.S.C. § 581(b).

[7] P.L. 101-648, 104 Stat. 4969 (1990). It should be noted that the ACUS has fallen to the 1995 budget ax.

[8] "But who is to guard the guards themselves?", Juvenal, *Satires,* vi, p. 347 (Lewis Evans translation).

[9] Executive Order 12778, 56 *Federal Register* 55195 (1991).

[10] Volume 3, World Arbitration & Mediation Reports (Bureau of National Affairs, 1992), p. 214. On April 3, 1995, House Bill No. 1050 added a new chapter to title 32 of the North Dakota Century Code which concerns Health Care Malpractice Claims. This new chapter requires an attorney for either the claimant or the health care provider to advise about all reasonably available alternative dispute resolution options that may be available to the parties. In addition, both the claimant and the health care provider are required to make a good-faith effort to resolve part or all of the health care malpractice claim through ADR before the claimant initiates an action. Where either the attorney or parties have failed to comply with these statutory requirements, the court has the authority to impose sanctions, including an award of reasonable actual and statutory costs and attorney fees to the prevailing party.

[11] California has passed several specific disclosure laws that apply in different types of disputes, and Minnesota has passed a bill which appears to apply to all binding arbitrations.

[12] For more information on this topic, see Frank Dukes, "Understanding Community Dispute Resolution," 8 *Mediation Quarterly* (Fall 1990), p. 27.

[13] Jerry Greenberg, spokesperson for the Los Angeles County Bar Association, as quoted in the *Santa Monica Outlook,* 27 March 1993, p. B2. Introducing peaceful conflict resolution into schools seems to have begun in 1972, with a program called Children's Creative Response to Conflict by the Society of Friends (Quakers) in New York.

[14] For a look at ADR (especially mediation) in schools from a psychological perspective, see Jennifer P. Maxwell, "Mediation in the Schools: Self-Regulation, Self-Esteem and Self-Discipline," 7 *Mediation Quarterly* (Winter 1989), p. 149.

[15] The heavy emphasis on litigation and paucity of courses on ADR in most American law schools is both stunning and disappointing.

[16] Hon. William W. Schwarzer, "ADR and the Federal Courts: Questions and Decisions for the Future," 7 *FJC Directions* (Federal Judicial Center, Dec. 1994), p. 3.

"That's not exactly the whole truth, Your Honor, but I think you'll agree that it makes an excellent story!"

Published 1983, American Bar Association

Appendix A

FEDERAL AND STATE ARBITRATION LAWS

The United States Arbitration Act (Domestic)
Title 9, U.S. Code § § 1—16

Chapter 1. GENERAL PROVISIONS

§ 1. "Maritime transactions" and "commerce" defined; exceptions to operation of title

"Maritime transaction", as herein defined, means charter parties, bills of lading of water carriers, agreements relating to wharfage, supplies furnished vessels or repairs to vessels, collisions, or any other matters in foreign commerce which, if the subject of controversy, would be embraced within admiralty jurisdiction; "commerce", as herein defined, means commerce among the several States or with foreign nations, or in any Territory of the United States or in the District of Columbia, or between any such Territory and another, or between any such Territory and any State or foreign nation, or between the District of Columbia and any State or Territory or foreign nation, but nothing herein contained shall apply to contracts of employment of seamen, railroad employees, or any other class of workers engaged in foreign or interstate commerce.

§ 2. Validity, irrevocability, and enforcement of agreements to arbitrate

A written provision in any maritime transaction or a contract evidencing a transaction involving commerce to settle by arbitration a controversy thereafter arising out of such contract or transaction, or the refusal to perform the whole or any part thereof, or an agreement in writing to submit to arbitration an existing controversy arising out of such a contract, transaction, or refusal, shall be valid, irrevocable, and enforceable, save upon such grounds as exist at law or in equity for the revocation of any contract.

§ 3. Stay of proceedings where issue therein referable to arbitration

If any suit or proceeding be brought in any of the courts of the United States upon any issue referable to arbitration under an agreement in writing for such arbitration, the court in which such suit is pending, upon being satisfied that the issue involved in such suit or proceeding is referable to arbitration under such an agreement, shall on application of one of the parties stay the trial of the action until such arbitration has been had in accordance with the terms of the agreement, providing the applicant for the stay is not in default in proceeding with such arbitration.

§ 4. Failure to arbitrate under agreement; petition to United States court having jurisdiction for order to compel arbitration; notice and service thereof; hearing and determination

A party aggrieved by the alleged failure, neglect, or refusal of another to arbitrate under a written agreement for arbitration may petition any United States district court which, save for such agreement, would have jurisdiction under Title 28, in a civil action or in admiralty of the subject matter of a suit arising out of the controversy between the parties, for an order directing that such arbitration proceed in the manner provided for in such agreement. Five days' notice in writing of such application shall be served upon the party in default. Service thereof shall be made in the manner provided by the Federal Rules of Civil Procedure. The court shall hear the parties, and upon being satisfied that the making of the agreement for arbitration or the failure to comply therewith is not in issue, the court shall make an order directing the parties to proceed to arbitration in accordance with the terms of the agreement. The hearing and proceedings, under such agreement, shall be within the district in which the petition for an order directing such arbitration is filed. If the making of the arbitration agreement or the failure, neglect, or refusal to perform the same be in issue, the court shall proceed summarily to the trial thereof. If no jury trial be demanded by the party alleged to be in default, or if the matter in dispute is within admiralty jurisdiction, the court shall hear and determine such issue. Where such an issue is raised, the party alleged to be in default may, except in cases of admiralty, on or before the return day of the notice of application, demand a jury trial of such issue, and upon such demand the court shall make an order referring the issue or issues to a jury in the manner provided by the Federal Rules of Civil Procedure, or may specially call a jury for that purpose. If the jury find that no agreement in writing for arbitration was made or that there is no default in proceeding thereunder, the proceeding shall be dismissed. If the jury find that an agreement for arbitration was made in writing and that there is a default in proceeding thereunder, the court shall make an order summarily directing the parties to proceed with the arbitration in accordance with the terms thereof.

§ 5. Appointment of arbitrators or umpire

If in the agreement provision be made for a method of naming or appointing an arbitrator or arbitrators or an umpire, such method shall be followed; but if no method be provided therein, or if a method be provided and any party thereto shall fail to avail himself of such method, or if for any other reason there shall be a lapse in the naming of an arbitrator or arbitrators or umpire, or in filling a vacancy, then upon the application of either party to the controversy the court shall designate and appoint an arbitrator or arbitrators or umpire, as the case may require, who shall act under the said agreement with the same force and effect as if he or they had been specifically named therein; and unless otherwise provided in the agreement the arbitration shall be by a single arbitrator.

§ 6. Application heard as motion

Any application to the court hereunder shall be made and heard in the manner provided by law for the making and hearing of motions, except as otherwise herein expressly provided.

§ 7. Witnesses before arbitrators; fees; compelling attendance

The arbitrators selected either as prescribed in this title or otherwise, or a majority of them, may summon in writing any person to attend before them or any of them as a witness and in a proper case to bring with him or them any book, record, document, or paper which may be deemed material as evidence in the case. The fees for such attendance shall be the same as the fees of witnesses before masters of the United States courts. Said summons shall issue in the name of the arbitrator or arbitrators, or a majority of them, and shall be signed by the arbitrators, or a majority of them, and shall be directed to the said person and shall be served in the same manner as subpoenas to appear and testify before the court; if any person or persons so summoned to testify shall refuse or neglect to obey said summons, upon petition the United States district court for the district in which such arbitrators, or a majority of them, are sitting may compel the attendance of such person or persons before said arbitrator or arbitrators, or punish said person or persons for contempt in the same manner provided by law for securing the attendance of witnesses or their punishment for neglect or refusal to attend in the courts of the United States.

§ 8. Proceedings begun by libel in admiralty and seizure of vessel or property

If the basis of jurisdiction be a cause of action otherwise justiciable in admiralty, then, notwithstanding anything herein to the contrary, the party claiming to be aggrieved may begin his proceeding hereunder by libel and seizure of the vessel or other property of the other party according to the usual course of admiralty proceedings, and the court shall then have jurisdiction to direct the parties to proceed with the arbitration and shall retain jurisdiction to enter its decree upon the award.

§ 9. Award of arbitrators; confirmation; jurisdiction; procedure

If the parties in their agreement have agreed that a judgment of the court shall be entered upon the award made pursuant to the arbitration, and shall specify the court, then at any time within one year after the award is made any party to the arbitration may apply to the court so specified for an order confirming the award, and thereupon the court must grant such an order unless the award is vacated, modified, or corrected as prescribed in sections 10 and 11 of this title. If no court is specified in the agreement of the parties, then such application may be made to the United States court in and for the district within which such award was made. Notice of the application shall be served upon the adverse party, and thereupon the court shall have jurisdiction of such party as though he had appeared generally in the proceeding. If the adverse party is a resident of the district within which the award was made, such service shall be made upon the adverse party or his attorney as prescribed by law for service of notice of motion in an action in the same court. If the adverse party shall be a nonresident, then the notice of the application shall be served by the marshal of any district within which the adverse party may be found in like manner as other process of the court.

§ 10. Same; vacation; grounds; rehearing

(a) In any of the following cases the United States court in and for the district wherein the award was made may make an order vacating the award upon the application of any party to the arbitration—

(1) Where the award was procured by corruption, fraud, or undue means.

(2) Where there was evident partiality or corruption in the arbitrators, or either of them.

(3) Where the arbitrators were guilty of misconduct in refusing to postpone the hearing, upon sufficient cause shown, or in refusing to hear evidence pertinent and material to the controversy; or of any other misbehavior by which the rights of any party have been prejudiced.

(4) Where the arbitrators exceeded their powers, or so imperfectly executed them that a mutual, final, and definite award upon the subject matter submitted was not made.

(5) Where an award is vacated and the time within which the agreement required the award to be made has not expired the court may, in its discretion, direct a rehearing by the arbitrators.

(b) The United States district court for the district wherein an award was made that was issued pursuant to section 590 of title 5 may make an order vacating the award upon the application of a person, other than a party to the arbitration, who is adversely affected or aggrieved by the award, if the use of arbitration or the award is clearly inconsistent with the factors set forth in section 582 of title 5.

§ 11. Same; modification or correction; grounds; order

In either of the following cases the United States court in and for the district wherein the award was made may make an order modifying or correcting the award upon the application of any party to the arbitration—

(a) Where there was an evident material miscalculation of figures or an evident material mistake in the description of any person, thing, or property referred to in the award.

(b) Where the arbitrators have awarded upon a matter not submitted to them, unless it is a matter not affecting the merits of the decision upon the matter submitted.

(c) Where the award is imperfect in matter of form not affecting the merits of the controversy.

The order may modify and correct the award, so as to effect the intent thereof and promote justice between the parties.

§ 12. Notice of motions to vacate or modify; service; stay of proceedings

Notice of a motion to vacate, modify, or correct an award must be served upon the adverse party or his attorney within three months after the award is filed or delivered. If the adverse party is a resident of the district within which the award was made, such service shall be made upon the adverse party or his attorney as prescribed by law for service of notice of motion in an action in the same court. If the adverse party shall be a nonresident then the notice of the application shall be served by the marshal of any district within which the adverse party may be found in like manner as other process of the court. For the purposes of the motion any judge who might make an order to stay the proceedings in an action brought in the same court may make an order, to be served with the notice of motion, staying the proceedings of the adverse party to enforce the award.

§ 13. Papers filed with order on motions; judgment; docketing; force and effect; enforcement

The party moving for an order confirming, modifying, or correcting an award shall, at the time such order is filed with the clerk for the entry of judgment thereon, also file the following papers with the clerk:

(a) The agreement; the selection or appointment, if any, of an additional arbitrator or umpire; and each written extension of the time, if any, within which to make the award.

(b) The award.

(c) Each notice, affidavit, or other paper used upon an application to confirm, modify, or correct the award, and a copy of each order of the court upon such an application.

The judgment shall be docketed as if it was rendered in an action.

The judgment so entered shall have the same force and effect, in all respects, as, and be subject to all the provisions of law relating to, a judgment in an action; and it may be enforced as if it had been rendered in an action in the court in which it is entered.

§ 14. Contracts not affected

This title shall not apply to contracts made prior to January 1, 1926.

§ 15. Inapplicability of the Act of State doctrine

Enforcement of arbitral agreements, confirmation of arbitral awards, and execution upon judgments based on orders confirming such awards shall not be refused on the basis of the Act of State doctrine.

§ 16. Appeals

(a) An appeal may be taken from—

(1) an order—

(A) refusing a stay of any action under section 3 of this title,

(B) denying a petition under section 4 of this title to order arbitration to proceed,

(C) denying an application under section 206 of this title to compel arbitration,

(D) confirming or denying confirmation of an award or partial award, or

(E) modifying, correcting, or vacating an award;

(2) an interlocutory order granting, continuing, or modifying an injunction against an arbitration that is subject to this title; or

(3) a final decision with respect to an arbitration that is subject to this title.

(b) Except as otherwise provided in section 1292(b) of title 28, an appeal may not be taken from an interlocutory order—

(1) granting a stay of any action under section 3 of this title;

(2) directing arbitration to proceed under section 4 of this title;

(3) compelling arbitration under section 206 of this title; or

(4) refusing to enjoin an arbitration that is subject to this title.

Uniform Arbitration Act (1955)

§ 1. Validity of Arbitration Agreement

A written agreement to submit any existing controversy to arbitration or a provision in a written contract to submit to arbitration any controversy thereafter arising between the parties is valid, enforceable and irrevocable, save upon such grounds as exist at law or in equity for the revocation of any contract. This act also applies to arbitration agreements between employers and employees or between their respective representatives [unless otherwise provided in the agreement].

§ 2. Proceedings to Compel or Stay Arbitration

(a) On application of a party showing an agreement described in Section 1, and the opposing party's refusal to arbitrate, the Court shall order the parties to proceed with arbitration, but if the opposing party denies the existence of the agreement to arbitrate, the Court shall proceed summarily to the determination of the issue so raised and shall order arbitration if found for the moving party, otherwise, the application shall be denied.

(b) On application, the court may stay an arbitration proceeding commenced or threatened on a showing that there is no agreement to arbitrate. Such an issue, when in substantial and bona fide dispute, shall be forthwith and summarily tried and the stay ordered if found for the moving party. If found for the opposing party, the court shall order the parties to proceed to arbitration.

(c) If an issue referable to arbitration under the alleged agreement is involved in an action or proceeding pending in a court having jurisdiction to hear applications under subdivision (a) of this Section, the application shall be made therein. Otherwise and subject to Section 18, the application may be made in any court of competent jurisdiction.

(d) Any action or proceeding involving an issue subject to arbitration shall be stayed if an order for arbitration or an application therefor has been made under this section or, if the issue is severable, the stay may be with respect thereto only. When the application is made in such action or proceeding, the order for arbitration shall include such stay.

(e) An order for arbitration shall not be refused on the ground that the claim in issue lacks merit or bona fides or because any fault or grounds for the claim sought to be arbitrated have not been shown.

§ 3. Appointment of Arbitrators by Court

If the arbitration agreement provides a method of appointment of arbitrators, this method shall be followed. In the absence thereof, or if the agreed method fails or for any reason cannot be followed, or when an arbitrator appointed fails or is unable to act and his successor has not been duly appointed, the court on application of a party shall appoint one or more arbitrators. An arbitrator so appointed has all the powers of one specifically named in the agreement.

§ 4. Majority Action by Arbitrators

The powers of the arbitrators may be exercised by a majority unless otherwise provided by the agreement or by this act.

§ 5. Hearing

Unless otherwise provided by the agreement:

(a) The arbitrators shall appoint a time and place for the hearing and cause notification to the parties to be served personally or by registered mail not less than five days before the hearing. Appearance at the hearing waives such notice. The arbitrators may adjourn the hearing from time to time as necessary and, on request of a party and for good cause, or upon their own motion may postpone the hearing to a time not later than the date fixed by the agreement for making the award unless the parties consent to a later date. The arbitrators may hear and determine the controversy upon the evidence produced notwithstanding the failure of a party duly notified to appear. The court on application may direct the arbitrators to proceed promptly with the hearing and determination of the controversy.

(b) The parties are entitled to be heard, to present evidence material to the controversy and to cross-examine witnesses appearing at the hearing.

(c) The hearing shall be conducted by all the arbitrators but a majority may determine any question and render a final award. If, during the course of the hearing, an arbitrator for any reason ceases to act, the remaining arbitrator or arbitrators appointed to act as neutrals may continue with the hearing and determination of the controversy.

§ 6. Representation by Attorney

A party has the right to be represented by an attorney at any proceeding or hearing under this act. A waiver thereof prior to the proceeding or hearing is ineffective.

§ 7. Witnesses, Subpoenas, Depositions

(a) The arbitrators may issue (cause to be issued) subpoenas for the attendance of witnesses and for the production of books, records, documents and other evidence, and shall have the power to administer oaths. Subpoenas so issued shall be served, and upon application to the Court by a party or the arbitrators, enforced, in the manner provided by law for the service and enforcement of subpoenas in a civil action.

(b) On application of a party and for use as evidence, the arbitrators may permit a deposition to be taken, in the manner and upon the terms designated by the arbitrators, of a witness who cannot be subpoenaed or is unable to attend the hearing.

(c) All provisions of law compelling a person under subpoena to testify are applicable.

(d) Fees for attendance as a witness shall be the same as for a witness in the .... Court.

§ 8. Award

(a) The award shall be in writing and signed by the arbitrators joining in the award. The arbitrators shall deliver a copy to each party personally or by registered mail, or as provided in the agreement.

(b) An award shall be made within the time fixed therefor by the agreement or, if not so fixed, within such time as the court orders on application of a party. The parties may extend the time in writing either before or after the expiration thereof. A party waives the objection that an award was not made within the time required unless he notifies the arbitrators of his objection prior to the delivery of the award to him.

§ 9. Change of Award by Arbitrators

On application of a party or, if an application to the court is pending under Sections 11, 12 or 13, on submission to the arbitrators by the court under such conditions as the court may order, the arbitrators may modify or correct the award upon the grounds stated in paragraphs (1) and (3) of subdivision (a) of Section 13, or for the purpose of clarifying the award. The application shall be made within twenty days after delivery of the award to the applicant. Written notice thereof shall be given forthwith to the opposing party, stating he must serve his objections thereto, if any, within ten days from the notice. The award so modified or corrected is subject to the provisions of Sections 11, 12 and 13.

§ 10. Fees and Expenses of Arbitration

Unless otherwise provided in the agreement to arbitrate, the arbitrators' expenses and fees, together with other expenses, not including counsel fees, incurred in the conduct of the arbitration, shall be paid as provided in the award.

§ 11. Confirmation of an Award

Upon application of a party, the Court shall confirm an award, unless within the time limits hereinafter imposed grounds are urged for vacating or modifying or correcting the award, in which case the court shall proceed as provided in Sections 12 and 13.

§ 12. Vacating an Award

(a) Upon application of a party, the court shall vacate an award where:

(1) The award was procured by corruption, fraud or other undue means;

(2) There was evident partiality by an arbitrator appointed as a neutral or corruption in any of the arbitrators or misconduct prejudicing the rights of any party;

(3) The arbitrators exceeded their powers;

(4) The arbitrators refused to postpone the hearing upon sufficient cause being shown therefor or refused to hear evidence material to the controversy or otherwise so conducted the hearing, contrary to the provisions of Section 5, as to prejudice substantially the rights of a party; or

(5) There was no arbitration agreement and the issue was not adversely determined in proceedings under Section 2 and the party did not participate in the arbitration hearing without raising the objection;

but the fact that the relief was such that it could not or would not be granted by a court of law or equity is not ground for vacating or refusing to confirm the award.

(b) An application under this Section shall be made within ninety days after delivery of a copy of the award to the applicant, except that, if predicated upon corruption, fraud or other undue means, it shall be made within ninety days after such grounds are known or should have been known.

(c) In vacating the award on grounds other than stated in clause (5) of Subsection (a) the court may order a rehearing before new arbitrators chosen as provided in the agreement, or in the absence thereof, by the court in accordance with Section 3, or if the award is vacated on grounds set forth in clauses (3) and

(4) of Subsection (a) the court may order a rehearing before the arbitrators who made the award or their successors appointed in accordance with Section 3. The time within which the agreement requires the award to be made is applicable to the rehearing and commences from the date of the order.

(d) If the application to vacate is denied and no motion to modify or correct the award is pending, the court shall confirm the award. As amended Aug. 1956.

§ 13. Modification or Correction of Award

(a) Upon application made within ninety days after delivery of a copy of the award to the applicant, the court shall modify or correct the award where:

   (1) There was an evident miscalculation of figures or an evident mistake in the description of any person, thing or property referred to in the award;

   (2) The arbitrators have awarded upon a matter not submitted to them and the award may be corrected without affecting the merits of the decision upon the issues submitted; or

   (3) The award is imperfect in a matter of form, not affecting the merits of the controversy.

(b) If the application is granted, the court shall modify and correct the award so as to effect its intent and shall confirm the award as so modified and corrected. Otherwise, the court shall confirm the award as made.

(c) An application to modify or correct an award may be joined in the alternative with an application to vacate the award.

§ 14. Judgment or Decree on Award

Upon the granting of an order confirming, modifying or correcting an award, judgment or decree shall be entered in conformity therewith and be enforced as any other judgment or decree. Costs of the application and of the proceedings subsequent thereto, and disbursements may be awarded by the court.

§ 15. Judgment Roll, Docketing

(a) On entry of judgment or decree, the clerk shall prepare the judgment roll consisting, to the extent filed, of the following:

   (1) The agreement and each written extension of the time within which to make the award;

   (2) The award;

   (3) A copy of the order confirming, modifying or correcting the award; and

(4) A copy of the judgment or decree.

(b) The judgment or decree may be docketed as if rendered in an action.

§ 16. Applications to Court

Except as otherwise provided, an application to the court under this act shall be by motion and shall be heard in the manner and upon the notice provided by law or rule of court for the making and hearing of motions. Unless the parties have agreed otherwise, notice of an initial application for an order shall be served in the manner provided by law for the service of a summons in an action.

§ 17. Court, Jurisdiction

The term "court" means any court of competent jurisdiction of this State. The making of an agreement described in Section 1 providing for arbitration in this State confers jurisdiction on the court to enforce the agreement under this Act and to enter judgment on an award thereunder.

§ 18. Venue

An initial application shall be made to the court of the [county] in which the agreement provides the arbitration hearing shall be held or, if the hearing has been held, in the county in which it was held. Otherwise the application shall be made in the [county] where the adverse party resides or has a place of business or, if he has no residence or place of business in this State, to the court of any [county]. All subsequent applications shall be made to the court hearing the initial application unless the court otherwise directs.

§ 19. Appeals

(a) An appeal may be taken from:

(1) An order denying an application to compel arbitration made under Section 2;

(2) An order granting an application to stay arbitration made under Section 2(b);

(3) An order confirming or denying confirmation of an award;

(4) An order modifying or correcting an award;

(5) An order vacating an award without directing a rehearing; or

(6) A judgment or decree entered pursuant to the provisions of this act.

(b) The appeal shall be taken in the manner and to the same extent as from orders or judgments in a civil action.

§ 20. Act Not Retroactive

This act applies only to agreements made subsequent to the taking effect of this act.

§ 21. Uniformity of Interpretation

This act shall be so construed as to effectuate its general purpose to make uniform the law of those states which enact it.

§ 22. Constitutionality

If any provision of this act or the application thereof to any person or circumstance is held invalid, the invalidity shall not affect other provisions or applications of the act which can be given effect without the invalid provision or application, and to this end the provisions of this act are severable.

§ 23. Short Title

This act may be cited as the Uniform Arbitration Act.

§ 24. Repeal

All acts or parts of acts which are inconsistent with the provisions of this act are hereby repealed.

§ 25. Time of Taking Effect

This act shall take effect ....

State Arbitration Laws

* These states follow the Uniform Arbitration Act ("UAA").

Ala. Code tit. 7, ch. 19, § § 6-6-1 *et seq.* (1977 & Supp. 1993).

* Alaska Stat. § § 09.43.010 to 09.43.180 (1962 & Supp. 1992).

* Ariz. Rev. Stat. Ann. § § 12-1501 *et seq.* (West 1982 & Supp. 1993).

* Ark. Code Ann. § § 16-108-201 *et seq.* (1987 & Supp. 1992).

Cal. Civ. Proc. Code § § 1280 *et seq.* (Deering 1981 & Supp. 1993).

* Colo. Rev. Stat. § § 13-22-201 *et seq.* (West 1989 & Supp. 1993).

Conn. Gen. Stat. § § 52-408 *et seq.* (West 1991 & Supp. 1992).

* Del. Code Ann. tit. 10, § § 5701 *et seq.* (1975 & Supp. 1992).

* D.C. Code tit. 16, § § 16-4301 *et seq.* (Michie 1981 & Supp. 1992).

* Fla. Stat. § § 682.01 *et seq.* (West 1992).

Ga. Code Ann. § § 9-9-1 *et seq.* (Construction disputes only) (1982 & Supp. 1992).

Haw. Rev. Stat. § § 658-1 *et seq.* (Michie 1988 & Supp. 1992).

* Idaho Code § § 7-901 *et seq.* (Michie 1948 & Supp. 1992).

* Ill. Comp. Stat. ch. 710, ILCS § § 5/1 *et seq.* (West 1992).

* Ind. Code § § 34-4-1-1 *et seq.* (West 1983 & Supp. 1993).

* Iowa Code § § 679A.1 *et seq.* (West 1987 & Supp. 1992).

* Kan. Stat. Ann. § § 5-401 *et seq.* (1990).

* Ky. Rev. Stat. Ann. § § 417.045 *et seq.* (Michie 1971 & Supp. 1992).

La. Rev. Stat. Ann. § § 9:4201 *et seq.* (West 1992).

* Me. Rev. Stat. Ann. tit. 14, § § 5927 *et seq.* (West 1980 & Supp. 1993).

* Md. Cts. & Jud. Proc. Code Ann. § § 3-201 *et seq.* (Michie 1992).

* Mass. Gen. Laws Ann. ch. 251, § § 1 *et seq.* (West 1988 & Supp. 1992).

* Mich. Comp. Laws § § 600.5001 *et seq.* (West 1992).

* Minn. Stat. § § 572.08 *et seq.* (West 1993).

Miss. Code Ann. § § 11-15-101 *et seq.* (Construction disputes only) (1991).

* Mo. Rev. Stat. § § 435.012 *et seq.* (West 1992).

* Mont. Code Ann. § § 27-5-111 *et seq.* (1978 & Supp. 1991).

* Neb. Rev. Stat. § § 25-2601 *et seq.* (1954 & Supp. 1992).

* Nev. Rev. Stat. § § 38.015 *et seq.* (Michie 1986 & Supp. 1991).

* N.C. Gen. Stat. § § 1-567.1 *et seq.* (Michie 1944 & Supp. 1992).

* N.D. Cent. Code tit. 32, ch. 32-29.2, § § 32-29.2-01 *et seq.* (Michie 1987 & Supp. 1992).

N.H. Rev. Stat. Ann. § § 542:1 *et seq.* (Equity 1991).

N.J. Stat. Ann. § § 2A:24-1 *et seq.* (West 1992).

* N.M. Stat. Ann. § § 44-7-1 *et seq.* (1978 & Supp. 1992).

N.Y. Civ. Prac. L. & R. §§7501 *et seq.* (McKinney 1980 & Supp. 1993).

Ohio Rev. Code Ann. §§2711.01 *et seq.* (Anderson 1912 & Supp. 1992).

* Okla. Stat. Ann. tit. 15, §§801 *et seq.* (West 1993).

Or. Rev. Stat. §§36.300 *et seq.* (1991).

* Pa. Con. Stat. Ann. tit. 42, ch. 73, §§7301 *et seq.* (West 1982 & Supp. 1992).

R.I. Gen. Laws §§10-3-1 *et seq.* (Michie 1957 & Supp. 1992).

* S.C. Code §§15-48-10 *et seq.* (1991).

* S.D. Codified Laws §21-25A-1 *et seq.* (1968 & Supp. 1992).

* Tenn. Code Ann. §§29-5-301 *et seq.* (1955 & Supp. 1992).

* Tex. Rev. Civ. Stat. Ann. tit. 10, Art. 224 *et seq.* (Vernon 1973 Supp. 1992).

* Utah Code Ann. §§78-31a-1 *et seq.* (Michie 1986 & Supp. 1992).

* Vt. Stat. Ann. tit. 12, §§5651 *et seq.* (1991).

* Va. Code Ann. §§8.01-581.01 *et seq.* (Michie 1992).

Wash. Rev. Code §§7.04.010 *et seq.* (West 1992).

W.Va. Code of 1966, ch. 55, §§55-10-1 to 55-10-8 (Michie 1966 and Supp. 1992).

Wis. Stat. §§788.01 *et seq.* (West 1992).

* Wyo. Stat. Ann. §§1-36-101 *et seq.* (1977 & Supp. 1992).

See also P.R. Laws. Ann. tit. 32, §§3201 *et seq.* (1991).

Appendix B
SELECTED MEDIATION AND ARBITRATION RULES

AAA Commercial Mediation Rules

(AAA rules reprinted by permission of the American Arbitration Association.)

1. Agreement of Parties

Whenever, by stipulation or in their contract, the parties have provided for mediation or conciliation of existing or future disputes under the auspices of the American Arbitration Association (AAA) or under these rules, they shall be deemed to have made these rules, as amended and in effect as of the date of the submission of the dispute, a part of their agreement.

2. Initiation of Mediation

Any party or parties to a dispute may initiate mediation by filing with the AAA a submission to mediation or a written request for mediation pursuant to these rules, together with the appropriate administrative fee contained in the Fee Schedule. Where there is no submission to mediation or contract providing for mediation, a party may request the AAA to invite another party to join in a submission to mediation. Upon receipt of such a request, the AAA will contact the other parties involved in the dispute and attempt to obtain a submission to mediation.

3. Request for Mediation

A request for mediation shall contain a brief statement of the nature of the dispute and the names, addresses, and telephone numbers of all parties to the dispute and those who will represent them, if any, in the mediation. The initiating party shall simultaneously file two copies of the request with the AAA and one copy with every other party to the dispute.

4. Appointment of Mediator

Upon receipt of a request for mediation, the AAA will appoint a qualified mediator to serve. Normally, a single mediator will be appointed unless the parties agree otherwise or the AAA determines otherwise. If the agreement of the parties names a mediator or specifies a method of appointing a mediator, that designation or method shall be followed.

5. Qualifications of Mediator

No person shall serve as a mediator in any dispute in which that person has any financial or personal interest in the result of the mediation, except by the written consent of all parties. Prior to accepting an appointment, the prospective mediator shall disclose any circumstance likely to create a presumption of bias or prevent a prompt meeting with the parties. Upon receipt of such information, the AAA shall either replace the mediator or immediately communicate the information to the parties for their comments. In the event that the parties disagree as to whether the mediator shall serve, the AAA will appoint another mediator. The AAA is authorized to appoint another mediator if the appointed mediator is unable to serve promptly.

6. Vacancies

If any mediator shall become unwilling or unable to serve, the AAA will appoint another mediator, unless the parties agree otherwise.

7. Representation

Any party may be represented by persons of the party's choice. The names and addresses of such persons shall be communicated in writing to all parties and to the AAA.

8. Date, Time, and Place of Mediation

The mediator shall fix the date and the time of each mediation session. The mediation shall be held at the appropriate regional office of the AAA, or at any other convenient location agreeable to the mediator and the parties, as the mediator shall determine.

9. Identification of Matters in Dispute

At least ten days prior to the first scheduled mediation session, each party shall provide the mediator with a brief memorandum setting forth its position with regard to the issues that need to be resolved. At the discretion of the mediator, such memoranda may be mutually exchanged by the parties.

At the first session, the parties will be expected to produce all information reasonably required for the mediator to understand the issues presented.

The mediator may require any party to supplement such information.

10. Authority of Mediator

The mediator does not have the authority to impose a settlement on the parties but will attempt to help them reach a satisfactory resolution of their dispute. The mediator is authorized to conduct joint and separate meetings with the parties and to make oral and written recommendations for settlement. Whenever necessary, the mediator may also obtain expert advice concerning technical aspects of the dispute, provided that the parties agree and assume the expenses of obtaining such advice. Arrangements for obtaining such advice shall be made by the mediator or the parties, as the mediator shall determine.

The mediator is authorized to end the mediation whenever, in the judgment of the mediator, further efforts at mediation would not contribute to a resolution of the dispute between the parties.

11. Privacy

Mediation sessions are private. The parties and their representatives may attend mediation sessions. Other persons may attend only with the permission of the parties and with the consent of the mediator.

12. Confidentiality

Confidential information disclosed to a mediator by the parties or by witnesses in the course of the mediation shall not be divulged by the mediator. All records, reports, or other documents received by a mediator while serving in that capacity shall be confidential. The mediator shall not be compelled to divulge such records or to testify in regard to the mediation in any adversary proceeding or judicial forum.

The parties shall maintain the confidentiality of the mediation and shall not rely on, or introduce as evidence in any arbitral, judicial, or other proceeding:

(a) views expressed or suggestions made by another party with respect to a possible settlement of the dispute;

(b) admissions made by another party in the course of the mediation proceedings;

(c) proposals made or views expressed by the mediator; or

(d) the fact that another party had or had not indicated willingness to accept a proposal for settlement made by the mediator.

13. No Stenographic Record

There shall be no stenographic record of the mediation process.

14. Termination of Mediation

The mediation shall be terminated:

(a) by the execution of a settlement agreement by the parties;

(b) by a written declaration of the mediator to the effect that further efforts at mediation are no longer worthwhile; or

(c) by a written declaration of a party or parties to the effect that the mediation proceedings are terminated.

15. Exclusion of Liability

Neither the AAA nor any mediator is a necessary party in judicial proceedings relating to the mediation.

Neither the AAA nor any mediator shall be liable to any party for any act or omission in connection with any mediation conducted under these rules.

16. Interpretation and Application of Rules

The mediator shall interpret and apply these rules insofar as they relate to the mediator's duties and responsibilities. All other rules shall be interpreted and applied by the AAA.

17. Expenses

The expenses of witnesses for either side shall be paid by the party producing such witnesses. All other expenses of the mediation, including required traveling and other expenses of the mediator and representatives of the AAA, and the expenses of any witness and the cost of any proofs or expert advice produced at the direct request of the mediator, shall be borne equally by the parties unless they agree otherwise.

Administrative Fees

The case filing or set-up fee is $300. This fee is to be borne equally or as otherwise agreed by the parties.

Additionally, the parties are charged a fee based on the number of hours of mediator time. The hourly fee is for the compensation of both the mediator and the AAA and varies according to region. Check with your local office for specific availability and rates.

There is no charge to the filing party where the AAA is requested to invite other parties to join in a submission to mediation. However, if a case settles after AAA involvement but prior to dispute resolution, the filing party will be charged a $150 filing fee.

The expenses of the AAA and the mediator, if any, are generally borne equally by the parties. The parties may vary this arrangement by agreement.

Where the parties have attempted mediation under these rules but have failed to reach a settlement, the AAA will apply the administrative fee on the mediation toward subsequent AAA arbitration, which is filed with the AAA within ninety days of the termination of the mediation.

Deposits

Before the commencement of mediation, the parties shall each deposit such portion of the fee covering the cost of mediation as the AAA shall direct and all appropriate additional sums that the AAA deems necessary to defray the expenses of the proceeding. When the mediation has terminated, the AAA shall render an accounting and return any unexpended balance to the parties.

Refunds

Once the parties agree to mediate, no refund of the administrative fee will be made.

AAA Commercial Arbitration Rules

(AAA rules reprinted by permission of the American Arbitration Association.)

1. Agreement of Parties

The parties shall be deemed to have made these rules a part of their arbitration agreement whenever they have provided for arbitration by the American Arbitration Association (hereinafter AAA) or under its Commercial Arbitration Rules. These rules and any amendment of them shall apply in the form obtaining at the time the demand for arbitration or submission agreement is received by the AAA. The parties, by written agreement, may vary the procedures set forth in these rules.

2. Name of Tribunal

Any tribunal constituted by the parties for the settlement of their dispute under these rules shall be called the Commercial Arbitration Tribunal.

3. Administrator and Delegation of Duties

When parties agree to arbitrate under these rules, or when they provide for arbitration by the AAA and an arbitration is initiated under these rules, they thereby authorize the AAA to administer the arbitration. The authority and duties of the AAA are prescribed in the agreement of the parties and in these rules, and may be carried out through such of the AAA's representatives as it may direct.

4. National Panel of Arbitrators

The AAA shall establish and maintain a National Panel of Commercial Arbitrators and shall appoint arbitrators as provided in these rules.

5. Regional Offices

The AAA may, in its discretion, assign the administration of an arbitration to any of its regional offices.

6. Initiation under an Arbitration

Provision in a Contract Arbitration under an arbitration provision in a contract shall be initiated in the following manner:

(a) The initiating party (hereinafter claimant) shall, within the time period, if any, specified in the contract(s), give written notice to the other party (hereinafter respondent) of its intention to arbitrate (demand), which notice shall contain a statement setting forth the nature of the dispute, the amount involved, if any, the remedy sought, and the hearing locale requested, and

(b) shall file at any regional office of the AAA three copies of the notice and three copies of the arbitration provisions of the contract, together with the appropriate filing fee as provided in the schedule [below].

The AAA shall give notice of such filing to the respondent or respondents. A respondent may file an answering statement in duplicate with the AAA within ten days after notice from the AAA, in which event the respondent shall at the same time send a copy of the answering statement to the claimant. If a counterclaim is asserted, it shall contain a statement setting forth the nature of the counterclaim, the amount involved, if any, and the remedy sought. If a counterclaim is made, the appropriate fee provided in the schedule [below] shall be forwarded to the AAA with the answering statement. If no answering statement is filed within the stated time, it will be treated as a denial of the claim. Failure to file an answering statement shall not operate to delay the arbitration.

7. Initiation under a Submission

Parties to any existing dispute may commence an arbitration under these rules by filing at any regional office of the AAA three copies of a written submission to arbitrate under these rules, signed by the parties. It shall contain a statement of the matter in dispute, the amount involved, if any, the remedy sought, and the hearing locale requested, together with the appropriate filing fee as provided in the schedule [below].

8. Changes of Claim

After filing of a claim, if either party desires to make any new or different claim or counterclaim, it shall be made in writing and filed with the AAA, and a copy shall be mailed to the other party, who shall have a period of ten days from the date of such mailing within which to file an answer with the AAA. After the arbitrator is appointed, however, no new or different claim may be submitted except with the arbitrator's consent.

9. Applicable Procedures

Unless the AAA in its discretion determines otherwise, the Expedited Procedures shall be applied in any case where no disclosed claim or counterclaim exceeds $50,000, exclusive of interest and arbitration costs. Parties may also agree to using the Expedited Procedures in cases involving claims in excess of $50,000. The Expedited Procedures shall be applied as described in Sections 53 through 57 of these rules, in addition to any other portion of these rules that is not in conflict with the Expedited Procedures.

All other cases shall be administered in accordance with Sections 1 through 52 of these rules.

10. Administrative Conference, Preliminary Hearing, and Mediation Conference

At the request of any party or at the discretion of the AAA, an administrative conference with the AAA and the parties and/or their representatives will be scheduled in appropriate cases to expedite the arbitration proceedings. There is no administrative fee for this service.

In large or complex cases, at the request of any party or at the discretion of the arbitrator or the AAA, a preliminary hearing with the parties and/or their representatives and the arbitrator may be scheduled by the arbitrator to specify the issues to be resolved, to stipulate to uncontested facts, and to consider any other matters that will expedite the arbitration proceedings. Consistent with the expedited nature of arbitration, the arbitrator may, at the preliminary hearing, establish (i) the extent of and schedule for the production of relevant documents and other information, (ii) the identification of any witnesses to be called, and (iii) a schedule for further hearings to resolve the dispute. There is no administrative fee for the first preliminary hearing.

With the consent of the parties, the AAA at any stage of the proceeding may arrange a mediation conference under the Commercial Mediation Rules, in order to facilitate settlement. The mediator shall not be an arbitrator appointed to the case. Where the parties to a pending arbitration agree to mediate under the AAA's rules, no additional administrative fee is required to initiate the mediation.

11. Fixing of Locale

The parties may mutually agree on the locale where the arbitration is to be held. If any party requests that the hearing be held in a specific locale and the other party files no objection thereto within ten days after notice of the request has been sent to it by the AAA, the locale shall be the one requested. If a party objects to the locale requested by the other party, the AAA shall have the power to determine the locale and its decision shall be final and binding.

12. Qualifications of an Arbitrator

Any neutral arbitrator appointed pursuant to Section 13, 14, 15, or 54, or selected by mutual choice of the parties or their appointees, shall be subject to disqualification for the reasons specified in Section 19. If the parties specifically so agree in writing, the arbitrator shall not be subject to disqualification for those reasons.

Unless the parties agree otherwise, an arbitrator selected unilaterally by one party is a party-appointed arbitrator and is not subject to disqualification pursuant to Section 19.

The term "arbitrator" in these rules refers to the arbitration panel, whether composed of one or more arbitrators and whether the arbitrators are neutral or party appointed.

13. Appointment from Panel

If the parties have not appointed an arbitrator and have not provided any other method of appointment, the arbitrator shall be appointed in the following manner: immediately after the filing of the demand or submission, the AAA shall send simultaneously to each party to the dispute an identical list of names of persons chosen from the panel.

Each party to the dispute shall have ten days from the transmittal date in which to strike names objected to, number the remaining names in order of preference, and return the list to the AAA. In a single-arbitrator case, each party may strike three names on a peremptory basis. In a multiarbitrator case, each party may strike five names on a peremptory basis. If a party does not return the list within the time specified, all persons named therein shall be deemed acceptable. From among the persons who have been approved on both lists, and in accordance with the designated order of mutual preference, the AAA shall invite the acceptance of an arbitrator to serve. If the parties fail to agree on any of the persons named, or if acceptable arbitrators are unable to act, or if for any other reason the appointment cannot be made from the submitted lists, the AAA shall have the power to make the appointment from among other members of the panel without the submission of additional lists.

14. Direct Appointment by a Party

If the agreement of the parties names an arbitrator or specifies a method of appointing an arbitrator, that designation or method shall be followed. The notice of appointment, with the name and address of the arbitrator, shall be filed with the AAA by the appointing party. Upon the request of any appointing party, the AAA shall submit a list of members of the panel from which the party may, if it so desires, make the appointment.

If the agreement specifies a period of time within which an arbitrator shall be appointed and any party fails to make the appointment within that period, the AAA shall make the appointment.

If no period of time is specified in the agreement, the AAA shall notify the party to make the appointment. If within ten days thereafter an arbitrator has not been appointed by a party, the AAA shall make the appointment.

15. Appointment of Neutral Arbitrator by Party-Appointed Arbitrators or Parties

If the parties have selected party-appointed arbitrators, or if such arbitrators have been appointed as provided in Section 14, and the parties have authorized them to appoint a neutral arbitrator within a specified time and no appointment is made within that time or any agreed extension, the AAA may appoint a neutral arbitrator, who shall act as chairperson.

If no period of time is specified for appointment of the neutral arbitrator and the party-appointed arbitrators or the parties do not make the appointment within ten days from the date of the appointment of the last party-appointed arbitrator, the AAA may appoint the neutral arbitrator, who shall act as chairperson.

If the parties have agreed that their party-appointed arbitrators shall appoint the neutral arbitrator from the panel, the AAA shall furnish to the party-appointed arbitrators, in the manner provided in Section 13, a list selected from the panel, and the appointment of the neutral arbitrator shall be made as provided in that section.

16. Nationality of Arbitrator in International Arbitration

Where the parties are nationals or residents of different countries, any neutral arbitrator shall, upon the request of either party, be appointed from among the nationals of a country other than that of any of the parties. The request must be made prior to the time set for the appointment of the arbitrator as agreed by the parties or set by these rules.

17. Number of Arbitrators

If the arbitration agreement does not specify the number of arbitrators, the dispute shall be heard and determined by one arbitrator, unless the AAA, in its discretion, directs that a greater number of arbitrators be appointed.

18. Notice to Arbitrator of Appointment

Notice of the appointment of the neutral arbitrator, whether appointed mutually by the parties or by the AAA, shall be sent to the arbitrator by the AAA, together with a copy of these rules, and the signed acceptance of the arbitrator shall be filed with the AAA prior to the opening of the first hearing.

19. Disclosure and Challenge Procedure

Any person appointed as neutral arbitrator shall disclose to the AAA any circumstance likely to affect impartiality, including any bias or any financial or personal interest in the result of the arbitration or any past or present relationship with the parties or their representatives. Upon receipt of such information from the arbitrator or another source, the AAA shall communicate the information to the parties and, if it deems it appropriate to do so, to the arbitrator and others. Upon objection of a party to the continued service of a neutral arbitrator, the AAA shall determine whether the arbitrator should be disqualified and shall inform the parties of its decision, which shall be conclusive.

20. Vacancies

If for any reason an arbitrator is unable to perform the duties of the office, the AAA may, on proof satisfactory to it, declare the office vacant. Vacancies shall be filled in accordance with the applicable provisions of these rules.

In the event of a vacancy in a panel of neutral arbitrators after the hearings have commenced, the remaining arbitrator or arbitrators may continue with the hearing and determination of the controversy, unless the parties agree otherwise.

21. Date, Time, and Place of Hearing

The arbitrator shall set the date, time, and place for each hearing. The AAA shall send a notice of hearing to the parties at least ten days in advance of the hearing date, unless otherwise agreed by the parties.

22. Representation

Any party may be represented by counsel or other authorized representative. A party intending to be so represented shall notify the other party and the AAA of the name and address of the representative at least three days prior to the date set for the hearing at which that person is first to appear. When such a representative initiates an arbitration or responds for a party, notice is deemed to have been given.

23. Stenographic Record

Any party desiring a stenographic record shall make arrangements directly with a stenographer and shall notify the other parties of these arrangements in advance of the hearing. The requesting party or parties shall pay the cost of the record. If the transcript is agreed by the parties to be, or determined by the arbitrator to be, the official record of the proceeding, it must be made available to the arbitrator and to the other parties for inspection, at a date, time, and place determined by the arbitrator.

24. Interpreters

Any party wishing an interpreter shall make all arrangements directly with the interpreter and shall assume the costs of the service.

25. Attendance at Hearings

The arbitrator shall maintain the privacy of the hearings unless the law provides to the contrary. Any person having a direct interest in the arbitration is entitled to attend hearings. The arbitrator shall otherwise have the power to require the exclusion of any witness, other than a party or other essential person, during the testimony of any other witness. It shall be discretionary with the arbitrator to determine the propriety of the attendance of any other person.

26. Postponements

The arbitrator for good cause shown may postpone any hearing upon the request of a party or upon the arbitrator's own initiative, and shall also grant such postponement when all of the parties agree.

27. Oaths

Before proceeding with the first hearing, each arbitrator may take an oath of office and, if required by law, shall do so. The arbitrator may require witnesses to testify under oath administered by any duly qualified person and, if it is required by law or requested by any party, shall do so.

28. Majority Decision

All decisions of the arbitrators must be by a majority. The award must also be made by a majority unless the concurrence of all is expressly required by the arbitration agreement or by law.

29. Order of Proceedings and Communication with Arbitrator

A hearing shall be opened by the filing of the oath of the arbitrator, where required; by the recording of the date, time, and place of the hearing, and the presence of the arbitrator, the parties, and their representatives, if any; and by the receipt by the arbitrator of the statement of the claim and the answering statement, if any.

The arbitrator may, at the beginning of the hearing, ask for statements clarifying the issues involved. In some cases, part or all of the above will have been accomplished at the preliminary hearing conducted by the arbitrator pursuant to Section 10.

The complaining party shall then present evidence to support its claim. The defending party shall then present evidence supporting its defense. Witnesses for each party shall submit to questions or other examination. The arbitrator has the discretion to vary this procedure but shall afford a full and equal opportunity to all parties for the presentation of any material and relevant evidence.

Exhibits, when offered by either party, may be received in evidence by the arbitrator. The names and addresses of all witnesses and a description of the exhibits in the order received shall be made a part of the record.

There shall be no direct communication between the parties and a neutral arbitrator other than at oral hearing, unless the parties and the arbitrator agree otherwise. Any other oral or written communication from the parties to the neutral arbitrator shall be directed to the AAA for transmittal to the arbitrator.

30. Arbitration in the Absence of a Party or Representative

Unless the law provides to the contrary, the arbitration may proceed in the absence of any party or representative who, after due notice, fails to be present or fails to obtain a postponement. An award shall not be made solely on the default of a party. The arbitrator shall require the party who is present to submit such evidence as the arbitrator may require for the making of an award.

31. Evidence

The parties may offer such evidence as is relevant and material to the dispute and shall produce such evidence as the arbitrator may deem necessary to an understanding and determination of the dispute. An arbitrator or other person authorized by law to subpoena witnesses or documents may do so upon the request of any party or independently.

The arbitrator shall be the judge of the relevance and materiality of the evidence offered, and conformity to legal rules of evidence shall not be necessary. All evidence shall be taken in the presence of all of the arbitrators and all of the parties, except where any of the parties is absent in default or has waived the right to be present.

32. Evidence by Affidavit and Posthearing Filing of Documents or Other Evidence

The arbitrator may receive and consider the evidence of witnesses by affidavit, but shall give it only such weight as the arbitrator deems it entitled to after consideration of any objection made to its admission.

If the parties agree or the arbitrator directs that documents or other evidence be submitted to the arbitrator after the hearing, the documents or other evidence shall be filed with the AAA for transmission to the arbitrator. All parties shall be afforded an opportunity to examine such documents or other evidence.

33. Inspection or Investigation

An arbitrator finding it necessary to make an inspection or investigation in connection with the arbitration shall direct the AAA to so advise the parties. The arbitrator shall set the date and time and the AAA shall notify the parties. Any party who so desires may be present at such an inspection or investigation. In the event that one or all parties are not present at the inspection or investigation, the arbitrator shall make a verbal or written report to the parties and afford them an opportunity to comment.

34. Interim Measures

The arbitrator may issue such orders for interim relief as may be deemed necessary to safeguard the property that is the subject matter of the arbitration, without prejudice to the rights of the parties or to the final determination of the dispute.

35. Closing of Hearing

The arbitrator shall specifically inquire of all parties whether they have any further proofs to offer or witnesses to be heard. Upon receiving negative replies or if satisfied that the record is complete, the arbitrator shall declare the hearing closed.

If briefs are to be filed, the hearing shall be declared closed as of the final date set by the arbitrator for the receipt of briefs. If documents are to be filed as provided in Section 32 and the date set for their receipt is later than that set for the receipt of briefs, the later date shall be the date of closing the hearing. The time limit within which the arbitrator is required to make the award shall commence to run, in the absence of other agreements by the parties, upon the closing of the hearing.

36. Reopening of Hearing

The hearing may be reopened on the arbitrator's initiative, or upon application of a party, at any time before the award is made. If reopening the hearing would prevent the making of the award within the specific time agreed on by the parties in the contract(s) out of which the controversy has arisen, the matter may not be reopened unless the parties agree on an extension of time. When no specific date is fixed in the contract, the arbitrator may reopen the hearing and shall have thirty days from the closing of the reopened hearing within which to make an award.

37. Waiver of Oral Hearing

The parties may provide, by written agreement, for the waiver of oral hearings in any case. If the parties are unable to agree as to the procedure, the AAA shall specify a fair and equitable procedure.

38. Waiver of Rules

Any party who proceeds with the arbitration after knowledge that any provision or requirement of these rules has not been complied with and who fails to state an objection in writing shall be deemed to have waived the right to object.

39. Extensions of Time

The parties may modify any period of time by mutual agreement. The AAA or the arbitrator may for good cause extend any period of time established by these rules, except the time for making the award. The AAA shall notify the parties of any extension.

40. Serving of Notice

Each party shall be deemed to have consented that any papers, notices, or process necessary or proper for the initiation or continuation of an arbitration under these rules; for any court action in connection therewith; or for the entry of judgment on any award made under these rules may be served on a party by mail addressed to the party or its representative at the last known address or by personal service, in or outside the state where the arbitration is to be held, provided that reasonable opportunity to be heard with regard thereto has been granted to the party.

The AAA and the parties may also use facsimile transmission, telex, telegram, or other written forms of electronic communication to give the notices required by these rules.

41. Time of Award

The award shall be made promptly by the arbitrator and, unless otherwise agreed by the parties or specified by law, no later than thirty days from the date of closing the hearing, or, if oral hearings have been waived, from the date of the AAA's transmittal of the final statements and proofs to the arbitrator.

42. Form of Award

The award shall be in writing and shall be signed by a majority of the arbitrators. It shall be executed in the manner required by law.

43. Scope of Award

The arbitrator may grant any remedy or relief that the arbitrator deems just and equitable and within the scope of the agreement of the parties, including, but not limited to, specific performance of a contract. The arbitrator shall, in the award, assess arbitration fees, expenses, and compensation as provided in Sections 48, 49, and 50 in favor of any party and, in the event that any administrative fees or expenses are due the AAA, in favor of the AAA.

44. Award upon Settlement

If the parties settle their dispute during the course of the arbitration, the arbitrator may set forth the terms of the agreed settlement in an award. Such an award is referred to as a consent award.

45. Delivery of Award to Parties

Parties shall accept as legal delivery of the award the placing of the award or a true copy thereof in the mail addressed to a party or its representative at the last known address, personal service of the award, or the filing of the award in any other manner that is permitted by law.

46. Release of Documents for Judicial Proceedings

The AAA shall, upon the written request of a party, furnish to the party, at its expense, certified copies of any papers in the AAA's possession that may be required in judicial proceedings relating to the arbitration.

47. Applications to Court and Exclusion of Liability

    (a) No judicial proceeding by a party relating to the subject matter of the arbitration shall be deemed a waiver of the party's right to arbitrate.

    (b) Neither the AAA nor any arbitrator in a proceeding under these rules is a necessary party in judicial proceedings relating to the arbitration.

    (c) Parties to these rules shall be deemed to have consented that judgment upon the arbitration award may be entered in any federal or state court having jurisdiction thereof.

    (d) Neither the AAA nor any arbitrator shall be liable to any party for any act or omission in connection with any arbitration conducted under these rules.

48. Administrative Fees

As a not-for-profit organization, the AAA shall prescribe filing and other administrative fees and service charges to compensate it for the cost of providing administrative services. The fees in effect when the fee or charge is incurred shall be applicable.

The filing fee shall be advanced by the initiating party or parties, subject to final apportionment by the arbitrator in the award.

The AAA may, in the event of extreme hardship on the part of any party, defer or reduce the administrative fees.

49. Expenses

The expenses of witnesses for either side shall be paid by the party producing such witnesses. All other expenses of the arbitration, including required travel and other expenses of the arbitrator, AAA representatives, and any witness and the cost of any proof produced at the direct request of the arbitrator, shall be borne equally by the parties, unless they agree otherwise or unless the arbitrator in the award assesses such expenses or any part thereof against any specified party or parties.

50. Neutral Arbitrator's Compensation

Unless the parties agree otherwise, members of the National Panel of Commercial Arbitrators appointed as neutrals will serve without compensation for the first day of service.

Thereafter, compensation shall be based on the amount of service involved and the number of hearings. An appropriate daily rate and other arrangements will be discussed by the administrator with the parties and the arbitrator. If the parties fail to agree to the terms of compensation, an appropriate rate shall be established by the AAA and communicated in writing to the parties.

Any arrangement for the compensation of a neutral arbitrator shall be made through the AAA and not directly between the parties and the arbitrator.

51. Deposits

The AAA may require the parties to deposit in advance of any hearings such sums of money as it deems necessary to cover the expense of the arbitration, including the arbitrator's fee, if any, and shall render an accounting to the parties and return any unexpended balance at the conclusion of the case.

52. Interpretation and Application of Rules

The arbitrator shall interpret and apply these rules insofar as they relate to the arbitrator's powers and duties. When there is more than one arbitrator and a difference arises among them concerning the meaning or application of these rules, it shall be decided by a majority vote. If that is not possible, either an arbitrator or a party may refer the question to the AAA for final decision. All other rules shall be interpreted and applied by the AAA.

Expedited Procedures

53. Notice by Telephone

The parties shall accept all notices from the AAA by telephone. Such notices by the AAA shall subsequently be confirmed in writing to the parties. Should there be a failure to confirm in writing any notice hereunder, the proceeding shall nonetheless be valid if notice has, in fact, been given by telephone.

54. Appointment and Qualifications of Arbitrator

(a) Where no disclosed claim or counterclaim exceeds $50,000, exclusive of interest and arbitration costs, the AAA shall appoint a single arbitrator, from the National Panel of Commercial Arbitrators, without submission of lists of proposed arbitrators.

(b) Where all parties request that a list of proposed arbitrators be sent, the AAA upon payment of the service charge as provided in the Administrative Fees shall submit simultaneously to each party an identical list of five proposed arbitrators, drawn from the National Panel of Commercial Arbitrators, from which one arbitrator shall be appointed. Each party may strike two names from the list on a peremptory basis. The list is returnable to the AAA within seven days from the date of the AAA's mailing to the parties.

If for any reason the appointment of an arbitrator cannot be made from the list, the AAA may make the appointment from among other members of the panel without the submission of additional lists.

(c) The parties will be given notice by telephone by the AAA of the appointment of the arbitrator, who shall be subject to disqualification for the reasons specified in Section 19. The parties shall notify the AAA, by telephone, within seven days of any objection to the arbitrator appointed. Any objection by a party to the arbitrator shall be confirmed in writing to the AAA with a copy to the other party or parties.

55. Date, Time, and Place of Hearing

The arbitrator shall set the date, time, and place of the hearing. The AAA will notify the parties by telephone, at least seven days in advance of the hearing date. A formal notice of hearing will also be sent by the AAA to the parties.

56. The Hearing

Generally, the hearing shall be completed within one day, unless the dispute is resolved by submission of documents under Section 37. The arbitrator, for good cause shown, may schedule an additional hearing to be held within seven days.

57. Time of Award

Unless otherwise agreed by the parties, the award shall be rendered not later than fourteen days from the date of the closing of the hearing.

Administrative Fees

The AAA's administrative charges are based on filing and service fees. Arbitrator compensation, if any, is not included in this schedule. Unless the parties agree otherwise, arbitrator compensation and administrative fees are subject to allocation by the arbitrator in the award.

Filing Fees

A nonrefundable filing fee is payable in full by a filing party when a claim, counterclaim or additional claim is filed, as provided below.

Amount of Claim	Filing Fee
Up to $10,000	$500
Above $10,000 to $50,000 . . .	$750
Above $50,000 to $250,000 . .	$1,500
Above $250,000 to $500,000 .	$3,000
Above $500,000 to $1,000,000	$4,000
Above $1 million	$5,000

When no amount can be stated at the time of filing, the minimum filing fee is $1,500, subject to increase when the claim or counterclaim is disclosed.

When a claim or counterclaim is not for a monetary amount, an appropriate filing fee will be determined by the AAA. The minimum filing fee for any case having three or more arbitrators is $1,500.

Expedited Procedures, outlined in sections 53-57 of the rules, are applied in any case where no disclosed claim or counterclaim exceeds $50,000, exclusive of interest and arbitration costs. Under those procedures, arbitrators are directly appointed by the AAA. Where the parties request a list of proposed arbitrators under those procedures, a service charge of $150 will be payable by each party.

Hearing Fees

For each day of hearing held before a single arbitrator, an administrative fee of $150 is payable by each party.

For each day of hearing held before a multiarbitrator panel, an administrative fee of $200 is payable by each party.

There is no hearing fee for the initial hearing in cases administered under the Expedited Procedures.

Postponement/Cancellation Fees

A fee of $150 is payable by a party causing a postponement of any hearing scheduled before a single arbitrator.

A fee of $200 is payable by a party causing a postponement of any hearing scheduled before a multiarbitrator panel.

Processing Fees

On single-arbitrator cases, a processing fee of $150 per party is payable 180 days after the case is initiated, and every 90 days thereafter, until the case is withdrawn or settled or the hearings are closed by the arbitrator.

On multiarbitrator cases, a processing fee of $200 per party is payable 180 days after the case is initiated, and every 90 days thereafter, until the case is withdrawn or settled or the hearings are closed by the arbitrators.

Suspension for Nonpayment

If arbitrator compensation or administrative charges have not been paid in full, the AAA may so inform the parties in order that one of them may advance the required payment. If such payments are not made, the arbitrator may order the suspension or termination of the proceedings. If no arbitrator has yet been appointed, the AAA may suspend the proceedings.

Hearing Room Rental

The Hearing Fees described above do not cover the rental of hearing rooms, which are available on a rental basis. Check with our local office for availability and rates.

The CPR Model Mediation Procedure for Business Disputes*

1. Proposing Mediation

Any party to a business dispute may propose the use of mediation to the other party or parties orally or in writing. If the parties have made a contractual commitment to mediate disputes between them, or if they have subscribed to the CPR Corporate Policy Statement on Alternatives to Litigation, or to another commitment to engage in alternative dispute resolution (ADR), that commitment or policy may be invoked. Sometimes a neutral organization may help persuade a party to engage in mediation. CPR may be requested to play that role.

2. Selecting the Mediator

Once the parties have agreed in principle to a mediation process, or at least to seriously consider mediation, they will discuss the selection of a mediator. Unless the parties agree otherwise, the mediator shall be selected from the CPR Panels of Neutrals. If the parties cannot agree promptly on a mediator, they will notify CPR of their need for assistance in selecting a mediator, informing CPR of any preferences as to matters such as candidates' mediation style, subject matter expertise or geographic location.

CPR will convene the parties, in person or by telephone, to attempt to select a mediator by agreement. If the parties do not promptly reach agreement, CPR will submit to the parties the names of not less than three candidates, with their resumes and hourly rates. If the parties are unable to agree on a candidate from the list within seven days following receipt of the list, each party will, within 15 days following receipt of the list, send to CPR the list of candidates ranked in descending order of preference. The candidate with the lowest combined score will be appointed as the mediator by CPR. CPR will break any tie.

Before proposing any mediator candidate, CPR will request the candidate to disclose any circumstances known to him or her that would cause reasonable doubt regarding the candidate's impartiality. If a clear conflict is disclosed, the individual will not be proposed. Other circumstances a candidate discloses to CPR will be disclosed to the parties. A party may challenge a mediator candidate if it knows of any circumstances giving rise to reasonable doubt regarding the candidate's impartiality.

The mediator's rate of compensation will be determined before appointment. Such compensation, and any other costs of the process, will be shared equally by the parties unless they otherwise agree. If a party withdraws from a multiparty mediation but the procedure continues, the withdrawing party will not be responsible for any costs incurred after it has notified the mediator and the other parties of its withdrawal.

Before appointment, the mediator will assure the parties of his or her availability to conduct the proceeding expeditiously. It is strongly advised that the parties and the mediator enter into a retention agreement. A model agreement is attached hereto as Form 2 [not reproduced].

3. Ground Rules of Proceeding

The following ground rules will apply, subject to any changes on which the parties and the mediator agree.

(a) The process is voluntary and non-binding.

(b) Each party may withdraw at any time after attending the first session, and before execution of a written agreement, by written notice to the mediator and the other party or parties.

(c) The mediator shall be neutral and impartial.

(d) The mediator shall control the procedural aspects of the mediation. The parties will cooperate fully with the mediator.

    i.   The mediator is free to meet and communicate separately with each party.

    ii.   The mediator will decide when to hold joint meetings with the parties and when to hold separate meetings. The mediator will fix the time and place of each session and its agenda in consultation with the parties. There will be no stenographic record of any meeting. Formal rules of evidence or procedure will not apply.

(e) Each party will be represented at each mediation conference by a business executive authorized to negotiate a resolution of the dispute, unless excused by the mediator as to a particular conference. Each party may be represented by more than one person, e.g. a business executive and an attorney. The mediator may limit the number of persons representing each party.

(f) The process will be conducted expeditiously. Each representative will make every effort to be available for meetings.

(g) The mediator will not transmit information received in confidence from any party to any other party or any third party unless authorized to do so by the party transmitting the information, or unless ordered to do so by a court of competent jurisdiction.

(h) Unless the parties agree otherwise, they will refrain from pursuing litigation or any administrative or judicial remedies during the mediation process or for a set period of time, insofar as they can do so without prejudicing their legal rights.

(i) Unless all parties and the mediator otherwise agree in writing, the mediator and any persons assisting the mediator will be disqualified as a witness, consultant or expert in any pending or future investigation, action or proceeding relating to the subject matter of the mediation (including any investigation, action or proceeding which involves persons not party to this mediation).

(j) If the dispute goes into arbitration, the mediator shall not serve an arbitrator, unless the parties and the mediator otherwise agree in writing.

(k) The mediator may obtain assistance and independent expert advice, with the prior agreement of and at the expense of the parties. Any person proposed as an independent expert also will be required to disclose any circumstances known to him or her that would cause reasonable doubt regarding the candidate's impartiality.

(l) Neither CPR nor the mediator shall be liable for any act or omission in connection with the mediation, except for its/his/her own willful misconduct.

(m) The mediator may withdraw at any time by written notice to the parties (i) for serious personal reasons, (ii) if the mediator believes that a party is not acting in good faith, or (iii) if the mediator concludes that further mediation efforts would not be useful. If the mediator withdraws pursuant to (i) or (ii), he or she need not state the reason for withdrawal.

(n) At the inception of the mediation process, each party and representative will agree in writing to all provisions of this Model Procedure, as modified by agreement of the parties. A model Submission Agreement is attached hereto as Form 1 [not reproduced].

4. Exchange of Information

If any party has a substantial need for documents or other material in the possession of another party, the parties shall attempt to agree on an exchange of documents or other material. Should they fail to agree, either party may request a joint consultation with the mediator who shall assist the parties in reaching agreement. The parties and mediator may, of their own option, establish a schedule for discovery that may facilitate a settlement.

At the conclusion of the mediation process, upon the request of a party which provided documents or other material to one or more other parties, the recipients shall return the same to the originating party without retaining copies thereof.

5. Presentation to the Mediator

Before dealing with the substance of the dispute, the parties and the mediator will discuss preliminary matters, such as possible modification of the ground rules, place and time of meetings, and each party's need for documents or other information in the possession of the other.

At least five business days before the first substantive mediation conference, unless otherwise agreed, each party will submit to the mediator a written statement summarizing the background and present status of the dispute and such other material and information as it deems helpful to familiarize the mediator with the dispute. The parties may agree to submit jointly certain records and other materials. The mediator may request any party to provide clarification and additional information.

The parties are encouraged to exchange written statements and other materials they submit to the mediator to further each party's understanding of the other party's viewpoints. Except as the parties otherwise agree, the mediator shall keep confidential any written materials or information that are submitted to him or her. The parties and their representatives are not entitled to receive or review any materials or information submitted to the mediator by another party or representative without the concurrence of the latter. At the conclusion of the mediation process, upon request of a party, the mediator will return to that party all written materials and information which that party had provided to the mediator without retaining copies thereof.

6. Negotiation of Terms

The mediator may promote settlement in any manner the mediator believes is appropriate. The mediator will help the parties focus on their underlying interests and concerns, explore resolution alternatives and develop settlement options. The mediator will decide when to hold joint meetings, and when to confer separately with each party.

The parties are expected to initiate and convey to the mediator proposals for settlement. Each party shall provide a rationale for any settlement terms proposed.

Finally, if the parties fail to develop mutually acceptable settlement terms, before terminating the procedure, and only with the consent of the parties, (a) the mediator may submit to the parties a final settlement proposal which the mediator considers fair and equitable to all parties; and (b) if the mediator believes he/she is qualified to do so, the mediator may give the parties an evaluation (which if the parties choose will be in writing) of the likely outcome of the case if it were tried to final judgment. Thereupon, the mediator may suggest further discussions to explore whether the mediator's evaluation or proposal may lead to a resolution.

Efforts to reach a settlement will continue until (a) a written settlement is reached, or (b) the mediator concludes and informs the parties that further efforts would not be useful, or (c) one of the parties or the mediator withdraws from the process. However, if there are more than two parties, the remaining parties may elect to continue following the withdrawal of a party.

7. Settlement

If a settlement is reached, the mediator, or a representative of a party, will draft a written settlement document incorporating all settlement terms, which may include mutual general releases from all liability relating to the subject matter of the dispute. This draft will be circulated among the parties, amended as necessary, and formally executed. Initially, a preliminary memorandum of understanding may be prepared at the mediation and executed by the parties.

If litigation is pending, the settlement may provide that the parties will request dismissal of the case promptly upon execution of the settlement agreement. The parties also may request the court to enter the settlement agreement as a consent judgment.

8. Failure to Agree

If a resolution is not reached, the mediator will discuss with the parties the possibility of their agreeing on advisory or binding arbitration, "last offer" arbitration or another form of ADR. If the parties agree in principle, the mediator may offer to assist them in structuring a procedure designed to result in a prompt, economical process. The mediator will not serve as arbitrator, unless all parties agree.

9. Confidentiality

The entire mediation process is confidential. Unless agreed among all the parties or required to do so by law, the parties and the mediator shall not disclose to any person who is not associated with participants in the process, including any judicial officer, any information regarding the process (including pre-process exchanges and agreements), contents (including written and oral information), settlement terms or outcome of the proceeding. If litigation is pending, the participants may, however, advise the court of the schedule and overall status of the mediation for purposes of litigation management.

Under this procedure, the entire process is a compromise negotiation subject to Federal Rule of Evidence 408 and all state counterparts, together with any applicable statute protecting the confidentiality of mediation. All offers, promises, conduct and statements, whether oral or written, made in the course of the proceeding by any of the parties, their agents, employees, experts and attorneys, and by the mediator are confidential. Such offers, promises, conduct and statements are privileged under any applicable mediation privilege and are inadmissible and not discoverable for any purpose, including impeachment, in litigation between the parties. However, evidence that is otherwise admissible or discoverable shall not be rendered inadmissible or non-discoverable solely as a result of its presentation or use during the mediation.

The exchange of any tangible material shall be without prejudice to any claim that such material is privileged or protected as work-product within the meaning of Federal Rule of Civil Procedure 26 and all state and local counterparts.

The mediator and any documents and information in the mediator's possession will not be subpoenaed in any such investigation, action or proceeding, and all parties will oppose any effort to have the mediator or documents subpoenaed. The mediator will promptly advise the parties of any attempt to compel him/her to divulge information received in mediation.

Mediators and participating attorneys should be familiar with applicable law governing the confidentiality and discoverability of material exchanged in a mediation.

AAA Supplementary Procedures for Large, Complex Disputes

(AAA procedures reprinted by permission of the American Arbitration Association.)

1. Applicability

(a) The Supplementary Procedures for Large, Complex Disputes (hereinafter "Procedures") shall apply to all cases administered by the American Arbitration Association (hereinafter "AAA") under any of its rules in which the claim or counterclaim of any party is at least $1,000,000 exclusive of interest, costs and fees or is undetermined, and in which either: (1) all parties have elected to have the Procedures apply to the resolution of their dispute; or (2) a court or governmental agency of competent jurisdiction has determined that a dispute should be resolved before the AAA pursuant to the Procedures. Parties may also agree to using the Supplementary Procedures for Large, Complex Disputes in cases involving claims under $1,000,000. The Procedures are designed to complement the rules selected by the parties to govern their dispute. To the extent that there is any variance between such rules and these Procedures, the Procedures shall control. Any such cases are herein referred to as "Large, Complex Cases."

(b) The parties to any arbitration proceeding that is to be subject to the Procedures may, by consent of all parties, agree to eliminate, modify or alter any of the Procedures, and, in such case, the Procedures as so modified or altered shall apply to that particular case.

2. Administrative Conference

Prior to the dissemination of a list of potential arbitrators, the AAA shall, unless it determines the same to be unnecessary, conduct an administrative conference with the parties or their attorneys or other representatives, either in person or by conference call, at the discretion of the AAA. Such administrative conference shall be conducted for the following purposes and for such additional purposes as the parties or the AAA may deem appropriate:

(a) to obtain additional information about the nature and magnitude of the dispute and the anticipated length of hearing and scheduling;

(b) to discuss the views of the parties about the technical and other qualifications of the arbitrators; and

(c) to consider, with the parties, whether mediation or other non-adjudicative methods of dispute resolution might be appropriate.

3. Arbitrators

(a) Large, Complex Cases shall be heard and determined by either one or three arbitrators, as may be agreed upon by the parties. If the parties are unable to agree upon the number of arbitrators, then one arbitrator shall hear and determine the case unless AAA shall determine otherwise.

(b) The AAA shall appoint arbitrators as agreed by the parties. If they are unable to agree on a method of appointment, the AAA shall appoint arbitrators as provided in the rules under which the case is being administered.

(c) Compensation for the arbitrators shall be based upon the magnitude and complexity of the case and shall be arranged by the AAA with the parties and the arbitrators prior to the commencement of the arbitration hearings. If the parties fail to agree to the terms of compensation, an appropriate rate shall be established by the AAA.

4. Preliminary Hearing

As promptly as practicable after the selection of the arbitrators, a preliminary hearing shall be held among the parties or their attorneys or other representatives and the arbitrators. With the consent of the arbitrators and the parties, the preliminary hearing may: (1) be conducted by the Chair of the panel of arbitrators rather than all the arbitrators; and/or (2) be conducted by telephone conference call rather than in person; or (3) be omitted. At the preliminary hearing the matters that may be considered shall include, without limitation by specification: (a) service of a detailed statement of claims, damages and defenses, a statement of the issues asserted by each party and positions with respect thereto, and any legal authorities the parties may wish to bring to the attention of the arbitrators; (b) stipulations to uncontested facts; (c) exchange and premarking of those documents which each party believes may be offered at the hearing; (d) the identification and availability of witnesses, including experts, and such matters with repect to witnesses including their biographies and expected testimony as may be appropriate; (e) whether, and the extent to which, any sworn statements and/or depositions shall be permitted; (f) whether a stenographic or other official record of the proceedings shall be maintained; and (g) the possibility of utilizing mediation or other non-adjudicative methods of dispute resolution.

5. Management of Proceedings

(a) Arbitrators shall take such steps as they may deem necessary or desirable to avoid delay and to achieve a just, speedy and cost-effective resolution of Large, Complex Cases.

(b) Parties shall cooperate in the exchange of documents, exhibits and information within such party's control if the arbitrators consider such production to be consistent with the goal of achieving a just, speedy and cost-effective resolution of a Large, Complex Case.

(c) The parties may conduct such discovery as may be agreed to by all the parties provided, however, that the arbitrators may provide for or place such limitations on the conduct of such discovery as the arbitrators may deem appropriate.

(d) At the request of a party, the arbitrators may order the conduct of the deposition of, or the propounding of interrogatories to, such persons who may possess information determined by the arbitrators to be necessary to a determination of a Large, Complex Case and who will not be available to testify at the hearings.

6. Form of Award

If requested by all parties, the award of the arbitrators shall be accompanied by a statement of the reasons upon which such award is based. If requested by one party the arbitrators may, in their discretion, issue such a statement.

7. Interest, Fees and Costs

The award of the arbitrators may include: (a) interest at such rate and from such date as the arbitrators may deem appropriate; (b) an apportionment between the parties of all or part of the fees and expenses of the AAA and the compensation and expenses of the arbitrators; and (c) an award of attorneys' fees if all parties have requested or authorized such an award.

Panel Qualification Criteria

1. Experience and Competence

(a) Fifteen-year business or professional practice involving complex legal or business matters;

(b) Extensive experience in dispute resolution;

(c) Strong academic background and professional/business credentials preferred;

(d) Scholarship and continuing education preferred.

2. Neutrality

(a) Commitment to impartiality and objectivity;

(b) Freedom from national or cultural prejudice;

(c) Independence and open-mindedness.

3. Judicial Capacity

(a) Dispute management skills;

(b) Judicious temperament: impartiality, patience, courtesy;

(c) Talent for adjudication, negotiation, and conciliation.

4. Reputation

(a) Highest respect of Bar and/or business community;

(b) Integrity, patience, courtesy.

5. Commitment and Availability

(a) A willingness to serve if nominated, and general availability to serve in accordance with the needs of the parties;

(b) Ability to devote time and effort to major disputes;

(c) Successful completion of an advanced AAA panelist training course.

6. Quality Control

(a) Careful attention paid to selecting panelists to meet the needs of the particular dispute and the desires of the parties;

(b) Periodic review of the panel.

Appendix C

COMPENDIUM OF STATE LAWS REGARDING PRIVATE JUDGING

[**Note:** This appendix does not include state rules of civil procedure providing for special masters. Many states have a "Rule of Civil Procedure 53," patterned after the Federal Rule of Civil Procedure 53. Under these rules, the master is appointed by the judge in a pending action, and normally does *not* hear all issues in the action. *See, e.g.,* Alabama Rule of Civil Procedure 53; Nevada Rule of Civil Procedure 53; Vermont Rule of Civil Procedure 53. Similarly, statutes providing for referees are not included when they fail to specify certain basic elements of true private judging (such as: the parties can select and compensate the neutral). *See, e.g.,* Nebraska Revised Statutes Sections 25-1129 to 25-1132; South Dakota Codified Laws Annotated Section 15-20-6.

Also, this appendix does not include provisions where the court or the state set the amount of compensation to be paid to the temporary judge or referee or where such compensation is paid by the state or charged to the parties as part of court costs. *See, e.g.,* Connecticut General Statutes Section 52-434; Kansas Statute Annotated Sections 20-310a, 20-310b; Maine Rule of Civil Procedure 53; Missouri Revised Statutes Section 515.220; North Carolina Rule of Civil Procedure 53; Oklahoma Statutes, Title 12, Sections 619 and Title 20, Section 103.1; Washington Revised Code Section 2.08.180. One state allows a retired judge to try the case and to be paid by the parties, but the decision of the judge is *not* appealable, which makes the process more like arbitration than private judging. Also excluded are statutes providing for a regular judge to appoint temporary judges to hear cases in order to relieve the court's caseload, or when the regular judge is disqualified for some reason. *See, e.g.,* Alabama Constitution Amendment 328, Section 6.10; Arizona Revised Statutes Annotated Sections 12-141, 12-142; New Mexico Constitution Article VI, Section 15; North Dakota Century Code Sections 27-24-01 and following.]

ARKANSAS

On stipulation of the parties, any court of the state may order a civil action to be tried by a temporary judge who is licensed in the state to practice law. Temporary judges are empowered to act until final determination of the action. It is not clear, however, whether trial by a temporary judge can take place outside of the courthouse. The stipulation of the parties includes the amount of compensation to be paid the temporary judge for trying the case and the method of paying that compensation. *See,* Arkansas Code Annotated Section 16-10-115.

CALIFORNIA

On stipulation of the parties, the court may order an action to be tried by a privately-compensated temporary judge who is named in the stipulation and is a member of the state bar. The use of a private judge is an election by the parties to have proceedings outside the courthouse, and court facilities and personnel are not to be used except upon a finding by the presiding judge that their use would further justice. The court may also order that the case in front of the temporary judge be heard at a site easily accessible to the public. A private judge must disclose other alternative dispute resolution proceedings in which the judge has been privately compensated by any party, attorney, or law firm participating in the case in front of him or her during the past 18 months. *See,* California Constitution Article VI, Section 21; California Rules of Court 244, 532, 880.

Cases already pending in state Superior Court may also be voluntarily referred to a referee. The reference may be made upon agreement of the parties or on motion of a party to a written contract or lease which requires that controversies arising under the instrument must be heard by reference. The scope of reference—usually agreed to by the parties and approved by court order—range from all issues in an action or proceeding (general reference) to a particular fact necessary of the court to determine an action or proceeding (special reference).

Special references (any reference of less than the whole action) are quite popular. Litigants are able to obtain a separate advance decision on some issues in the action and have the trial judge take a critical look at that decision before adopting it. The normal rules of procedure and evidence will apply unless the parties agree otherwise. Like the use of a private judge, the use of a privately compensated referee is an election by the parties to have proceedings outside the courthouse, and court facilities and personnel are not to be used except upon a finding by the presiding judge that their use would further justice. The court may also order that the case in front of the referee be heard at a site easily accessible to the public. A referee must disclose the other alternative dispute resolution proceedings in which the referee has been privately compensated by any party, attorney, or law firm participating in the case in front of him or her during the past 18 months.

A referee's appointment concludes with the filing of a report with the court. When the report deals exclusively with facts, it has the effect of a special verdict (finding by a jury on one or more specific facts). Examples of issues which are frequently referred include complicated damage claims, and conflicting expert testimony. Referees are frequently chosen for their experience and expertise in the subject matter of the controversy. Unlike temporary judges, they need not be attorneys.

When the parties do not agree to a reference, the court may direct a reference on its own motion or on application of a party. Unlike voluntary reference, the circumstances of court-ordered reference are specifically defined by statute:

(a) when the trial of an issue of fact requires the examination of long account;

(b) when the taking of an account is necessary for the information of the court;

(c) when a question of fact (other than on the pleadings) arises on motion or otherwise;

(d) when necessary for the information of the court in a special proceeding;

(e) when the court decides that a reference is needed to hear one or more discovery disputes of motions.

While the judge decides who the referee will be, many courts give serious consideration to someone recommended by the litigants. As with voluntary references, the referee need not be an attorney. *See,* California Code of Civil Procedure Sections 638-640; California Rules of Court 244.1, 532.1.

COLORADO

If the parties to a civil action agree to have a retired judge of a court assigned to hear the action and agree to pay the per diem salary of the assigned judge, the chief justice may assign such person. The judgment rendered may be enforced or appealed and has the same force and effect as a judgment rendered after a hearing or trial by a regularly-serving judge. *See,* Colorado Revised Statutes Section 13-3-111.

IDAHO

An action in the District Court may be tried by a judge pro tem, who must be a member of the bar and agreed upon by the parties. The judge pro tem has all the powers of a district judge except the "inherent powers" of the court such as contempt power. The parties agree upon the compensation to be paid to the judge pro tem. If the parties stipulate, and the judge pro tem approves, the hearing or trial may be held outside the regular courtroom. *See,* Idaho Constitution, Article V, Section 12; Idaho Court Administrative Rule 4.

INDIANA

Parties to an action may agree to have the case heard by a private judge. A private judge must (1) be a resident of the state; (2) be admitted to the practice of law in the state; and (3) must have been, but not currently be, a judge of a Circuit, Superior, Criminal, Probate,

Municipal or County Court who has served for at least four consecutive years. A private judge has the same powers as a judge of the Circuit Court and an appeal from a judgment rendered by a private judge may be taken. The place where the case is heard may be at any time and any place in Indiana mutually agreeable to all parties and the private judge. *See,* Indiana Code Sections 33-13-15-2 and following.

MASSACHUSETTS

The parties in a civil action may agree to select a master, who must be an attorney, to hear evidence in connection with any action and report facts. Although the master's compensation may be charged to the parties in an amount set by the court or charged to the state, a provision is made in the latter situation for the parties to pay additional compensation to the master if approved by the court.

The order of reference may specify or limit the master's powers. The court will accept the master's findings of fact unless they are clearly erroneous or contain errors of law. The court may adopt the master's report, modify, or remand it back to the master for further actions. Adoption of the report is deemed to be entry of judgment by the court. *See,* Massachusetts Annotated Laws Rule of Civil Procedure 53.

MINNESOTA

In the judicial districts including greater Minneapolis-St. Paul, where the amount in controversy exceeds $50,000 the presiding judge may, with the consent of all parties, submit to the parties a list of retired judges or qualified attorneys who are available to serve as Special Magistrates for binding proceedings. If the parties agree on a selection from the list, the Special Magistrate may preside over any pretrial and trial matters as determined by the presiding judge. The Special Magistrate's fees and expenses are borne by the parties on a basis determined by the presiding judge, upon recommendation by the special magistrate. If there is a right to a jury trial, the Special Master must conduct the jury trial pursuant to the rules of the court and must use the jury pool of the county in which the action is venued. The presiding judge may adopt the rulings and findings of Special Magistrates and the results of any jury trial without modification. The parties have a right to appeal from the presiding judge's ruling and findings and from the special verdict as in other civil matters. *See,* Minnesota Statute Section 484.74.

MONTANA

Upon agreement of the parties, a civil action in the District Court may be tried by a judge pro tem, who must be a member of the bar of the state. Any judgment rendered by the judge pro tem has the same force and effect as if rendered by the District Court with a regular judge presiding. The parties can stipulate to trial being held outside the courthouse. A judge pro tem may be (1) a member of the bar of the state who meets the qualification for a judge of the District court; (2) a retired judge of the District Court; or (3) a retired justice of the state Supreme Court. *See,* Montana Code Annotated Section 3-5-117.

NEW JERSEY

Contractual disputes may be resolved by alternative resolution proceedings, even in the absence of a contractual provision for such process, if the parties mutually agree. In an alternative dispute resolution proceeding, an umpire or umpires are designated by the parties or the court to hear the dispute. An umpire has full and complete authority to determine all claims, issues and disputes arising from the agreement. An umpire's award must be accompanied by written findings of fact and conclusions of law. Review consists of an expedited summary review before the Chancery Division of the state Superior Court. Limited intermediate review is also permitted. *See,* New Jersey Statute Annotated Sections 2A:23A-1 and following.

NEW YORK

As to all motions, actions, or proceedings submitted to an official referee by stipulation of the parties, the referee proceeds with the same power and authority as a presiding justice. Unless otherwise specified in the order of reference, the referee must conduct the trial in the same manner as the court trying the issue without a jury. The decision of the referee must comply with other requirements for a decision by the court and stands as the decision of a court. The parties can designate any number of referees. Except by consent of the parties, a person designated must be an attorney. *See,* New York Judiciary Law Sections 117, 119, New York Civil Practice Law & Rules Sections 4301-4321.

OHIO

The parties to any civil action may choose to have the action referred for adjudication by a judge who has registered with the court. A voluntarily retired judge is eligible to be registered with the clerk. A retired judge has all the powers, duties and authority of an active judge of the court in which the proceeding or action is pending. The parties must enter into a written agreement with the retired judge that provides that the parties will be responsible for facilities and equipment needed by the retired judge to consider the action, and provides for the retired judge's compensation. *See,* Ohio Revised Code Annotated Section 2701.10.

OREGON

Each circuit court may establish a panel of reference judges for trial and disposition of civil actions. The state Chief Justice and the presiding circuit court judge appoint members of the state bar for service on the panel as a reference judge. The parties to an action may request referral of the action to a particular reference judge on the panel, which will be granted by the presiding judge. The compensation for the reference judge is paid equally by the parties unless they agree to a different allocation. The reference judge has all the judicial powers and duties of a judge of the circuit court during the proceedings of the action on reference. The judgment of the reference judge, when filed in a final report, is entered as the judgment of the court in the action. *See,* Oregon Revised Statute Sections 3.300 and following.

RHODE ISLAND

The parties in any pending civil action may stipulate to refer the action to one or more referees, to be agreed on by the parties. The parties must also agree on the procedure to be used, the expenses, the time and manner in which the referees make their report, and the time and manner of issuing execution on the judgment which the court will enter upon receiving the report. *See,* Rhode Island General Laws Section 9-15-1 and following.

SOUTH CAROLINA

In cases where a cause can be shown, the presiding Circuit Court judge, upon agreement of the parties, may appoint a special referee who has all the powers of a master-in-equity (a judge of the Equity Court, which is a division of the Circuit Court). The special referee is compensated by the parties. The decisions of a special referee are appealable to the Circuit Court. *See,* South Carolina Code Annotated Sections 14-11-60, 14-11-85, 15-31-150.

TENNESSEE

If the parties to a civil action desire the matter to be disposed of expeditiously, they may agree to have the case heard by a retired or former judge. The parties are responsible for making arrangements of the place, date and time of the trial. The parties are also responsible for compensating the retired or former judge. The finding of the retired or former judge becomes the finding of the court and judgment may be rendered as if the action had been tried by the court. Appeal is available from the findings of a retired or former judge and judgment entered. *See,* Tennessee Code Annotated Sections 17-2-106, 17-2-108, 17-2-121.

TEXAS

The parties to a civil action may file a motion to have the matter referred to a special judge, who is a retired or former district, statutory, county court or appellate judge. While serving, a special judge has the powers of a district court judge except the power to hold a person in contempt of court unless that person is a witness before the special judge. The proceeding cannot be held in a public courtroom, but the right to an appeal is preserved. *See,* Texas Civil Practice & Remedies Code Annotated Sections 151.002 and following.

Also, a county judge for good cause may appoint a licensed attorney selected by the parties to be a special judge for any pending matter. A special judge so appointed has the same powers as a county judge in the matter. *See,* Texas Government Code Annotated Section 26.022.

VIRGINIA

The parties to a civil action pending in Circuit Court may enter into a written stipulation appointing a licensed attorney as a judge pro tem. A judge pro tem has the same power and authority as a regularly elected judge, and is compensated by the parties as agreed upon in their stipulation. The parties may, by the terms of their stipulation, limit the power of the judge pro tem (temporary) to the trial and determination of any specified issue or issues in the case. *See,* Virginia Code Annotated Section 17-9.

Appendix D
INTERNATIONAL TREATIES AND RULES

Convention on the Recognition and Enforcement of Foreign Arbitral Awards

Article I

1. This Convention shall apply to the recognition and enforcement of arbitral awards made in the territory of a State other than the State where the recognition and enforcement of such awards are sought, and arising out of differences between persons, whether physical or legal. It shall also apply to arbitral awards not considered as domestic awards in the State where their recognition and enforcement are sought.

2. The term "arbitral awards" shall include not only awards made by arbitrators appointed for each case but also those made by permanent arbitral bodies to which the parties have submitted.

3. When signing, ratifying or acceding to this Convention, or notifying extension under article X hereof any State may on the basis of reciprocity declare that it will apply the Convention to the recognition and enforcement of awards made only in the territory of another Contracting State. It may also declare that it will apply the Convention only to differences arising out of legal relationships, whether contractual or not, which are considered as commercial under the national law of the State making such declaration.

Article II

1. Each Contracting State shall recognize an agreement in writing under which the parties undertake to submit to arbitration all or any differences which have arisen or which may arise between them in respect of a defined legal relationship, whether contractual or not, concerning a subject matter capable of settlement by arbitration.

2. The term "agreement in writing" shall include an arbitral clause in a contract or an arbitration agreement, signed by the parties or contained in an exchange of letters or telegrams.

3. The court of a Contracting State, when seized of an action in a matter in respect to which the parties have made an agreement within the meaning of this article, shall, at the request of one of the parties, refer the parties to arbitration, unless it finds that the said agreement is null and void, inoperative or incapable of being performed.

Article III

Each Contracting State shall recognize arbitral awards as binding and enforce them in accordance with the rules of procedure of the territory where the award is relied upon, under the conditions laid down in the following articles. There shall not be imposed substantially more onerous conditions or higher fees or charges on the recognition or enforcement of arbitral awards to which this Convention applies than are imposed on the recognition or enforcement of domestic arbitral awards.

Article IV

1. To obtain the recognition and enforcement mentioned in the preceding article, the party applying for recognition and enforcement shall, at the time of the application, supply:

(a) The duly authenticated original award or a duly certified copy thereof;

(b) The original agreement referred to in article II or a duly certified copy thereof.

2. If the said award or agreement is not made in an official language of the country in which the award is relied upon, the party applying for recognition and enforcement of the award shall produce a translation of these documents into such language. The translation shall be certified by an official or sworn translator or by a diplomatic or consular agent.

Article V

1. Recognition and enforcement of the award may be refused, at the request of the party against whom it is invoked, only if that party furnishes to the competent authority where the recognition and enforcement is sought, proof that:

(a) The parties to the agreement referred to in article II were, under the law applicable to them, under some incapacity, or the said agreement is not valid under the law to which the parties have subjected it or, failing any indication thereon, under the law of the country where the award was made; or

(b) The party against whom the award is invoked was not given proper notice of the appointment of the arbitrator or of the arbitration proceedings or was otherwise unable to present his case; or

(c) The award deals with a difference not contemplated by or not falling within the terms of the submission to arbitration, or it contains decisions on matters beyond the scope of the submission to arbitration, provided that, if the decisions on matters submitted to arbitration can be separated from those not so submitted, that part of the award which contains decisions on matters submitted to arbitration may be recognized and enforced; or

(d) The composition of the arbitral authority or the arbitral procedure was not in accordance with the agreement of the parties, or, failing such agreement, was not in accordance with the law of the country where the arbitration took place; or

(e) The award has not yet become binding on the parties, or has been set aside or suspended by a competent authority of the country in which, or under the law of which, that award was made.

2. Recognition and enforcement of an arbitral award may also be refused if the competent authority in the country where recognition and enforcement in sought finds that:

(a) The subject matter of the difference is not capable of settlement by arbitration under the law of that country; or

(b) The recognition or enforcement of the award would be contrary to the public policy of that country.

Article VI

If an application for the setting aside or suspension of the award has been made to a competent authority referred to in article V(1)(e), the authority before which the award is sought to be relied upon may, if it considers it proper, adjourn the decision on the enforcement of the award and may also, on the application of the party claiming enforcement of the award, order the other party to give suitable security.

Article VII

1. The provisions of the present Convention shall not affect the validity of multilateral or bilateral agreements concerning the recognition and enforcement of arbitral awards entered into by the Contracting States nor deprive any interest party of any right he may have to avail himself of an arbitral award in the manner and to the extent allowed by the law or the treaties of the country where such award is sought to be relied upon.

2. The Geneva Protocol on Arbitration Clauses of 1923 and the Geneva Convention on the Execution of Foreign Arbitral Awards of 1927 shall cease to have effect between Contracting States on their becoming bound and to the extent that they become bound, by this Convention.

Article VIII

1. This Convention shall be open until 31 December 1958 for signature on behalf of any Member of the United Nations and also on behalf of any other State which is or hereafter becomes a member of any specialized agency of the United Nations, or which is or hereafter becomes a party to the Statute of the International Court of Justice, or

any other State to which an invitation has been addressed by the General Assembly of the United Nations.

2. This Convention shall be ratified and the instrument of ratification shall be deposited with the Secretary-General of the United Nations.

Article IX

1. This Convention shall be open for accession to all States referred to in article VIII.

2. Accession shall be effected by the deposit of an instrument of accession with the Secretary-General of the United Nations.

Article X

1. Any State may, at the time of signature, ratification or accession, declare that this Convention shall extend to all or any of the territories for the international relations of which it is responsible. Such a declaration shall take effect when the Convention enters into force for the State concerned.

2. At any time thereafter any such extension shall be made by notification addressed to the Secretary-General of the United Nations and shall take effect as from the ninetieth day after the day of receipt by the Secretary-General of the United Nations of this notification, or as from the date of entry into force of the Convention for the State concerned, whichever is the later.

3. With respect to those territories to which this Convention is not extended at the time of signature, ratification or accession, each State concerned shall consider the possibility of taking the necessary steps in order to extend the application of this Convention to such territories, subject, where necessary for constitutional reasons, to the consent of the Governments of such territories.

Article XI

In the case of a federal or non-unitary State the following provisions shall apply:

(a) With respect to those articles of this Convention that come within the legislative jurisdiction of the federal authority, the obligations of the federal Government shall to the extent be the same as those of Contracting States which are not federal States;

(b) With respect to those articles of this Convention that come within the legislative jurisdiction of constituent states of provinces which are not, under the constitutional system of the federation, bound to take legislative action, the federal Government shall bring such articles with a favourable recommendation to the notice of the appropriate authorities of constituent states or provinces at the earliest possible moment;

(c) A federal State Party to this Convention shall, at the request of any other Contracting State transmitted through the Secretary-General of the United Nations, supply a statement of the law and practice of the federation and its constituent units in regard to any particular provision of this Convention, showing the extent to which effect has been given to that provision by legislative or other action.

Article XII

1. This Convention shall come into force on the ninetieth day following the date of deposit of the third instrument of ratification or accession.

2. For each State ratifying or acceding to this Convention after the deposit of the third instrument of ratification or accession, this Convention shall enter into force on the ninetieth day after deposit by such State of its instrument of ratification or accession.

Article XIII

1. Any Contracting State may denounce this Convention by a written notification to the Secretary-General of the United Nations. Denunciation shall take effect one year after the date of receipt of the notification by the Secretary-General.

2. Any State which has made a declaration or notification under article X may, at any time thereafter, by notification to the Secretary-General of the United Nations, declare that this Convention shall cease to extend to the territory concerned one year after the date of the receipt of the notification by the Secretary-General.

3. This Convention shall continue to be applicable to arbitral awards in respect of which recognition or enforcement proceedings have been instituted before the denunciation takes effect.

Article XIV

A Contracting State shall not be entitled to avail itself of the present Convention against other Contracting States except to the extent that it is itself bound to apply the Convention.

Article XV

The Secretary-General of the United Nations shall notify the States contemplated in article VIII of the following:

(a) Signatures and ratifications in accordance with article VIII;

(b) Accessions in accordance with article IX;

(c) Declarations and notifications under articles I, X and XI;

(*d*) The date upon which this Convention enters into force in acordance with article XII;

(*e*) Denunciations and notifications in accordance with article XIII.

Article XVI

1. This Convention, of which the Chinese, English, French, Russian and Spanish texts shall be equally authentic, shall be deposited in the archives of the United Nations.

2. The Secretary-General of the United Nations shall transmit a certified copy of this Convention to the States contemplated in article VIII.

Convention on the Recognition and Enforcement of Foreign Arbitral Awards. Done at New York June 10, 1958; entered into force for the United States December 29, 1970, subject to declarations.*

---

* The United States of America will apply the Convention, on the basis of reciprocity, to the recognition and enforcement of only those awards made in the territory of another Contracting State.
The United States of America will apply the Convention only to differences arising out of legal relationships, whether contractual or not, which are considered as commercial under the national law of the United States.

The Convention applies to all of the territories for the international relations of which the United States of America is responsible.

Inter-American Convention on International Commercial Arbitration

The Governments of the Member States of the Organization of American States, desirous of concluding a convention on international commercial arbitration, have agreed as follows:

Article 1

An agreement in which the parties undertake to submit to arbitral decision any differences that may arise or have arisen between them with respect to a commercial transaction is valid. The agreement shall be set forth in an instrument signed by the parties, or in the form of an exchange of letters, telegrams, or telex communications.

Article 2

Arbitrators shall be appointed in the manner agreed upon by the parties. Their appointment may be delegated to a third party, whether a natural or juridical person.

Arbitrators may be nationals or foreigners.

Article 3

In the absence of an express agreement between the parties, the arbitration shall be conducted in accordance with the rules of procedure of the Inter-American Commercial Arbitration Commission.

Article 4

An arbitral decision or award that is not appealable under the applicable law or procedural rules shall have the force of a final judicial judgment. Its execution or recognition may be ordered in the same manner as that of decisions handed down by national or foreign ordinary courts, in accordance with the procedural laws of the country where it is to be executed and the provisions of international treaties.

Article 5

1. The recognition and execution of the decision may be refused, at the request of the party against which it is made, only if such party is able to prove to the competent authority of the State in which recognition and execution are requested:

   a. That the parties to the agreement were subject to some incapacity under the applicable law or that the agreement is not valid under the law to which the parties have submitted it, or, if such law is not specified, under the law of the State in which the decision was made: or

   b. That the party against which the arbitral decision has been made was not duly notified of the appointment of the arbitrator or of the arbitration procedure to be followed, or was unable, for any other reason, to present his defense; or

c. That the decision concerns a dispute not envisaged in the agreement between the parties to submit to arbitration; nevertheless, if the provisions of the decision that refer to issues submitted to arbitration can be separated from those not submitted to arbitration, the former may be recognized and executed; or

d. That the constitution of the arbitral tribunal or the arbitration procedure has not been carried out in accordance with the terms of the agreement signed by the parties or, in the absence of such agreement, that the constitution of the arbitral tribunal or the arbitration procedure has not been carried out in accordance with the law of the State where the arbitration took place; or

e. That the decision is not yet binding on the parties or has been annulled or suspended by a competent authority of the State in which, or according to the law of which, the decision has been made

2. The recognition and execution of an arbitral decision may also be refused if the competent authority of the State in which the recognition and execution is requested finds:

a. That the subject of the dispute cannot be settled by arbitration under the law of that State; or

b. That the recognition or execution of the decision would be contrary to the public policy ("ordre public") of that State.

Article 6

If the competent authority mentioned in Article 5.1.e has been requested to annul or suspend the arbitral decision, the authority before which such decision is invoked may, if it deems it appropriate, postpone a decision on the execution of the arbitral decision and, at the request of the party requesting execution, may also instruct the other party to provide appropriate guaranties.

Article 7

This Convention shall be open for signature by the Member States of the Organization of American States.

Article 8

This Convention is subject to ratification. The instruments of ratification shall be deposited with the General Secretariat of the Organization of American States.

Article 9

This Convention shall remain open for accession by any other State. The instruments of accession shall be deposited with the General Secretariat of the Organization of American States.

Article 10

This Convention shall enter into force on the thirtieth day following the date of deposit of the second instrument of ratification.

For each State ratifying or acceding to the Convention after the deposit of the second instrument of ratification, the Convention shall enter into force on the thirtieth day after deposit by such State of its instrument of ratification or accession.

Article 11

If a State Party has two or more territorial units in which different systems of law apply in relation to the matters dealt with in this Convention, it may, at the time of signature, ratification or accession, declare that this Convention shall extend to all its territorial units or only to one or more of them.

Such declaration may be modified by subsequent declarations, which shall expressly indicate the territorial unit or units to which the Convention applies. Such subsequent declarations shall be transmitted to the General Secretariat of the Organization of American States, and shall become effective thirty days after the date of their receipt.

Article 12

This Convention shall remain in force indefinitely, but any of the States Parties may denounce it. The instrument of denunciation shall be deposited with the General Secretariat of the Organization of American States. After one year from the date of deposit of the instrument of denunciation, the Convention shall no longer be in effect for the denouncing State, but shall remain in effect for the other States Parties.

Article 13

The original instrument of this Convention, the English, French, Portuguese and Spanish texts of which are equally authentic, shall be deposited with the General Secretariat of the Organization of American States. The Secretariat shall notify the Member States of the Organization of American States and the States that have acceded to the Convention of the signatures, deposits of instruments of ratification, accession, and denunciation as well as of reservations, if any. It shall also transmit the declarations referred to in Article 11 of this Convention.

IN WITNESS WHEREOF the undersigned Plenipotentiaries, being duly authorized thereto by their respective Governments, have signed this Convention.

DONE AT PANAMA CITY, Republic of Panama, this thirtieth day of January one thousand nine hundred and seventy-five.

UNCITRAL Arbitration Rules

Section I. Introductory Rules

Scope of Application

Article 1

1. Where the parties to a contract have agreed in writing that disputes in relation to that contract shall be referred to arbitration under the UNCITRAL Arbitration Rules, then such disputes shall be settled in accordance with these Rules subject to such modification as the parties may agree in writing.

2. These Rules shall govern the arbitration except that where any of these Rules is in conflict with a provision of the law applicable to the arbitration from which the parties cannot derogate, that provision shall prevail.

Notice, Calculation of Periods of Time

Article 2

1. For the purposes of these Rules, any notice, including a notification, communication or proposal, is deemed to have been received if it is physically delivered to the addressee or if it is delivered at his habitual residence, place of business or mailing address, or, if none of these can be found after making reasonable inquiry, then at the addressee's last known residence or place of business. Notice shall be deemed to have been received on the day it is so delivered.

2. For the purposes of calculating a period of time under these Rules, such period shall begin to run on the day following the day when a notice, notification, communication or proposal is received. If the last day of such period is an official holiday or a non-business day at the residence or place of business of the addressee, the period is extended until the first business day which follows. Official holidays or non-business days occurring during the running of the period of time are included in calculating the period.

Notice of Arbitration

Article 3

1. The party initiating recourse to arbitration (hereinafter called the "claimant") shall give to the other party (hereinafter called the "respondent") a notice of arbitration.

2. Arbitral proceedings shall be deemed to commence on the date on which the notice of arbitration is received by the respondent.

3. The notice of arbitration shall include the following:

(a) A demand that the dispute be referred to arbitration;

(b) The names and addresses of the parties;

(c) A reference to the arbitration clause or the separate arbitration agreement that is invoked;

(d) A reference to the contract out of or in relation to which the dispute arises;

(e) The general nature of the claim and an indication of the amount involved, if any;

(f) The relief or remedy sought;

(g) A proposal as to the number of arbitrators (i.e., one or three), if parties have not previously agreed thereon.

4. The notice of arbitration may also include:

(a) The proposals for the appointment of a sole arbitrator and an appointing authority referred to in article 6, paragraph 1;

(b) The notification of the appointment of an arbitrator referred to in article 7;

(c) The statement of claim referred to in article 18.

Representation and Assistance

Article 4

The parties may be represented or assisted by persons of their choice. The names and addresses of such persons must be communicated in writing to the other party; such communication must specify whether the appointment is being made for purposes of representation or assistance.

Section II. Composition of the Arbitral Tribunal

Number of Arbitrators

Article 5

If the parties have not previously agreed on the number of arbitrators (i.e., one or three), and if within fifteen days after the receipt by the respondent of the notice of arbitration the parties have not agreed that there shall be only one arbitrator, three arbitrators shall be appointed.

Appointment of Arbitrators (Articles 6 to 8)

Article 6

1. If a sole arbitrator is to be appointed, either party may propose to the other:

(a) The names of one or more persons, one of whom would serve as the sole arbitrator; and

(b) If no appointing authority has been agreed upon by the parties, the name or names of one or more institutions or persons, one of whom would serve as appointing authority.

2. If within thirty days after receipt by a party of a proposal made in accordance with paragraph 1 the parties have not reached agreement on the choice of a sole arbitrator, the sole arbitrator shall be appointed by the appointing authority agreed upon by the parties. If no appointing authority has been agreed upon by the parties, or if the appointing authority agreed upon refuses to act or fails to appoint the arbitrator within sixty days of the receipt of a party's request therefor, either party may request the Secretary-General of the Permanent Court of Arbitration at The Hague to designate an appointing authority.

3. The appointing authority shall, at the request of one of the parties, appoint the sole arbitrator as promptly as possible. In making the appointment the appointing authority shall use the following list-procedure, unless both parties agree that the list-procedure should not be used or unless the appointing authority determines in its discretion that the use of the list-procedure is not appropriate for the case:

(a) At the request of one of the parties the appointing authority shall communicate to both parties an identical list containing at least three names;

(b) Within fifteen days after the receipt of this list, each party may return the list to the appointing authority after having deleted the name or names to which he objects and numbered the remaining names on the list in the order of his preference;

(c) After the expiration of the above period of time the appointing authority shall appoint the sole arbitrator from among the names approved on the lists returned to it and in accordance with the order of preference indicated by the parties;

(d) If for any reason the appointment cannot be made according to this procedure, the appointing authority may exercise its discretion in appointing the sole arbitrator.

4. In making the appointment, the appointing authority shall have regard to such considerations as are likely to secure the appointment of an independent and impartial arbitrator and shall take into account as well the advisability of appointing an arbitrator of a nationality other than the nationalities of the parties.

Article 7

1. If three arbitrators are to be appointed, each party shall appoint one arbitrator. The two arbitrators thus appointed shall choose the third arbitrator, who will act as the presiding arbitrator of the tribunal.

2. If within thirty days after the receipt of a party's notification of the appointment of an arbitrator, the other party has not notified the first party of the arbitrator he has appointed:

(a) The first party may request the appointing authority previously designated by the parties to appoint the second arbitrator; or

(b) If no such authority has been previously designated by the parties, or if the appointing authority previously designated refuses to act or fails to appoint the arbitrator within thirty days after receipt of a party's request therefor, the first party may request the Secretary-General of the Permanent Court of Arbitration at The Hague to designate the appointing authority. The first party may then request the appointing authority so designated to appoint the second arbitrator. In either case, the appointing authority may exercise its discretion in appointing the arbitrator.

3. If within thirty days after the appointment of the second arbitrator the two arbitrators have not agreed on the choice of the presiding arbitrator, the presiding arbitrator shall be appointed by the appointing authority in the same way as a sole arbitrator would be appointed under article 6.

Article 8

1. When the appointing authority is requested to appoint an arbitrator pursuant to article 6 or article 7, the party which makes the request shall send to the appointing authority a copy of the notice of arbitration, a copy of the contract out of or in relation to which the dispute has arisen and a copy of the arbitration agreement if it is not contained in the contract. The appointing authority may require from either party such information as it deems necessary to fulfill its function.

2. Where the names of one or more persons are proposed for appointment as arbitrators, their full names, addresses and nationalities shall be indicated, together with a description of their qualifications.

Challenge of Arbitrators (Articles 9 to 12)

Article 9

A prospective arbitrator shall disclose to those who approach him in connection with his possible appointment any circumstances likely to give rise to justifiable doubts as to his impartiality or independence. An arbitrator, once appointed or chosen, shall disclose such circumstances to the parties unless they have already been informed by him of these circumstances.

Article 10

1. Any arbitrator may be challenged if circumstances exist that give rise to justifiable doubts as to the arbitrator's impartiality or independence.

2. A party may challenge the arbitrator appointed by him only for reasons of which he becomes aware after the appointment has been made.

Article 11

1. A party who intends to challenge an arbitrator shall send notice of his challenge within fifteen days after the appointment of the challenged arbitrator has been notified to the challenging party or within fifteen days after the circumstances mentioned in articles 9 and 10 became known to that party.

2. The challenge shall be notified to the other party, to the arbitrator who is challenged and to the other members of the arbitral tribunal. The notification shall be in writing and shall state the reasons for the challenge.

3. When an arbitrator has been challenged by one party, the other party may agree to the challenge. The arbitrator may also, after the challenge, withdraw from his office. In neither case does this imply acceptance of the validity of the grounds for the challenge. In both cases the procedure provided in article 6 or 7 shall be used in full for the appointment of the substitute arbitrator, even if during the process of appointing the challenged arbitrator a party had failed to exercise his right to appoint or to participate in the appointment.

Article 12

1. If the other party does not agree to the challenge and the challenged arbitrator does not withdraw, the decision on the challenge will be made:

(a) When the initial appointment was made by an appointing authority, by that authority;

(b) When the initial appointment was not made by an appointing authority, but an appointing authority has been previously designated, by that authority;

(c) In all other cases, by the appointing authority to be designated in accordance with the procedure for designating an appointing authority as provided for in article 6.

2. If the appointing authority sustains the challenge, a substitute arbitrator shall be appointed or chosen pursuant to the procedure applicable to the appointment or choice of an arbitrator as provided in articles 6 to 9.

Replacement of an Arbitrator

Article 13

1. In the event of the death or resignation of an arbitrator during the course of the arbitral proceedings, a substitute arbitrator shall be appointed or chosen pursuant to the procedure provided for in articles 6 to 9 that was applicable to the appointment or choice of the arbitrator being replaced.

2. In the event that an arbitrator fails to act or in the event of the *de jure* or *de facto* impossibility of his performing his functions, the procedure in respect of the challenge and replacement of an arbitrator as provided in the preceding articles shall apply.

Repetition of Hearings in the Event of the Replacement of an Arbitrator

Article 14

If under articles 11 to 13 the sole or presiding arbitrator is replaced, any hearings held previously shall be repeated; if any other arbitrator is replaced, such prior hearings may be repeated at the discretion of the arbitral tribunal.

Section III. Arbitral Proceedings

General Provisions

Article 15

1. Subject to these Rules, the arbitral tribunal may conduct the arbitration in such manner as it considers appropriate, provided that the parties are treated with equality and that at any stage of the proceedings each party is given a full opportunity of presenting his case.

2. If either party so requests at any stage of the proceedings, the arbitral tribunal shall hold hearings for the presentation of evidence by witnesses, including expert witnesses, or for oral argument. In the absence of such a request, the arbitral tribunal shall decide whether to hold such hearings or whether the proceedings shall be conducted on the basis of documents and other materials.

3. All documents or information supplied to the arbitral tribunal by one party shall at the same time be communicated by that party to the other party.

Place of Arbitration

Article 16

1. Unless the parties have agreed upon the place where the arbitration is to be held, such place shall be determined by the arbitral tribunal, having regard to the circumstances of the arbitration.

2. The arbitral tribunal may determine the locale of the arbitration within the country agreed upon by the parties. It may hear witnesses and hold meetings for consultation among its members at any place it deems appropriate, having regard to the circumstances of the arbitration.

3. The arbitral tribunal may meet at any place it deems appropriate for the inspection of goods, other property or documents. The parties shall be given sufficient notice to enable them to be present at such inspection.

4. The award shall be made at the place of arbitration.

Language

Article 17

1. Subject to an agreement by the parties, the arbitral tribunal shall, promptly after its appointment, determine the language or languages to be used in the proceedings. This determination shall apply to the statement of claim, the statement of defense, and any further written statements and, if oral hearings take place, to the language or languages to be used in such hearings.

2. The arbitral tribunal may order that any documents annexed to the statement of claim or statement of defense, and any supplementary documents or exhibits submitted in the course of the proceedings, delivered in their original language, shall be accompanied by a translation into the language or languages agreed upon by the parties or determined by the arbitral tribunal.

Statement of Claim

Article 18

1. Unless the statement of claim was contained in the notice of arbitration, within a period of time to be determined by the arbitral tribunal, the claimant shall communicate his statement of claim in writing to the respondent and to each of the arbitrators. A copy of the contract, and of the arbitration agreement if not contained in the contract, shall be annexed thereto.

2. The statement of claim shall include the following particulars:

(a) The names and addresses of the parties;

(b) A statement of the facts supporting the claim;

(c) The points at issue;

(d) The relief or remedy sought.

The claimant may annex to his statement of claim all documents he deems relevant or may add a reference to the documents or other evidence he will submit.

Statement of Defense

Article 19

1. Within a period of time to be determined by the arbitral tribunal, the respondent shall communicate his statement of defense in writing to the claimant and to each of the arbitrators.

2. The statement of defense shall reply to the particulars (b), (c) and (d) of the statement of claim (article 18, para. 2). The respondent may annex to his statement the documents on which he relies for his defense or may add a reference to the documents or other evidence he will submit.

3. In his statement of defense, or at a later stage in the arbitral proceedings if the arbitral tribunal decides that the delay was justified under the circumstances, the respondent may make a counter-claim arising out of the same contract or rely on a claim arising out of the same contract for the purpose of a set-off.

4. The provisions of article 18, paragraph 2, shall apply to a counter-claim and a claim relied on for the purpose of a set-off.

Amendments to the Claim or Defense

Article 20

During the course of arbitral proceedings either party may amend or supplement his claim or defense unless the arbitral tribunal considers it inappropriate to allow such amendment having regard to the delay in making it or prejudice to the other party or any other circumstances. However, a claim may not be amended in such a manner that the amended claim falls outside the scope of the arbitration clause or separate arbitration agreement.

Pleas as to the Jurisdiction of the Arbitral Tribunal

Article 21

1. The arbitral tribunal shall have the power to rule on objections that it has no jurisdiction, including any objections with respect to the existence or validity of the arbitration clause or of the separate arbitration agreement.

2. The arbitral tribunal shall have the power to determine the existence or the validity of the contract of which an arbitration clause forms a part. For the purposes of article 21, an arbitration clause which forms part of a contract and which provides for arbitration under these Rules shall be treated as an agreement independent of the other terms of the contract. A decision by the arbitral tribunal that the contract is null and void shall not entail *ipso jure* the invalidity of the arbitration clause.

3. A plea that the arbitral tribunal does not have jurisdiction shall be raised not later than in the statement of defense or, with respect to a counter-claim, in the reply to the counter-claim.

4. In general, the arbitral tribunal should rule on a plea concerning its jurisdiction as a preliminary question. However, the arbitral tribunal may proceed with the arbitration and rule on such a plea in their final award.

Further Written Statements

Article 22

The arbitral tribunal shall decide which further written statements, in addition to the statement of claim and the statement of defense, shall be required from the parties or may be presented by them and shall fix the periods of time for communicating such statements.

Periods of Time

Article 23

The periods of time fixed by the arbitral tribunal for the communication of written statements (including the statement of claim and statement of defense) should not exceed forty-five days. However, the arbitral tribunal may extend the time limits if it concludes that an extension is justified.

Evidence and Hearings (Articles 24 and 25)

Article 24

1. Each party shall have the burden of proving the facts relied on to support his claim or defense.

2. The arbitral tribunal may, if it considers it appropriate, require a party to deliver to the tribunal and to the other party, within such a period of time as the arbitral tribunal shall decide, a summary of the documents and other evidence which that party intends to present in support of the facts in issue set out in his statement of claim or statement of defense.

3. At any time during the arbitral proceedings the arbitral tribunal may require the parties to produce documents, exhibits or other evidence within such a period of time as the tribunal shall determine.

Article 25

1. In the event of an oral hearing, the arbitral tribunal shall give the parties adequate advance notice of the date, time and place thereof.

2. If witnesses are to be heard, at least fifteen days before the hearing each party shall communicate to the arbitral tribunal and to

the other party the names and addresses of the witnesses he intends to present, and the subject upon and the languages in which such witnesses will give their testimony.

3. The arbitral tribunal shall make arrangements for the translation of oral statements made at a hearing and for a record of the hearing if either is deemed necessary by the tribunal under the circumstances of the case, or if the parties have agreed thereto and have communicated such agreement to the tribunal at least fifteen days before the hearing.

4. Hearings shall be held *in camera* unless the parties agree otherwise. The arbitral tribunal may require the retirement of any witness or witnesses during the testimony of other witnesses. The arbitral tribunal is free to determine the manner in which witnesses are examined.

5. Evidence of witnesses may also be presented in the form of written statements signed by them.

6. The arbitral tribunal shall determine the admissibility, relevance, materiality and weight of the evidence offered.

Interim Measures of Protection

Article 26

1. At the request of either party, the arbitral tribunal may take any interim measures it deems necessary in respect of the subject matter of the dispute, including measures for the conservation of the goods forming the subject matter in dispute, such as ordering their deposit with a third person or the sale of perishable goods.

2. Such interim measures may be established in the form of an interim award. The arbitral tribunal shall be entitled to require security for the costs of such measures.

3. A request for interim measures addressed by any party to a judicial authority shall not be deemed incompatible with the agreement to arbitrate, or as a waiver of that agreement.

Experts

Article 27

1. The arbitral tribunal may appoint one or more experts to report to it, in writing, on specific issues to be determined by the tribunal. A copy of the expert's terms of reference, established by the arbitral tribunal, shall be communicated to the parties.

2. The parties shall give the expert any relevant information or produce for his inspection any relevant documents or goods that he may require of them. Any dispute between a party and such expert as

to the relevance of the required information or production shall be referred to the arbitral tribunal for decision.

3. Upon receipt of the expert's report, the arbitral tribunal shall communicate a copy of the report to the parties who shall be given the opportunity to express, in writing, their opinion on the report. A party shall be entitled to examine any document on which the expert has relied in his report.

4. At the request of either party the expert, after delivery of the report, may be heard at a hearing where the parties shall have the opportunity to be present and to interrogate the expert. At this hearing either party may present expert witnesses in order to testify on the points at issue. The provisions of article 25 shall be applicable to such proceedings.

Default

Article 28

1. If, within the period of time fixed by the arbitral tribunal, the claimant has failed to communicate his claim without showing sufficient cause for such failure, the arbitral tribunal shall issue an order for the termination of the arbitral proceedings. If, within the period of time fixed by the arbitral tribunal, the respondent has failed to communicate his statement of defense without showing sufficient cause for such failure, the arbitral tribunal shall order that the proceedings continue.

2. If one of the parties, duly notified under these Rules, fails to appear at a hearing, without showing sufficient cause for such failure, the arbitral tribunal may proceed with the arbitration.

3. If one of the parties, duly invited to produce documentary evidence, fails to do so within the established period of time, without showing sufficient cause for such failure, the arbitral tribunal may make the award on the evidence before it.

Closure of Hearings

Article 29

1. The arbitral tribunal may inquire of the parties if they have any further proofs to offer or witnesses to be heard or submissions to make and, if there are none, it may declare the hearings closed.

2. The arbitral tribunal may, if it considers it necessary owing to exceptional circumstances, decide, on its own motion or upon application of a party, to reopen the hearings at any time before the award is made.

Waiver of Rules

Article 30

A party who knows that any provision of, or requirement under, these Rules has not been complied with and yet proceeds with the arbitration without promptly stating his objection to such noncompliance shall be deemed to have waived his right to object.

Section IV. The Award

Decisions

Article 31

1. When there are three arbitrators, any award or other decision of the arbitral tribunal shall be made by a majority of the arbitrators.

2. In the case of questions of procedure, when there is no majority or when the arbitral tribunal so authorizes, the presiding arbitrator may decide on his own, subject to revision, if any, by the arbitral tribunal.

Form and Effect of the Award

Article 32

1. In addition to making a final award, the arbitral tribunal shall be entitled to make interim, interlocutory, or partial awards.

2. The award shall be made in writing and shall be final and binding on the parties. The parties undertake to carry out the award without delay.

3. The arbitral tribunal shall state the reasons upon which the award is based, unless the parties have agreed that no reasons are to be given.

4. An award shall be signed by the arbitrators and it shall contain the date on which and the place where the award was made. Where there are three arbitrators and one of them fails to sign, the award shall state the reason for the absence of the signature.

5. The award may be made public only with the consent of both parties.

6. Copies of the award signed by the arbitrators shall be communicated to the parties by the arbitral tribunal.

7. If the arbitration law of the country where the award is made requires that the award be filed or registered by the arbitral tribunal, the tribunal shall comply with this requirement within the period of time required by law.

Applicable Law, *Amiable Compositeur*
Article 33

1. The arbitral tribunal shall apply the law designated by the parties as applicable to the substance of the dispute. Failing such designation by the parties, the arbitral tribunal shall apply the law determined by the conflict of laws rules which it considers applicable.

2. The arbitral tribunal shall decide as *amiable compositeur* or *ex aequo et bono* only if the parties have expressly authorized the arbitral tribunal to do so and if the law applicable to the arbitral procedure permits such arbitration.

3. In all cases, the arbitral tribunal shall decide in accordance with the terms of the contract and shall take into account the usages of the trade applicable to the transaction.

Settlement or Other Grounds for Termination
Article 34

1. If, before the award is made, the parties agree on a settlement of the dispute, the arbitral tribunal shall either issue an order for the termination of the arbitral proceedings or, if requested by both parties and accepted by the tribunal, record the settlement in the form of an arbitral award on agreed terms. The arbitral tribunal is not obliged to give reasons for such an award.

2. If, before the award is made, the continuation of the arbitral proceedings becomes unnecessary or impossible for any reason not mentioned in paragraph 1, the arbitral tribunal shall inform the parties of its intention to issue an order for the termination of the proceedings. The arbitral tribunal shall have the power to issue such an order unless a party raises justifiable grounds for objection.

3. Copies of the order for termination of the arbitral proceedings or of the arbitral award on agreed terms, signed by the arbitrators, shall be communicated by the arbitral tribunal to the parties. Where an arbitral award on agreed terms is made, the provisions of article 32, paragraphs 2 and 4 to 7, shall apply.

Interpretation of the Award
Article 35

1. Within thirty days after the receipt of the award, either party, with notice to the other party, may request that the arbitral tribunal give an interpretation of the award.

2. The interpretation shall be given in writing within forty-five days after the receipt of the request. The interpretation shall form part of the award and the provisions of article 32, paragraphs 2 to 7, shall apply.

Correction of the Award

Article 36

1. Within thirty days after the receipt of the award, either party, with notice to the other party, may request the arbitral tribunal to correct in the award any errors in computation, any clerical or typographical errors, or any errors of similar nature. The arbitral tribunal may within thirty days after the communication of the award make such corrections on its own initiative.

2. Such corrections shall be in writing, and the provisions of article 32, paragraphs 2 to 7, shall apply.

Additional Award

Article 37

1. Within thirty days after the receipt of the award, either party, with notice to the other party, may request the arbitral tribunal to make an additional award as to claims presented in the arbitral proceedings but omitted from the award.

2. If the arbitral tribunal considers the request for an additional award to be justified and considers that the omission can be rectified without any further hearings or evidence, it shall complete its award within sixty days after the receipt of the request.

3. When an additional award is made, the provisions of article 32, paragraphs 2 to 7, shall apply.

Costs (Articles 38 to 40)

Article 38

The arbitral tribunal shall fix the costs of arbitration in its award. The term "costs" includes only:

(a) The fees of the arbitral tribunal to be stated separately as to each arbitrator and to be fixed by the tribunal itself in accordance with article 39;

(b) The travel and other expenses incurred by the arbitrators;

(c) The costs of expert advice and of other assistance required by the arbitral tribunal;

(d) The travel and other expenses of witnesses to the extent such expenses are approved by the arbitral tribunal;

(e) The costs for legal representation and assistance of the successful party if such costs were claimed during the arbitral proceedings, and only to the extent that the arbitral tribunal determines that the amount of such costs is reasonable;

(f) Any fees and expenses of the appointing authority as well as the expenses of the Secretary-General of the Permanent Court of Arbitration at The Hague.

Article 39

1. The fees of the arbitral tribunal shall be reasonable in amount, taking into account the amount in dispute, the complexity of the subject matter, the time spent by the arbitrators and any other relevant circumstances of the case.

2. If an appointing authority has been agreed upon by the parties or designated by the Secretary-General of the Permanent Court of Arbitration at The Hague, and if that authority has issued a schedule of fees for arbitrators in international cases which it administers, the arbitral tribunal in fixing its fees shall take that schedule of fees into account to the extent that it considers appropriate in the circumstances of the case.

3. If such appointing authority has not issued a schedule of fees for arbitrators in international cases, any party may at any time request the appointing authority to furnish a statement setting forth the basis for establishing fees which is customarily followed in international cases in which the authority appoints arbitrators. If the appointing authority consents to provide such a statement, the arbitral tribunal in fixing its fees shall take such information into account to the extent that it considers appropriate in the circumstances of the case.

4. In cases referred to in paragraphs 2 and 3, when a party so requests and the appointing authority consents to perform the function, the arbitral tribunal shall fix its fees only after consultation with the appointing authority which may make any comment it deems appropriate to the arbitral tribunal concerning the fees.

Article 40

1. Except as provided in paragraph 2, the costs of arbitration shall in principle be borne by the unsuccessful party. However, the arbitral tribunal may apportion each of such costs between the parties if it determines that apportionment is reasonable, taking into account the circumstances of the case.

2. With respect to the costs of legal representation and assistance referred to in article 38, paragraph (e), the arbitral tribunal, taking into account the circumstances of the case, shall be free to determine which party shall bear such costs or may apportion such costs between the parties if it determines that apportionment is reasonable.

3. When the arbitral tribunal issues an order for the termination of the arbitral proceedings or makes an award on agreed terms, it shall fix

the costs of arbitration referred to in article 38 and article 39, paragraph 1, in the text of that order or award.

4. No additional fees may be charged by an arbitral tribunal for interpretation or correction or completion of its award under articles 35 to 37.

Deposit of Costs

Article 41

1. The arbitral tribunal, on its establishment, may request each party to deposit an equal amount as an advance for the costs referred to in article 38, paragraphs (a), (b) and (c).

2. During the course of the arbitral proceedings the arbitral tribunal may request supplementary deposits from the parties.

3. If an appointing authority has been agreed upon the parties or designated by the Secretary-General of the Permanent Court of Arbitration at The Hague, and when a party so requests, the arbitral tribunal shall fix the amounts of any deposits or supplementary deposits only after consultation with the appointing authority which may make any comments to the arbitral tribunal which it deems appropriate concerning the amounts of such deposits and supplementary deposits.

4. If the required deposits are not paid in full within thirty days after the receipt of the request, the arbitral tribunal shall so inform the parties in order that one or another of them may make the required payment. If such payment is not made, the arbitral tribunal may order the suspension or termination of the arbitral proceedings.

5. After the award has been made, the arbitral tribunal shall render an accounting to the parties of the deposits received and return any unexpended balance to the parties.

ICC Rules of Conciliation and Arbitration (1988)*

The ICC Rules set forth herein have been translated in many different languages. However, the English and French versions are the only authoritative texts.

Rules of Optional Conciliation

The revised ICC Rules for Conciliation entered into force on January 1, 1988. Conciliation is a process independent of arbitration. It remains entirely optional unless the parties have otherwise agreed. The ICC Rules do not require an effort at conciliation prior to commencing an arbitration. So too, the Rules permit conciliation to be attempted without any requirement to engage thereafter in arbitration if the conciliation effort is unsucessful.

Rules of Optional Conciliation

Preamble

Settlement is a desirable solution for business disputes of an international character.

The International Chamber of Commerce therefore sets out these Rules of Optional Conciliation in order to facilitate the amicable settlement of such disputes.

Article 1

All business disputes of an international character may be submitted to conciliation by a sole conciliator appointed by the International Chamber of Commerce.

Article 2

The party requesting conciliation shall apply to the Secretariat of the International Court of Arbitration of the International Chamber of Commerce setting out succinctly the purpose of the request and accompanying it with the fee required to open the file, as set out in Appendix III hereto.

Article 3

The Secretariat of the International Court of Arbitration shall, as soon as possible, inform the other party of the request for conciliation. That party will be given a period of 15 days to inform the Secretariat whether it agrees or declines to participate in the attempt to conciliate.

If the other party agrees to participate in the attempt to conciliate it shall so inform the Secretariat within such period.

---

* ICC No. 447-3, *ICC Rules of Conciliation and Arbitration,* © 1993 by ICC Publishing S.A. Reprinted with the permission of ICC Publishing, Inc., in New York.

In the absence of any reply within such period or in the case of a negative reply the request for conciliation shall be deemed to have been declined. The Secretariat shall, as soon as possible, so inform the party which had requested conciliation.

Article 4

Upon receipt of an agreement to attempt conciliation, the Secretary General of the International Court of Arbitration shall appoint a conciliator as soon as possible. The conciliator shall inform the parties of his appointment and set a time-limit for the parties to present their respective arguments to him.

Article 5

The conciliator shall conduct the conciliation process as he thinks fit, guided by the principles of impartiality, equity and justice.

With the agreement of the parties, the conciliator shall fix the place for conciliation.

The conciliator may at any time during the conciliation process request a party to submit to him such additional information as he deems necessary.

The parties may, if they so wish, be assisted by counsel of their choice.

Article 6

The confidential nature of the conciliation process shall be respected by every person who is involved in it in whatever capacity.

Article 7

The conciliation process shall come to an end:

(a) Upon the parties signing an agreement. The parties shall be bound by such agreement. The agreement shall remain confidential unless and to the extent that its execution or application require disclosure.

(b) Upon the production by the conciliator of a report recording that the attempt to conciliate has not been successful. Such report shall not contain reasons.

(c) Upon notification to the conciliator by one or more parties at any time during the conciliation process of an intention no longer to pursue the conciliation process.

Article 8

Upon termination of the conciliation, the conciliator shall provide the Secretariat of the International Court of Arbitration with the settlement agreement signed by the parties or with his report of lack of success or with a notice from one or more parties of the intention no longer to pursue the conciliation process.

Article 9

Upon the file being opened, the Secretariat of the International Court of Arbitration shall fix the sum required to permit the process to proceed, taking into consideration the nature and importance of the dispute. Such sum shall be paid in equal shares by the parties.

This sum shall cover the estimated fees of the conciliator, expenses of the conciliation, and the administrative expenses as set out in Appendix III hereto.

In any case where, in the course of the conciliation process, the Secretariat of the Court shall decide that the sum originally paid is insufficient to cover the likely total costs of the conciliation, the Secretariat shall require the provision of an additional amount which shall be paid in equal shares by the parties.

Upon termination of the conciliation, the Secretariat shall settle the total costs of the process and advise the parties in writing.

All the above costs shall be borne in equal shares by the parties except and insofar as a settlement agreement provides otherwise.

A party's other expenditures shall remain the responsibility of that party.

Article 10

Unless the parties agree otherwise, a conciliator shall not act in any judicial or arbitration proceeding relating to the dispute which has been the subject of the conciliation process whether as an arbitrator, representative or counsel of a party.

The parties mutually undertake not to call the conciliator as a witness in any such proceedings, unless otherwise agreed between them.

Article 11

The parties agree not to introduce in any judicial or arbitration proceeding as evidence or in any manner whatsoever:

(a) any views expressed or suggestions made by any party with regard to the possible settlement of the dispute;

(b) any proposals put forward by the conciliator;

(c) the fact that a party had indicated that it was ready to accept some proposal for a settlement put forward by the conciliator.

Rules of Arbitration

Article 1

International Court of Arbitration

1. The International Court of Arbitration of the International Chamber of Commerce is the arbitration body attached to the International Chamber of Commerce. Members of the Court are appointed by the Council of the International Chamber of Commerce. The function of the Court is to provide for the settlement by arbitration of business disputes of an international character in accordance with these Rules.

2. In principle, the Court meets once a month. It draws up its own internal regulations.

3. The Chairman of the International Court of Arbitration or his deputy shall have power to take urgent decisions on behalf of the Court, provided that any such decision shall be reported to the Court at its next session.

4. The Court may, in the manner provided for in its internal regulations, delegate to one or more groups of its members the power to take certain decisions provided that any such decision shall be reported to the Court at its next session.

5. The Secretariat of the International Court of Arbitration shall be at the Headquarters of the International Chamber of Commerce.

Article 2

The arbitral tribunal

1. The International Court of Arbitration does not itself settle disputes. Insofar as the parties shall not have provided otherwise, it appoints, or confirms the appointments of, arbitrators in accordance with the provisions of this Article. In making or confirming such appointment, the Court shall have regard to the proposed arbitrator's nationality, residence and other relationships with the countries of which the parties or the other arbitrators are nationals.

2. The disputes may be settled by a sole arbitrator or by three arbitrators. In the following Articles the word "arbitrator" denotes a single arbitrator or three arbitrators as the case may be.

3. Where the parties have agreed that the disputes shall be settled by a sole arbitrator, they may, by agreement, nominate him for confirmation by the Court. If the parties fail so to nominate a sole arbitrator within 30 days from the date when the Claimant's Request for Arbitration has been communicated to the other party, the sole arbitrator shall be appointed by the Court.

4. Where the dispute is to be referred to three arbitrators, each party shall nominate in the Request for Arbitration and the Answer

thereto respectively one arbitrator for confirmation by the Court. Such person shall be independent of the party nominating him. If a party fails to nominate an arbitrator, the appointment shall be made by the Court.

The third arbitrator, who will act as chairman of the arbitral tribunal, shall be appointed by the Court, unless the parties have provided that the arbitrators nominated by them shall agree on the third arbitrator within a fixed time-limit. In such a case the Court shall confirm the appointment of such third arbitrator. Should the two arbitrators fail, within the time-limit fixed by the parties or the Court, to reach agreement on the third arbitrator, he shall be appointed by the Court.

5. Where the parties have not agreed upon the number of arbitrators, the Court shall appoint a sole arbitrator, save where it appears to the Court that the dispute is such as to warrant the appointment of three arbitrators. In such a case the parties shall each have a period of 30 days within which to nominate an arbitrator.

6. Where the Court is to appoint a sole arbitrator or the chairman of an arbitral tribunal, it shall make the appointment after having requested a proposal from a National Committee of the ICC that it considers to be appropriate. If the Court does not accept the proposal made, or if said National Committee fails to make the proposal requested within the time-limit fixed by the Court, the Court may repeat its request or may request a proposal from another appropriate National Committee.

Where the Court considers that the circumstances so demand, it may choose the sole arbitrator or the chairman of the arbitral tribunal from a country where there is no National Committee, provided that neither of the parties objects within the time-limit fixed by the Court.

The sole arbitrator or the chairman of the arbitral tribunal shall be chosen from a country other than those of which the parties are nationals. However, in suitable circumstances and provided that neither of the parties objects within the time-limit fixed by the Court, the sole arbitrator or the chairman of the arbitral tribunal may be chosen from a country of which any of the parties is a national.

Where the Court is to appoint an arbitrator on behalf of a party which has failed to nominate one, it shall make the appointment after having requested a proposal from the National Committee of the country of which the said party is a national. If the Court does not accept the proposal made, or if said National Committee fails to make the proposal requested within the time-limit fixed by the Court, or if the country of which the said party is a national has no National Committee, the Court shall be at liberty to choose any person whom it regards as suitable, after having informed the National Committee of the country of which such person is a national, if one exists.

7. Every arbitrator appointed or confirmed by the Court must be and remain independent of the parties involved in the arbitration.

Before appointment or confirmation by the Court, a prospective arbitrator shall disclose in writing to the Secretary General of the Court any facts or circumstances which might be of such a nature as to call into question the arbitrator's independence in the eyes of the parties. Upon receipt of such information, the Secretary General of the Court shall provide it to the parties in writing and fix a time-limit for any comments from them.

An arbitrator shall immediately disclose in writing to the Secretary General of the Court and the parties any facts or circumstances of a similar nature which may arise between the arbitrator's appointment or confirmation by the Court and the notification of the final award.

8. A challenge of an arbitrator, whether for an alleged lack of independence or otherwise, is made by the submission to the Secretary General of the Court of a written statement specifying the facts and circumstances on which the challenge is based.

For a challenge to be admissible, it must be sent by a party either within 30 days from receipt by that party of the notification of the appointment or confirmation of the arbitrator by the Court; or within 30 days from the date when the party making the challenge was informed of the facts and circumstances on which the challenge is based, if such date is subsequent to the receipt of the aforementioned notification.

9. The Court shall decide on the admissibility, and at the same time if need be on the merits, of a challenge after the Secretary General of the Court has accorded an opportunity for the arbitrator concerned, the parties and any other members of the arbitral tribunal to comment in writing within a suitable period of time.

10. An arbitrator shall be replaced upon his death, upon the acceptance by the Court of a challenge, or upon the acceptance by the Court of the arbitrator's resignation.

11. An arbitrator shall also be replaced when the Court decides that he is prevented *de jure* or *de facto* from fulfilling his functions, or that he is not fulfilling his functions in accordance with the Rules or within the prescribed time-limits.

When, on the basis of information that has come to its attention, the Court considers applying the preceding subparagraph, it shall decide on the matter after the Secretary General of the Court has provided such information in writing to the arbitrator concerned, the parties and any other members of the arbitral tribunal, and accorded an opportunity to them to comment in writing within a suitable period of time.

12. In each instance where an arbitrator is to be replaced, the procedure indicated in the preceding paragraphs 3, 4, 5 and 6 shall be followed. Once reconstituted, and after having invited the parties to comment, the arbitral tribunal shall determine if and to what extent prior proceedings shall again take place.

13. Decisions of the Court as to the appointment, confirmation, challenge or replacement of an arbitrator shall be final.

The reasons for decisions by the Court as to the appointment, confirmation, challenge, or replacement of an arbitrator on the grounds that he is not fulfilling his functions in accordance with the Rules or within the prescribed time-limits, shall not be communicated.

Article 3

Request for Arbitration

1. A party wishing to have recourse to arbitration by the International Chamber of Commerce shall submit its Request for Arbitration to the Secretariat of the International Court of Arbitration, through its National Committee or directly. In this latter case the Secretariat shall bring the Request to the notice of the National Committee concerned.

The date when the Request is received by the Secretariat of the Court shall, for all purposes, be deemed to be the date of commencement of the arbitral proceedings.

2. The Request for Arbitration shall *inter alia* contain the following information:

(a) names in full, description, and addresses of the parties,

(b) a statement of the Claimant's case,

(c) the relevant agreements, and in particular the agreement to arbitrate, and such documentation or information as will serve clearly to establish the circumstances of the case,

(d) all relevant particulars concerning the number of arbitrators and their choice in accordance with the provisions of Article 2 above.

3. The Secretariat shall send a copy of the Request and the documents annexed thereto to the Defendant for his Answer.

Article 4

Answer to the Request

1. The Defendant shall within 30 days from the receipt of the documents referred to in paragraph 3 of Article 3 comment on the

proposals made concerning the number of arbitrators and their choice and, where appropriate, nominate an arbitrator. He shall at the same time set out his defence and supply relevant documents. In exceptional circumstances the Defendant may apply to the Secretariat for an extension of time for the filing of his defence and his documents. The application must, however, include the Defendant's comments on the proposals made with regard to the number of arbitrators and their choice and also, where appropriate, the nomination of an arbitrator. If the Defendant fails so to do, the Secretariat shall report to the International Court of Arbitration, which shall proceed with the arbitration in accordance with these Rules.

2. A copy of the Answer and of the documents annexed thereto, if any, shall be communicated to the Claimant for his information.

Article 5

Counter-claim

1. If the Defendant wishes to make a counter-claim, he shall file the same with the Secretariat, at the same time as his Answer as provided for in Article 4.

2. It shall be open to the Claimant to file a Reply with the Secretariat within 30 days from the date when the counter-claim was communicated to him.

Article 6

Pleadings and written statements, notifications or communications

1. All pleadings and written statements submitted by the parties, as well as all documents annexed thereto, shall be supplied in a number of copies sufficient to provide one copy for each party, plus one for each arbitrator, and one for the Secretariat.

2. All notifications or communications from the Secretariat and the arbitrator shall be validly made if they are delivered against receipt or forwarded by registered post to the address or last known address of the party for whom the same are intended as notified by the party in question or by the other party as appropriate.

3. Notification or communication shall be deemed to have been effected on the day when it was received, or should, if made in accordance with the preceding paragraph, have been received by the party itself or by its representative.

4. Periods of time specified in the present Rules or in the Internal Rules or set by the International Court of Arbitration pursuant to its authority under any of these Rules shall start to run on the day following the date a notification or communication is deemed to have

been effected in accordance with the preceding paragraph. When, in the country where the notification or communication is deemed to have been effected, the day next following such date is an official holiday or a non-business day, the period of time shall commence on the first following working day. Official holidays and non-working days are included in the calculation of the period of time. If the last day of the relevant period of time granted is an official holiday or a non-business day in the country where the notification or communication is deemed to have been effected, the period of time shall expire at the end of the first following working day.

Article 7

Absence of agreement to arbitrate

Where there is no *prima facie* agreement between the parties to arbitrate or where there is an agreement but it does not specify the International Chamber of Commerce, and if the Defendant does not file an Answer within the period of 30 days provided by paragraph 1 of Article 4 or refuses arbitration by the International Chamber of Commerce, the Claimant shall be informed that the arbitration cannot proceed.

Article 8

Effect of the agreement to arbitrate

1. Where the parties have agreed to submit to arbitration by the International Chamber of Commerce, they shall be deemed thereby to have submitted *ipso facto* to the present Rules.

2. If one of the parties refuses or fails to take part in the arbitration, the arbitration shall proceed notwithstanding such refusal or failure.

3. Should one of the parties raise one or more pleas concerning the existence or validity of the agreement to arbitrate, and should the International Court of Arbitration be satisfied of the *prima facie* existence of such an agreement, the Court may, without prejudice to the admissibility or merits of the plea or pleas, decide that the arbitration shall proceed. In such a case any decision as to the arbitrator's jurisdiction shall be taken by the arbitrator himself.

4. Unless otherwise provided, the arbitrator shall not cease to have jurisdiction by reason of any claim that the contract is null and void or allegation that it is inexistent provided that he upholds the validity of the agreement to arbitrate. He shall continue to have jurisdiction, even though the contract itself may be inexistent or null and void, to determine the respective rights of the parties and to adjudicate upon their claims and pleas.

5. Before the file is transmitted to the arbitrator, and in exceptional circumstances even thereafter, the parties shall be at liberty to apply to any competent judicial authority for interim or conservatory measures, and they shall not by so doing be held to infringe the agreement to arbitrate or to affect the relevant powers reserved to the arbitrator.

Any such application and any measures taken by the judicial authority must be notified without delay to the Secretariat of the International Court of Arbitration. The Secretariat shall inform the arbitrator thereof.

Article 9

Advance to cover costs of arbitration

1. The International Court of Arbitration shall fix the amount of the advance on costs in a sum likely to cover the costs of arbitration of the claims which have been referred to it.

Where, apart from the principal claim, one or more counter-claims are submitted, the Court may fix separate advances on costs for the principal claim and the counter-claim or counter-claims.

2. The advance on costs shall be payable in equal shares by the Claimant or Claimants and the Defendant or Defendants. However, any one party shall be free to pay the whole of the advance on costs in respect of the claim or the counter-claim should the other party fail to pay its share.

3. The Secretariat may make the transmission of the file to the arbitrator conditional upon the payment by the parties or one of them of the whole or part of the advance on costs to the International Chamber of Commerce.

4. When the Terms of Reference are communicated to the Court in accordance with the provisions of Article 13, the Court shall verify whether the requests for the advance on costs have been complied with.

The Terms of Reference shall only become operative and the arbitrator shall only proceed in respect of those claims for which the advance on costs has been duly paid to the International Chamber of Commerce.

Article 10

Transmission of the file to the arbitrator

Subject to the provisions of Article 9, the Secretariat shall transmit the file to the arbitrator as soon as it has received the Defendant's Answer to the Request for Arbitration, at the latest upon the expiry of the time-limits fixed in Articles 4 and 5 above for the filing of these documents.

Article 11

Rules governing the proceedings

The rules governing the proceedings before the arbitrator shall be those resulting from these Rules and, where these Rules are silent, any rules which the parties (or, failing them, the arbitrator) may settle, and whether or not reference is thereby made to a municipal procedural law to be applied to the arbitration.

Article 12

Place of arbitration

The place of arbitration shall be fixed by the International Court of Arbitration, unless agreed upon by the parties.

Article 13

Terms of Reference

1. Before proceeding with the preparation of the case, the arbitrator shall draw up, on the basis of the documents or in the presence of the parties and in the light of their most recent submissions, a document defining his Terms of Reference. This document shall include the following particulars:

(a) the full names and description of the parties,

(b) the addresses of the parties to which notifications or communications arising in the course of the arbitration may validly be made,

(c) a summary of the parties' respective claims,

(d) definition of the issues to be determined,

(e) the arbitrator's full name, description and address,

(f) the place of arbitration,

(g) particulars of the applicable procedural rules and, if such is the case, reference to the power conferred upon the arbitrator to act as amiable compositeur,

(h) such other particulars as may be required to make the arbitral award enforceable in law, or may be regarded as helpful by the International Court of Arbitration or the arbitrator.

2. The document mentioned in paragraph 1 of this Article shall be signed by the parties and the arbitrator. Within two months of the date when the file has been transmitted to him, the arbitrator shall transmit to the Court the said document signed by himself and by the parties. The Court may, pursuant to a reasoned request from the arbitrator or if need be on its own initiative, extend this time-limit if it decides it is necessary to do so.

Should one of the parties refuse to take part in the drawing up of the said document or to sign the same, the Court, if it is satisfied that the case is one of those mentioned in paragraphs 2 and 3 of Article 8, shall take such action as is necessary for its approval. Thereafter the Court shall set a time-limit for the signature of the statement by the defaulting party and on expiry of that time-limit the arbitration shall proceed and the award shall be made.

3. The parties shall be free to determine the law to be applied by the arbitrator to the merits of the dispute. In the absence of any indication by the parties as to the applicable law, the arbitrator shall apply the law designated as the proper law by the rule of conflict which he deems appropriate.

4. The arbitrator shall assume the powers of an amiable compositeur if the parties are agreed to give him such powers.

5. In all cases the arbitrator shall take account of the provisions of the contract and the relevant trade usages.

Article 14

The arbitral proceedings

1. The arbitrator shall proceed within as short a time as possible to establish the facts of the case by all appropriate means. After study of the written submissions of the parties and of all documents relied upon, the arbitrator shall hear the parties together in person if one of them so requests; and failing such a request he may of his own motion decide to hear them.

In addition, the arbitrator may decide to hear any other person in the presence of the parties or in their absence provided they have been duly summoned.

2. The arbitrator may appoint one or more experts, define their Terms of Reference, receive their reports and/or hear them in person.

3. The arbitrator may decide the case on the relevant documents alone if the parties so request or agree.

Article 15

1. At the request of one of the parties or if necessary on his own initiative, the arbitrator, giving reasonable notice, shall summon the parties to appear before him on the day and at the place appointed by him and shall so inform the Secretariat of the International Court of Arbitration.

2. If one of the parties, although duly summoned, fails to appear, the arbitrator, if he is satisfied that the summons was duly received and the party is absent without valid excuse, shall have power to

proceed with the arbitration, and such proceedings shall be deemed to have been conducted in the presence of all parties.

3. The arbitrator shall determine the language or languages of the arbitration, due regard being paid to all the relevant circumstances and in particular to the language of the contract.

4. The arbitrator shall be in full charge of the hearings, at which all the parties shall be entitled to be present. Save with the approval of the arbitrator and of the parties, persons not involved in the proceedings shall not be admitted.

5. The parties may appear in person or through duly accredited agents. In addition, they may be assisted by advisers.

Article 16

The parties may make new claims or counter-claims before the arbitrator on condition that these remain within the limits fixed by the Terms of Reference provided for in Article 13 or that they are specified in a rider to that document, signed by the parties and communicated to the International Court of Arbitration.

Article 17

Award by consent

If the parties reach a settlement after the file has been transmitted to the arbitrator in accordance with Article 10, the same shall be recorded in the form of an arbitral award made by consent of the parties.

Article 18

Time-limit for award

1. The time-limit within which the arbitrator must render his award is fixed at six months. Once the terms of Article 9 (4) have been satisfied, such time-limit shall start to run from the date of the last signature by the arbitrator or of the parties of the document mentioned in Article 13, or from the expiry of the time-limit granted to a party by virtue of Article 13(2), or from the date that the Secretary General of the International Court of Arbitration notifies the arbitrator that the advance on costs is paid in full, if such notification occurs later.

2. The Court may, pursuant to a reasoned request from the arbitrator or if need be on its own initiative, extend this time-limit if it decides it is necessary to do so.

3. Where no such extension is granted and, if appropriate, after application of the provisions of Article 2 (11), the Court shall determine the manner in which the dispute is to be resolved.

Article 19

Award by three arbitrators

When three arbitrators have been appointed, the award is given by a majority decision. If there be no majority, the award shall be made by the Chairman of the arbitral tribunal alone.

Article 20

Decision as to costs of arbitration

1. The arbitrator's award shall, in addition to dealing with the merits of the case, fix the costs of the arbitration and decide which of the parties shall bear the costs or in what proportions the costs shall be borne by the parties.

2. The costs of the arbitration shall include the arbitrator's fees and the administrative costs fixed by the International Court of Arbitration in accordance with the scale annexed to the present Rules, the expenses, if any, of the arbitrator, the fees and expenses of any experts, and the normal legal costs incurred by the parties.

3. The Court may fix the arbitrator's fees at a figure higher or lower than that which would result from the application of the annexed scale if in the exceptional circumstances of the case this appears to be necessary.

Article 21

Scrutiny of award by the Court

Before signing an award, whether partial or definitive, the arbitrator shall submit it in draft form to the International Court of Arbitration. The Court may lay down modifications as to the form of the award and, without affecting the arbitrator's liberty of decision, may also draw his attention to points of substance. No award shall be signed until it has been approved by the Court as to its form.

Article 22

Making of award

The arbitral award shall be deemed to be made at the place of the arbitration proceedings and on the date when it is signed by the arbitrator.

Article 23

Notification of award to parties

1. Once an award has been made, the Secretariat shall notify to the parties the text signed by the arbitrator; provided always that the costs of the arbitration have been fully paid to the International Chamber of Commerce by the parties or by one of them.

2. Additional copies certified true by the Secretary General of the International Court of Arbitration shall be made available, on request and at any time, to the parties but to no one else.

3. By virtue of the notification made in accordance with paragraph 1 of this article, the parties waive any other form of notification or deposit on the part of the arbitrator.

Article 24

Finality and enforceability of award

1. The arbitral award shall be final.

2. By submitting the dispute to arbitration by the International Chamber of Commerce, the parties shall be deemed to have undertaken to carry out the resulting award without delay and to have waived their right to any form of appeal insofar as such waiver can validly be made.

Article 25

Deposit of award

An original of each award made in accordance with the present Rules shall be deposited with the Secretariat of the International Court of Arbitration.

The arbitrator and the Secretariat of the Court shall assist the parties in complying with whatever further formalities may be necessary.

Article 26

General rule

In all matters not expressly provided for in these Rules, the International Court of Arbitration and the arbitrator shall act in the spirit of these Rules and shall make every effort to make sure that the award is enforceable at law.

Appendix I—Statutes of the International Court of Arbitration

Article 1

Appointment of members

The members of the International Court of Arbitration of the International Chamber of Commerce are appointed for a term of three years by the Council of that Chamber pursuant to Article 5.3.c of the Constitution, on the proposal of each National Committee.

Article 2

Composition

The International Court of Arbitration shall be composed of a Chairman and of Vice-Chairmen chosen by the Council of the International Chamber of Commerce either from among the members of the Court or apart from them, and of one member for, and appointed by, each National Committee.

The chairmanship may be exercised by two Co-Chairmen; in this case, they shall have equal rights, and the expression "the Chairman", used in the Rules of Conciliation and Arbitration, shall apply to either of them equally.

In exceptional cases, on the proposal of the Chairman of the Court, the Council may appoint an alternate member for a member of the Court.

If the Chairman is unable to attend a session of the Court, he shall be replaced by one of the Vice-Chairmen.

Article 3

Function and powers

The function of the International Court of Arbitration is to ensure the application of the Rules of Conciliation and Arbitration of the International Chamber of Commerce, and the Court has all the necessary powers for that purpose. It is further entrusted, if need be, with laying before the Commission on International Arbitration any proposals for modifying the Rules of Conciliation and Arbitration of the International Chamber of Commerce which it considers necessary.

Article 4

Deliberations and quorum

The decisions of the International Court of Arbitration shall be taken by a majority vote, the Chairman having a casting vote in the event of a tie. The deliberations of the Court shall be valid when at least six members are present.

The Secretary General of the International Chamber of Commerce, the Secretary General, the General Counsel and Deputy Secretary General of the Court shall attend in an advisory capacity only, as well as the Counsels of the Court for their respective cases.

Appendix II—Internal Rules of the International Court of Arbitration

Role of the International Court of Arbitration

1. The International Court of Arbitration may accept jurisdiction over business disputes not of an international business nature, if it has jurisdiction by reason of an arbitration agreement.

Confidential character of the work of the International Court of Arbitration

2. The work of the International Court of Arbitration is of a confidential character which must be respected by everyone who participates in that work in whatever capacity.

3. The sessions of the International Court of Arbitration, whether plenary or those of a Committee of the Court, are open only to its members and to the Secretariat.

However, in exceptional circumstances and, if need be, after obtaining the opinion of members of the Court, the Chairman of the International Court of Arbitration may invite honorary members of the Court and authorize observers to attend. Such persons must respect the confidential character of the work of the Court.

4. The documents submitted to the Court or drawn up by it in the course of the proceedings it conducts are communicated only to the members of the Court and to the Secretariat.

The Chairman or the Secretary General of the Court may nevertheless authorize researchers undertaking work of a scientific nature on international trade law to acquaint themselves with certain documents of general interest, with the exception of memoranda, notes, statements and documents remitted by the parties within the framework of arbitration proceedings.

Such authorization shall not be given unless the beneficiary has undertaken to respect the confidential character of the documents made available and to refrain from any publication in their respect without having previously submitted the text for approval to the Secretary General of the Court.

Participation of members of the International Court of Arbitration in ICC arbitration

5. Owing to the special responsibilities laid upon them by the ICC Rules of Arbitration, the Chairman, the Vice-Chairmen and the Secretariat of the International Court of Arbitration may not personally act as arbitrators or as counsel in cases submitted to ICC arbitration.

The members of the International Court of Arbitration may not be directly appointed as co-arbitrators, sole arbitrator or Chairman of an arbitral tribunal by the International Court of Arbitration. They may however be proposed for such duties by one or more of the parties, subject to confirmation by the Court.

6. When the Chairman, a Vice-Chairman or a member of the Court is involved, in any capacity whatsoever, in proceedings pending before the Court, he must inform the Secretary General of the Court as soon as he becomes aware of such involvement.

He must refrain from participating in the discussions or in the decisions of the Court concerning the proceedings and he must be absent from the courtroom whenever the matter is considered.

He will not receive documentation or information submitted to the Court during the proceedings.

Relations between the members of the Court and the ICC National Committees

7. By virtue of their capacity, the members of the International Court of Arbitration are independent of the ICC National Committees which proposed them for nomination by the ICC Council.

Furthermore, they must regard as confidential, vis-à-vis the said National Committees, any information concerning individual disputes with which they have become acquainted in their capacity as members of the Court except when they have been requested, by the Chairman of the Court or by its Secretary General, to communicate that information to their respective National Committees.

Committee of the Court

8. In accordance with the provisions of Article 1 (4) of the ICC Rules of Arbitration, the International Court of Arbitration hereby establishes a Committee of the Court composed as follows, and with the following powers.

9. The Committee consists of a Chairman and two members. The Chairman of the International Court of Arbitration acts as the Chairman of the Committee. He may nevertheless designate a Vice-Chairman of the Court to replace him during a session of the Committee.

The other two members of the Committee are appointed by the Court from among the Vice-Chairmen or the other members of the Court. At each meeting of the Court it appoints the members who are to attend the meeting of the Committee to be held before the next plenary session of the Court.

10. The Committee meets when convened by its Chairman, in principle twice a month.

11. (a) The Committee is empowered to take any decision within the jurisdiction of the Court, with the exception of decisions concerning challenges of arbitrators (Arts. 2 (8) and 2 (9) of the ICC Rules of Arbitration), allegations that an arbitrator is not fulfilling his functions (Art. 2 (11) of the ICC Rules of Arbitration) and approval of draft awards other than awards made with the consent of the parties.

(b) The decisions of the Committee are taken unanimously.

(c) When the Committee cannot reach a decision or deems it preferable to abstain, it transfers the case to the next plenary session of the Court, making any suggestions it deems appropriate.

(d) The Committee's proceedings are brought to the notice of the Court at its next plenary session.

Absence of an arbitration agreement

12. Where there is no *prima facie* arbitration agreement between the parties or where there is an agreement but it does not specify the ICC, the Secretariat draws the attention of the Claimant to the provisions laid down in Article 7 of the Rules of Arbitration. The Claimant is entitled to require the decision to be taken by the International Court of Arbitration.

This decision is of an administrative nature. If the Court decides that the arbitration solicited by the Claimant cannot proceed, the parties retain the right to ask the competent jurisdiction whether or not they are bound by an arbitration agreement in the light of the law applicable.

If the Court considers *prima facie* that the proceedings may take place, the arbitrator appointed has the duty to decide as to his own jurisdiction and, where such jurisdiction exists, as to the merits of the dispute.

Joinder of claims in arbitration proceedings

13. When a party presents a Request for Arbitration in connection with a legal relationship already submitted to arbitration proceedings by the same parties and pending before the International Court of Arbitration, the Court may decide to include that claim in the existing proceedings, subject to the provisions of Article 16 of the ICC Rules of Arbitration.

Advances to cover costs of arbitration

14. When the International Court of Arbitration has set separate advances on costs for a specific case in accordance with Article 9 (1) (sub para. 2) of the ICC Rules of Arbitration, the Secretariat requests each of the parties to pay the amount corresponding to its claims, without prejudice to the right of the parties to pay the said advances on costs in equal shares, if they deem it advisable.

15. When a request for an advance on costs has not been complied with, the Secretariat may set a time-limit, which must not be less than 30 days, on the expiry of which the relevant claim, whether principal claim or counter-claim, shall be considered as withdrawn. This does not prevent the party in question from lodging a new claim at a later date.

Should one of the parties wish to object to this measure, he must make a request, within the aforementioned period, for the matter to be decided by the Court.

16. If one of the parties claims a right to a set-off with regard to either a principal claim or counter-claim, such set-off is taken into account in determining the advance to cover the costs of arbitration, in the same way as a separate claim, insofar as it may require the arbitrators to consider additional matters.

Arbitral awards: form

17. When it scrutinizes draft arbitral awards in accordance with Article 21 of the ICC Rules of Arbitration, the International Court of Arbitration pays particular attention to the respect of the formal requirements laid down by the law applicable to the proceedings and, where relevant, by the mandatory rules of the place of arbitration, notably with regard to the reasons for awards, their signature and the admissibility of dissenting opinions.

Arbitrators' fees

18. In setting the arbitrators' fees on the basis of the scale attached to the ICC Rules of Arbitration, the International Court of Arbitration takes into consideration the time spent, the rapidity of the proceedings and the complexity of the dispute, so as to arrive at a figure within the limits specified or, when circumstances require, higher or lower than those limits (Art. 20(3) of the ICC Rules of Arbitration).

Appendix III—Schedule of Conciliation and Arbitration Costs

1. Costs of conciliation

(a) The administrative expenses for a conciliation procedure shall be fixed at one-quarter of the amount calculated in accordance with the scale of administrative expenses hereinafter set out. Where the sum in dispute in a conciliation procedure is not stated, the Secretary General of the International Court of Arbitration shall fix the administrative expenses at his discretion.

(b) The fee of the conciliator to be paid by the parties shall be fixed by the Secretary General of the Court. Such fee shall be reasonable in amount, taking into consideration the time spent, the complexity of the dispute and any other relevant circumstances.

2. Costs of arbitration

(a) The advance on costs fixed by the International Court of Arbitration comprises the fee(s) of the arbitrator(s), any personal expenses of the arbitrator(s) and the administrative expenses.

(b) The submission of any claim or counter-claim to the arbitrator(s) shall be made only after at least half of the advance on costs fixed by the Court has been satisfied. Terms of Reference shall only become operative and the arbitrator(s) shall only proceed in respect of those claims and counter-claims for which the totality of the advance on costs fixed by the Court has been satisfied.

(c) The Court shall fix the administrative expenses of each arbitration in accordance with the scale hereinafter set out or, where the sum in dispute is not stated, at its discretion. If exceptional circumstances so require, the Court may fix the administrative expenses at a lower or higher figure than that which would result from application of said scale, provided that such expenses shall in no event exceed US $65,500. Further, the Court may require the payment of administrative expenses in addition to those provided for in the scale of administrative expenses as a condition to holding an arbitration in abeyance at the request of the parties or one of them with the acquiescence of the other(s).

(d) Subject to Article 20(3) of the ICC Rules of Arbitration, the Court shall fix the fee(s) of the arbitrator(s) in accordance with the scale hereinafter set out or, where the sum in dispute is not stated, at its discretion.

(e) When a case is submitted to more than one arbitrator, the Court, at its discretion, shall have the right to increase the total fees up to a maximum of three times the fee payable to one arbitrator.

(f) When arbitration is preceded by attempted conciliation, one-half of the administrative expenses paid in respect of the said attempt shall be credited to the administrative expenses of the arbitration.

(g) Before any expertise can be commenced, the parties, or one of them, shall pay an advance on costs fixed by the arbitrator(s) sufficient to cover the expected fee and expenses of the expert as determined by the arbitrator(s).

3. Advance on administrative expenses

(a) Each party to a dispute submitted to conciliation under the Rules of Optional Conciliation of the ICC is required to make an advance payment of US $500 on the administrative expenses.

(b) Each request to open an arbitration pursuant to the ICC Rules of Arbitration must be accompanied by an advance payment of US $2,000 on the administrative expenses.

(c) No request for conciliation or arbitration will be entertained unless accompanied by the appropriate payment. This payment is not recoverable and becomes the property of the ICC. Such payment by a party shall be credited to its portion of the administrative expenses for the conciliation or arbitration, as the case may be.

4. Appointment of arbitrators

A registration fee of US $2,000 is payable by the requesting party in respect of each request made to the ICC to appoint an arbitrator for any arbitration not conducted under the ICC Rules of Arbitration. No request for appointment of an arbitrator will be entertained unless accompanied by said fee, which is not recoverable and becomes the property of the ICC.

Such fee shall cover any additional services rendered by the ICC regarding the appointment, such as decisions on a challenge of the arbitrator and the appointment of a substitute arbitrator.

5. Scales of administrative expenses and of arbitrator's fees

To calculate the administrative expenses and the arbitrator's fees, the amounts calculated for each successive slice of the sum in dispute **must be added together,** (*) (**) except that where the sum in dispute is over US $80 million, a flat amount of US $65,500 shall constitute the entirety of the administrative expenses.

A. Administrative Expenses

Sum in Dispute (in U.S. Dollars)	Administrative Expenses (*)
Up to 50,000	$2,000
From 50,001 to 100,000	3.00%
From 100,001 to 500,000	1.50%
From 500,001 to 1,000,000	1.00%
From 1,000,001 to 2,000,000	0.50%
From 2,000,001 to 5,000,000	0.20%
From 5,000,001 to 10,000,000	0.10%
From 10,000,001 to 80,000,000	0.05%
Over 80,000,000	$65,500

(*)(For illustrative purposes only, the table on the following page indicates the resulting administrative expenses in US $ when the proper calculations have been made.)

B. Arbitrator's Fees

Sum in Dispute (in U.S. Dollars)	Fees (**)	
	Minimum	Maximum
Up to 50,000	$2,000	15.00%
From 50,001 to 100,000	1.50%	10.00%
From 100,001 to 500,000	0.80%	5.00%
From 500,001 to 1,000,000	0.50%	3.00%
From 1,000,001 to 2,000,000	0.30%	2.50%
From 2,000,001 to 5,000,000	0.20%	0.80%
From 5,000,001 to 10,000,000	0.10%	0.50%
From 10,000,001 to 50,000,000	0.05%	0.15%
From 50,000,001 to 100,000,000	0.02%	0.10%
Over 100,000,000	0.01%	0.05%

(**)(For illustrative purposes only, the table on the following page indicates the resulting range of fees when the proper calculations have been made.)

Sum in Dispute (in U.S. Dollars)	A. Administrative Expenses (*) (in U.S. Dollars) Administrative Expenses	B. Arbitrator's Fees (**) (in U.S. Dollars) Minimum	Maximum
Up to 50,000	2,000	2,000	15.00% of the Sum in Dispute
From 50,001 to 100,000	2,000 + 3.00% of Amt. over 50,000	2,000 + 1.50% of Amt. over 50,000	7,500 + 10.00% of Amt. over 50,000
From 100,001 to 500,000	3,500 + 1.50% of Amt. over 100,000	2,750 + 0.80% of Amt. over 100,000	12,500 + 5.00% of Amt. over 100,000
From 500,001 to 1,000,000	9,500 + 1.00% of Amt. over 500,000	5,950 + 0.50% of Amt. over 500,000	32,500 + 3.00% of Amt. over 500,000
From 1,000,001 to 2,000,000	14,500 + 0.50% of Amt. over 1,000,000	8,450 + 0.30% of Amt. over 1,000,000	47,500 + 2.50% of Amt. over 1,000,000
From 2,000,001 to 5,000,000	19,500 + 0.20% of Amt. over 2,000,000	11,450 + 0.20% of Amt. over 2,000,000	72,500 + 0.80% of Amt. over 2,000,000
From 5,000,001 to 10,000,000	25,500 + 0.10% of Amt. over 5,000,000	17,450 + 0.10% of Amt. over 5,000,000	96,500 + 0.50% of Amt. over 5,000,000
From 10,000,001 to 50,000,000	30,500 + 0.05% of Amt. over 10,000,000	22,450 + 0.05% of Amt. over 10,000,000	121,500 + 0.15% of Amt. over 10,000,000
From 50,000,001 to 80,000,000	50,500 + 0.05% of Amt. over 50,000,000	42,450 + 0.02% of Amt. over 50,000,000	181,500 + 0.10% of Amt. over 50,000,000
From 80,000,001 to 100,000,000	65,500	48,450 + 0.02% of Amt. over 80,000,000	211,500 + 0.10% of Amt. over 80,000,000
Over 100,000,000	65,500	52,450 + 0.01% of Amt. over 100,000,000	231,500 + 0.05% of Amt. over 100,000,000

(*) (**) See preceding page

AAA International Arbitration Rules

(AAA rules reprinted by permission of the American Arbitration Association.)

Article 1

1. Where parties have agreed in writing to arbitrate disputes under these International Arbitration Rules, the arbitration shall take place in accordance with their provisions, as in effect at the date of commencement of the arbitration, subject to whatever modifications the parties may adopt in writing.

2. These rules govern the arbitration, except that, where any such rule is in conflict with any provision of the law applicable to the arbitration from which the parties cannot derogate, that provision shall prevail.

3. These rules specify the duties and responsibilities of the administrator, the American Arbitration Association. The administrator may provide services through its own facilities or through the facilities of arbitral institutions with whom it has agreements of cooperation.

I. Commencing the Arbitration

Notice of Arbitration and Statement of Claim

Article 2

1. The party initiating arbitration ("claimant") shall give written notice of arbitration to the administrator and to the party or parties against whom a claim is being made ("respondent(s)").

2. Arbitral proceedings shall be deemed to commence on the date on which the notice of arbitration is received by the administrator.

3. The notice of arbitration shall include the following:

(a) a demand that the dispute be referred to arbitration;

(b) the names and addresses of the parties;

(c) a reference to the arbitration clause or agreement that is invoked;

(d) a reference to any contract out of or in relation to which the dispute arises;

(e) a description of the claim and an indication of the facts supporting it;

(f) the relief or remedy sought and the amount claimed; and

(g) may include proposals as to the number of arbitrators, the place of arbitration and the language(s) of the arbitration.

Upon receipt of such notice, the administrator will communicate with all parties with respect to the arbitration, including the matters set forth in (g) above, if the parties have not already agreed on these matters, and will acknowledge the commencement of the arbitration.

Statement of Defense and Counterclaim

Article 3

1. Within forty-five days after the date of the commencement of the arbitration, a respondent shall file a statement of defense in writing with the claimant and any other parties, and with the administrator for transmittal to the tribunal when appointed.

2. At the time a respondent submits its statement of defense, a respondent may make counterclaims or assert set-offs as to any claim covered by the agreement to arbitrate, as to which the claimant shall within forty-five days file a statement of defense.

3. A respondent shall respond to the administrator, the claimant and other parties within forty-five days as to any proposals the claimant may have made as to the number of arbitrators, the place of the arbitration or the language(s) of the arbitration, except to the extent that the parties have previously agreed as to these matters.

Amendments to Claims

Article 4

During the arbitral proceedings, any party may amend or supplement its claim, counterclaim or defense, unless the tribunal considers it inappropriate to allow such amendment because of the party's delay in making it or of prejudice to the other parties or any other circumstances. A claim or counterclaim may not be amended if the amendment would fall outside the scope of the agreement to arbitrate.

II. The Tribunal

Number of Arbitrators

Article 5

If the parties have not agreed on the number of arbitrators, one arbitrator shall be appointed unless the administrator determines in its discretion that three arbitrators are appropriate because of the large size, complexity or other circumstances of the case.

Appointment of Arbitrators

Article 6

1. The parties may mutually agree upon any procedure for appointing arbitrators and shall inform the administrator as to such procedure.

2. The parties may mutually designate arbitrators, with or without the assistance of the administrator. When such designations are made, the parties shall notify the administrator so that notice of the appoint-

ment can be communicated to the arbitrators, together with a copy of these rules.

3. If within sixty days after the commencement of the arbitration, all of the parties have not mutually agreed on a procedure for appointing the arbitrator(s) or have not mutually agreed on the designation of the arbitrator(s), the administrator shall, at the written request of any party, appoint the arbitrator(s) and designate the presiding arbitrator. If all of the parties have mutually agreed upon a procedure for appointing the arbitrator(s), but all appointments have not been made within the time limits provided in that procedure, the administrator shall, at the written request of any party, perform all functions provided for in that procedure.

4. In making such appointments, the administrator, after inviting consultation with the parties, shall endeavor to select suitable arbitrators. At the request of any party or on its own initiative, the administrator may appoint nationals of a country other than that of any of the parties.

Challenge of Arbitrators

Article 7

Unless the parties agree otherwise, arbitrators acting under these rules shall be impartial and independent. Prior to accepting appointment, a prospective arbitrator shall disclose to the administrator any circumstance likely to give rise to justifiable doubts as to the arbitrator's impartiality or independence. Once appointed, an arbitrator shall disclose any additional such information to the parties and to the administrator. Upon receipt of such information from an arbitrator or a party, the administrator shall communicate it to the parties and to the arbitrator.

Article 8

1. A party may challenge any arbitrator whenever circumstances exist that give rise to justifiable doubts as to the arbitrator's impartiality or independence. A party wishing to challenge an arbitrator shall send notice of the challenge to the administrator within fifteen days after being notified of the appointment of the arbitrator, or within fifteen days after the circumstances giving rise to the challenge became known to that party.

2. The challenge shall state in writing the reasons for the challenge.

3. Upon receipt of such a challenge, the administrator shall notify the other parties of the challenge. When an arbitrator has been challenged by one party, the other parties may agree to the acceptance of the challenge and, if there is agreement, the arbitrator shall withdraw. The challenged arbitrator may also withdraw from office in the absence

of such agreement. In neither case does this imply acceptance of the validity of the grounds for the challenge.

Article 9

If the other party or parties do not agree to the challenge or the challenged arbitrator does not withdraw, the decision on the challenge shall be made by the administrator in its sole discretion.

Replacement of an Arbitrator

Article 10

If an arbitrator withdraws after a challenge, or the administrator sustains the challenge, or the administrator determines that there are sufficient reasons to accept the resignation of an arbitrator, or an arbitrator dies, a substitute arbitrator shall be appointed pursuant to the provisions of Article 6, unless the parties otherwise agree.

Article 11

1. If an arbitrator on a three-person tribunal fails to participate in the arbitration, the two other arbitrators shall have the power in their sole discretion to continue the arbitration and to make any decision, ruling or award, notwithstanding the failure of the third arbitrator to participate. In determining whether to continue the arbitration or to render any decision, ruling or award without the participation of an arbitrator, the two other arbitrators shall take into account the stage of the arbitration, the reason, if any, expressed by the third arbitrator for such nonparticipation, and such other matters as they consider appropriate in the circumstances of the case. In the event that the two other arbitrators determine not to continue the arbitration without the participation of the third arbitrator, the administrator on proof satisfactory to it shall declare the office vacant, and a substitute arbitrator shall be appointed pursuant to the provisions of Article 6, unless the parties otherwise agree.

2. If a substitute arbitrator is appointed, the tribunal shall determine at its sole discretion whether all or part of any prior hearings shall be repeated.

III. General Conditions

Representation

Article 12

Any party may be represented in the arbitration. The names, addresses and telephone numbers of representatives shall be communicated in writing to the other parties and to the administrator. Once the tribunal has been established, the parties or their representatives may communicate in writing directly with the tribunal.

Place of Arbitration

Article 13

1. If the parties disagree as to the place of arbitration, the place of arbitration may initially be determined by the administrator, subject to the power of the tribunal to determine finally the place of arbitration within sixty days after its constitution. All such determinations shall be made having regard for the contentions of the parties and the circumstances of the arbitration.

2. The tribunal may hold conferences or hear witnesses or inspect property or documents at any place it deems appropriate. The parties shall be given sufficient written notice to enable them to be present at any such proceedings.

Language

Article 14

If the parties have not agreed otherwise, the language(s) of the arbitration shall be that of the docments containing the arbitration agreement, subject to the power of the tribunal to determine otherwise based upon the contentions of the parties and the circumstances of the arbitration. The tribunal may order that any documents delivered in another language shall be accompanied by a translation into such language or languages.

Pleas as to Jurisdiction

Article 15

1. The tribunal shall have the power to rule on its own jurisdiction, including any objections with respect to the existence or validity of the arbitration agreement.

2. The tribunal shall have the power to determine the existence or validity of a contract of which an arbitration clause forms a part. Such an arbitration clause shall be treated as an agreement independent of the other terms of the contract.

3. Objections to the arbitrability of a claim must be raised no later than forty-five days after the commencement of the arbitration and, in respect to a counterclaim, no later than forty-five days after filing the counterclaim.

Conduct of the Arbitration

Article 16

1. Subject to these rules, the tribunal may conduct the arbitration in whatever manner it considers appropriate, provided that the parties are treated with equality and that each party has the right to be heard and is given a fair opportunity to present its case.

2. Documents or information supplied to the tribunal by one party shall at the same time be communicated by that party to the other party or parties.

Further Written Statements

Article 17

The tribunal may decide whether any written statements, in addition to statements of claims and counterclaims and statements of defense, shall be required from the parties or may be presented by them, and shall fix the periods of time for submitting such statements.

Periods of Time

Article 18

The periods of time fixed by the tribunal for the communication of written statements should not exceed forty-five days. However, the tribunal may extend such time limits if it considers such an extension justified.

Notices

Article 19

1. Unless otherwise agreed by the parties or ordered by the tribunal, all notices, statements and written communications may be served on a party by air mail or air courier addressed to the party or its representative at the last known address or by personal service. Facsimile transmission, telex, telegram, or other written forms of electronic communication may be used to give any such notices, statements or written communications.

2. For the purpose of calculating a period of time under these rules, such period shall begin to run on the day following the day when a notice, statement or written communication is received. If the last day of such period is an official holiday at the place received, the period is extended until the first business day which follows. Official holidays occurring during the running of the period of time are included in calculating the period.

Evidence

Article 20

1. Each party shall have the burden of proving the facts relied on to support its claim or defense.

2. The tribunal may order a party to deliver to the tribunal and to the other parties a summary of the documents and other evidence which that party intends to present in support of its claim, counterclaim or defense.

3. At any time during the proceedings, the tribunal may order parties to produce other documents, exhibits or other evidence it deems necessary or appropriate.

Hearings

Article 21

1. The tribunal shall give the parties at least thirty days' advance notice of the date, time and place of the initial oral hearing. The tribunal shall give reasonable notice of subsequent hearings.

2. At least fifteen days before the hearings, each party shall give the tribunal and the other parties the names and addresses of any witnesses it intends to present, the subject of their testimony and the languages in which such witnesses will give their testimony.

3. At the request of the tribunal or pursuant to mutual agreement of the parties, the administrator shall make arrangements for the interpretation of oral testimony or for a record of the hearing.

4. Hearings are private unless the parties agree otherwise or the law provides to the contrary. The tribunal may require any witness or witnesses to retire during the testimony of other witnesses. The tribunal may determine the manner in which witnesses are examined.

5. Evidence of witnesses may also be presented in the form of written statements signed by them.

6. The admissibility, relevance, materiality and weight of the evidence offered by any party shall be determined by the tribunal.

Interim Measures of Protection

Article 22

1. At the request of any party, the tribunal may take whatever interim measures it deems necessary in respect of the subject-matter of the dispute, including measures for the conservation of the goods which are the subject-matter in dispute, such as ordering their deposit with a third person or the sale of perishable goods.

2. Such interim measures may be taken in the form of an interim award and the tribunal may require security for the costs of such measures.

3. A request for interim measures addressed by a party to a judicial authority shall not be deemed incompatible with the agreement to arbitrate or a waiver of the right to arbitrate.

Experts

Article 23

1. The tribunal may appoint one or more independent experts to report to it, in writing, on specific issues designated by the tribunal and communicated to the parties.

2. The parties shall provide such an expert with any relevant information or produce for inspection any relevant documents or goods that the expert may require. Any dispute between a party and the expert as to the relevance of the requested information or goods shall be referred to the tribunal for decision.

3. Upon receipt of an expert's report, the tribunal shall send a copy of the report to all parties, who shall be given an opportunity to express, in writing, their opinion on the report. A party may examine any document on which the expert has relied in such a report.

4. At the request of any party, the parties shall be given an opportunity to question the expert at a hearing. At this hearing, parties may present expert witnesses to testify on the points at issue.

Default

Article 24

1. If a party fails to file a statement of defense within the time established by the tribunal without showing sufficient cause for such failure, as determined by the tribunal, the tribunal may proceed with the arbitration.

2. If a party, duly notified under these rules, fails to appear at a hearing without showing sufficient cause for such failure, as determined by the tribunal, the tribunal may proceed with the arbitration.

3. If a party, duly invited to produce evidence, fails to do so within the time established by the tribunal without showing sufficient cause for such failure, as determined by the tribunal, the tribunal may make the award on the evidence before it.

Closure of Hearing

Article 25

1. After asking the parties if they have any further testimony or evidentiary submissions and upon receiving negative replies or if satisfied that the record is complete, the tribunal may declare the hearings closed.

2. If it considers it appropriate, on its own motion or upon application of a party, the tribunal may reopen the hearings at any time before the award is made.

Waiver of Rules

Article 26

A party who knows that any provision of the rules or requirement under the rules has not been complied with, but proceeds with the arbitration without promptly stating an objection in writing thereto, shall be deemed to have waived the right to object.

Awards, Decisions and Rulings

Article 27

1. When there is more than one arbitrator, any award, decision or ruling of the arbitral tribunal shall be made by a majority of the arbitrators.

2. When the parties or the tribunal so authorize, decisions or rulings on questions of procedure may be made by the presiding arbitrator, subject to revision by the tribunal.

Form and Effect of the Award

Article 28

1. Awards shall be made in writing, promptly by the tribunal, and shall be final and binding on the parties. The parties undertake to carry out any such award without delay.

2. The tribunal shall state the reasons upon which the award is based, unless the parties have agreed that no reasons need be given.

3. An award signed by a majority of the arbitrators shall be sufficient. Where there are three arbitrators and one of them fails to sign, the award shall be accompanied by a statement of whether the third arbitrator was given the opportunity to sign. The award shall contain the date and the place where the award was made, which shall be the place designated pursuant to Article 13.

4. An award may be made public only with the consent of all parties or as required by law.

5. Copies of the award shall be communicated to the parties by the administrator.

6. If the arbitration law of the country where the award is made requires the award to be filed or registered, the tribunal shall comply with such requirement.

7. In addition to making a final award, the tribunal may make interim, interlocutory, or partial orders and awards.

Applicable Laws

Article 29

1. The tribunal shall apply the substantive law or laws designated by the parties as applicable to the dispute. Failing such a designation by the parties, the tribunal shall apply such law or laws as it determines to be appropriate.

2. In arbitrations involving the application of contracts, the tribunal shall decide in accordance with the terms of the contract and shall take into account usages of the trade applicable to the contract.

3. The tribunal shall not decide as *amiable compositeur* or *ex aequo et bono* unless the parties have expressly authorized it to do so.

Settlement or Other Reasons for Termination

Article 30

1. If the parties settle the dispute before an award is made, the tribunal shall terminate the arbitration and, if requested by all parties, may record the settlement in the form of an award on agreed terms. The tribunal is not obliged to give reasons for such an award.

2. If the continuation of the proceedings becomes unnecessary or impossible for any other reason, the tribunal shall inform the parties of its intention to terminate the proceedings. The tribunal shall thereafter issue an order terminating the arbitration, unless a party raises justifiable grounds for objection.

Interpretation or Correction of the Award

Article 31

1. Within thirty days after the receipt of an award, any party, with notice to the other parties, may request the tribunal to interpret the award or correct any clerical, typographical or computation errors or make an additional award as to claims presented but omitted from the award.

2. If the tribunal considers such a request justified, after considering the contentions of the parties, it shall comply with such a request within thirty days after the request.

Costs

Article 32

The tribunal shall fix the costs of arbitration in its award. The tribunal may apportion such costs among the parties if it determines that such apportionment is reasonable, taking into account the circumstances of the case. Such costs may include:

(a) the fees and expenses of the arbitrators;

(b) the costs of assistance required by the tribunal, including its experts;

(c) the fees and expenses of the administrator;

(d) the reasonable costs for legal representation of a successful party.

Compensation of Arbitrators

Article 33

Arbitrators shall be compensated based upon their amount of service, taking into account the size and complexity of the case. An appropriate daily or hourly rate, based on such considerations, shall be arranged by the administrator with the parties and the arbitrators prior to the commencement of the arbitration. If the parties fail to agree on the terms of compensation, an appropriate rate shall be established by the administrator and communicated in writing to the parties.

Deposit of Costs

Article 34

1. When claims are filed, the administrator may request the filing party to deposit appropriate amounts, as an advance for the costs referred to in Article 32, paragraphs (a), (b) and (c).

2. During the course of the arbitral proceedings, the tribunal may request supplementary deposits from the parties.

3. If the deposits requested are not paid in full within thirty days after the receipt of the request, the administrator shall so inform the parties, in order that one or the other of them may make the required payment. If such payments are not made, the tribunal may order the suspension or termination of the proceedings.

4. After the award has been made, the administrator shall render an accounting to the parties of the deposits received and return any unexpended balance to the parties.

Confidentiality

Article 35

Confidential information disclosed during the proceedings by the parties or by witnesses shall not be divulged by an arbitrator or by the administrator. Unless otherwise agreed by the parties, or required by applicable law, the members of the tribunal and the administrator shall keep confidential all matters relating to the arbitration or the award.

Exclusion of Liability

Article 36

The members of the tribunal and the administrator shall not be liable to any party for any act or omission in connection with any arbitration conducted under these rules.

Interpretation of Rules

Article 37

The tribunal shall interpret and apply these rules insofar as they relate to its powers and duties. All other rules shall be interpreted and applied by the administrator.

Administrative Fees

The AAA's administrative charges are based on filing and service fees. Arbitrator compensation, if any, is not included in this schedule. Unless the parties agree otherwise, arbitrator compensation and administrative fees are subject to allocation by the arbitrator in the award.

Filing Fees

A nonrefundable filing fee is payable in full by a filing party when a claim, counterclaim or additional claim is filed, as provided below.

Amount of Claim	Filing Fee
Up to $10,000	$500
Above $10,000 to $50,000 . . .	$750
Above $50,000 to $250,000 . .	$1,500
Above $250,000 to $500,000 .	$3,000
Above $500,000 to $1,000,000	$4,000
Above $1 million	$5,000

When no amount can be stated at the time of filing, the minimum filing fee is $1,500, subject to increase when the claim or counterclaim is disclosed.

When a claim or counterclaim is not for a monetary amount, an appropriate filing fee will be determined by the AAA.

The minimum filing fee for any case having three or more arbitrators is $1,500.

Hearing Fees

For each day of hearing held before a single arbitrator, an administrative fee of $150 is payable by each party.

For each day of hearing held before a multiarbitrator panel, an administrative fee of $200 is payable by each party.

Postponement/Cancellation Fees

A fee of $150 is payable by a party causing a postponement of any hearing scheduled before a single arbitrator.

A fee of $200 is payable by a party causing a postponement of any hearing scheduled before a multiarbitrator panel.

Processing Fees

On single-arbitrator cases, a processing fee of $150 per party is payable 180 days after the case is initiated, and every 90 days thereafter, until the case is withdrawn or settled or the hearings are closed by the arbitrator.

On multiarbitrator cases, a processing fee of $200 per party is payable 180 days after the case is initiated, and every 90 days thereafter, until the case is withdrawn or settled or the hearings are closed by the arbitrators.

Suspension for Nonpayment

If arbitrator compensation or administrative charges have not been paid in full, the AAA may so inform the parties in order that one of them may advance the required payment. If such payments are not made, the arbitrator may order the suspension or termination of the proceedings. If no arbitrator has yet been appointed, the AAA may suspend the proceedings.

Hearing Room Rental

The Hearing Fees described above do not cover the rental of hearing rooms, which are available on a rental basis. Check with our local office for availability and rates.

Convention on the Settlement of Investment Disputes Between States and Nationals of Other States (ICSID Convention)

Source of text: Done at Washington, D.C., March 18, 1965, entered into force for the United States, October 14, 1966, 17 U.S.T. 1270, T.I.A.S. No. 6090, 575 U.N.T.S. 159, Doc. ICSID/15 (1985), reprinted in 4 I.L.M. 532 (1965).

Preamble

The Contracting States

Considering the need for international cooperation for economic development, and the role of private international investment therein,

Bearing in mind the possibility that from time to time disputes may arise in connection with such investment between Contracting States and nationals of other Contracting States;

Recognizing that while such disputes would usually be subject to national legal processes, international methods of settlement may be appropriate in certain cases;

Attaching particular importance to the availability of facilities for international conciliation or arbitration to which Contracting States and nationals of other Contracting States may submit such disputes if they so desire;

Desiring to establish such facilities under the auspices of the International Bank for Reconstruction and Development;

Recognizing that mutual consent by the parties to submit such disputes to conciliation or to arbitration through such facilities constitutes a binding agreement which requires in particular that due consideration be given to any recommendation of conciliators, and that any arbitral award be complied with; and

Declaring that no Contracting State shall by the mere fact of its ratification, acceptance or approval of this Convention and without its consent be deemed to be under any obligation to submit any particular dispute to conciliation or arbitration,

Have agreed as follows:

Chapter I
International Centre for Settlement of Investment Disputes

Section 1
Establishment and Organization

Article 1

1. There is hereby established the International Centre for Settlement of Investment Disputes (hereinafter called the Centre).

2. The purpose of the Centre shall be to provide facilities for conciliation and arbitration of investment disputes between Contracting States and nationals of other Contracting States in accordance with the provisions of this Convention.

Article 2

The seat of the Centre shall be at the principal office of the International Bank for Reconstruction and Development (hereinafter called the Bank). The seat may be moved to another place by decision of the Administrative Council adopted by a majority two-thirds of its members.

Article 3

The Centre shall have an Administrative Council and a Secretariat and shall maintain a Panel of Conciliators and a Panel of Arbitrators.

Section 2

The Administrative Council

Article 4

1. The Administrative Council shall be composed of one representative of each Contracting State. An alternate may act as representative in case of his principal's absence from a meeting or inability to act.

2. In the absence of a contrary designation, each governor and alternate governor of the Bank appointed by a Contracting State shall be ex officio its representative and its alternate respectively.

Article 5

The President of the Bank shall be ex officio Chairman of the Administrative Council (hereinafter called the Chairman) but shall have no vote. During his absence or inability to act and during any vacancy in the office of President of the Bank, the person for the time being acting as President shall act as Chairman of the Administrative Council.

Article 6

1. Without prejudice to the powers and functions vested in it by other provisions of this Convention, the Administrative Council shall

(a) adopt the administrative and financial regulations of the Centre;

(b) adopt the rules of procedure for the institution of conciliation and arbitration proceedings;

(c) adopt the rules of procedure for conciliation and arbitration proceedings (hereinafter called the Conciliation Rules and the Arbitration Rules);

(d) approve arrangements with the Bank for the use of the Bank's administrative facilities and services;

(e) determine the conditions of service of the Secretary-General and of any Deputy Secretary-General;

(f) adopt the annual budget of revenues and expenditures of the Centre;

(g) approve the annual report on the operation of the Centre.

The decisions referred to in sub-paragraphs (a), (b), (c) and (f) above shall be adopted by a majority of two-thirds of the members of the Administrative Council.

2. The Administrative Council may appoint such committees as it considers necessary.

3. The Administrative Council shall also exercise such other powers and perform such other functions as it shall determine to be necessary for the implementation of the provisions of this Convention.

Article 7

1. The Administrative Council shall hold an annual meeting and such other meetings as may be determined by the Council, or convened by the Chairman, or convened by the Secretary-General at the request of not less than five members of the Council.

2. Each member of the Administrative Council shall have one vote and, except as otherwise herein provided, all matters before the Council shall be decided by a majority of the votes cast.

3. A quorum for any meeting of the Administrative Council shall be a majority of its members.

4. The Administrative Council may establish, by a majority of two-thirds of its members, a procedure whereby the Chairman may seek a vote of the Council without convening a meeting of the Council. The vote shall be considered valid only if the majority of the members of the Council cast their votes within the time limit fixed by the said procedure.

Article 8

Members of the Administrative Council and the Chairman shall serve without remuneration from the Centre.

Section 3

The Secretariat

Article 9

The Secretariat shall consist of a Secretary-General, one or more Deputy Secretaries-General and staff.

Article 10

1. The Secretary-General and any Deputy Secretary-General shall be elected by the Administrative Council by a majority of two-thirds of its members upon the nomination of the Chairman for a term of service not exceeding six years and shall be eligible for re-election. After consulting the members of the Administrative Council, the Chairman shall propose one or more candidates for each such office.

2. The offices of Secretary-General and Deputy Secretary-General shall be incompatible with the exercise of any political function. Neither the Secretary-General nor any Deputy Secretary-General may hold any other employment or engage in any other occupation except with the approval of the Administrative Council.

3. During the Secretary-General's absence or inability to act, and during any vacancy of the office of Secretary-General, the Deputy Secretary-General shall act as Secretary-General. If there shall be more than one Deputy Secretary-General, the Administrative Council shall determine in advance the order in which they shall act as Secretary-General.

Article 11

The Secretary-General shall be the legal representative and the principal officer of the Centre and shall be responsible for its administration, including the appointment of staff, in accordance with the provisions of this Convention and the rules adopted by the Administrative Council. He shall perform the function of registrar and shall have the power to authenticate arbitral awards rendered pursuant to this Convention, and to certify copies thereof.

Section 4

The Panels

Article 12

The Panel of Conciliators and the Panel of Arbitrators shall each consist of qualified persons, designated as hereinafter provided, who are willing to serve thereon.

Article 13

1. Each Contracting State may designate to each Panel four persons who may but need not be its nationals.

2. The Chairman may designate ten persons to each Panel. The persons so designated to a Panel shall each have a different nationality.

Article 14

1. Persons designated to serve on the Panels shall be persons of high moral character and recognized competence in the fields of law,

commerce, industry or finance, who may be relied upon to exercise independent judgment. Competence in the field of law shall be of particular importance in the case of persons on the Panel of Arbitrators.

2. The Chairman, in designating persons to serve on the Panels, shall in addition pay due regard to the importance of assuring representation on the Panels of the principal legal systems of the world and of the main forms of economic activity.

Article 15

1. Panel members shall serve for renewable periods of six years.

2. In case of death or resignation of a member of a Panel, the authority which designated the member shall have the right to designate another person to serve for the remainder of that member's term.

3. Panel members shall continue in office until their successors have been designated.

Article 16

1. A person may serve on both Panels.

2. If a person shall have been designated to serve on the same Panel by more than one Contracting State, or by one or more Contracting States and the Chairman, he shall be deemed to have been designated by the authority which first designated him or, if one such authority is the State of which he is a national, by that State.

3. All designations shall be notified to the Secretary-General and shall take effect from the date on which the notification is received.

Section 5

Financing the Centre

Article 17

If the expenditure of the Centre cannot be met out of charges for the use of its facilities, or out of other receipts, the excess shall be borne by Contracting States which are members of the Bank in proportion to their respective subscriptions to the capital stock of the Bank, and by Contracting States which are not members of the Bank in accordance with rules adopted by the Administrative Council.

Section 6

Status, Immunities and Privileges

Article 18

The Centre shall have full international legal personality. The legal capacity of the Centre shall include the capacity

(a) to contract;

(b) to acquire and dispose of movable and immovable property;

(c) to institute legal proceedings.

Article 19

To enable the Centre to fulfil its functions, it shall enjoy in the territories of each Contracting State the immunities and privileges set forth in this Section.

Article 20

The Centre, its property and assets shall enjoy immunity from all legal process, except when the Centre waives this immunity.

Article 21

The Chairman, the members of the Administrative Council, persons acting as conciliators or arbitrators or members of a Committee appointed pursuant to paragraph 3 of Article 52, and the officers and employees of the Secretariat

(a) shall enjoy immunity from legal process with respect to acts performed by them in the exercise of their functions, except when the Centre waives this immunity;

(b) not being local nationals, shall enjoy the same immunities from immigration restrictions, alien registration requirements and national service obligations, the same facilities as regards exchange restrictions and the same treatment in respect of travelling facilities as are accorded by Contracting States to the representatives, officials and employees of comparable rank of other Contracting States.

Article 22

The provisions of Article 21 shall apply to persons appearing in proceedings under this Convention as parties, agents, counsel, advocates, witnesses or experts; provided, however, that sub-paragraph (b) thereof shall apply only in connection with their travel to and from, and their stay at, the place where the proceedings are held.

Article 23

1. The archives of the Centre shall be inviolable, wherever they may be.

2. With regard to its official communications, the Centre shall be accorded by each Contracting State treatment not less favourable than that accorded to other international organizations.

Article 24

1. The Centre, its assets, property and income, and its operations and transactions authorized by this Convention shall be exempt from

all taxation and customs duties. The Centre shall also be exempt from liability for the collection or payment of any taxes or customs duties.

2. Except in the case of local nationals, no tax shall be levied on or in respect of expense allowances paid by the Centre to the Chairman or members of the Administrative Council, or on or in respect of salaries, expense allowances or other emoluments paid by the Centre to officials or employees of the Secretariat.

3. No tax shall be levied on or in respect of fees or expense allowances received by persons acting as conciliators, or arbitrators, or members of a Committee appointed pursuant to paragraph 3 of Article 52, in proceedings under this Convention, if the sole jurisdictional basis for such tax is the location of the Centre or the place where such proceedings are conducted or the place where such fees or allowances are paid.

Chapter II
Jurisdiction of the Centre

Article 25

1. The jurisdiction of the Centre shall extend to any legal dispute arising directly out of an investment, between a Contracting State (or any constituent subdivision or agency of a Contracting State designated to the Centre by that State) and a national of another Contracting State, which the parties to the dispute consent in writing to submit to the Centre. When the parties have given their consent, no party may withdraw its consent unilaterally.

2. "National of another Contracting State" means:

(a) any natural person who had the nationality of a Contracting State other than the State party to the dispute on the date on which the parties consented to submit such dispute to conciliation or arbitration as well as on the date on which the request was registered pursuant to paragraph 3 of Article 28 or paragraph 3 of Article 36, but does not include any person who on either date also had the nationality of the Contracting State party to the dispute; and

(b) any juridical person which had the nationality of a Contracting State other than the State party to the dispute on the date on which the parties consented to submit such dispute to conciliation or arbitration and any juridical person which had the nationality of the Contracting State party to the dispute on that date and which, because of foreign control, the parties have agreed should be treated as a national of another Contracting State for the purposes of this Convention.

3. Consent by a constituent subdivision or agency of a Contracting State shall require the approval of that State unless that State notifies the Centre that no such approval is required.

4. Any Contracting State may, at the time of ratification, acceptance or approval of this Convention or at any time thereafter, notify the Centre of the class or classes of disputes which it would or would not consider submitting to the jurisdiction of the Centre. The Secretary-General shall forthwith transmit such notification to all Contracting States. Such notification shall not constitute the consent required by paragraph 1.

Article 26

Consent of the parties to arbitration under this Convention shall, unless otherwise stated, be deemed consent to such arbitration to the exclusion of any other remedy. A Contracting State may require the exhaustion of local administrative or judicial remedies as a condition of its consent to arbitration under this Convention.

Article 27

1. No Contracting State shall give diplomatic protection, or bring an international claim, in respect of a dispute which one of its nationals and another Contracting State shall have consented to submit or shall have submitted to arbitration under this Convention, unless such other Contracting State shall have failed to abide by and comply with the award rendered in such dispute.

2. Diplomatic protection, for the purposes of paragraph 1, shall not include informal diplomatic exchanges for the sole purpose of facilitating a settlement of the dispute.

Chapter III
Conciliation

Section 1
Request for Conciliation

Article 28

1. Any Contracting State or any national of a Contracting State wishing to institute conciliation proceedings shall address a request to that effect in writing to the Secretary-General who shall send a copy of the request to the other party.

2. The request shall contain information concerning the issues in dispute, the identity of the parties and their consent to conciliation in accordance with the rules of procedure for the institution of conciliation and arbitration proceedings.

3. The Secretary-General shall register the request unless he finds, on the basis of the information contained in the request, that the

dispute is manifestly outside the jurisdiction of the Centre. He shall forthwith notify the parties of registration or refusal to register.

Section 2

Constitution of the Conciliation Commission

Article 29

1. The Conciliation Commission (hereinafter called the Commission) shall be constituted as soon as possible after registration of a request pursuant to Article 28.

2.(a) The Commission shall consist of a sole conciliator or any uneven number of conciliators appointed as the parties shall agree.

(b) Where the parties do not agree upon the number of conciliators and the method of their appointment, the Commission shall consist of three conciliators, one conciliator appointed by each party and the third, who shall be the president of the Commission, appointed by agreement of the parties.

Article 30

If the Commission shall not have been constituted within 90 days after notice of registration of the request has been dispatched by the Secretary-General in accordance with paragraph 3 of Article 28, or such other period as the parties may agree, the Chairman shall, at the request of either party and after consulting both parties as far as possible, appoint the conciliator or conciliators not yet appointed.

Article 31

1. Conciliators may be appointed from outside the Panel of Conciliators, except in the case of appointments by the Chairman pursuant to Article 30.

2. Conciliators appointed from outside the Panel of Conciliators shall possess the qualities stated in paragraph 1 of Article 14.

Section 3

Conciliation Proceedings

Article 32

1. The Commission shall be the judge of its own competence.

2. Any objection by a party to the dispute that dispute is not within the jurisdiction of the Centre, or for other reasons is not within the competence of the Commission, shall be considered by the Commission which shall determine whether to deal with it as a preliminary question or to join it to the merits of the dispute.

Article 33

Any conciliation proceeding shall be conducted in accordance with the provisions of this Section and, except as the parties otherwise agree, in accordance with the Conciliation Rules in effect on the date on which the parties consented to conciliation. If any question of procedure arises which is not covered by this Section or the Conciliation Rules or any rules agreed by the parties, the Commission shall decide the question.

Article 34

1. It shall be the duty of the Commission to clarify the issues in dispute between the parties and to endeavour to bring about agreement between them upon mutually acceptable terms. To that end, the Commission may at any stage of the proceedings and from time to time recommend terms of settlement to the parties. The parties shall cooperate in good faith with the Commission in order to enable the Commission to carry out its functions, and shall give their most serious consideration to its recommendations.

2. If the parties reach agreement, the Commission shall draw up a report noting the issues in dispute and recording that the parties have reached agreement. If, at any stage of the proceedings, it appears to the Commission that there is no likelihood of agreement between the parties, it shall close the proceedings and shall draw up a report noting the submission of the dispute and recording the failure of the parties to reach agreement. If one party fails to appear or participate in the proceedings, the Commission shall close the proceedings and shall draw up a report noting that party's failure to appear or participate.

Article 35

Except as the parties to the dispute shall otherwise agree, neither party to a conciliation proceeding shall be entitled in any other proceeding, whether before arbitrators or in a court of law or otherwise, to invoke or rely on any views expressed or statements or admissions or offers of settlement made by the other party in the conciliation proceedings, or the report or any recommendations made by the Commission.

Chapter IV
Arbitration

Section 1
Request for Arbitration

Article 36

1. Any Contracting State or any national of a Contracting State wishing to institute arbitration proceedings shall address a request to

that effect in writing to the Secretary-General who shall send a copy of the request to the other party.

2. The request shall contain information concerning the issues in dispute, the identity of the parties and their consent to arbitration in accordance with the rules of procedure for the institution of conciliation and arbitration proceedings.

3. The Secretary-General shall register the request unless he finds, on the basis of the information contained in the request, that the dispute is manifestly outside the jurisdiction of the Centre. He shall forthwith notify the parties of registration or refusal to register.

Section 2

Constitution of the Tribunal

Article 37

1. The Arbitral Tribunal (hereinafter called the Tribunal) shall be constituted as soon as possible after registration of a request pursuant to Article 36.

2.(a) The Tribunal shall consist of a sole arbitrator or any uneven number of arbitrators appointed as the parties shall agree.

(b) Where the parties do not agree upon the number of arbitrators and the method of their appointment, the Tribunal shall consist of three arbitrators, one arbitrator appointed by each party and the third, who shall be the president of the Tribunal, appointed by agreement of the parties.

Article 38

If the Tribunal shall not have been constituted within 90 days after notice of registration of the request has been dispatched by the Secretary-General in accordance with paragraph 3 of Article 36, or such other period as the parties may agree, the Chairman shall, at the request of either party and after consulting both parties as far as possible, appoint the arbitrator or arbitrators not yet appointed. Arbitrators appointed by the Chairman pursuant to this article shall not be nationals of the Contracting State party to the dispute or of the Contracting State whose national is a party to the dispute.

Article 39

The majority of the arbitrators shall be nationals of States other than the Contracting State party to the dispute and the Contracting State whose national is a party to the dispute; provided, however, that the foregoing provisions of this article shall not apply if the sole arbitrator or each individual member of the Tribunal has been appointed by agreement of the parties.

Article 40

1. Arbitrators may be appointed from outside the Panel of Arbitrators, except in the case of appointments by the Chairman pursuant to Article 38.

2. Arbitrators appointed from outside the Panel of Arbitrators shall possess the qualities stated in paragraph 1 of Article 14.

Section 3

Powers and Functions of the Tribunal

Article 41

1. The Tribunal shall be the judge of its own competence.

2. Any objection by a party to the dispute that dispute is not within the jurisdiction of the Centre, or for other reasons is not within the competence of the Tribunal, shall be considered by the Tribunal which shall determine whether to deal with it as a preliminary question or to join it to the merits of the dispute.

Article 42

1. The Tribunal shall decide a dispute in accordance with such rules of law as may be agreed by the parties. In the absence of such agreement, the Tribunal shall apply the law of the Contracting State party to the dispute (including its rules on the conflict of laws) and such rules of international law as may be applicable.

2. The Tribunal may not bring in a finding of non liquet on the ground of silence or obscurity of the law.

3. The provisions of paragraphs 1 and 2 shall not prejudice the power of the Tribunal to decide a dispute ex aequo et bono if the parties so agree.

Article 43

Except as the parties otherwise agree, the Tribunal may, if it deems it necessary at any stage of the proceedings,

(a) call upon the parties to produce documents or other evidence, and

(b) visit the scene connected with the dispute, and conduct such inquiries there as it may deem appropriate.

Article 44

Any arbitration proceeding shall be conducted in accordance with the provisions of this Section and, except as the parties otherwise agree, in accordance with the Arbitration Rules in effect on the date on which the parties consented to arbitration. If any question of procedure arises which is not covered by this Section or the Arbitration Rules or any rules agreed by the parties, the Tribunal shall decide the question.

Article 45

1. Failure of a party to appear or to present his case shall not be deemed an admission of the other party's assertions.

2. If a party fails to appear or to present his case at any stage of the proceedings the other party may request the Tribunal to deal with the questions submitted to it and to render an award. Before rendering an questions submitted to it and to render an award. Before rendering an award, the Tribunal shall notify, and grant a period of grace to, the party failing to appear or to present its case, unless it is satisfied that party does not intend to do so.

Article 46

Except as the parties otherwise agree, the Tribunal shall, if requested by a party, determine any incidental or additional claims or counter-claims arising directly out of the subject-matter of the dispute provided that they are within the scope of the consent of the parties and are otherwise within the jurisdiction of the Centre.

Article 47

Except as the parties otherwise agree, the Tribunal may, if it considers that the circumstances so require, recommend any provisional measures which should be taken to preserve the respective rights of either party.

Section 4

The Award

Article 48

1. The Tribunal shall decide questions by a majority of the votes of all its members.

2. The award of the Tribunal shall be in writing and shall be signed by the members of the Tribunal who voted for it.

3. The award shall deal with every question submitted to the Tribunal, and shall state the reasons upon which it is based.

4. Any member of the Tribunal may attach his individual opinion to the award, whether he dissents from the majority or not, or a statement of his dissent.

5. The Centre shall not publish the award without the consent of the parties.

Article 49

1. The Secretary-General shall promptly dispatch certified copies of the award to the parties. The award shall be deemed to have been rendered on the date on which the certified copies were dispatched.

2. The Tribunal upon the request of a party made within 45 days after the date on which the award was rendered may after notice to the other party decide any question which it had omitted to decide in the award, and shall rectify any clerical, arithmetical or similar error in the award. Its decision shall become part of the award and shall be notified to the parties in the same manner as the award. The periods of time provided for under paragraph 2 of Article 51 and paragraph 2 of Article 52 shall run from the date on which the decision was rendered.

Section 5

Interpretation, Revision and Annulment of the Award

Article 50

1. If any dispute shall arise between the parties as to the meaning or scope of an award, either party may request interpretation of the award by an application in writing addressed to the Secretary-General.

2. The request shall, if possible, be submitted to the Tribunal which rendered the award. If this shall not be possible, a new Tribunal shall be constituted in accordance with Section 2 of this chapter. The Tribunal may, if it considers that the circumstances so require, stay enforcement of the award pending its decision.

Article 51

1. Either party may request revision of the award by an application in writing addressed to the Secretary-General on the ground of discovery of some fact of such a nature as decisively to affect the award, provided that when the award was rendered that fact was unknown to the Tribunal and to the applicant and that the applicant's ignorance of that fact was not due to negligence.

2. The application shall be made within 90 days after the discovery of such fact and in any event within three years after the date on which the award was rendered.

3. The request shall, if possible, be submitted to the Tribunal which rendered the award. If this shall not be possible, a new Tribunal shall be constituted in accordance with Section 2 of this chapter.

4. The Tribunal may, if it considers that the circumstances so require, stay enforcement of the award pending its decision. If the applicant requests a stay of enforcement of the award in his application, enforcement shall be stayed provisionally until the Tribunal rules on such request.

Article 52

1. Either party may request annulment of the award by an application in writing addressed to the Secretary-General on one or more of the following grounds:

(a) that the Tribunal was not properly constituted;

(b) that the Tribunal has manifestly exceeded it powers;

(c) that there was corruption on the part of a member of the Tribunal;

(d) that there has been a serious departure from a fundamental rule of procedure; or

(e) that the award has failed to state the reasons on which it is based.

2. The application shall be made within 120 days after the date on which the award was rendered except that when annulment is requested on the ground of corruption such application shall be made within 120 days after discovery of the corruption and in any event within three years after the date on which the award was rendered.

3. On receipt of the request the Chairman shall forthwith appoint from the Panel of Arbitrators an ad hoc Committee of three persons. None of the members of the Committee shall have been a member of the Tribunal which rendered the award, shall be of the same nationality as any such member, shall be a national of the State party to the dispute or of the State whose national is a party to the dispute, shall have been designated to the Panel of Arbitrators by either of those States, or shall have acted as a conciliator in the same dispute. The Committee shall have the authority to annul the award or any part thereof on any of the grounds set forth in paragraph 1.

4. The provisions of Articles 41 to 45, 48, 49, 53 and 54, and of Chapters VI and VII shall apply mutatis mutandis to proceedings before the Committee.

5. The Committee may, if it considers that the circumstances so require, stay enforcement of the award pending its decision. If the applicant requests a stay of enforcement of the award in his application, enforcement shall be stayed provisionally until the Committee rules on such request.

6. If the award is annulled the dispute shall, at the request of either party, be submitted to a new Tribunal constituted in accordance with Section 2 of this chapter.

Section 6

Recognition and Enforcement of the Award

Article 53

1. The award shall be binding on the parties and shall not be subject to any appeal or to any other remedy except those provided for in this Convention. Each party shall abide by and comply with the terms of the award except to the extent that enforcement shall have been stayed pursuant to the relevant provisions of this Convention.

2. For the purposes of this Section, "award" shall include any decision interpreting, revising or annulling such award pursuant to Articles 50, 51 or 52.

Article 54

1. Each Contracting State shall recognize an award rendered pursuant to this Convention as binding and enforce the pecuniary obligations imposed by that award within its territories as if it were a final judgment of a court in that State. A Contracting State with a federal constitution may enforce such an award in or through its federal courts and may provide that such courts shall treat the award as if it were a final judgment of the courts of a constituent state.

2. A party seeking recognition or enforcement in the territories of a Contracting State shall furnish to a competent court or other authority which such State shall have designated for this purpose a copy of the award certified by the Secretary-General. Each Contracting State shall notify the Secretary-General of the designation of the competent court or other authority for this purpose and of any subsequent change in such designation.

3. Execution of the award shall be governed by the laws concerning the execution of judgments in force in the State in whose territories such execution is sought.

Article 55

Nothing in Article 54 shall be construed as derogating from the law in force in any Contracting State relating to immunity of that State or of any foreign State from execution.

Chapter V

Replacement and Disqualification of Conciliators and Arbitrators

Article 56

1. After a Commission or a Tribunal has been constituted and proceedings have begun, its composition shall remain unchanged; provided, however, that if a conciliator or an arbitrator should die, become incapacitated, or resign, the resulting vacancy shall be filled in accor-

dance with the provisions of Section 2 of Chapter III or Section 2 of Chapter IV.

2. A member of a Commission or Tribunal shall continue to serve in that capacity notwithstanding that he shall have ceased to be a member of the Panel.

3. If a conciliator or arbitrator appointed by a party shall have resigned without the consent of the Commission or Tribunal of which he was a member, the Chairman shall appoint a person from the appropriate Panel to fill the resulting vacancy.

Article 57

A party may propose to a Commission or Tribunal the disqualification of any of its members on account of any fact indicating a manifest lack of the qualities required by paragraph 1 of Article 14. A party to arbitration proceedings may, in addition, propose the disqualification of an arbitrator on the ground that he was ineligible for appointment to the Tribunal under Section 2 of Chapter IV.

Article 58

The decision on any proposal to disqualify a conciliator or arbitrator shall be taken by the other members of the Commission or Tribunal as the case may be, provided that where those members are equally divided, or in the case of a proposal to disqualify a sole conciliator or arbitrator, or a majority of the conciliators or arbitrators, the Chairman shall take that decision. If it is decided that the proposal is well-founded the conciliator or arbitrator to whom the decision relates shall be replaced in accordance with the provisions of Section 2 of Chapter III or Section 2 of Chapter IV.

Chapter VI
Cost of Proceedings

Article 59

The charges payable by the parties for the use of the facilities of the Centre shall be determined by the Secretary-General in accordance with the regulations adopted by the Administrative Council.

Article 60

1. Each Commission and each Tribunal shall determine the fees and expenses of its members within limits established from time to time by the Administrative Council and after consultation with the Secretary-General.

2. Nothing in paragraph I of this article shall preclude the parties from agreeing in advance with the Commission or Tribunal concerned upon the fees and expenses of its members.

Article 61

1. In the case of conciliation proceedings the fees and expenses of members of the Commission as well as the charges for the use of the facilities of the Centre, shall be borne equally by the parties. Each party shall bear any other expenses it incurs in connection with the proceedings.

2. In the case of arbitration proceedings the Tribunal shall, except as the parties otherwise agree, assess the expenses incurred by the parties in connection with the proceedings, and shall decide how and by whom those expenses, the fees and expenses of the members of the Tribunal and the charges for the use of the facilities of the Centre shall be paid. Such decision shall form part of the award.

Chapter VII
Place of Proceedings

Article 62

Conciliation and arbitration proceedings shall be held at the seat of the Centre except as hereinafter provided.

Article 63

Conciliation and arbitration proceedings may be held, if the parties so agree,

(a) at the seat of the Permanent Court of Arbitration or of any other appropriate institution, whether private or public, with which the Centre may make arrangements for that purpose; or

(b) at any other place approved by the Commission or Tribunal after consultation with the Secretary-General.

Chapter VIII
Disputes between Contracting States

Article 64

Any dispute arising between Contracting States concerning the interpretation or application of this Convention which is not settled by negotiation shall be referred to the International Court of Justice by the application of any party to such dispute, unless the States concerned agree to another method of settlement.

Chapter IX
Amendment

Article 65

Any Contracting State may propose amendment of this Convention. The text of a proposed amendment shall be communicated to the Secretary-General not less than 90 days prior to the meeting of the Administrative Council at which such amendment is to be considered and shall forthwith be transmitted by him to all the members of the Administrative Council.

Article 66

1. If the Administrative Council shall so decide by a majority of two-thirds of its members, the proposed amendment shall be circulated to all Contracting States for ratification, acceptance or approval. Each amendment shall enter into force 30 days after dispatch by the depositary of this Convention of a notification to Contracting States that all Contracting States have ratified, accepted or approved the amendment.

2. No amendment shall affect the rights and obligations under this Convention of any Contracting State or of any of its constituent subdivisions or agencies, or of any national of such State arising out of consent to the jurisdiction of the Centre given before the date of entry into force of the amendment.

Chapter X
Final Provisions

Article 67

This Convention shall be open for signature on behalf of States members of the Bank. It shall also be open for signature on behalf of any other State which is a party to the Statute of the International Court of Justice and which the Administrative Council, by a vote of two-thirds of its members, shall have invited to sign the Convention.

Article 68

1. This Convention shall be subject to ratification, acceptance or approval by the signatory States in accordance with their respective constitutional procedures.

2. This Convention shall enter into force 30 days after the date of deposit of the 20th instrument of ratification, acceptance or approval. It shall enter into force for each State which subsequently deposits its instrument of ratification, acceptance or approval 30 days after the date of such deposit.

Article 69

Each Contracting State shall take such legislative or other measures as may be necessary for making the provisions of this Convention effective in its territories.

Article 70

This Convention shall apply to all territories for whose international relations a Contracting State is responsible, except those which are excluded by such State by written notice to the depositary of this

Convention either at the time of ratification, acceptance or approval or subsequently.

Article 71

Any Contracting State may denounce this Convention by written notice to the depositary of this Convention. The denunciation shall take effect six months after receipt of such notice.

Article 72

Notice by a Contracting State pursuant to Articles 70 or 71 shall not affect the rights or obligations under this Convention of that State or of any of its constituent subdivisions or agencies or of any national of that State arising out of consent to the jurisdiction of the Centre given by one of them before such notice was received by the depositary.

Article 73

Instruments of ratification, acceptance or approval of this Convention and of amendments thereto shall be deposited with the Bank which shall act as the depositary of this Convention The depositary shall transmit certified copies of this Convention to States members of the Bank and to any other State invited to sign the Convention.

Article 74

The depositary shall register this Convention with the Secretariat of the United Nations in accordance with Article 102 of the Charter of the United Nations and the Regulations thereunder adopted by the General Assembly.

Article 75

The depositary shall notify all signatory States of the following:

(a) signatures in accordance with Article 67;

(b) deposits of instruments of ratification, acceptance and approval in accordance with Article 73;

(c) the date on which this Convention enters into force in accordance with Article 68;

(d) exclusions from territorial application pursuant to Article 70;

(e) the date on which any amendment of this Convention enters into force in accordance with Article 66; and

(f) denunciations in accordance with Article 71.

The United States Arbitration Act (International)
Title 9, U.S. Code § § 201-208, 301-307
Chapter 2. CONVENTION ON THE RECOGNITION AND ENFORCEMENT OF FOREIGN ARBITRAL AWARDS

§ 201. Enforcement of Convention

The Convention on the Recognition and Enforcement of Foreign Arbitral Awards of June 10, 1958, shall be enforced in United States courts in accordance with this chapter.

§ 202. Agreement or award falling under the Convention

An arbitration agreement or arbitral award arising out of a legal relationship, whether contractual or not, which is considered as commercial, including a transaction, contract, or agreement described in section 2 of this title, falls under the Convention. An agreement or award arising out of such a relationship which is entirely between citizens of the United States shall be deemed not to fall under the Convention unless that relationship involves property located abroad, envisages performance or enforcement abroad, or has some other reasonable relation with one or more foreign states. For the purpose of this section a corporation is a citizen of the United States if it is incorporated or has its principal place of business in the United States.

§ 203. Jurisdiction; amount in controversy

An action or proceeding falling under the Convention shall be deemed to arise under the laws and treaties of the United States. The district courts of the United States (including the courts enumerated in section 460 of title 28) shall have original jurisdiction over such an action or proceeding, regardless of the amount in controversy.

§ 204. Venue

An action or proceeding over which the district courts have jurisdiction pursuant to section 203 of this title may be brought in any such court in which save for the arbitration agreement an action or proceeding with respect to the controversy between the parties could be brought, or in such court for the district and division which embraces the place designated in the agreement as the place of arbitration if such place is within the United States.

§ 205. Removal of cases from State courts

Where the subject matter of an action or proceeding pending in a State court relates to an arbitration agreement or award falling under the Convention, the defendant or the defendants may, at any time before the trial thereof, remove such action or proceeding to the district court of the United States for the district and division embracing the place where the action or proceeding is pending. The procedure for removal of causes otherwise provided by law shall apply, except that the ground for removal provided in this section need not appear on the face of the complaint but may be shown in the petition for removal. For the purposes of Chapter 1 of this title any action or proceeding removed under this section shall be deemed to have been brought in the district court to which it is removed.

§ 206. Order to compel arbitration; appointment of arbitrators

A court having jurisdiction under this chapter may direct that arbitration be held in accordance with the agreement at any place therein provided for, whether that place is within or without the United States. Such court may also appoint arbitrators in accordance with the provisions of the agreement.

§ 207. Award of arbitrators; confirmation; jurisdiction; proceeding

Within three years after an arbitral award falling under the Convention is made, any party to the arbitration may apply to any court having jurisdiction under this chapter for an order confirming the award as against any other party to the arbitration. The court shall confirm the award unless it finds one of the grounds for refusal or deferral of recognition or enforcement of the award specified in the said Convention.

§ 208. Chapter 1; residual application

Chapter 1 applies to actions and proceedings brought under this chapter to the extent that chapter is not in conflict with this chapter or the Convention as ratified by the United States.

Chapter 3. INTER-AMERICAN CONVENTION ON INTERNATIONAL COMMERCIAL ARBITRATION

§ 301. Enforcement of Convention

The Inter-American Convention on International Commercial Arbitration of January 30, 1975, shall be enforced in United States courts in accordance with this chapter.

§ 302. Incorporation by reference

Sections 202, 203, 204, 205, and 207 of this title shall apply to this chapter as if specifically set forth herein, except that for the purposes of this chapter "the Convention" shall mean the Inter-American Convention.

§ 303. Order to compel arbitration; appointment of arbitrators; locale

(a) A court having jurisdiction under this chapter may direct that arbitration be held in accordance with the agreement at any place therein provided for, whether that place is within or without the United States. The court may also appoint arbitrators in accordance with the provisions of the agreement.

(b) In the event the agreement does not make provision for the place of arbitration or the appointment of arbitrators, the court shall direct that the arbitration shall be held and the arbitrators be appointed in accordance with Article 3 of the Inter-American Convention.

§ 304. Recognition and enforcement of foreign arbitral decisions and awards; reciprocity

Arbitral decisions or awards made in the territory of a foreign State shall, on the basis of reciprocity, be recognized and enforced under this chapter only if that State has ratified or acceded to the Inter-American Convention.

§ 305. Relationship between the Inter-American Convention and the Convention on the Recognition and Enforcement of Foreign Arbitral Awards of June 10, 1958

When the requirements for application of both the Inter-American Convention and the Convention on the Recognition and Enforcement of Foreign Arbitral Awards of June 10, 1958, are met, determination as to which Convention applies shall, unless otherwise expressly agreed, be made as follows:

(1) If a majority of the parties to the arbitration agreement are citizens of a State or States that have ratified or acceded to the Inter-American Convention and are member States of the Organization of American States, the Inter-American Convention shall apply.

(2) In all other cases the Convention on the Recognition and Enforcement of Foreign Arbitral Awards of June 10, 1958, shall apply.

§ 306. Applicable rules of Inter-American Commercial Arbitration Commission

(a) For the purposes of this chapter the rules of procedure of the Inter-American Commercial Arbitration Commission referred to in Article 3 of the Inter-American Convention shall, subject to subsection (b) of this section, be those rules as promulgated by the Commission on July 1, 1988.

(b) In the event the rules of procedure of the Inter-American Commercial Arbitration Commission are modified or amended in accordance with the procedures for amendment of the rules of that Commission, the Secretary of State, by regulation in accordance with section 553 of title 5, consistent with the aims and purposes of this Convention, may prescribe that such modifications or amendments shall be effective for purposes of this chapter.

§ 307. Chapter 1; residual application

Chapter 1 applies to actions and proceedings brought under this chapter to the extent chapter 1 is not in conflict with this chapter or the Inter-American Convention as ratified by the United States.

The United States Foreign Sovereign Immunities Act

90 Stat. 2891, 28 U.S.C.A. § § 1330, 1332, 1391, 1602—1611 (1976), as amended
by PL 100-640, 102 Stat. 3333 (1988) and PL 100-669, 102 Stat. 3969 (1988)

§ 1330. Actions against foreign states

(a) The district courts shall have original jurisdiction without regard to amount in controversy of any nonjury civil action against a foreign state as defined in section 1603(a) of this title as to any claim for relief in personam with respect to which the foreign state is not entitled to immunity either under sections 1605-1607 of this title or under any applicable international agreement.

(b) Personal jurisdiction over a foreign state shall exist as to every claim for relief over which the district courts have jurisdiction under subsection (a) where service has been made under section 1608 of this title.

(c) For purposes of subsection (b), an appearance by a foreign state does not confer personal jurisdiction with respect to any claim for relief not arising out of any transaction or occurrence enumerated in sections 1605-1607 of this title.

§ 1332. Diversity of citizenship; amount in controversy; costs

(a) The district courts shall have original jurisdiction of all civil actions where the matter in controversy exceeds the sum or value of $50,000, exclusive of interest and costs, and is between—

(1) citizens of different States;

(2) citizens of a State and citizens or subjects of a foreign state;

(3) citizens of different States and in which citizens or subjects of a foreign state are additional parties; and

(4) a foreign state, defined in section 1603(a) of this title, as plaintiff and citizens of a State or of different States. For the purposes of this section, section 1335, and section 1441, an alien admitted to the United States for permanent residence shall be deemed a citizen of the State in which such alien is domiciled.

* * *

§ 1391. Venue generally

* * *

(f) A civil action against a foreign state as defined in section 1603(a) of this title may be brought—

(1) in any judicial district in which a substantial part of the events or omissions giving rise to the claim occurred, or a substantial part of property that is the subject of the action is situated;

(2) in any judicial district in which the vessel or cargo of a foreign state is situated, if the claim is asserted under section 1605(b) of this title;

(3) in any judicial district in which the agency or instrumentality is licensed to do business or is doing business, if the action is brought against an agency or instrumentality of a foreign state as defined in section 1603(b) of this title; or

(4) in the United States District Court for the District of Columbia if the action is brought against a foreign state or political subdivision thereof.

§ 1441. Actions removable generally

* * *

(d) Any civil action brought in a State court against a foreign state as defined in section 1603(a) of this title may be removed by the foreign state to the district court of the United States for the district and division embracing the place where such action is pending. Upon removal the action shall be tried by the court without jury. Where removal is based upon this subsection, the time limitations of section 1446(b) of this chapter may be enlarged at any time for cause shown.

* * *

§ 1602. Findings and declaration of purpose

The Congress finds that the determination by United States courts of the claims of foreign states to immunity from the jurisdiction of such courts would serve the interests of justice and would protect the rights of both foreign states and litigants in United States courts. Under international law, states are not immune from the jurisdiction of foreign courts insofar as their commercial activities are concerned, and their commercial property may be levied upon for the satisfaction of judgments rendered against them in connection with their commercial activities. Claims of foreign states to immunity should henceforth be decided by courts of the United States and of the States in conformity with the principles set forth in this chapter.

§ 1603. Definitions

For purposes of this chapter—

(a) A "foreign state", except as used in section 1608 of this title, includes a political subdivision of a foreign state or an agency or instrumentality of a foreign state as defined in subsection (b).

(b) An "agency or instrumentality of a foreign state" means any entity—

(1) which is a separate legal person, corporate or otherwise, and

(2) which is an organ of a foreign state or political subdivision thereof, or a majority of whose shares or other ownership interest is owned by a foreign state or political subdivision thereof, and

(3) which is neither a citizen of a State of the United States as defined in section 1332(c) and (d) of this title, nor created under the laws of any third country.

(c) The "United States" includes all territory and waters, continental or insular, subject to the jurisdiction of the United States.

(d) A "commercial activity" means either a regular course of commercial conduct or a particular commercial transaction or act. The commercial character of an activity shall be determined by reference to the nature of the course of conduct or particular transaction or act, rather than by reference to its purpose.

(e) A "commercial activity carried on in the United States by a foreign state" means commercial activity carried on by such state and having substantial contact with the United States.

§ 1604. Immunity of a foreign state from jurisdiction

Subject to existing international agreements to which the United States is a party at the time of enactment of this Act a foreign state shall be immune from the jurisdiction of the courts of the United States and of the States except as provided in sections 1605 to 1607 of this chapter.

§ 1605. General exceptions to the jurisdictional immunity of a foreign state

(a) A foreign state shall not be immune from the jurisdiction of courts of the United States or of the States in any case—

(1) in which the foreign state has waived its immunity either explicitly or by implication, notwithstanding any withdrawal of the waiver which the foreign state may purport to effect except in accordance with the terms of the waiver;

(2) in which the action is based upon a commercial activity carried on in the United States by the foreign state; or upon an act performed in the United States in connection with a commercial activity of the foreign state elsewhere; or upon an act outside the territory of the United States in connection with a commercial activity of the foreign state elsewhere and that act causes a direct effect in the United States;

(3) in which rights in property taken in violation of international law are in issue and that property or any property exchanged for such property is present in the United States in connection with a commercial activity carried on in the United States by the foreign state; or that property or any property exchanged for such property is owned or operated by an agency or instrumentality of the foreign state and that agency or instrumentality is engaged in a commercial activity in the United States;

(4) in which rights in property in the United States acquired by succession or gift or rights in immovable property situated in the United States are in issue;

(5) not otherwise encompassed in paragraph (2) above, in which money damages are sought against a foreign state for personal injury or death, or damage to or loss of property, occurring in the United States and caused by the tortious act or omission of that foreign state or of any official or employee of that foreign state while acting within the scope of his office or employment; except this paragraph shall not apply to—

(A) any claim based upon the exercise or performance or the failure to exercise or perform a discretionary function regardless of whether the discretion be abused, or

(B) any claim arising out of malicious prosecution, abuse of process, libel, slander, misrepresentation, deceit, or interference with contract rights; or

(6) in which the action is brought, either to enforce an agreement made by the foreign state with or for the benefit of a private party to submit to arbitration all or any differences which have arisen or which may arise between the parties with respect to a defined legal relationship, whether contractual or not, concerning a subject matter capable of settlement by arbitration under the laws of the United States, or to confirm an award made pursuant to such an agreement to arbitrate, if (A) the arbitration

takes place or is intended to take place in the United States, (B) the agreement or award is or may be governed by a treaty or other international agreement in force for the United States calling for the recognition and enforcement of arbitral awards, (C) the underlying claim, save for the agreement to arbitrate, could have been brought in a United States court under this section or section 1607, or (D) paragraph (1) of this subsection is otherwise applicable.

(b) A foreign state shall not be immune from the jurisdiction of the courts of the United States in any case in which a suit in admiralty is brought to enforce a maritime lien against a vessel or cargo of the foreign state, which maritime lien is based upon a commercial activity of the foreign state: Provided, That—

(1) notice of the suit is given by delivery of a copy of the summons and of the complaint to the person, or his agent, having possession of the vessel or cargo against which the maritime lien is asserted; and if the vessel or cargo is arrested pursuant to process obtained on behalf of the party bringing the suit, the service of process of arrest shall be deemed to constitute valid delivery of such notice, but the party bringing the suit shall be liable for any damages sustained by the foreign state as a result of the arrest if the party bringing the suit had actual or constructive knowledge that the vessel or cargo of a foreign state was involved; and

(2) notice to the foreign state of the commencement of suit as provided in section 1608 of this title is initiated within ten days either of the delivery of notice as provided in paragraph (1) of this subsection or, in the case of a party who was unaware that the vessel or cargo of a foreign state was involved, of the date such party determined the existence of the foreign state's interest.

(c) Whenever notice is delivered under subsection (b)(1), the suit to enforce a maritime lien shall thereafter proceed and shall be heard and determined according to the principles of law and rules of practice of suits in rem whenever it appears that had the vessel been privately owned and possessed, a suit in rem might have been maintained. A decree against the foreign state may include costs of the suit and, if the decree is for a money judgment. interest as ordered by the court, except that the court may not award judgment against the foreign state in an amount greater than the value of the vessel or cargo upon which the maritime lien arose. Such value shall be determined as of the time notice is served under subsection (b)(1). Decrees shall be subject to appeal and revision as provided in other cases of admiralty and maritime jurisdiction. Nothing shall preclude the plaintiff in any proper case from seeking relief in personam in the same action brought to enforce a maritime lien as provided in this section.

(d) A foreign state shall not be immune from the jurisdiction of the courts of the United States in any action brought to foreclose a preferred mortgage, as defined in the Ship Mortgage Act, 1920 (46 U.S.C. 911 and following). Such action shall be brought, heard, and determined in accordance with the provisions of that Act and in accordance with the principles of law and rules of practice of suits in rem, whenever it appears that had the vessel been privately owned and possessed a suit in rem might have been maintained.

§ 1606. Extent of liability

As to any claim for relief with respect to which a foreign state is not entitled to immunity under section 1605 or 1607 of this chapter, the foreign state shall be liable in the same manner and to the same extent as a private individual under like circumstances; but a foreign state except for an agency or instrumentality thereof shall not be liable for punitive damages; if, however, in any case wherein death was caused, the law of the place where the action or omission occurred provides, or has been construed to provide, for damages only punitive in nature, the foreign state shall be liable for actual or compensatory damages measured by the pecuniary injuries resulting from such death which were incurred by the persons for whose benefit the action was brought.

§ 1607. Counterclaims

In any action brought by a foreign state, or in which a foreign state intervenes, in a court of the United States or of a State, the foreign state shall not be accorded immunity with respect to any counterclaim—

(a) for which a foreign state would not be entitled to immunity under section 1605 of this chapter had such claim been brought in a separate action against the foreign state; or

(b) arising out of the transaction or occurrence that is the subject matter of the claim of the foreign state; or

(c) to the extent that the counterclaim does not seek relief exceeding in amount or differing in kind from that sought by the foreign state.

§ 1608. Service; time to answer; default

(a) Service in the courts of the United States and of the States shall be made upon a foreign state or political subdivision of a foreign state:

  (1) by delivery of a copy of the summons and complaint in accordance with any special arrangement for service between the plaintiff and the foreign state or political subdivision; or

  (2) if no special arrangement exists, by delivery of a copy of the summons and complaint in accordance with an applicable international convention on service of judicial documents; or

  (3) if service cannot be made under paragraphs (1) or (2), by sending a copy of the summons and complaint and a notice of suit, together with a translation of each into the official language of the foreign state, by any form of mail requiring a signed receipt, to be addressed and dispatched by the clerk of the court to the head of the ministry of foreign affairs of the foreign state concerned, or

  (4) if service cannot be made within 30 days under paragraph (3), by sending two copies of the summons and complaint and a notice of suit, together with a translation of each into the official language of the foreign state, by any form of mail requiring a signed receipt, to be addressed and dispatched by the clerk of the court to the Secretary of State in Washington, District of Columbia, to the attention of the Director of Special Consular Services—and the Secretary shall transmit one copy of the papers through diplomatic channels to the foreign state and shall send to the clerk of the court a certified copy of the diplomatic note indicating when the papers were transmitted.

As used in this subsection, a "notice of suit" shall mean a notice addressed to a foreign state and in a form prescribed by the Secretary of State by regulation.

(b) Service in the courts of the United States and of the States shall be made upon an agency or instrumentality of a foreign state:

  (1) by delivery of a copy of the summons and complaint in accordance with any special arrangement for service between the plaintiff and the agency or instrumentality; or

  (2) if no special arrangement exists, by delivery of a copy of the summons and complaint either to an officer, a managing or general agent, or to any other agent authorized by

appointment or by law to receive service of process in the United States; or in accordance with an applicable international convention on service of judicial documents; or

(3) if service cannot be made under paragraphs (1) or (2), and if reasonably calculated to give actual notice, by delivery of a copy of the summons and complaint, together with a translation of each into the official language of the foreign state—

(A) as directed by an authority of the foreign state or political subdivision in response to a letter rogatory or request or

(B) by any form of mail requiring a signed receipt, to be addressed and dispatched by the clerk of the court to the agency or instrumentality to be served, or

(C) as directed by order of the court consistent with the law of the place where service is to be made.

(c) Service shall be deemed to have been made—

(1) in the case of service under subsection (a)(4), as of the date of transmittal indicated in the certified copy of the diplomatic note; and

(2) in any other case under this section, as of the date of receipt indicated in the certification, signed and returned postal receipt, or other proof of service applicable to the method of service employed.

(d) In any action brought in a court of the United States or of a State, a foreign state, a political subdivision thereof, or an agency or instrumentality of a foreign state shall serve an answer or other responsive pleading to the complaint within sixty days after service has been made under this section.

(e) No judgment by default shall be entered by a court of the United States or of a State against a foreign state, a political subdivision thereof, or an agency or instrumentality of a foreign state, unless the claimant establishes his claim or right to relief by evidence satisfactory to the court. A copy of any such default judgment shall be sent to the foreign state or political subdivision in the manner prescribed for service in this section.

§ 1609. Immunity from attachment and execution of property of a foreign state

Subject to existing international agreements to which the United States is a party at the time of enactment of this Act the property in the United States of a foreign state shall be immune from attachment arrest and execution except as provided in sections 1610 and 1611 of this chapter.

§ 1610. Exceptions to the immunity from attachment or execution

   (a) The property in the United States of a foreign state, as defined in section 1603(a) of this chapter, used for a commercial activity in the United States, shall not be immune from attachment in aid of execution, or from execution, upon a judgment entered by a court of the United States or of a State after the effective date of this Act, if—

      (1) the foreign state has waived its immunity from attachment in aid of execution or from execution either explicitly or by implication, notwithstanding any withdrawal of the waiver the foreign state may purport to effect except in accordance with the terms of the waiver, or

      (2) the property is or was used for the commercial activity upon which the claim is based, or

      (3) the execution relates to a judgment establishing rights in property which has been taken in violation of international law or which has been exchanged for property taken in violation of international law, or

      (4) the execution relates to a judgment establishing rights in property—

         (A) which is acquired by succession or gift, or

         (B) which is immovable and situated in the United States:

Provided, That such property is not used for purposes of maintaining a diplomatic or consular mission or the residence of the Chief of such mission, or

      (5) the property consists of any contractual obligation or any proceeds from such a contractual obligation to indemnify or hold harmless the foreign state or its employees under a policy of automobile or other liability or casualty insurance covering the claim which merged into the judgment, or

      (6) the judgment is based on an order confirming an arbitral award rendered against the foreign state, provided that attachment in aid of execution, or execution, would not be inconsistent with any provision in the arbitral agreement.

   (b) In addition to subsection (a), any property in the United States of an agency or instrumentality of a foreign state engaged in commercial activity in the United States shall not be immune from attachment in aid of execution, or from execution, upon a judgment entered by a court of the United States or of a State after the effective date of this Act, if—

(1) the agency or instrumentality has waived its immunity from attachment in aid of execution or from execution either explicitly or implicitly, notwithstanding any withdrawal of the waiver the agency or instrumentality may purport to effect except in accordance with the terms of the waiver, or

(2) the judgment relates to a claim for which the agency or instrumentality is not immune by virtue of section 1605(a)(2), (3), or (5), or 1605(b) of this chapter, regardless of whether the property is or was used for the activity upon which the claim is based.

(c) No attachment or execution referred to in subsections (a) and (b) of this section shall be permitted until the court has ordered such attachment and execution after having determined that a reasonable period of time has elapsed following the entry of judgment and the giving of any notice required under section 1608(e) of this chapter.

(d) The property of a foreign state, as defined in section 1603(a) of this chapter, used for a commercial activity in the United States, shall not be immune from attachment prior to the entry of judgment in any action brought in a court of the United States or of a State, or prior to the elapse of the period of time provided in subsection (c) of this section, if—

(1) the foreign state has explicitly waived its immunity from attachment prior to judgment, notwithstanding any withdrawal of the waiver the foreign state may purport to effect except in accordance with the terms of the waiver, and

(2) the purpose of the attachment is to secure satisfaction of a judgment that has been or may ultimately be entered against the foreign state, and not to obtain jurisdiction.

(e) The vessels of a foreign state shall not be immune from arrest in rem, interlocutory sale, and execution in actions brought to foreclose a preferred mortgage as provided in section 1605(d).

§ 1611. Certain types of property immune from execution

(a) Notwithstanding the provisions of section 1610 of this chapter, the property of those organizations designated by the President as being entitled to enjoy the privileges, exemptions, and immunities provided by the International Organizations Immunities Act shall not be subject to attachment or any other judicial process impeding the disbursement of funds to, or on the order of, a foreign state as the result of an action brought in the courts of the United States or of the States.

(b) Notwithstanding the provisions of section 1610 of this chapter, the property of a foreign state shall be immune from attachment and from execution, if—

  (1) the property is that of a foreign central bank or monetary authority held for its own account, unless such bank or authority, or its parent foreign government, has explicitly waived its immunity from attachment in aid of execution, or from execution, notwithstanding any withdrawal of the waiver which the bank, authority or government may purport to effect except in accordance with the terms of the waiver; or

  (2) the property is, or is intended to be, used in connection with a military activity and

  (A) is of a military character, or

  (B) is under the control of a military authority or defense agency.

Selected Bibliography

Acret, James. *Construction Arbitration Handbook.* Shepard's/McGraw-Hill, Inc., 1985.

Aggarwal, Arjun P. "Arbitral Review of Sexual Harassment in the Canadian Workplace." *Arbitration Journal,* March 1991.

Aitken, Robert, and Overly, Michael. "Confidentiality Agreements and the First Amendment: The Right to Say Nothing." *California Litigation,* December 1991.

American Arbitration Association. *Code of Ethics for Arbitrators in Commercial Disputes.* New York: American Arbitration Association, 1977.

American Arbitration Association. *Drafting Dispute Resolution Clauses: A Practical Guide.* New York: American Arbitration Association, 1992.

American Arbitration Association. *A Guide for the AAA Mediator.* New York: American Arbitration Association, 1985.

American Arbitration Association. *Insurance ADR Manual.* Shepard's/McGraw-Hill, Inc., 1993.

American Arbitration Association. *Pioneers in Dispute Resolution: A History of the American Arbitration Association on Its 65th Anniversary (1926-1991).* New York: American Arbitration Association, 1991.

American Arbitration Association. *Lawyers' Arbitration Letters.* Ardsley-on-Hudson, New York: Transnational Juris Publications, Inc., 1990.

Arnold, Tom; Fletcher, Michael G.; and McAughan, Jr., Robert A. *Patent Alternative Dispute Resolution Handbook.* Clark Boardman Callaghan, 1991.

Aufses, Arthur H. III. "Thinking About ADR." *Litigation* 16. American Bar Association, Spring 1990.

Axelrod, R. *The Evolution of Cooperation.* New York: Basic Books, 1984.

Barrett, Jerome T. "The Past Version of Win-Win Bargaining." *Dispute Resolution and Democracy in the 1990s: Shaping the Agenda.* Washington, D.C.: Society of Professionals in Dispute Resolution 17th International Conference, [1990].

Baruch-Bush, Robert A., and Folger, Joseph P. *The Promise Of Mediation.* San Francisco: Jossey-Bass, 1994.

Barzini, L. *The Europeans.* New York: Simon and Schuster, 1983.

Bayer and Abrahams. "The Trouble With Arbitration." 11 *Litigation* 31 (Winter 1985).

Bazerman, M.H., and Lewicki, R.J., eds. *Negotiations in Organizations.* Beverly Hills, Cal.: Sage, 1983.

Binnendijk, H., ed. *National Negotiating Styles.* Washington, D.C.: U.S. Department of State Foreign Service Institute, 1987.

Brams, S.J. *Game Theory and Politics.* New York: Macmillan, 1975.

Brascher, T.W. "Partnering Public Works Projects," State of Washington, Department of General Administration, 1992.

Brazil, Wayne, et al. "Early Neutral Evaluation: An Experimental Effort to Expedite Dispute Resolution." 69 *Judicature* (American Judicature Society, 1986): p. 280.

Breggin, P. *Beyond Conflict: From Self-Help and Psychotherapy to Peacemaking*. New York: St. Martin's Press, 1992.

Brooks, John W. *Relevant Factors and Drafting Elements in International Arbitration Clauses*. San Diego: Society of Professionals in Dispute Resolution 19th Annual International Conference, [1992].

Brunet. *Questioning the Quality of ADR*. 62 Tul. L. Rev. 1 (1987).

Bunker, Barbara Benedict, and Rubin, Jeffrey Z. & assoc. *Conflict, Cooperation, and Justice*. San Francisco: Jossey-Bass, 1995.

Calder, James J.; Kleinberg, James P.; Lipsky, Jr., Abbott B.; and Varner, Carlton A. "A New Alternative to Antitrust Litigation: Arbitration of Antitrust Disputes." *Antitrust*, Spring 1989.

Calero, Henry H., and Oskan, Bob. *Negotiating the Deal You Want*. New York: Dodd Mead & Co., 1983.

Carbonneau, Thomas E. *Alternative Dispute Resolution: Melting the Lances and Dismounting the Steeds*. Urbana, Ill.: University of Illinois Press, 1989.

Carbonneau, Thomas E. *Resolving Transnational Disputes Through International Arbitration*. Charlottesville, Va.: University Press of Virginia, 1984.

Carlisle, J.A., and Parker, R.C. *Beyond Negotiation: Redeeming Customer-Supplier Relationships*. New York: John Wiley and Sons, Ltd., 1989.

Carvajal, Doreen. "Civil Verdicts Delayed for Years in New York's Clogged U.S. Court." *New York Times*, 17 April 1995, p. A1.

Christian, Thomas F., ed. *Expanding Horizons: Theory and Research in Dispute Resolution*. Syracuse, N.Y.: American Bar Association, 1989.

Chu, C. *The Asian Mind Game: Unlocking the Hidden Agenda of the Asian Business Culture—A Westerner's Survival Manual*. New York: Rawson Associates, 1991.

Chung, K.C.; Haffner, P.; and Kaplan, F.M. *The Korea Guidebook*. Boston, Mass.: Houghton Mifflin Company, 1991.

Cohen, A.R., and Bradford, D.L. *Influence Without Authority*. New York: John Wiley and Sons, Inc., 1990.

Coombe, George W., Jr. "State of the Art ADR: The Growing Influence of Asia." *American Bar Association International Commercial Arbitration Committee Newsletter* 4 (Fall 1994): 3.

Costello, Edward J., Jr. *Alternative Dispute Resolution in California: An Overview*. Dispute Resolution Alternatives 1994. New York: Practising Law Insitute, [1994].

Costello, Edward J., Jr. *Focus Group Report: Business and Construction Litigators View Alternative Dispute Resolution.* American Arbitration Association, 31 August 1991, p. 7.

Costello, Edward J., Jr. *Operational Thinking: A Workout for the Mind.* Los Angeles: CIG Publishing, 1991.

Coulson, Robert. *Business Arbitration—What You Need to Know.* New York: American Arbitration Association, 1987.

Craver, Charles B. *Effective Legal Negotiation and Settlement.* Charlottesville, Va.: The Michie Company, 1987.

Creel, Thomas L., ed. *Guide to Patent Arbitration.* Washington, D.C.: The Bureau of National Affairs, Inc., 1987.

Crowley, Thomas E. *Settle It Out of Court: How to Resolve Business and Personal Disputes Using Mediation, Arbitration, and Negotiation.* Wiley Law Publications, 1994.

Dauer, Edward A. *Manual of Dispute Resolution.* McGraw-Hill, 1994.

Dawson, R. *The Facts About Negotiation.* Nightingale-Conant Corp., 1989.

Dawson, R. *You Can Get Anything You Want But You Have to Do More Than Ask: Secrets of Power Negotiating.* New York: Simon and Schuster, 1985.

Dellapenna, Joseph W. *Suing Foreign Governments and Their Corporations.* Washington, D.C.: The Bureau of National Affairs, Inc., 1988.

Deutsch, M. *The Resolution of Conflict: Constructive and Destructive Processes.* New Haven, Conn.: Yale University Press, 1973.

Dilliard, Irving, ed. *The Spirit of Liberty: Papers and Addresses of Learned Hand.* New York: Vintage Books, 1959.

Doyle, Michael, and Strauss, David. *How to Make Meetings Work.* New York: Jove Books, 1976.

Doyle, Stephen Patrick, and Haydock, Roger Silve. "Arbitration Procedures Without the Punches." *Resolving Disputes Without Litigation.* Minnesota: Equilaw Inc., 1991.

Dukes, Frank. "Understanding Community Dispute Resolution." 8 *Mediation Quarterly* (Fall 1990): 27.

Eastern District of Wisconsin. *Introduction to Civil Justice Expense and Delay Reduction Plan Adopted Pursuant to the Civil Justice Reform Act of 1990.* (1991), p. 4.

Eco, U. *Travels in Hyperreality.* San Diego, Cal.: Harcourt Brace Jovanovich, 1986.

"The Defense Rests: America's Biggest Companies Are Tired of Making Lawyers Rich." *Economist,* 10 November 1990, p. 89.

Ennis, Anne B. *Basic Documents on Commercial Arbitration.* New York: American Arbitration Association, 1986.

Feinberg, Kenneth R. *Advancing Justice: Avoiding Litigation Through Non-binding Mediation.* Schaumburg, Ill.: Alliance of American Insurers, 1987.

Fine, Erika S. *ADR and the Courts.* New York: Center for Public Resources, 1987.

Fine, Erika S., ed., and Plapinger, Elizabeth S., asst. ed. *The CPR Legal Program—ADR and The Courts: A Manual for Judges and Lawyers.* New York: Butterworth Legal Publishers, 1987.

Fisher, Roger, et al. *Beyond Machiavelli: Tools for Coping with Conflict.* Cambridge, Mass.: Harvard University Press, 1994.

Fisher, R. and Brown, S. *Getting Together: Building a Relationship That Gets to Yes.* Boston, Mass.: Houghton Mifflin Company, 1988.

Fisher, Roger, and Ury, William. *Getting to Yes: Negotiating Agreement Without Giving In.* Boston, Mass.: Houghton Mifflin Company, 1981.

Folberg, Jay, and Taylor, Alison. *Mediation: A Comprehensive Guide to Resolving Conflicts Without Litigation.* San Francisco: Jossey-Bass, 1984.

Folsom, Gordon, and Spanogle. *International Business Transactions* (West, 1992).

Fox, Lawrence J. "Mini-trials." 19 *Litigation* 4 (Summer 1993): p. 36.

Fraser, N., and Hipel, K. *Conflict Analysis.* Amsterdam: Elsevier, 1984.

Fuller, George. *The Negotiator's Handbook.* Englewood Cliffs, N.J.: Prentice Hall, 1991.

Gilligan, C. *In a Different Voice: Psychological Theory and Women's Development.* Cambridge, Mass.: Harvard University Press, 1982.

Goldberg, S.; Green, E.; and Sander, F. *Dispute Resolution.* Boston, Mass.: Little Brown, 1985.

Gottlieb, M., and Healy, W.J. *Making Deals: The Business of Negotiating.* New York: New York Institute of Finance, 1990.

Gray, Barbara. *Collaborating.* San Francisco: Jossey-Bass, 1989.

Guccione, Jean. "Selling Justice." *California Lawyer,* October 1991.

Habeeb, W.M. *Power and Tactics in International Negotiation.* Baltimore, Md.: Johns Hopkins University Press, 1988.

Hagedorn, Ann. "Special Masters Offer Judicial Relief But Experts Are Skeptical About Trend." *Wall Street Journal,* 11 October 1988, p. B8.

Hancher, Donn E. "In Search of Partnering Excellence: Final Report of the Partnering Task Force of the Construction Industry Institute." University of Texas at Austin: Construction Industry Institute, February 1991.

Harbaugh, Joseph D. *Negotiation: Winning Tactics and Techniques.* New York: Practicing Law Institute, 1988.

Harragan, B.L. *Games Mother Never Taught You: Corporate Gamesmanship for Women.* New York: Warner Books, Inc., 1977.

Harris, P.R., and Moran, R.T. *Managing Cultural Differences.* Houston: Gulf Publishing Company, 1987.

Henry, James F., and Lieberman, Jethro K. *The Manager's Guide to Resolving Legal Disputes: Better Results Without Litigation.* New York: Harper and Row, 1985.

Hensler, Deborah R. *Court-Ordered Arbitration: An Alternative View.* Santa Monica, Cal.: RAND Corp., 1990.

Hensler, Deborah R. *Science in the Court: Is There a Role for Alternative Dispute Resolution?* Santa Monica, Cal.: RAND Corp., 1991.

Hermann, M.G., and Kogan, N. "Effects of Negotiators' Personalities on Negotiating Behavior." In *Negotiation: Social-Psychological Perspectives,* edited by D. Druckman. Beverly Hills, Cal.: Sage, 1977.

Hinchcliff, Carole L. *Dispute Resolution: A Selected Bibliography 1987-1988.* American Bar Association, 1991.

Hoellering, Michael F. *Alternative Dispute Resolution Report.* (Bureau of National Affairs, 5 January 1989), p. 13.

Hoeniger, Berthold H. *Commercial Arbitration Handbook.* Parker-Griffin Publishing Co., 1990.

Howard, William M. "The Evolution of Contractually Mandated Arbitration." *Arbitration Journal* 48 (September 1993): 27.

Ide, William III. "Summoning Our Resolve: Alternative Dispute Resolution Aims for Settlement Without Litigation." *American Bar Association Journal,* October 1993.

Jacobs, Margaret A. "Mandatory Arbitration Agreement Faces Direct Challenge by EEOC." *Wall Street Journal,* 12 April 1995, p. B6.

Jacobs, Margaret A. "Workers Call Some Private Justice Unjust." *Wall Street Journal,* 26 January 1995, p. B1.

Janis, Mark W. *An Introduction to International Law.* Toronto: Little Brown & Co., 1988.

Johnson, David P. "Partnering in Government Contracts: The Ultimate in Dispute Resolution?" *World Arbitration and Mediation Report* 1, No. 7, November 1990.

Jones, William J. "Implementing A Corporate ADR Program." *Dispute Resolution and Democracy in the 1990s: Shaping the Agenda.* Washington, D.C.: Society of Professionals in Dispute Resolution 17th International Conference, [1990].

Judicial Council of California. "Judicial Statistics for Fiscal Year 1991-92." *Annual Report* 2 (1993).

Kanowitz, Leo. *Cases and Materials on Alternative Dispute Resolution.* St. Paul, Minn.: West Publishing Co., 1985.

Kanter, Rosabeth Moss. *When Giants Learn to Dance.* New York: Simon and Schuster, 1989.

Kapoor, A. *Planning for International Business Negotiation.* Cambridge, Mass.: Ballinger Publishing Company, 1975.

Karalis, John P. *International Joint Ventures: A Practical Guide.* West Publications, 1992: sec. 5.39.

Karlins, M., and Abelson, H. *Persuasion.* New York: Springer Publishing, 1970.

Karrass, C.L. *The Negotiating Game.* New York: Crowell, 1970.

Karrass, G. *Negotiate to Close: How to Make More Successful Deals.* New York: Simon and Schuster, 1985.

Keirsey, D., and Bates, M. *Please Understand Me: Character and Temperament Types.* Del Mar, Cal.: Prometheus Nemesis Book Company, 1984.

Keller, Robert E. *Sales Negotiating Handbook.* Englewood Cliffs, N.J.: Prentice Hall, 1988.

Kellerman, B., and Rubin, J.Z., eds. *Leadership and Negotiation in the Middle East.* New York: Praeger, 1988.

Keltner, John W. *The Management of Struggle: Elements of Dispute Resolution Through Negotiation, Mediation and Arbitration.* Annadale, Va.: Cresskil, N.J. and Speech Communication Assoc., Hampton Press, Inc., 1994.

Kennedy, G. *Everything is Negotiable.* London: Century Business, 1989.

Kennedy, G. *Negotiate Everywhere: Doing Business Abroad.* London: Business Books Ltd., 1985.

Kennedy, G.; Benson, J.; and McMillan, J. *Managing Negotiations.* London: Business Books Ltd., 1985.

Kolb, Deborah M. and assoc. *When Talk Works.* San Francisco: Jossey-Bass, 1994.

Kremenyuk, V.A. *International Negotiation.* San Francisco: Jossey-Bass Publishers, 1991.

Kritek, Phyllis Beck. *Negotiating at an Uneven Table: Developing Moral Courage in Resolving Our Conflicts.* San Francisco: Jossey-Bass, 1994.

Lake, Laura M. *Environmental Mediation, the Search for Consensus.* Boulder, Colo.: Western Press, 1980.

Lax, David A., and Sebenius, James K. *The Manager as Negotiator.* New York: The Free Press, a Division of Macmillan, 1986.

Leeson, Susan M., and Johnston, Bryan M. *Ending It: Dispute Resolution in America.* Cincinnati, Ohio: Anderson Publishing Co., 1988.

Lewicki, R.J., and Litterrer, J.A. *Negotiation.* Homewood, Ill.: Irwin, 1985.

Lind, E. Allan, et al. *The Perception of Justice.* Santa Monica, Cal.: RAND Corporation, 1989.

Lovenheim, Peter. *Mediate, Don't Litigate: How to Resolve Disputes Quickly, Privately, and Inexpensively—Without Going to Court.* New York: McGraw-Hill Publishing Company, 1989.

McGillis, Daniel. *Community Dispute Resolution Programs and Public Policy.* Washington, D.C.: National Institute of Justice, 1986.

McKay, Robert B. "Ethical Considerations in Alternative Dispute Resolution." *The Arbitration Journal* 45, No. 1, March 1990.

Macneil, Ian R. *American Arbitration Law.* New York: Oxford University Press, 1992.

McPhee, John. *The Control of Nature.* Farrar, Straus and Giroux, 1989.

Maggiolo, Walter. *Techniques of Mediation.* New York: Oceana Publications, 1985.

March, R.M. *The Japanese Negotiator: Subtlety and Strategy Beyond Western Logic.* Tokyo: Kodansha International, 1990.

Maxwell, Jennifer P. "Mediation in the Schools: Self-Regulation, Self-Esteem and Self-Discipline." 7 *Mediation Quarterly* (Winter 1989): 149.

Meason, and Smith. "Non-Lawyers in International Commercial Arbitration: Gathering Splinters on the Bench." *Journal of International Law & Business* 12 (1991): 31.

Meili, Stephen, and Packard, Tamara. "Alternative Dispute Resolution in a New Health Care System: Will it Work for Everyone?" *Ohio State Journal on Dispute Resolution* 10, No. 1, 1994.

Millhauser, Marguerite W. *Sourcebook, Federal Agency Use of Alternative Means of Dispute Resolution.* Washington, D.C.: The Conference, 1987.

Milwid, B. *Working With Men: Professional Women Talk About Power, Sexuality and Ethics.* Hillsboro, Ore.: Beyond Words Publishing, Inc., 1990.

Murray, John S.; Rau, Alan Scott; and Sherman, Edward F. *Processes of Dispute Resolution: The Role of Lawyers.* Westbury, N.Y.: The Foundation Press, Inc., 1989.

Nagel, Stuart S., and Mills, Miriam K. *Multi-Criteria Methods for Alternative Dispute Resolution: With Microcomputer Software Applications.* New York: Quorum Books, 1990.

Nanus, Burt. *Visionary Leadership.* San Francisco: Jossey-Bass, 1992.

Nirenberg, Gerald I. *Fundamentals of Negotiating.* New York: Perennial Library, 1973.

Polak, Aaron J. "Punitive Damages in Commercial Contract Arbitration-Still an Issue After All These Years." *Ohio State Journal on Dispute Resolution* 10, No. 1, 1994.

Program Materials of a Conference on International Litigation, American Bar Assoc., 1989.

Raiffa, H. *The Art and Science of Negotiation.* Cambridge, Mass.: Harvard University Press, 1982.

Rakoff, Todd D. "Contracts of Adhesion: An Essay in Reconstruction," *Harvard Law Review* 96, (1983): 1173.

The Recorder (San Francisco), 18 April 1995, p. 1.

Reuben, Richard C. "Get-Tough Stance Draws Fiscal Criticism." *American Bar Association Journal,* January 1995: 16.

Riskin, Leonard L., and Westbrook, James E. *Dispute Resolution and Lawyers.* St. Paul, Minn.: West Publishing Company, 1987.

Rogers, Nancy H., and McEwen, Craig A. *Mediation: Law, Policy, Practice.* Rochester, N.Y.: Lawyers Co-Operative Publishing Co., 1989.

Rosenberg, Joshua P. "Keeping the Lid on Confidentiality: Mediation Privilege and Conflict of Laws," *Ohio State Journal on Dispute Resolution* 10, No. 1, 1994.

Rubinstein, Moshe F. *Tools for Thinking and Problem Solving.* Englewood Cliffs, N.J.: Prentice-Hall, 1986.

Sander, Frank E.A. "Paying for ADR: To Make it Work, We Have to Provide Funds For It." *American Bar Association Journal,* February 1992.

Sander, F., and Goldberg, S. "Fitting the Forum to the Fuss: A User-Friendly Guide to Selecting an Alternative Dispute Resolution Procedure." *Negotiation Journal* 10 (1994).

Sands, John E. *Alternative Dispute Resolution and Risk Management: Controlling Conflict and its Costs.* New York: Practicing Law Institute, 1987.

Schoenfield, Mark K., and Schoenfield, Richard M. *Legal Negotiations: Getting Maximum Results.* Colorado Springs, Colo.: Shepards'/McGraw-Hill, 1988.

Schubert, Glendon. *Dispassionate Justice: A Synthesis of the Judicial Opinions of Robert H. Jackson.* Indianapolis, In.: The Bobbs-Merrill Co., Inc., 1969.

Schuyler, Nina, mod. "Coercive Harmony: An Anthropologist and a Former Federal Judge Debate the Purpose of Mandatory ADR." *California Lawyer,* (May 1995): 37.

Schwarz, Robert M. *The Skilled Facilitator: Practical Wisdom for Developing Effective Groups.* San Francisco: Jossey-Bass, 1994.

Seide, Katherine. *A Dictionary of Arbitration and its Terms; Labor, Commercial, International; a Concise Encyclopedia of Peaceful Dispute Settlement.* Dobbs Ferry, N.Y.: Oceana Publications, 1970.

Silberman, Alan D. *Implementing the Prtnering Process: Guidelines for Facilitators.* American Arbitration Association, 1993.

Simmonds, Kenneth R., and Hill, Brian H.W., "Commercial Arbitration Law in Asia and the Pacific." *International Commercial Arbitration.* New York: Oceana Publications Incorporated, 1987.

Singer, Linda R. *Settling Disputes.* Westview Press, 1990.

Solum, Lawrence B. "Alternative Court Structures in the Future of the California Judiciary: 20/20 Vision." *University of Southern California Law Review* 66 (1993): 2121.

Stern, David B. "Rent-A-Judge, Rent-A-Wimp." *Los Angeles Lawyer,* October 1991.

Stipanowich. *Rethinking American Arbitration.* 63 Ind. L.J. 425, 435nn. (1987).

Susskind, Lawrence, and Cruikshank, Jeffrey. *Breaking the Impasse.* New York: Basic Books, 1987.

Tagliere, Daniel A. *How to Meet, Think and Work to Consensus.* San Diego, Cal.: Pfeiffer & Company, 1992.

Tannen, D. *That's Not What I Meant: How Conversational Style Makes or Breaks Relationships.* New York: Ballantine Books, 1986.

Tannen, D. *You Just Don't Understand: Women and Men in Conversation.* New York: Ballantine Books, 1990.

Ury, William. *Getting Past No: Negotiating With Difficult People.* New York: Bantam Books, 1991.

Ury, William; Brett, J.M.; and Goldberg, S.B. *Getting Disputes Resolved: Designing Systems to Cut the Costs of Conflict.* San Francisco: Jossey-Bass, 1989.

Varchaver, Nicholas. "Dispute Revolution." *The American Lawyer,* April 1992.

Vermont Law School. *A Study of Barriers to the Use of Alternative Methods of Dispute Resolution.* South Royalton: Vermont Law School, 1984.

Wallace, J. Clifford, Hon. "Tackling the Caseload Crisis." *American Bar Association Journal,* June 1994: 88.

Webb, Susan L. *Step Forward: Sexual Harassment in the Workplace.* MasterMedia Limited, USA (1991).

Widiss, Alan I., ed. *Arbitration: Commercial Disputes, Insurance, and Tort Claims.* New York: Practising Law Institute, 1979.

Woolf, B. *Friendly Persuasion.* New York: Berkeley Books, 1990.

Yarn, Douglas H. "Commercial Arbitration in Olde England." *Dispute Resolution Journal* 50, No. 1 (January 1995): 68.

Zamora, Stephen, and Brand, Ronald A., gen. eds. *Basic Documents of International Economic Law 2,* (Commerce Clearing House, Inc. 1990).

Glossary

Ad hoc arbitration: Arbitration without formalized rules and procedures which is not conducted or administered by an institution.

Adhesion contract: A standard form of contract that must be signed, as is, by all who engage in a specific activity or purchase a given product or service, *e.g.,* insurance policy.

Adjudication: The process of hearing and deciding a case; any dispute resolution process in which a decision maker hears testimony and renders a decision is an adjudicatory process.

Adverse precedent: Prior legal decision which stands against a position.

Alternative dispute resolution (ADR): A widely used term referring to the entire range of out-of-court dispute resolution options.

Arbitration: A dispute resolution process in which the parties (and/or their attorneys) present their cases to a decision maker, called the arbitrator, who renders a decision which is not appealable.

Arbitrator: The neutral decision maker in an arbitration.

Award: The decision of the arbitrator.

Bench trial: A court trial presided over by a judge without a jury.

Binding: Legally enforceable; a binding decision in a case is a decision that the disputants must accept.

Common law: The body of law developed in England from judicial decisions used as precedent, not written in statutes. This body of law is the basis for the legal system in England and all the United States except Louisiana.

Conciliation: A process that facilitates dispute resolution, in which a neutral third party, called a conciliator, acts as a go-between, communicating each side's position to the other, relaying settlement options, and sometimes offering nonbinding advice in an effort to bring the sides closer to settlement. This process is similar to mediation.

Contracting state: A country which has agreed to be bound by a convention.

Convention: An international agreement drafted by a number of countries or an international organization.

Court annexed: The part of the dispute resolution process available through the court system.

Deposition: The process, carried out prior to a trial or to an arbitration hearing, through which disputants in a case or their attorneys jointly question a witness and record the witness's testimony. The recorded testimony may be used later as evidence during the trial or arbitration hearing.

Discovery: The process, carried out prior to a trial or sometimes to an arbitration hearing, in which the disputants exchange documents and other information pertinent to that case.

Early neutral evaluation (ENE): A dispute resolution process designed to expedite settlement of court cases in their early pretrial stage. Attorneys and their clients who have filed a case in federal or state court meet with a neutral, sometimes voluntarily or at the behest of the court, in an effort to encourage negotiation and settlement. The neutral assesses the strengths and weaknesses of each side's position and offers an opinion of how the case will fare at trial.

Ex parte (Latin): Contact with the arbitrator or judge by one side in a dispute without the other side(s) being present (or on the telephone or sending a written communication to the arbitrator or judge without sending a copy to all other parties).

ICSID Convention: A multinational treaty providing a means for resolving disputes between a country and a foreign investor in that country.

Injunction: A remedy which requires a party to either do or refrain from doing a particular act or activity.

Joint caucus: Meeting in mediation where all parties are present.

Judge pro tem: A temporary judge.

Legal precedent: A court decision which establishes a principle applicable to future legal disputes.

Med/Arb: A dispute resolution procedure that combines aspects of both mediation and arbitration. By agreement of the parties, a neutral attempts to mediate a dispute, but if any or all issues cannot be resolved, the parties must proceed to binding arbitration (whether carried out by the same neutral or not).

Mediation: A voluntary, nonbinding dispute resolution process in which a neutral third party meets in private caucuses with each party, as well as in joint session, and guides the parties to a mutually beneficial resolution by defusing hostilities, narrowing the issues, and helping the parties gain realistic assessments of the merits of their cases.

Mediator: The neutral who carries out the dispute resolution process called mediation.

Mini-trial: A dispute resolution process designed for business disputes where attorneys argue their clients' cases before a panel of decision makers comprised of top executives from each of the disputing organizations. The panel hears arguments and then tries to negotiate a resolution, sometimes with the assistance of a third-party neutral.

Misdemeanor: A class of criminal offenses consisting of those offenses less serious than felonies and which are sanctioned by less severe penalties.

National: A citizen or legal resident of a country (state).

Neutral: Any independent, impartial individual who helps parties reach agreement through any dispute resolution process.

New York Convention: Convention on the Recognition and Enforcement of Foreign Arbitral Awards.

Ombudsman: A neutral empowered to receive and investigate complaints about any institution, organization, or business. Sometimes he or she is also given the authority to recommend or to facilitate solutions to problems.

Panama Convention: Inter-American Convention on Commercial Arbitration.

Partnering: A technique designed to prevent business disputes from occurring by establishing working relationships between or among business partners, based on open communication, joint problem solving, teamwork, and shared risks and rewards.

Private caucus: A private meeting between the mediator and one of the parties in a mediation.

Private judging: A procedure, allowed in some jurisdictions, where parties agree to hire a private judge (usually a retired judge or practicing attorney), who hears the case and renders a decision which is appealable (sometimes called Rent-A-Judge).

Provisional remedy: A temporary order made by a judge or an arbitrator to preserve the status quo between disputing parties, until final disposition of a matter can occur.

Remedy: The means employed to redress an injury.

Restitution: Giving back what was wrongly taken, or otherwise returning a party to its previous position before being wronged.

Settlement conference: A meeting with a judge, lawyer, or other person experienced in professional dispute resolution who listens to the parties and attempts to facilitate settlement.

Specific performance: A remedy for a breach of an agreement whereby the breaching party is ordered to perform the obligations contained within the agreement.

State: Sovereign political unit, such as a country or a state of the United States.

Statute of limitations: A law setting a certain time period, after which rights cannot be enforced by legal action.

Stipulation: An agreement in writing or recorded in the official records of a proceeding.

Treaty: An agreement between sovereign states.

UNCITRAL: United Nations Commission on International Trade Law; sponsored international commercial arbitration/conciliation rules which bear its name.

[The next page is 501.]

Topical Index

All references are to page numbers.